Unfinished Revolution

JEFFERSONIAN AMERICA

JAN ELLEN LEWIS, PETER S. ONUF, AND ANDREW O'SHAUGHNESSY
EDITORS

UNFINISHED

⚜ The Early American Republic in a British World ⚜

REVOLUTION

SAM W. HAYNES

University of Virginia Press · Charlottesville and London

University of Virginia Press
© 2010 by the Rector and Visitors of the University of Virginia
All rights reserved
Printed in the United States of America on acid-free paper

First published 2010

1 3 5 7 9 8 6 4 2

LIBRARY OF CONGRESS CATALOGING-IN-PUBLICATION DATA

Haynes, Sam W. (Sam Walter), 1956–
    Unfinished revolution : the early American republic in a British world /
Sam W. Haynes.
        p.   cm. — (Jeffersonian America)
    Includes bibliographical references and index.
    ISBN 978-0-8139-3068-8 (cloth : alk. paper) — ISBN 978-0-8139-3080-0 (e-book)
    1. United States—History—1783–1865. 2. United States—Relations—Great Britain.
3. Great Britain—Relations—United States. 4. Great Britain—Foreign public opinion,
American—History—19th century. 5. United States—Public opinion—History—19th
century. 6. United States—Territorial expansion—History—19th century. I. Title.
    E338.H39 2010
    973.3'1—dc22

2010018010

To Grace, Bonnie and Chas

Contents

Acknowledgments

In writing this book I have been obliged to take on the role of free-range historian, trespassing upon several subfields in order to fully explore the extent to which anti-British sentiment informed American attitudes. I have incurred many debts along the way, calling upon the aid of historians whose expertise in certain areas far exceeds my own. At the University of Texas at Arlington, Christopher Morris, Stephen Maizlish, Joyce Goldberg, and David Narrett each read parts of the manuscript and offered perceptive analysis. I would also like to thank the members of the Dallas Area Social History Group, who twice listened to working papers on the issues contained in this book, as well as the host of other scholars who helped me to refine my understanding of this subject at numerous academic conferences in the United States and Great Britain where I presented portions of my research. In addition, a number of scholars either lent support and/or offered valuable advice along the way, including John Belohlavek, Jimmy Bryan, Guy Chet, Matthew Hale, Thomas Hietala, Robert W. Johannsen, James Kirby Martin, Robert May, Steven Mintz, Donald Ratcliffe, Lelia Roeckell, Marco Sioli, and David J. Weber. Dick Holway, History Editor at the University of Virginia Press, was an early supporter of my work; I would also like to thank everyone at the press who worked on this project and offered helpful suggestions, especially my copy editor, Ruth Steinberg.

As my academic home for the better part of two decades, the University of Texas at Arlington deserves special recognition here. UTA's Office of the Provost provided me with a semester off and a generous travel grant when I first conceived of this project many years ago. Along the way I also received financial assistance from the Office of the College of Liberal Arts and the Center for Greater Southwestern Studies. In addition, the Center has for several years provided me with the services of a part-time research assistant, a position that has been filled by a string of graduate students, too numerous to mention here individually, who combed through American newspapers of the period for evidence of anti-British sentiment. During the past year I have benefited enormously from the Center's administrative staff, Ann Jennings and Amanda Harris, who helped prepare the final draft of the manuscript. This project began as a result of my interest in the role Great Britain played as an obstacle to U.S. continental expansionism. It has therefore been a joy and a privilege to have an office only a few feet away from one of the best repositories of archival materials on the nineteenth-century American Southwest, and I am grateful to the knowledgeable Special Collections staff who work there. Special thanks also go to the always helpful Diana Hines, who tracked down countless source materials through interlibrary loan. I am grateful, too, to Lisa Berry, who read several portions of this manuscript as it was nearing completion with a critical eye. Finally, I would be remiss if I did not also thank the many students in UT Arlington's Transatlantic History Program whom I have worked with over the years, especially those who took my Anglo-American Connections colloquium and seminar in the spring and fall of 2005.

Several other academic institutions also helped to bring this project to fruition. I received three much-needed research fellowships: a Visiting Scholar fellowship from the Beinecke Library, Yale University; an Andrew W. Mellon Foundation fellowship from the Library Company of Philadelphia; and a William Gilmore Simms Visiting Research Professor award from the South Caroliniana Library, University of South Carolina. I would like to thank the helpful staffs at these venerable institutions, as well as those at the many other libraries where the research for this book was conducted, especially the American Antiquarian Society; the Dolph Briscoe Center for American History, University of Texas at Austin; the Harvard Theatre Collection and Houghton Library, Harvard University; the Huntington Library; the New York Public Library; and, at Southern Methodist University, the Bridwell, Fondren, and Harmon Libraries.

Finally, I would like to acknowledge the support of my entire family, some of whom I suspect never really understood my fixation with the "special relationship." But *Unfinished Revolution* is dedicated to just three of them. I am especially grateful for the support of my brother, Charles, and my sister, Bonnie. I have been promising for years to dedicate a book to them; this work is their modest reward for their unflagging patience. It is dedicated, too, to my mother, Grace. Though not trained as an academic, she is nonetheless the other historian in the family, and the most voracious reader I have ever known. She has pored over several drafts of this manuscript and followed the project from beginning to end with keen interest. Authors customarily dedicate books to their parents, but my need to recognize her here has little to do with a sense of filial obligation. Rather, I do so with the knowledge that the enormous intellectual debt I owe her can never fully be repaid.

Unfinished Revolution

Introduction

During the early decades of the nineteenth century, American attitudes toward Great Britain were both conflicted and complex. Some Americans continued to look to Great Britain for standards of taste and refinement, for direction in the realm of arts and letters, and for moral guidance on the issue of slavery. At the same time, a great many Americans maintained that the world's dominant empire still posed the most serious threat to the republic's security and well-being. The British lion took on a wide range of threatening guises: an industrial hegemon bent on destroying domestic manufactures by inundating the republic with cheaply made goods; a banking colossus that could arrest the flow of transatlantic credit, bringing the American economy to a standstill; an evangelical antislavery movement that had set its sights on the abolition of American slave labor as its next great crusade; and a government in London that seemed to be coordinating these various activities with masterful precision while pursuing its own policy of hemispheric territorial aggrandizement.[1]

For all its many contradictions, the American relationship with Great Britain nonetheless played a crucial role in the process of national self-definition. It could hardly be otherwise. With John Bull intruding upon virtually every aspect of public life, from politics to economic development to literature to the performing arts, Brother Jonathan was constantly reminded of his subordinate status in the transatlantic equation. Unabashed Anglophiles, of course, were untroubled by the disparity. But a majority of Americans were at least willing to pay lip service to the goal of divesting the republic of its Old World influences. As earnest republicans, they instinctively sought to sever the ties that still connected the two nations, as if in so doing they could prove themselves worthy of the legacy bequeathed to them by the Revolutionary generation. Wrestling with feelings of inferiority, they endeavored to fashion—albeit fitfully, and with varying degrees of commitment and success—a sense of Americanness in contradistinction to British norms.

If this welter of insecurities has not garnered the scholarly attention it deserves, the oversight may be due in part to the fact that we do not really think of the early republic as a developing nation, at least not in any traditional sense. The United States during this formative period is generally regarded as the arbiter of its own fate, a virile, self-confident nation well on its way to establishing itself as a continental power. As a result, we tend to view the challenges it faced—a volatile marketplace, territorial expansion, slavery—as those entirely of its own making. But the American relationship with Great Britain helps to remind us that the process by which nation-states in the early stages of development arrive at a coherent self-image rarely occurs in isolation. Rather, it may also be driven—even for those nations that later become superpowers— by external, other-directed influences. The bonds of national belonging that create an "imagined" sense of community, to borrow from Benedict Anderson, are not always indigenous. More often than not, collective identities are informed to no small degree by how we imagine them to be perceived by others.[2]

So it was for the United States after 1815. While the nation's historical trajectory might seem straight and self-assured in retrospect, citizens of the early republic were in no way conscious of a "manifest destiny." For all its vaunted claims of distinctiveness, the young republic exhibited a set of anxieties not uncommon among nation-states that have emerged from long periods of colonial rule. This is not to ignore the many differences between settler colonies and those of conquered peoples. But the challenge of reconciling two fundamentally opposing impulses—the desire to repudiate *and* emulate the ancien regime—is one that has confronted the descendants of colonizers and colonized alike. As elsewhere, Americans struggled to define their precise relationship to the imperial parent, with many still fearing its ambitions and resenting its lingering influences, even as they remained desperate for its validation. To ignore these inherent tensions is to view the early American experience through the lens of another age, to see in the young republic the colossus it would become.

The need for a new perspective is especially timely, perhaps, as it becomes possible to imagine the age of American empire drawing to a close. When the day comes when Americans cease to think of themselves as citizens of the world's reigning superpower—a day that may not be far off—they will almost certainly think of their past differently too. In writing *Unfinished Revolution,* I have tried to contribute in some way to that discussion.

The Axials of Independence

Uncle John call'd aloud for his boys to come home,
"we'll rest now awhile, and let them alone;
But we will still watch; an eye on them keep,
If we can e'er catch them a dazing in sleep,
We will yet pay them, with interest tenfold,
For their impudence given and haughtiness bold.
—"A Story of Uncle Sam"

T he Fourth of July was a noisy affair in every city and town in America during the early decades of the nineteenth century, and nowhere was it more so than in New York City. In 1842, as in years past, the celebration commenced at dawn with an artillery salute on the Battery, at the southern edge of Manhattan Island. For the remainder of the day the air was filled with the sound of squibs and firecrackers, the pealing of church bells, and the celebratory fusillades of militia companies on parade. During the morning hours Gotham's residents began to congregate along the Battery, where the harbor teemed with vessels of every size and description, all festooned with flags, streamers, and patriotic bunting. By mid-day an immense throng had gathered to watch the festivities, which included the obligatory artillery displays of the city's harbor defenses. At noon, Castle Williams, the hulking, red-brick fortress on Governor's Island built to protect the city from the British during the War of 1812, fired its guns to salute the event, a heavy barrage that continued until the fortress was enveloped in a dense cloud of smoke.

As Americans celebrated past conflicts against Great Britain, their present relationship with the island nation was never far from their minds. This was especially true in 1842. Diplomatic relations between the two countries had become strained in recent years over a wide range of territorial and maritime issues. A rebellion in Canada had received the active support of many Americans, prompting angry talk of war on both sides of the Atlantic. But as the nation observed the 66th anniversary of its independence, there was every reason to believe that a rapprochement between the British empire and its former colonies was imminent. Some months earlier, the British government had dispatched a special envoy, Lord Ashburton, to Washington to address long-standing American grievances. By the summer, Ashburton and his U.S. counterpart, Secretary of State Daniel Webster, were said to be on the verge of an historic accord.

With public interest in Ashburton's mission running high in New York, a city that owed its very existence to the transatlantic trade, the harbor ceremonies honoring the national holiday took on special significance. Lying at anchor a short distance from shore was the HMS *Warspite*, a fifty gun man-of-war that had ferried Lord Ashburton across the Atlantic on his diplomatic errand and was now waiting to carry the British envoy back to England. With a crew of more than five hundred, the *Warspite* was a fitting emblem of British sea power. Particularly impressive was its heavy armament, the vessel having recently been outfitted with new, 68-pound Paixhans guns. Revolutionary in design, the Paixhans represented a breakthrough in the development of naval ordnance, firing exploding shells rather than conventional solid-iron shot. A "perfect" fighting ship, enthused one writer for a military magazine, the *Warspite* "cannot fail to excite the admiration of all persons capable of forming a judgment of what a man-of-war should be."[1]

When the cannonade from Castle Williams subsided, two U.S. warships in the harbor followed with artillery demonstrations of their own. The *North Carolina*, until recently the flagship of the Pacific fleet and one of the largest ships of the line in the U.S. Navy, delivered a thunderous salute, which was promptly echoed by the frigate *Columbia*, flagship of the Home Squadron. As a cheer went up from the thousands gathered along the Battery, one thought was on the minds of many in the crowd: would the HMS *Warspite* follow suit and deign to honor the United States on the anniversary of its independence from Great Britain? When at last the report of the *Columbia*'s guns faded, a quiet fell upon the harbor, and all eyes along the Battery turned to the *Warspite*. The British man-of-war remained eerily silent, with no sign of activity on its decks, some distance from shore.

"The Britisher's out of gunpowder," cried one wag in the crowd. No sooner had he uttered the remark than a sudden flash appeared from the side of the British frigate, followed by a wisp of smoke. The boom of the heavy brass gun reverberated across the water, and in a moment a mighty crash, painful to the ear, reached the onlookers along the Battery. Again and again the *Warspite's* guns fired, rattling the window panes of the buildings facing the harbor in a deafening barrage that made the American ships' cannons sound, according to one Scottish tourist, like "popguns." The cannonade caused surprise and no little consternation to some in the crowd. Though clearly intended as a gesture of respect to the Americans and their national holiday, it left many onlookers "causelessly annoyed" that their own vessels had been outdone in so public a manner by a British ship of the line.[2]

This trivial moment in U.S.-British relations encapsulates the complex and often contradictory manner in which Americans regarded the nation that had given birth to their republic. No other people in the western hemisphere who had broken free of European colonialism celebrated their independence with such flamboyant enthusiasm. Yet none remained so connected to the imperial parent. John Bull still loomed large in the public consciousness, bound to his former colonies by ties of kinship, culture, and commerce. As a result, Americans remained inordinately sensitive to the opinion of Great Britain, "the only country," wrote one editorialist, "for whose respect we really care a straw."[3]

And therein lay a dilemma for American patriots. Though keen for their country to be regarded as Britain's equal, they sensed, for all their bravado, that this was a distinction that was not theirs to bestow. Instinctively, they sought validation from the highest possible authority, from Britain itself. Yet the very act of doing so offered compelling evidence that the United States remained very much the junior partner in this transatlantic relationship. In exhibiting a yearning for British approval, Americans revealed their own doubts about the country's stature on the world stage. Thus, on July 4th, the residents of Gotham, and by extension the nation at large, waited in eager anticipation for the British vessel's congratulatory cannonade. But when it finally came, it did little to allay American insecurities. Rather, the *Warspite's* salute served as a blunt reminder that the republic still stood in the shadow of Great Britain, and would continue to do so for some time to come.

"Conflicting Sensations" and the National Sense of Self

This study in Anglophone transatlantic relations begins in 1815, a year that Americans have traditionally regarded as a watershed moment in the history of their republic. The War of 1812, a war that seemed to mark the final chapter in the struggle for independence, had ended. The second conflict with Great Britain had been fraught with embarrassments, the burning of the nation's capital notably among them. Nonetheless, in the minds of many Americans, Andrew Jackson's spectacular victory at New Orleans had done much to wipe this stain from the national escutcheon, allowing them to claim that they had bested the armies that had defeated Napoleon. The utter rout of British troops on the plains of Chalmette had also laid to rest, at long last, fears of foreign invasion. Peace would bring a new sense of territorial security, which would in turn help to whet American expansionist appetites. Although the Treaty of Ghent had achieved little of substance, the agreement signaled the end of an historic British-Indian alliance in the Ohio River Valley that for years had impeded westward-moving whites. A veritable land rush followed, resulting in the admission of five new transmontane states during the period 1816–21. Meanwhile, the slow disintegration of Spain's colonial empire in the Americas would soon bring Florida under Washington's aegis and create a power vacuum in the Southwest that betokened further territorial acquisitions. In the years after 1815, then, it seemed as if the United States had at last managed to detach itself from its Atlantic moorings. The nation's center of gravity now shifted, as American citizens turned their gaze westward, eager to test the limits of the national domain.[4]

Republican pundits saw in these auguries a great nation on the rise, and they delighted in saying so, loudly and often. Never reluctant to exhibit their patriotic bona fides in the years prior to the war, they made nothing less than a cult of national devotion in the years afterward. All manner of civic discourse—from the public prints to the pulpit, on the campaign stump and national holiday orations—took up the theme of *amor patriae*. Citizens of the republic became enthralled as never before by the iconography of nationhood, viewing the eagle and the flag as sacred objects. These emblems were not only on prominent display on the Fourth of July, but could be seen adorning public buildings, hotels, theaters, and private homes throughout the year. "You see the 'star spangled banner' every where, even on the lowest pot-houses," observed one British traveler.[5] Americans covered their walls with engravings, woodcuts, and paintings of military engagements, while even "the panels of some of their stage-coaches are ornamented with representations of their frigates capturing their British antagonists," as one visitor noted. Not satisfied with the observance of a single national holiday, Americans found many opportunities to commemorate the recent past with banquets, parades, patriotic oratory, pyrotechnics, cannonade, and fireworks displays. Washington's birthday was observed in similar fashion, while communities throughout the United States celebrated annually their own contributions in the struggle for independence. The proliferation of these events was accompanied by a monument-building mania,

with communities taking up subscriptions to erect tributes to local military heroes. From one end of the country to the other, Americans sang
the praises of the young republic, creating a nationwide echo chamber
of self-congratulation that would reach a climactic crescendo with the
fiftieth anniversary of independence in 1826.[6]

Initially, these rituals of national belonging were not seen as an excuse to dredge up old animosities. On the contrary, Americans in the
immediate postwar years seemed to have made their peace with Great
Britain. Community leaders entrusted with the task of interpreting the
nation's creation narrative on these holidays rarely used the occasion to
engender popular enmity toward the British. Their declamations were
often generic homilies on the meaning of a republic, paeans to the feats
of military heroes, replete with exhortations to never forget those whose
sacrifices had helped forge a nation. At Fourth of July gatherings and
other public meetings, orators might just as often expound upon the
kindred ties between Great Britain and the United States as dwell on
the bitter memories of war. Britain's minister to Washington encountered no explicit anti-British feeling during the visit of the Revolutionary War hero, the Marquis de Lafayette, who toured the country in 1825,
or during the fiftieth anniversary celebrations the following year.[7] Indeed, some Independence Day orators in 1826 took pains to reflect on
the connections that bound the two peoples, expressing a willingness to
let bygones be bygones: "Oh, England, how many sublime and tender
associations gather around thy name!" North Carolina politician Robert
Strange declared. Though the republic had been spurned and abused by
the mother country, he continued, "the filial affections of America still
cling to thee with ardor."[8]

Yet these attachments were not nearly as firm as Strange would have
his audience believe. The transatlantic relationship had always been a
volatile one, and James Fenimore Cooper was a good deal closer to the
mark when he observed that Americans regarded Great Britain with
"conflicting sensations," an ambivalence that weighed the two countries'
many commonalities against their many differences. Anti-British feel
ing may have subsided after 1815, but it would soon reemerge, and by
the second quarter of the nineteenth century some observers believed
that the mood of the country was decidedly more hostile to Great Britain than it had been during the war. British visitors did not fail to notice
the change in tone. By the Jacksonian period, they complained, the oratory of national holidays had become little more than an "opportunity
for vituperation" of their country. This was certainly an exaggeration,
but there can be little doubt that a shift in public opinion was under way.
American political leaders both exploited and fed these feelings. Beard-

ing the British lion would become a conspicuous feature of the rhetoric of both parties during this period, with one British diplomat asserting that members of Congress considered it "anti-American" to speak favorably of England. The travel writer Basil Hall was so amused by the anti-British screeds he witnessed from the Capitol galleries that he wondered if there was a House rule that required members "to take a passing fling at the poor Old Country" at least once every speech.[9]

This gradual swelling of anti-British sentiment had many sources. For one thing, Americans by the mid-1820s were becoming more than a little irritated by the tone of haughty condescension that British observers saw fit to adopt when writing of the former colonies. In periodicals and scores of travel books, British authors derided the republic as a nation of money-grubbing, tobacco-chewing rubes, insults that hurt Americans all the more because they traditionally held the opinions of the British intellectual community in such high regard. Meanwhile, Britain's vast industrial and financial power stoked American economic anxieties. Residents of manufacturing states clamored for tariff protection from cheap British imports, while others saw a greater evil in the vast web of transatlantic financial connections that left the republic deeply in debt to London banking houses. Southern slaveholders, moreover, regarded with unmixed horror that country's leadership role in the crusade to eradicate slavery in the western hemisphere. Territorial issues, too, were cause for concern. By the 1840s, boundary disputes in Maine and Oregon brought the two nations dangerously close to war, while a conspicuous British presence in Texas and Mexico prompted fears that the empire might block U.S. territorial ambitions in the West.

American fears of British hegemony were not entirely without foundation. Enjoying an unrivalled position of economic and geopolitical power similar to that exercised in the next century by the United States, Great Britain emerged after the fall of Napoleon as a globe-girding colossus whose reach extended far beyond its territorial dominions. Still, citizens of the American republic tended to exaggerate the threat from abroad. Much like other peoples in the developing world who have feared foreign domination, they ascribed to the imperial power an omnipotence it did not possess. It was widely believed that Britain, having failed to subdue its wayward North American colonies by force of arms, would now seek to accomplish the same object by indirect means. The belief that the danger from Great Britain would henceforth appear in veiled form only made it more menacing for many conspiratorially minded Americans. Allowing their imaginations free rein, Anglophobes espied an evil empire of Mephistophelean dimensions, convinced that Whitehall was secretly marshalling the full resources of British power in a vast, insidious campaign against them. John Bull seemed to be "here, there, and everywhere, plotting mischief and injury," one British visitor observed. He added, archly: "If money is scarce, it is England that has occasioned it—if credit is bad, it is England—if eggs are not fresh or beef is tough, it is, it must be, England."[10]

Even when Americans quarreled among themselves, they found it difficult to set aside their deeply rooted suspicions of the nation's traditional adversary. By the mid-1820s, the Jeffersonian consensus had disintegrated, as an increasingly uncertain and volatile marketplace produced a bitter national debate over federal economic policy. Urban growing pains brought class and ethnic tensions suddenly to the fore in the Mid-Atlantic states. Most ominously of all, the early rumblings of antislavery sentiment in the North were beginning to reveal the fault lines of a regional divide that would grow ever wider in the years ahead. To a more secure nation, these developments would have been seen as domestic problems only, with little connection to the world beyond its borders. But Americans still regarded Great Britain as an imperial hegemon bent on their demise, and consequently looked for an overseas connection whenever internal crises arose. Rare was the political controversy which was not accompanied by charges of "foreign influence." Leaders of varying partisan hues accused parliamentary cabals of rigging elections and disseminating propaganda to subvert American institutions. When faced with unsatisfactory political outcomes, they came swiftly to the same conclusion: that a fifth column of crypto-Tories was at work, bought and paid for with British gold.

Americans, too, were becoming increasingly frustrated by the extent to which Great Britain continued to shape the world in which they lived. Americans were among the world's biggest consumers of British-made goods, which accounted for 40 percent of the total value of U.S. imports.[11] They ate on plates from the kilns of Staffordshire, using flatware made in Sheffield, and dressed in clothing from the textile mills of Lancashire. Culturally, too, Americans remained moored to William Cowper's "fast-anchor'd isle." American institutions of higher learning modeled their curricula after the great English universities; the American reading public devoured the most popular contemporary British novelists, while British-owned theater companies staged the latest London plays, often performed by visiting British actors. So great was the demand for information from Europe, and especially from Britain, that Eastern metropolitan newspapers usually devoted more space to foreign events than the latest news from the western states. By the 1830s, Gotham's biggest daily newspapers used fleet sailboats to meet the transatlantic steamships as they approached the Narrows at the mouth of

New York Harbor to obtain the most recent foreign papers, the contents of which could then be reprinted and made available to readers on the streets of the city in a matter of hours. Foreign travelers in the United States never failed to be surprised by Americans' knowledge of events in England. "There was great eagerness for English news," one observed; "all the names and actions of our public men seem quite as familiar to the Americans generally as to ourselves."[12]

The country's continued fascination with all things British had long been a sore point for those who had expected, naively perhaps, that a declaration of political independence would effect a complete separation from the Old World. Not only had the new republic been woefully unable to escape what Jefferson called "the broils of Europe" after the Revolution, but it had continued to be corrupted by "English books, English prejudices, [and] English manners," a state of affairs which, he believed, posed a greater danger than force of arms. After 1815, Americans became even more conscious of the web of transatlantic connections that rendered them, for all intents and purposes, a cultural and economic satellite of the British empire. This heightened awareness was due largely to the fact that the patriotic fervor of the postwar years encouraged them to address the issue of nationhood as never before. And the more they did so, the more they were struck by the ways in which complete independence still eluded them. As they sought to discover the bonds that connected them as a people, so they became alert as never before to the chains that still shackled them to their colonial past.[13]

Thus, Americans liked to think of the War of 1812 as a "second war for independence," as the coda in the struggle to free themselves from British rule. Some went even further, and in their more exuberant moments saw nothing less than their country's transfiguration from fledgling republic to continental power. But Americans were inclined to overstate the significance of 1815 as a watershed moment. Even as the nation grew westward, it remained firmly fixed on a transatlantic axis. Even as its citizens reveled in the ballyhoo of patriotic celebrations, they remained apprehensive of British power. Their anxiety stemmed in part from a vague feeling that Americans exercised less control over their own affairs than they liked to believe; it also arose from a growing sense that their much-vaunted national unity was not all it seemed. The return of peace may have signaled a new chapter in the republic's short history, but the fact remained that theirs was still a developing nation, one whose revolution remained unfinished, whose future remained uncertain.[14]

The Many Faces of John Bull

From the foregoing it should be clear that American attitudes toward the British defied simple analysis and broad generalization. For most citizens of the republic during this period, there was not one John Bull, but many. It could hardly be otherwise, given the farrago of issues—cultural, commercial, and geopolitical—that informed their point of view. One essayist for the *New York Review* commented at length on the diversity—and seeming inconsistency—of American feelings toward the imperial parent. "From the lips of one man you may hear the expressions of a deep-toned reverence for the 'old country,'" the writer noted. Then again, one might just as easily find, from individuals alike in every other respect, "the opposite feeling of dislike and repugnance . . . as if the best evidences of loyalty and love to our country were to be found in enmity to England and Englishmen."[15]

Nor was it a simple matter of subdividing Americans neatly into opposing camps of Anglophobes and Anglophiles. Sometimes, the *New York Review* essayist noted, the same citizen could be found "giving utterance, at different moments and under different impulses," to both viewpoints. This was frequently the case when Americans struggled to reconcile their fondness for British cultural life with their hostility toward British policies. The South Carolina lawyer and diplomat Joel R. Poinsett may serve as a case in point. Schooled in England, Poinsett established close friendships with classmates with whom he would faithfully correspond for the rest of his life. "I love England and never have forgotten my early impressions of its scenery and its people," he wrote to one in 1842. Yet these ties in no way compromised his unwavering republicanism, or his conviction that the United States must exercise constant vigilance against an opportunistic empire determined to extend its hegemony in the western hemisphere.[16] The ability to assume two essentially disjunctive roles—private Anglophile and public Anglophobe—was a trait Poinsett shared with many political elites. Those who occupied positions of privilege often had close ties to Great Britain, but were obliged to delineate between their personal associations and civic obligations. English virtues resided in the English people, English vices in its tyrannical system of government. In the middle of a fiery anti-British polemic on the floor of the House of Representatives in 1842, Virginia Whig Henry Wise paused to point out that he "derived every drop of the blood in his veins" from that country, praising the "fatherland" as the font of American culture. But although he "loved her, honored her; he loved her arts; he loved her learning," Wise declared that "he hated English arrogance; he hated English selfishness; he hated English ambition."[17] Venerable paterfamilias one minute, haughty, belligerent bully the next, John Bull was for many Americans a polymorphous figure, capable of assuming multiple personalities.

Still, a few general observations regarding American attitudes toward Great Britain can be safely made. Just as the colonial gentry had experienced divided loyalties during the Revolution, subsequent generations of well-to-do Americans would have a difficult time trying to reconcile their innate Anglophilia with the values of republicanism. The advent of a more democratic culture during the early decades of the nineteenth century did not make their dilemma any easier. Recoiling in horror at the leveling tendencies that were reshaping many aspects of American life, a cosmopolitan beau monde looked ever more wistfully at the hierarchical world across the Atlantic. Philadelphia aristocrat Sidney George Fisher, who unapologetically declared, "My hatred of democracy is stronger than my love of country," was one of many elites who clung to an idealized image of England. It mattered little that the island empire was experiencing its own forms of social upheaval as a result of industrialization. Fisher saw in England what he wanted to see: a well-ordered social system, where rank and status still mattered and the hoi polloi knew its proper place.[18] Looking to London for standards of taste and gentility, Americans of privilege insisted on "talking like the English, thinking like the English," and in other ways behaving like their transatlantic brethren. They read books and subscribed to highbrow magazines published in Britain, attended plays written and performed by Britons, and turned out en masse at the galas held to honor visiting British celebrities. London fashions were in such high demand among the upper classes that the latest styles for the summer season invariably made their appearance in northern cities by the fall or winter (prompting humorist James Kirke Paulding to speculate that this was the cause of the inordinately high rate of consumption among American women).[19]

For those who could afford it, the British experience was best discovered firsthand. The grand tour took on the character of a pilgrimage for some, who paid dutiful homage to Westminster Abbey, the birthplace of Sir Walter Scott, and many other sacred sites. Not all were drawn by the goal of cultural enrichment; many, in fact, seemed more intent on rubbing shoulders with as many blue bloods as possible. The object of much ridicule at home, American nabobs were said to abandon all republican pretensions once on British soil, as they sought to wheedle their way into London society. They returned stateside "rogues and fops," with little to show for their travels but "extravagant anti-American notions."[20] For a few, especially those who resented the inferior position in which they were held by their Anglophone cousins, the experience was not all they had hoped. South Carolina politician and lawyer Hugh S. Legaré, who prided himself on his intellectual attainments, bristled when an Oxford professor of classics did not treat him with due respect, and summed up his trip by stating that he had "learnt to be *an American.*" James Henry Hammond, a self-confessed lover of Old World pomp and ceremony, became so convinced that he was being fleeced at every turn by British tradespeople that he was moved to declare: "Although you are the land of my ancestors, I hate and detest you." More often than not, however, Americans of privilege saw a visit to the British Isles as an emotional homecoming. "When I touched English ground I could have fallen on my knees and kissed it," the novelist Catherine Maria Sedgwick wrote to a relative during a trip abroad.[21]

Even geopolitical crises that brought the two nations to the brink of war were sometimes not enough to shake American upper classes from their Anglophile reverie. When the British author Frederick Marryat toured the Northern states in the late 1830s at the height of the Canadian rebellions, which threatened to erupt into a wider, transatlantic conflict involving the United States, he was struck by the pains which New England gentlemen took to convince him that they felt no hostile feeling toward Great Britain. Visiting the same part of the country at the height of the Maine boundary crisis a few years later, a British army officer was similarly astonished by the Anglophile feeling he encountered among local elites, all of whom claimed to be descended from British royalty. "All-republican as they claim to be," he wrote, "I consider them the proudest and most aristocratic people I ever beheld."[22]

A very different image of John Bull prevailed in the working-class neighborhoods of American cities, where the republic's appetite for cheap, British-made consumer goods imperiled the livelihoods of craft laborers and unskilled workers alike. While most were native-born, even recent emigrants from the British Isles could be found stoking resentment of their homeland. Many took an active part in the nascent American trade union movement, urging their fellow laborers to take a stand against the advent of a mechanized, impersonal workplace similar to the one they had experienced in Britain. During the 1830s and 1840s, the ranks of Gotham's poor would be swelled by a wave of immigrants from Ireland, making Anglophobia a permanent feature of Tammany Hall campaign rhetoric. With a loathing of England that was seared into their cultural memory, the new immigrants "bring their feuds and their animosities with them," one essayist scornfully observed, adding that "such luggage ought to be considered contraband." Although tensions between native-born workers and the Irish would eventually help to undermine what little cohesion the urban labor movement enjoyed, hostility to Great Britain would remain constant, an article of faith shared by a wide cross-section of working-class groups.[23]

Regional identities, too, came into play in shaping American attitudes toward the imperial parent. Nowhere were Anglophile sentiments more in evidence than in New England. An Anglo-Saxon enclave in an increasingly polyglot nation, the region had managed to retain the folkways of its Puritan descendants, prompting some inhabitants to inform surprised Britons that "they are more English than we are."[24] Only in the northernmost states did British travelers feel truly at home during their tours of the United States. Consanguinity was not the only bond linking the peoples of Old and New England. Local mercantile interests exerted considerable political influence, and could be counted on to lobby heavily for amicable relations between the two countries. At the same time, no other part of the republic felt a greater admiration for Britain's cultural achievements. Home to the nation's oldest universities—the largely conservative bastions of an antiquarian intellectual tradition—New England exhibited the deepest reverence for English literature, jurisprudence, and political theory. The region's rich cultural life had given rise to a strong humanistic impulse that found common cause with like-minded Britons over a variety of reform issues, from public education to religious instruction to antislavery. These transatlantic bonds helped foster a political culture in which anti-British feeling played a relatively minor role. Indeed, only in New England could prominent politicians publicly express their fondness for Great Britain without risk to their careers. While speaking on the subject of U.S.-British relations during a campaign rally in Boston in 1844, Daniel Webster was interrupted by a heckler who cried out, "They are all slaves in England." The remark earned a stern rebuke from the imposing senator. "Who dares thus to libel the land of his ancestors?" he intoned, and proceeded to lecture the individual on the great cultural debt the republic owed to Great Britain. Webster's remonstrances, one reporter noted, "were received with general and hearty cheers" from the crowd.[25]

The South, not surprisingly, exhibited the most conflicted feelings toward Great Britain. Lord Cornwallis's ruthless campaign to root out guerrilla insurgents in Georgia and the Carolinas during the Revolution had left a lasting animus against the British in the Southeastern states. Nonetheless, the tidewater elite traditionally cherished the image of a pastoral England, aping the manners and mores of its landed nobility. With the rise of the cotton empire, the Deep South would become more firmly tied to Great Britain than any other region of the country. By the 1840s, the textile mills of the Midlands were purchasing roughly two-thirds of the South's cotton crop, three-fourths of Britain's total cotton imports. As incomes rose, a nouveau riche class of cotton lords exhibited a sentimental Anglophilia not unlike their Tidewater counterparts. Harboring aristocratic pretensions of their own, men like the Mississippi planter and Whig politician S. S. Prentiss expressed "a hearty affection for Old England." And yet these sentiments could evaporate in an instant when questions over the future of the peculiar institution arose. Alarmed by Parliament's historic decision in 1833 to abolish slavery in the West Indies, Southern planters responded to rumors that linked Great Britain to the American antislavery movement with paroxysms of wild-eyed, Anglophobic hysteria. A fondness for "the Mother Country" notwithstanding, Southern planters like Prentiss felt their interests, indeed their very way of life, to be more directly threatened by Whitehall's policies than any other group of Americans.[26]

The Trans-Appalachian States was the only region of the country where hostility toward Great Britain existed in unalloyed form. An historically Anglophobic Scots-Irish population had gravitated to the republic's western fringes in the late eighteenth and early nineteenth centuries. Western elites, in contrast to the urban parvenus of the eastern seaboard, had inherited the anti-British sentiments of their hardscrabble forbears. Few traveled abroad, and were thus less likely to ape the manners of British nabobs, or to assiduously follow the latest European fashion trends. Economically, the region was not as closely linked to Britain as other parts of the country. Farmers large and small resented Parliament's Corn Laws, which denied them access to lucrative British markets. Equally important, land hunger prompted western Americans to agitate for a program of territorial growth, putting them frequently at odds with Whitehall, which was committed to thwarting the expansion of its North American rival. Past conflicts with Great Britain, too, were part of the calculus of Anglophobia in the transmontane region. When it learned of rumors that the British government was seeking to prevent the United States from annexing Texas in the mid-1840s, the *Kentucky Yeoman* issued a bellicose call to arms. Recalling the heroics of an earlier generation, it declared that the "brave and chivalrous Kentuckians who met and vanquished the British Lion when he assailed our homes in 1812 . . . will again pour out rivers of blood before he shall set his polluting foot upon the soil of the young [Texas] republic."[27]

Popular attitudes toward Great Britain, it must be emphasized, were never static during the early decades of the nineteenth century. For many Americans, their feelings toward Great Britain were situational and subject to change. While Irish and Scots-Irish Americans exhibited a knee-jerk hostility toward England, most citizens were not Anglophobes by habit or by nature. For a few weeks in the summer of 1838, for example, the entire nation seemed to be swept up in a fever of Anglomania occasioned by the coronation of the nineteen-year-old Queen Victoria.[28] Notwithstanding the frequently adversarial official intercourse between the two governments, a majority of Americans were inclined to believe that the bonds of consanguinity made the United States and Great Britain natural allies, and held out the hope that amicable relations between the two countries would one day be restored.

The Postcolonial Predicament: Continuity vs. Originality

In a Thanksgiving Day sermon delivered in New Haven in 1840, the Congregationalist minister H. G. Ludlow reflected upon the blessings for which he and his congregation could be thankful. Painting an undeniably rosy view of the state of the republic (then in the throes of a severe economic downturn), Ludlow opined that theirs was a nation without broad distinctions of class and inequality of wealth. Theirs was a nation, too, where all citizens enjoyed access to educational opportunities and religious freedom. And as he pointed with patriotic pride to each of the republic's many virtues, he asked his congregation the same rhetorical question, "Is there any thing like this in England?"[29]

The answer, of course, did not hazard a doubt: the United States could claim a great many advantages over Great Britain. Yet in making the comparison at all, Ludlow underscored the fact that he, like so many Americans, was incapable of evaluating his country on its own terms. No matter how great the strides made by the republic, evidence of national progress was still measured by standards established abroad. When Americans took stock of their country, they invariably employed a transatlantic frame of reference. It was the only way they knew to gauge how far as a people they had come, and how far they still had to go.

In truth, Americans could not help but look to England for a sense of who they were. Even those who could not claim English descent were inclined to view the republic as the most recent point on an historical continuum in the Anglo-Saxon's quest for political liberty that had begun with the Magna Carta. Americans had no desire to repudiate the parliamentary tradition that had so inspired the leaders of the Revolution, believing that "every genuine American republican carries the spirit of John Hampden in his bosom."[30] After 1815 this line of reasoning became difficult to sustain, as many states abolished voting restrictions based on property and established a democratic system for white male citizens that bore little similarity to the parliamentary rule of British oligarchs. Nonetheless, most Anglo-Americans accepted as axiomatic the view that the republican tree of liberty was of English genus, transplanted and now flourishing in new, more fertile soil. Culturally, too, citizens of the republic were eager to appropriate the imperial parent's greatest achievements as their own. "The best English literature is ours," insisted the Southern novelist William Gilmore Simms, who believed that the former colonies' political separation could not deny Americans their "rich inheritance of blood and language." In drawing attention to their British antecedents, Americans claimed for their fledgling republic an instant legitimacy. Endowed with an unimpeachable pedigree and the language, laws, and literature of "the most civilized and improved nation of the world," the United States seemed eminently prepared to one day take its place among the first rank of great powers.[31]

American Anglophiles, of course, were the most eager to claim their transatlantic inheritance. In their view, an indissoluble bond existed between the two nations that had not been severed by independence. So enamored were they of Great Britain that they could only hope that its luster might continue to shine, however dimly, upon its American progeny. They routinely employed familial imagery to express the cultural debt which they owed the seat of the Anglophone world. At a public reception honoring a British diplomat in 1842, the mayor of Boston offered this toast: "So long as there is a tie to link a child to its parent, America will not forget that England is her mother." Mindful of the political upheavals which other fledgling nation-states had suffered, they credited the British parliamentary tradition with the success of American representative institutions. Indeed, to that country's parenting skills alone could be attributed the remarkable ease with which the young nation had endured those awkward developing years. Having been "well schooled in our boyhood," the republic was now ready to abandon its leading strings and stand alone.[32]

But not all Americans were so quick to look to Britain for their birthright. As they pondered the republic's relationship with the imperial parent, many found themselves questioning whether "these mighty boons" of English cultural achievement might not be a serious liability. If the United States had indeed "leaped, mature and panoplied, from the teeming brain of her progenitor," as one Virginia orator declared in 1839, could it really claim to be anything more than a copy, a mere simulacrum of British virtues? It was one thing to acknowledge a rich cultural heritage, quite another to argue, as did Ralph Waldo Emerson, that the genius of the United States was but a continuation of English genius under new and propitious conditions. Was there not, after all, something a little inappropriate about Americans' infatuation with a world steeped in the values of aristocracy and privilege? Even the staunchest Anglophiles were willing to concede that their reverence for English cultural life "may be perverted to our intellectual injury," by prohibiting the republic from achieving preeminence on its own merits. Most educated observers, regardless of their feelings toward Great Britain, recognized that the ligaments of colonialism were still deeply imbedded in American life, making it all but impossible for the nation to acquire a set of features it could call its own.[33]

By the second quarter of the nineteenth century, the imitativeness of American life had become something of an idée fixe for many Jacksonian pundits and essayists, who had come to realize that political sovereignty was only the first step in a much more elaborate and protracted process of national self-definition. Incessantly, they bemoaned the fact that the republic was as dependent on Great Britain for their "*laws, customs, manners, fashions, morals, literature arts, science, and manufactures,*" as it had ever been. Far from being analogous to the domestic relations of the family, the British connection to the United States seemed to many Americans more like the oppressive bonds that existed between master and slave. Adopting the imagery of bondage, they were reminded of Joshua's enslavement of the Gibeonites, and in their more fretful moments wondered if they were forever destined to remain "hewers of wood and drawers of water," to British masters. Complete liberation could never be won "if one nation is always to teach, and the other always to learn," wrote one Irish-born New Yorker. "Must we tread always in their steps, go where they go, be what they are, do what they do, and say what they say?"[34]

The need to mimic British forms and behaviors might not have seemed so objectionable had it not struck at one of the foundational pillars of the American narrative: the nation's sense of uniqueness. Even before the birth of their republic, Americans had entertained the notion they had been marked for a special destiny, regarding their system of representative government as a beacon of liberty that would bring light to the Stygian darkness of the Old World. The salons of Europe had helped fuel this conceit, hailing the American republican experiment as the acme of rational endeavor. But the Enlightenment had run its course, a victim of the political upheavals that had rocked Europe in the years between the fall of the Bastille and the Battle of Waterloo. This turbulent period would refocus the intellectual energies of post-Napoleonic Europe, giving rise to new political ideologies that emphasized the innate rather than the institutional. A distinct culture and language, a storied history—these were the attributes of nationhood that now seemed to matter most, qualities which were in short supply in Britain's former colonies. When the European Romantics spoke of a *volkgeist*, a national identity that was organic and immutable, it was clear they did not have Americans in mind.[35]

The stirrings of European nationalism were greeted with enthusiasm by highbrow periodicals in the United States, but also with undeniable feelings of dismay. Ever attuned to overseas intellectual trends, they studied ad nauseum the relevance of these developments to the American experience. In vain they searched for a "spirit" that might define so disparate and ethnically diverse a people. A national consciousness of any sort, an essayist for the *North American Review* opined, would be eminently preferable to the "second-hand" nationalism of a country still bound by the fetters of colonialism. This abject dependence prompted the historian Francis Parkman to observe that an "educated Englishman is an Englishman still; an educated Frenchman is often intensely French; but an educated American is apt to have no national character at all." Impatiently, they wondered how long it would be before the United States divested itself of its colonial appurtenances and developed an identity of its own. One Baltimore editor in 1819 predicted that it would take another generation, maybe two, before the national character was fully formed and Americans could think at last for themselves. James Fenimore Cooper offered an even gloomier prognosis: "We must make up our minds, I fear; to live our time as the inhabitants of a mere colony—A century hence things will improve, perhaps, but not in our day."[36]

Americans sought to reconcile this yearning for uniqueness with their claims to a British inheritance in imaginative ways. Some maintained that the political act of separation had had profound sociocultural implications, freeing citizens of the republic from all forms of foreign hegemony. Americans were the product of the best British traditions, said one writer, but their unnatural worship of the imperial parent had ceased at the precise moment that "the besotted ministry of George the Third determined to soil us of this heritage." In an address commemorating Washington's birthday in 1832, University of Nashville president Phillip Lindsley acknowledged that the heroes of the Revolution possessed "English hearts and English virtues," but in severing their political ties to the Crown they had freed themselves from English influence. Americans were thus entitled to all the advantages and privileges of a great cultural tradition, but unencumbered by the vestiges of a corrupt and archaic past. Lindsley dismissed out of hand the idea that the republic's origins had in any way diluted its special character. By its act of separation, the Revolutionary generation had forged a new nation from new materials, becoming a people as different from "British feeling and usage, as if we had sprung from a different race."[37]

For many intellectuals, however, the argument that a political event had somehow had an alchemical effect on the national DNA, transforming Britons magically into something else—Americans—seemed, at the very least, wishful thinking. To make the case for national distinctiveness an explicitly racial one, some patriots offered the argument that the nation's bloodline, despite its English origins, was nonetheless uniquely American. Such was the novel reasoning of the scholar and conservationist George Perkins Marsh, who regarded the English character as an amalgam of Roman and Gothic influences. To the former could be traced the Briton's "grasping ambition" and self-aggrandizement, to the latter his moral and intellectual power. The historic struggle for religious and political liberty in England, Marsh argued, was at its root a conflict in which the competing impulses of Roman tyranny and Gothic liberty battled for dominance. With the English migration to the Americas, this struggle had entered a new phase. Those who represented the best Gothic traditions had abandoned their homeland to Roman sybarites, leaving them to their sensual pleasures, their love of pomp and ceremony, their fondness of hereditary titles. Thus, Marsh ingeniously managed to turn on its head the idea, widely held even on his own side of the Atlantic, that the early colonists represented the offscourings of England. Rather, it was the dissolute who had been left behind! It was "the spirit of the Goth," he insisted, "that guided the May-Flower across the trackless ocean; the blood of the Goth that flowed at Bunker's Hill."[38]

In the end, these tortured turns of logic could do little to hide the fact that Brother Jonathan, as the young nation was often called, still bore a distinct resemblance to his more celebrated cousin. Frustrated, a great many social commentators urged their fellow citizens to disassociate themselves, root and branch, from the imperial parent. The fevered nationalism Americans exhibited during this period increasingly devolved into a simple rejection of anything even remotely associated with Great Britain, as public figures framed the American experience in terms of a contest between the Old World and the New. In literature and the arts, the emergence of a native-born author or actor was promptly hailed as a deliverer from cultural bondage. Political leaders who challenged British power were cheered as the true heirs of the Revolutionary generation. Indeed, anything which seemed to widen the divide between the two countries could be dubbed by patriotic pundits a new declaration of independence.

The desire to exorcize British influences from American life was, at times, carried to extremes. Among the most radical of these ideas was the codification movement, which called for the creation of an entirely new legal code to take the place of English common law. Forming the basis of the American legal system, common law arose out of the customs, rules, and social practices of Saxon England. Cumbrous, antiquated, and all but incomprehensible to the layperson, it seemed to many Americans wholly ill-suited to the needs of a democratic society. Codification had begun as a pet project of Jeremy Bentham and other British utilitarians who found their way to the United States during the Jeffersonian period, but would emerge as a full-fledged movement, gaining adherents and momentum, in the climate of intense nationalism around the time of the country's fiftieth anniversary. In an address to the New York Historical Society in 1823, William Sampson, an exiled Irish nationalist who had twice been imprisoned by the British government, delivered the first influential critique of the American legal system's English foundations. The address sparked a vigorous debate among the nation's legal scholars, with jurists from Boston to New York to South Carolina calling for a complete break with English forms. By the 1830s, radical Jacksonians joined in the clamor against common law, which they denounced as a tool of the rich to keep the working classes in a perpetual state of peonage. Although codification attracted a wide range of disparate constituencies, each with their own objections to legal tradition, all claimed higher, patriotic motives, upbraiding the nation's legal community for its obsequious servility to an Old World system that was inimical to American institutions.[39]

Even John Bull's claims to sole custody of the English language were seen as evidence of the nation's subordinate status. Long before Oscar Wilde observed that Great Britain and the United States were two countries separated by a common language, Britons had noticed that Americans were not reluctant to take liberties with the mother tongue. Although a few cultural nationalists like Noah Webster had led the way in defending the country's right to modify the King's English around the turn of the century, Americans did not become inordinately sensitive on the issue until the 1820s, when British writers began to cross the Atlantic in increasing numbers to witness these idiomatic transgressions for themselves. In response, Americans protested that Great Britain was no more entitled to a monopoly over the language than to the production of textiles or iron, and complained that they could not "presume to turn a noun into a verb, or add a monosyllable to the stock of English words," without incurring British displeasure. There were, as always, a few indignant patriots who went so far as to assert, without the benefit of evidence or plausibility, that the republic would always improve upon anything the Old World had to offer. The author of one geography primer for schoolchildren, for example, was willing to declare unequivocally that the English language "is spoken in far greater purity of idiom and intonation with us than in Great Britain." Most educated Americans sensed, however, even if they could not bring themselves to admit as much, that a bowdlerized language was not something they could point to with feelings of national pride. The debate over American colloquial speech was but another reminder of the ways in which the republic would always be judged by standards that were not its own. It was almost enough to make one frustrated editorialist wish that the nation could be as widely separated from the imperial parent "by a difference of language," as it was physically by the Atlantic Ocean.[40]

Obviously, there were limits to how far the republic could go in rooting out British influences. The young nation found itself perched uncomfortably on the horns of a dilemma: should it seek continuity, preserving the time-honored, venerable traditions of its past, or aspire to originality, jettisoning British forms and precedents in favor of a new order? A great many Americans, certainly, would have preferred to do both. William Gilmore Simms spoke for many of his fellow citizens when he stated that they would have to be judicious, deciding which aspects of English culture they wanted to discard, which ones they wanted to keep. "Our parents were English, but our garments need not be made by an English tailor. Our language is English, but such need not be the case with our literature. Our sense of liberty is English, but it does not follow that we might not rid ourselves of some of the brutalities of English law."[41]

Alas, it was not that simple. Even the selective appropriation of British norms implied a certain level of cultural indebtedness, a tacit admission of the republic's derivative character. Undeterred, Americans would continue to proclaim their exceptionalism, even as they remained more than a little unclear as to what that entailed.

❖❖

The years following the republic's second war for independence would find Americans more preoccupied with who they were, as a nation and a people, than at any time in their history. And while the idea of "Americanness" had become ever more important, it had also become ever more difficult to define. Inevitably, the figure of John Bull loomed large as they pondered these questions of identity. To a considerable extent, Americans still felt anchored in a British world, and acutely aware of their second-class standing within it. Most could agree—at least in theory—that the wholesale repudiation of Old World ideas should be a guiding principle for the young republic. Yet the centripetal pull of Britain's imperial orbit remained strong. It was easy enough to call for an end to British influences, but even the most strident Anglophobe often found it difficult to translate these convictions into practice.

In the final analysis, though, it was not the elusive goal of complete independence, but the search for it that mattered. Americans could never entirely disentangle their nation from the dense thicket of connections to Great Britain that had grown up around them over the past two hundred years. This did not stop them from trying, however. As the chapters that follow will seek to demonstrate, they strove to set themselves apart, self-consciously crafting a contrary set of attitudes and behaviors (albeit in a manner that was fitful and often inconsistent). Americans did not deliberately set about to create a national character. But in the process of distinguishing themselves from the British they were better able to arrive at one. Lacking a clear sense of what a national identity should be, they had to settle for what they knew it was not. To become more American, they would first have to become less British.

⊱ 2 ⊰

"What Do You Think of Our Country?"

Ye wandering scribblers who infest the land,
Spleen in your souls and papers in your hand;
Whose hearts a "goodly matter" do indite,
Who write to live—just heavens—and live to write . . .
Time was—ah! pity that the time is o'er—
When British fools ne'er left the shore,
Nor e'en indulg'd the slightest wish to roam,
Contented to be spurned and lashed at home.
—Frederick William Shelton, *The Trollopiad*

There was no greater testament to the limits of American independence than the extraordinary importance that citizens of the republic attached to British opinions. And of all those opinions, John Bull's views regarding their nation's prospects and development fascinated them most. Visitors from the British Isles would publish more than one hundred and fifty accounts of their travels in North America during the first half of the nineteenth century, while British literary quarterlies and magazines teemed with essays and editorials on the institutions, habits, and customs of the inhabitants of the United States. Though intended for a British readership, this enormous body of literature received far greater scrutiny stateside, poured over and debated endlessly by a self-conscious American public that exhibited a manic, almost compulsive need for foreign praise. To their great chagrin, Americans found that they did not always meet with John Bull's approval. They bristled at the Tory condescension that colored many of these critiques, and the almost gleeful eagerness with which some British writers drew attention to republican shortcomings. As a result, the unrequited desire for approbation soon bred feelings of deep resentment. More than any other single issue, the ongoing assault from British pens would serve to keep American animosities simmering long after the memories of military conflict had faded.[1]

One of the first Americans to take umbrage at British carping and rise to the defense of his country was Charles Jared Ingersoll. A young Philadelphia attorney, Ingersoll seemed an unlikely figure to lead the fight against the nation's foreign detractors. His prominent and well-connected family had come late to the Revolutionary cause, and in the years that followed remained steeped in the cultural traditions that bound the new republic fast to Great Britain. His father, Jared, a prominent Federalist, had been one of the "midnight judges" removed from the bench during Jefferson's first hours as president, and would be the party's vice-presidential nominee in 1812. During the son's early years, the apple did not fall far from the Federalist tree. Imbibing the political principles of his father, and the Anglophile proclivities that went with them, Charles Jared Ingersoll received his education at Princeton, then made the obligatory grand tour of Britain and the Continent. There he became the protégé and traveling companion of the Federalist luminary Rufus King, a family friend, who was then serving as the U.S. minister to the Court of St. James's. Upon his return stateside, Ingersoll was admitted to the bar, and like many of his social class, leavened his professional life with occasional forays into the belletristic sphere. Enjoying some success as a gentleman of letters, the young Philadelphia aristocrat penned a play and contributed verse to the literary journal favored by local highbrows, Jonathan Dennie's fiercely anti-democratic Port Folio.

The events leading up to the second war with Great Britain would bring about a seismic shift in Ingersoll's political worldview. When the British warship Leopard, in an effort to remove deserters of the Royal Navy, attacked the Chesapeake off the coast of Virginia in 1807, the Philadelphia attorney fired off a broadside of his own in the form of a pamphlet entitled "A View of the Rights and Wrongs, Power and Policy, of the United States of America." A defense of the commercial and maritime policies of the Jefferson administration, the tract marked his complete renunciation of the Federalist Party's pro-British principles. Ingersoll's growing unhappiness with the transatlantic relationship was not limited to the deteriorating political situation between the two countries. More and more, the young Philadelphian could not abide the slavish Anglophilia of his class, which affected English manners and habits while holding up to ridicule all that was American. Sending a copy to Rufus King, Ingersoll tried to prepare him for his apostasy from Federalist doctrines, warning his old friend that he would find within its pages "politics you do not admire, sentiments you can not concur in, arguments you consider false," but that his loyalty to country came before his attachment to party.[2]

That same year, 1807, Ingersoll read a copy of *The Stranger in America*, an account of Charles William Janson's thirteen-year residence in the United States. A failed English businessman who had never felt at home in the young republic, Janson was appalled by the "impudent freedom" that Americans enjoyed. Such a lack of restraint, he believed, was the root of all manner of social ills. It eroded the proper boundaries that defined relations between the classes and contributed to high rates of juvenile delinquency. Nor was this all; the leveling tendencies of republican society, Janson suggested, had even been the cause of an unseemly familiarity between the sexes.[3] Moved to issue a response, the twenty-eight-year-old Ingersoll published, in 1810, *Inchiquin, the Jesuit's Letters*, a series of letters purporting to be the correspondence of an Irish priest visiting the United States. Ingersoll's fictional correspondent credited the very same freedoms Janson deplored with creating a general prosperity and healthy moral climate, making Americans "the happiest and least depraved people in the world." Once again, Ingersoll did not limit his scorn to foreign critics, but chided the beau monde, whose preference for European manners and customs he now regarded as nothing less than an insidious form of treason.[4]

Some members of the Federalist Party regarded Ingersoll's defection as a personal betrayal, believing he had bowed to popular opinion to advance his political career. But the charge was unfair. Ingersoll was no opportunist who tacked toward the prevailing political winds; his conversion to Jeffersonian principles was deeply felt and lifelong. So too was his unyielding Anglophobia. In later years, ten of which would be spent in Congress, Ingersoll waged a personal crusade against British influences, using his position to draw attention to the many ways in which the imperial parent continued to hold sway over the United States. When Northern citizens denounced Southern slavery, Ingersoll assumed they had been gulled by British reformers. When the economy collapsed in the late 1830s, he accused British banks of deliberately precipitating the crisis. When some Americans objected to Washington's efforts to acquire more territory in the West, he assumed they were acting in the interests of a British government determined to thwart the republic's rise as a continental power.[5]

Before the country could successfully fend off these challenges, the Philadelphian believed, it would first have to break free of its reliance on foreign opinions. So long as Americans looked across the Atlantic for their intellectual aliment, so long as they craved the high esteem of the British, full and complete independence would remain elusive. Although he respected Great Britain—"It is impossible not to admire her grandeur," he would later write—Ingersoll argued that the United States would never develop an identity of its own until it learned to think for itself. Not until it emerged from the chrysalis of its postcolonial state could it reach its full maturity as a nation.[6]

Americans who harbored no special fondness for Great Britain would find it easy enough to endorse Ingersoll's plea for cultural independence. But what of the intellectual community, which had always deferred to, and sought the validation of, the London literati? With the publication of *Inchiquin*, Ingersoll called on the nation's highbrows to reject the judgments of British essayists and travel writers. To Americans who traditionally, even instinctively, sought the benediction of the imperial parent, this would be no easy task.

The "Paper War"

As was so often the case with books published in the United States during the early national period, *Inchiquin* would never have caused a stir had it not first attracted notice in Great Britain. In recent years, a pair of periodicals, the Whiggish *Edinburgh Review* and its Tory counterpart, the *Quarterly Review,* had come to enjoy wide influence among the British privileged classes, and despite the outbreak of war, could claim a devoted readership among the cognoscenti in the United States as well. Devoted primarily to criticism of recently published works in literature, science, and the arts, the journals allowed contributors a wide berth, with reviews often serving as points of embarkation for much more wide-ranging commentary. In the January 1814 issue of the *Quarterly Review,* there appeared a vitriolic attack on the United States in the form of a belated review of Ingersoll's *Inchiquin*, which would prove to be the opening salvo in a "paper war" between the two nations. The unsigned, thirty-seven-page essay, widely attributed to the poet Robert Southey, offered a churlish, wholesale indictment of the American people and their republican institutions. Borrowing from the already sizable canon of British travel literature on the United States, the author grumbled at the poor accommodations of American inns, characterized its lawmakers as uncouth rowdies, and dismissed its literary lions as men of mediocre talent. Even the country's greatest public figures were not spared the reviewer's contempt. To the great irritation of Americans, the author was willing to concede—grudgingly—that Washington had been "an honest man." His verdict of Benjamin Franklin was less charitable still; the famous Philadelphian was dismissed as a man of only modest intellectual abilities, who had acquired most of his knowledge during his sojourns in London.[7]

Southey's remarks posed a dilemma for American highbrows, who invariably deferred on cultural matters to the opinions of British periodicals. Despite the unpopularity of the war in Federalist circles, the *Quarterly Review* essay represented a direct attack on both the institutions of the United States and its most revered icons, and, as such, could not be allowed to go unchallenged. For those Eastern elites who had opposed the disruption of trade with the imperial parent, the verbal assault on the nation offered an opportunity to reaffirm their patriotic mettle. Timothy Dwight, president of Yale College, was characteristic of the conflicted loyalties of many well-to-do New Englanders, who took umbrage at British criticism but whose filiopietism remained undiminished. As a member of the group of poets known as the Connecticut Wits, Dwight had played a prominent role in the gestation of an American literary movement that aimed to distance itself, however tentatively, from British models. Yet he remained a man of staunch Federalist principles and English sensibilities, who lamented the rancor that had lately filled the pages of journals on both sides of the Atlantic. Dwight's rebuttal to Southey, therefore, was hardly the ringing defense of their country many Americans would have preferred. Sharing with the *Quarterly Review* an abhorrence of democratic republicanism, the Yale president responded in a tone more rueful than irate, tempering his defense of his country with an apology for the Jacobinical tendencies of Thomas Jefferson and James Madison. These were not the views of all Americans, he insisted, and counseled British critics to be patient with the United States. "We shall not always be ruled by men such as these."[8]

With the resumption of transatlantic travel after the War of 1812, the war of words was quickly ratcheted upward as a new wave of curious Britons washed upon American shores. The British reading public was developing a hearty appetite for literature by those who ventured to foreign parts, and to the former colonies in particular. There soon appeared, in quick succession, a spate of travel books highly critical of the United States. Americans often learned of these works—many of which were intended as guides for potential emigrants and were therefore not widely available stateside—through the British literary periodicals, whose reviews, like the one attributed to Southey, usually added to an increasingly unflattering portrait of the young republic.[9]

With American anger at British criticism escalating rapidly, Washington Irving, soon to be among the nation's most prominent literary figures, issued an appeal for calm. An expatriate living in England, Irving was an unabashed Anglophile, yet dismayed by the seemingly unending torrent of abuse from English writers. Irving regretted the misrepresentations of American society he had read in the British press, but he cautioned Americans against responding with similar invective. Troubled that anti-British polemics would "excite virulent national prejudices," he believed that relations between the two countries were too important to be governed by unreasonable passion. He deplored the Anglophobic feeling that had prompted some American writers to issue a blanket indictment against the old country, a posture that blinded them to its many virtues. While conceding that there were those who "admire and imitate everything English, merely because it is English," he urged Americans only to be more discriminating. As a young nation, the United States could not help but be anything but imitative, Irving believed; it should therefore strive to copy only the best the world had to offer. "There is no country more worthy of our study than England," he wrote, which should be held up as a model "to strengthen and to embellish our national character."[10]

But Irving, like Timothy Dwight, represented an ever-shrinking minority, as American intellectuals rallied to the defense of the national honor. The Philadelphia editor and essayist Robert Walsh Jr. offered the first direct reply to the nation's detractors with his *Appeal from the Judgments of Great Britain* (1819), which not only refused to acknowledge American cultural inferiority, but insisted that the republic was in many respects superior to the benighted land that had created it.[11] The principal American literary journals promptly closed rank behind Walsh. The Philadelphia *Port Folio*, once slavish in its deference to British opinion, now urged its readers to "lay aside forbearance" and abandon the "doctrines of passive obedience and nonresistance" which had hitherto characterized the American response to the aspersions of foreign essayists and travelers. Edward Everett, juggling his duties as a professor of Greek at Harvard University and editor of the *North American Review*, also departed from his unabashed admiration of Great Britain in an essay in defense of Walsh. Anti-British feeling, he was obliged to admit, now commanded "unusual unanimity" throughout the nation—a state of affairs that had not existed during the recent war. Still, Everett believed that the attacks on the republic were the work of a querulous minority, and did not represent the true feelings of the British people.[12]

In January 1820, before some American periodicals had time to comment on the growing controversy, the *Edinburgh Review* fired another broadside in the contest: a review by the Reverend Sydney Smith of Adam Seybert's *Statistical Annals of the United States*. Smith closed his brief essay with an indictment of the young republic in a tone that was equal parts snooty and truculent:

In the four quarters of the globe, who reads an American book? or goes to an American play? or looks at an American picture or statue? What does the world yet owe to American physicians or surgeons? What new substances have their chemists discovered, or what old ones have they analyzed? What new constellations have been discovered by the telescopes of Americans? What have they done in the mathematics? Who drinks out of American glasses? or eats from American plates? or wears American coats or gowns?[13]

While Seybert's book of statistics soon faded from public memory, Smith's rhetorical interrogatory would have repercussions that would frame the transatlantic cultural relationship for more than a quarter of a century. "Who reads an American book?" would serve as a rallying cry for American intellectuals in the struggle for cultural independence, prompting even New Englanders not normally given to anti-British expression to vent their frustration. In a Fourth of July oration that year, John Quincy Adams argued that the republic's contributions to the cause of liberty had already eclipsed those of the imperial parent. "In the half century which has elapsed since the declaration of American independence," he asked Britons with pointed indignation, "what have *you* done for the benefit of mankind?"[14]

What had prompted these unprovoked outbursts of hostility? Some patriotic pundits attributed British ire to American military successes in the two wars against the Crown. Others saw in the mounting tide of overseas criticism a deliberate, covert effort to portray the new nation in the worst possible light. According to this thesis, British oligarchs saw the upstart republic as a direct threat to the status quo on their own side of the Atlantic. A propaganda campaign to discredit the republic would serve a twofold purpose: discouraging potential emigrants to the United States, while lending support to entrenched elites at home anxious to resist the growing popular clamor for greater political representation. Allegations that the censorious tone of British travel memoirs and literary journals were the handiwork of Whitehall did not seem particularly far-fetched, for Americans were well-versed in a national creation myth that attributed their forbears' rupture with the Crown to the machinations of sinister parliamentary cabals. Viewing the British government as a monolithic hegemon with the power to impose its will in every corner of the globe, they had little reason to doubt, and every reason to believe, that it had dispatched paid hirelings to impugn their republic and its institutions.[15]

No American writer devoted himself more assiduously to the task of answering British critics than James Kirke Paulding, a New Yorker of Dutch descent. Born in 1778, Paulding carried no memories of the Revolution, though his family had experienced firsthand the wrenching upheavals of war. The conflict left Paulding's father financially ruined, while his maternal grandfather suffered a severe and permanent head injury when British soldiers beat him unconscious because he would not cry "God save the King." When Paulding was still in his teens he moved to New York City, where he was introduced into society by a brother-in-law, William Irving, and his younger brother, Washington. In 1807 the three men published *Salmagundi*, a pamphlet series satirizing the New York social scene.[16]

Paulding and Washington Irving would remain lifelong friends, but for Paulding, much as for Charles Jared Ingersoll, the War of 1812 awakened strong nationalist stirrings that would propel his literary career down a very different path. While Irving sailed for England at war's end, Paulding assumed a prominent position as one of his country's earliest defenders against the cavils of British writers. The year the war began Paulding published *The Diverting History of John Bull and Brother Jonathan*, a humorous allegory examining the relationship between the two countries. In 1813 he authored *The Lay of the Scottish Fiddle*, a parody of Sir Walter Scott's romantic poem, *The Lay of the Last Minstrel*, which attributed recent British war crimes against Americans to a desire to imitate "those mischievous books of chivalry" for which Scott was famous.[17] By war's end Paulding had weighed in on the growing controversy over the anti-American tone of the British periodicals with *The United States and England* (1815), in which he attacked the *Quarterly Review* for what he believed to be a growing catalog of deliberate misrepresentations of the United States.[18]

Offended though he was by the aspersions against his country, Paulding masked his indignation with an irreverent sense of humor. A successful playwright, he caricatured the obtuse British traveler in comedies such as *The Lion of the West*, one of the most popular plays written by an American during the Jacksonian period.[19] Having never set foot outside the United States, this did not deter him from penning a satirical travel memoir of his own, *A Sketch of Old England by a New England Man* (1822). Written not long after the Peterloo Massacre, in which British troops had fired upon a crowd of pro-democracy demonstrators, the book presented to American readers a sardonic picture of monarchical despotism run amok. In *John Bull in America* (1825), Paulding assumed the guise of an anonymous writer for the *Quarterly Review* on a visit to the Northern states. The author described a people of unimaginably bad manners, savage cruelty, and extraordinary boorishness. During his travels in Connecticut, John Bull observed: "The white people were for the most part employed in getting drunk at the taverns, running horses, fighting cocks, or gouging one another's eyes out—the women sitting along the road, chewing tobacco, and spitting in the faces of passers by; and the little boys and girls were pretty much engaged in beating their parents." Irritated by British condemnation of slavery, Paulding described a society in which cruelty to African Americans was unremitting and widespread: "The common amusement of young persons is to stick pins in their black attendants, while every boy has a little negro, of about his own age, to torture for his pastime." The Irish fared little better, reported the *Review* author, who found that they were summarily shot for being out after nine o'clock.[20]

The early travel books that were the object of Paulding's bemused scorn never managed more than a limited audience in the British Isles, and an even smaller one in the United States. As a result, during the decade following the War of 1812 the general public remained only dimly aware of the British critique of American institutions that had so many intellectuals up in arms. That would change with the release of Basil Hall's *Travels in North America* (1829). A retired captain in the Royal Navy, Hall had penned a number of travel books before visiting the United States, and was received warmly as a literary celebrity. Hall took note of the poor lodgings, rude innkeepers, and bad roads that so distressed other British travelers of the period, inconveniences which he bore only slightly better than most. But the Scottish-born sea captain was more interested in American democracy, which he witnessed in all its unbridled boisterousness during the presidential campaign of 1828. A staunch opponent of parliamentary reform in his own country, Hall saw nothing in the United States to change his mind, and he returned home more convinced than ever that only men of rank and distinction could be entrusted with a nation's public affairs.[21]

Hall had made no secret of his intention to write a book based on his travels, and its release was much anticipated by Americans anxious to know what a well-known British writer thought of them. The book became a best-seller in the United States, despite the drubbing it received from reviewers who, sputtering with aggrieved indignation, denounced it as a national insult. While all were willing to acknowledge that the republic had its faults, and that Americans could profit from foreign criticism, they insisted that Hall and others of his itinerant tribe were "so blinded by prejudice . . . so implacable in their hatred" of American political institutions that they could not be taken seriously as credible observers. That Hall used his sojourn in the United States to lecture Britons on the dangers of democracy only confirmed American suspicions that the Scotsman had been sent as an agent of his government, and that his real purpose was to undermine the growth of like-minded sentiments at home.[22]

Frances Trollope's America

But the harshest indictment of American society was yet to come. Captain Hall's study of the young republic was mildness itself compared with Frances Trollope's *Domestic Manners of the Americans*, published in 1832. Five years earlier, Trollope had accompanied the English radical Frances Wright to America, having decided, somewhat impulsively, to spend a few months at her friend's newly established utopian community at Nashoba, Tennessee. She was accompanied on the trip by three of her five children, a pair of servants, and a French artist, the latter a family friend lured to America with the promise of obtaining employment as a teacher. Disembarking at New Orleans, Trollope and her entourage journeyed by steamboat up the Mississippi. The voyage quickly became a Conradian nightmare for the forty-seven-year-old matron, who was unaccustomed and ill-suited to the rigors of frontier travel. The situation did not improve when she arrived at Nashoba, a rude collection of leaky cabins in a malarial marshland that bore absolutely no resemblance to the quaint, bucolic idyll Frances Wright had described. Fearing for the health of her family, she decamped ten days later, relocating the family in Cincinnati. There she opened a bazaar, which soon failed, and after two frustrating years in the Queen City, Trollope and company made their way east, eventually scraping together enough money for the voyage home.

Trollope had taken copious notes of her experiences in America, and upon her return to England she set about the task of penning a memoir of her four-year residence abroad. The first-time author could hardly claim to be an authority on the United States, having seen little of the South and bypassed New England during her travels altogether (had she visited the latter, which British travelers invariably found so agreeable and so much like their native land, she might have been moved to tem per her criticism). But the finished work did not claim to be a comprehensive survey of America and its institutions. Before Frances Trollope, the travel memoir had been an authorial vehicle enlisted in the service of a larger cause, allowing writers to offer exhaustive descriptions of flora and fauna, statistics on the country's potential as a destination for British immigrants, or, as in Basil Hall's case, extensive ruminations on the effects of popular sovereignty. Eschewing such ponderous matters, the dowager was content to dwell chiefly on the customs, habits, and peculiarities of its people. With a keen eye for colorful detail, Trollope managed to bring American society, with all its rough edges, to life, shining a spotlight upon the physiognomy of republicanism in a series of colorful vignettes. It was a light in which Americans did not appear to good advantage. Whereas Hall had at least maintained the pretense of objectivity, Trollope made no secret of her unvarnished contempt for all things American. "I do not like them," she wrote. "I do not like their principles, I do not like their manners, I do not like their opinions."[23] Some of Trollope's complaints had already been the subject of much comment by earlier visitors—the bad roads, the poor accommodations, the insolent and untrustworthy servants, the grotesque table manners, the mangling of the King's English, the incessant tobacco chewing, to name a few—though no one had chronicled them in such merciless detail. As Trollope herself put it, Americans had received Captain Hall and other visiting dignitaries "in full dress." She, on the other hand, a woman of modest means, without reputation or letters of introduction, had lived among the rustics and observed them in their natural state, unadorned and *deshabillé*.[24]

Trollope's book, liberally illustrated by the French artist who had accompanied the family (who seems to have enjoyed his sojourn in the republic no more than she), became a best-seller in England and caused an instant sensation when it appeared in the United States. As with earlier travel volumes that took an uncharitable view of the American republic, critics spied an ulterior motive. The book had been released during the parliamentary debates over the Reform Bill, prompting speculation that it was intended as yet another Tory indictment of democratic institutions. Once it became known that Basil Hall had used his influence to help publish the book, some critics opined that the work had actually been ghost-written by the British captain. Despite hostile reviews, public reaction proved to be more amused than indignant, the sheer mean-spiritedness of Trollope's memoir making it difficult to take seriously as a valid indictment of American society.[25]

With the release of *Domestic Manners*, the British critique against the United States was largely complete. Subsequent visitors would provide additional anecdotal detail, but for the most part they would do little more than echo the criticisms leveled by Trollope and her predecessors. In the compendium of republican shortcomings compiled by British travelers, one issue stood out as the root cause of the behaviors they abhorred: an unceasing pursuit of the main chance. What had come to be known in the colloquial parlance of the new nation as a "go-ahead" spirit, the foreign visitor regarded as an unrelenting quest for money and material goods. The leveling impulse of democracy had failed to produce great achievements in the arts, conservative Britons averred,

for all beauty and elegance had been trampled underfoot in the headlong rush to pay homage to the great god of commerce. Too busy in their
pursuit of profit either for personal reflection or meaningful social intercourse, Americans lacked wit, erudition, or any appreciation for aes-
thetics. Even the common courtesies that had become the hallmarks
of European bourgeois respectability seemed to have no place among a
people whose one consuming passion was their own self-interest. What
was worse, in such a rampantly acquisitive society, dishonesty and selfishness had become virtues; shrewdness and "smart dealing" (an American euphemism for deceptive business practices) passed for intellect.
Always wanting more, they seemed to Britons a restless, humorless, unhappy people, a nation of bottom feeders devoted to the bottom line.

Visitors took note of regional differences, yet there was one trait that
seemed to link Americans everywhere—North, South and West, from
the salons of the beau monde, to the poorest working-class wards, to the
most isolated hamlets on the trans-Appalachian frontier: an excessive,

FIGURE 1.

The Trollope Family. Sharply critical of American society, Frances Trollope's travel
memoir, *Domestic Manners of the Americans,* became a national sensation when it
was published in 1832. (Courtesy Library of Congress, Prints & Photographs Division, LC-USZ62-90145)

almost relentless desire for the approval of foreigners. Everywhere they went, they were constantly buttonholed with the query, "What do you think of our country?" To the visitor predisposed to look charitably on the young republic, the question seemed innocent enough, and could be interpreted as little more than a clumsy effort to initiate conversation.[26] Most travelers, on the other hand, viewed the perennial query as a desperate, pathetic plea for approbation, one that was posed so often and so insistently that it bordered on harassment. Basil Hall described the rapid-fire line of questioning as follows:

> Don't you think this is a wonderful country? Don't you allow that we deserve great credit for what we are doing? Do not we resemble the old country much more than you expected? Had you any idea of finding us so far advanced? Are not the western parts of our state improving very rapidly? Is not our canal the finest work in the world? Don't you admit that we are becoming a great nation? What do you think of us, upon the whole?[27]

When such prompting failed to elicit the desired response (as was usually the case), Americans did not hesitate to lavish encomiums upon themselves. European visitors were invariably struck by the fact that citizens of the republic harbored not the slightest doubt that they were "the greatest people under the canopy of heaven," a conviction drummed into their heads, as one noted in 1833, at every conceivable opportunity by Fourth of July orators, clerics, politicians, and newspaper editors. Americans, said another, were so determined to impress upon visitors the superiority of their institutions that "there was hardly room for us to slip in a word, edgewise." Should foreign travelers offer anything less than a wholehearted endorsement of such views, they were best advised to keep silent, for Americans were notoriously thin-skinned. Frances Trollope went further, moved to declare that they "have, apparently, no skins at all; they wince if a breeze blows over them, unless it be tempered with adulation." Even those who did not share Trollope's haughty condescension were obliged to concede this point. One British traveler who had little respect for Trollope's powers of observation admitted that he was utterly baffled by the "absolute puerility" which Americans exhibited when confronted with even "the slightest appearance of dispraise" from foreign visitors.[28]

Even the most astute observers, however, generally failed to realize that British fault-finding bore no small responsibility for the very behaviors they deplored. While earlier visitors had reported that Americans were indeed eager for praise, their irritation on this score paled beside those who followed in the path of Hall and Trollope, who were badgered incessantly by citizens eager to deliver loud paeans to the glories of their infant republic. By the 1830s British criticism and the American response to it had clearly become a self-perpetuating process. Having read the published works of earlier travelers, British visitors learned to anticipate American sensitivity, which in turn became all the more pronounced with each new indictment from abroad. Few foreigners could tour the United States without being buttonholed by citizens determined to educate them on their country's many virtues. And the more they complained of such practices, the more thin-skinned Americans became, determined to steal a march on their critics with chest-thumping bravado.[29]

The controversy over hostile foreign opinions, once confined to cosmopolitan elites in the years immediately following the second war with Great Britain, had become by the 1830s nothing less than a fixation for the public at large. A burgeoning publishing industry helped feed public interest in the transatlantic squabble. Whereas the book trade had once catered primarily to an urban readership, improved transportation and distribution networks now made it possible for American publishers to market their products throughout the country, with the result that copies of Basil Hall's *Travels in North America* could be found in every "city, town, village, and hamlet, steamboat and stagecoach" in the union.[30] Those who did not manage to procure the latest British travel memoir could usually find it extensively excerpted and reviewed in any number of the literary journals and monthly miscellanies that proliferated during the period. Americans would have also encountered the British traveler caricatured on the American stage, with Basil Hall and Frances Trollope both ridiculed in several popular plays of the period. Trollope, in particular, managed to achieve a prominence in American popular culture enjoyed by few foreigners, her name a byword for obnoxious prejudice and privileged *hauteur*. The book sparked a nationwide debate over the state of American manners, with citizens cheerfully poking fun at themselves by adopting new standards of public decorum. When male theater patrons were caught slouching in their seats with their feet on the gallery railings—a practice that Mrs. Trollope had viewed with undisguised horror—fellow patrons taunted them with cries of "Trollope! Trollope!" until they assumed a more dignified posture.[31]

With *Domestic Manners* a publishing phenomenon on both sides of the Atlantic, the British visitor with literary pretensions became a seemingly ubiquitous presence on the American scene. A veritable deluge of travel books followed, all hoping to repeat its extraordinary commercial success. In 1833 alone, the year after its release, no less than seven major works on America were published in Great Britain, and were soon widely available as reprints in the United States. Americans took it for granted that any traveling Briton they encountered would be writing a book about them upon their return home. It was not an unreasonable assumption. They hailed from all walks of life: actors and actresses fresh from theatrical engagements of the United States, social reformers on inspection tours of American penitentiaries and asylums, diplomatic representatives on official state business, clergymen attending ecclesiastical conferences, prospective immigrants who, like Frances Trollope, recorded their observations purely as a means of defraying their expenses. All saw their memoirs rushed into print by British and American publishing houses. On and on they came, with pens in hand, a never-ending conga line of the querulous, the censorious, and the simply curious.[32]

Some visitors taxed the forbearance of their American hosts more than others. When Frederick Marryat, a former officer in the British navy who had gained a considerable reputation as a novelist of seafaring adventures, embarked upon an eighteen month tour of the United States and Canada in 1837, he publicly disavowed any intention of writing a book of his travels, a pledge that was no doubt intended to put his American hosts at ease. Endowed with strong Tory sentiments and an utter want of tact, Marryat could not have been less suited to the role of goodwill ambassador. Even members of high society, so prone to fawn over visiting celebrities, found little to recommend the renowned author. After opening his home to the captain in Philadelphia, an exasperated Samuel Breck pronounced the English "a parcel of offensive smellfunguses, too prejudiced to see clearly, too supercilious to acknowledge the good they see and too disgustingly insolent in telling us of what they do not like."[33]

Controversy dogged Marryat's every move. His arrival in the United States coincided with the outbreak of insurrections in Canada, which received strong support from American citizens along the border. Still holding a captain's commission in the Royal Navy, Marryat promptly set out for Canada to report for duty, where he took part in the effort to quash the rebellion. In December 1837 a British force crossed the Niagara River and burned the steamer Caroline for supplying the rebels, provoking an outcry for war in the United States. In April the following year, at a public dinner in Toronto, Marryat delivered a toast applauding the military action, which was duly reported in the American press.[34] Excoriated by editorialists throughout the country, the British author was hanged in effigy in Detroit and St. Louis, as angry crowds staged book-burnings of his best-selling novels. Some months later, during a stop in Louisville, the intrepid captain found himself in hot water again, this time in a scandal of a more prurient nature. Caught in what appeared to be a compromising position with one of the guests at his hotel, the wife of a phrenologist, Marryat departed the city in some haste, and two months later sailed for England, having firmly established a reputation in the United States as both a boorish guest and an inveterate cad.[35]

"Their Ways Are Not Our Ways"

For all the widespread public furor, it remained for those in the world of letters to frame the response to foreign fault-finding. Having been governed more than most Americans by British opinions, they were naturally the most sensitive to British reproach. A few intellectuals responded with attempts at satire, following James Kirke Paulding's lead in parodying some of the better-known travel books. But they were, on the whole, a painfully self-conscious group, unable to laugh at themselves or to hide their wounded pride. Most failed to see the humor in British condescension, their frustration rising with each new philippic from abroad. Virtually every major literary figure of the period, and a great many lesser-known ones, felt obliged to respond publicly to the criticism.[36] They derived but little satisfaction from such efforts, for every rebuttal revealed just how much the good opinion of the British meant to them. Their hypersensitivity, their eagerness for praise, and their petulance when it was not forthcoming—all revealed deeply rooted feelings of inadequacy. "Were we to respect ourselves as we ought," one essayist admitted ruefully, the slings and arrows of foreign critics would have little effect.[37]

What made the captious tone of British observers all the more galling to American highbrows was their belief that the most serious defects in the national character could be traced back to Britain's doorstep. If Americans were a patriotic people, given to effusive self-adulation, then surely, they argued, the charge could be leveled with equal justice at subjects of the Crown. No less irritating was the frequent observation by foreigners that citizens of the republic were consumed by the pursuit of wealth. Again, few Americans denied the charge, but they vigorously complained that John Bull was an equally devoted acolyte of Mammon. If the Yankee had a reputation for "smart dealing," it was only because the people of New England were primarily of British origin. "Why, truly, there never existed a nation where the love of money, or the fury to obtain it, has been more ungovernable than in England," declared one editorialist.[38]

The complaint that Americans were not like their transatlantic cousins—a charge made by foreigners either directly or by insinuation—seems to have bothered urban elites almost as much as the criticism itself. In pointing to Great Britain as a source of their own shortcomings, American intellectuals sought to demonstrate, to themselves and to outsiders, the connections that still bound the two peoples. This emphasis on shared cultural cognates allowed them to trivialize British disapproval, and thereby mask their own irritation of it. By insisting that the defects and errors of Americans were merely "exaggerations of English imperfections," the ongoing contretemps could be characterized as little more than a family spat.[39] Such a response served a dual purpose, allowing American pundits to deflect British criticism even as they claimed a kinship with the world's most powerful nation-state. Thus, it was not the republic's lack of refinement that John Bull found so annoying, but the "*strong family resemblance to himself.*"[40] Again and again, they attempted in vain to argue that British irritability stemmed not from American inadequacies, but from American successes. "The more we become like them," James Kirke Paulding insisted, "the more they dislike us."[41]

Unreconstructed Anglophiles, who tended to be overrepresented in the American literary community, found such criticism especially difficult to bear, for it was they who were the most anxious of all Americans to prove that national character traits were "derived from our British ancestry."[42] Certainly there were some cosmopolites who snickered at the provincialisms described in *Domestic Manners* (Richard Henry Dana Jr., for example, found British criticism ungracious but generally accurate). But the image of Brother Jonathan as a slack-jawed rube was not one most elites wished to present to the outside world, and particularly not to the British reading public. Only by insisting that the cultural life of the new nation was, in fact, an extension of the colonial experience could they bask in England's reflected glory, could they see in their own society a likeness of English virtues. Seemingly untroubled by Basil Hall's detailed indictment of democracy, one editorialist for the *North American Review* was cut to the quick by the author's insinuation that Americans and Britons differed "more from one another in many essential respects," than any two nations in Europe. What two countries, the reviewer demanded to know, were "more like each other" than England and the United States? Instead of drawing attention to republican foibles, Americans believed, British critics should applaud the accomplishments of their transatlantic cousins, since they were "performed under the influence of English habits, feelings, and principles."[43]

Ironically, their profound exasperation with foreign criticism ultimately led some in the intellectual community to the conclusion that their antagonists were correct. Educated Americans had generally been comfortable with the knowledge that they were bound to Great Britain by a set of common cultural assumptions. But now, after years of transatlantic carping, many wondered if in fact Americans and Britons were not two distinct peoples. An emotional, combative patriotism thus became a common (if unconscious) coping strategy to deal with the assaults from abroad. Americans, many writers argued, had indeed morphed into a different species in the decades since the Revolution. "Their ways are not our ways," a Fourth of July orator declared in Albany, New York, in 1835. "They will buy with us, sell with us, talk with us . . . but they do not love us." A Western editor echoed these sentiments. "They do not resemble us in appearance or manners," he wrote. "There is not even a family likeness between us." Politically, too, the two countries seemed to be growing not closer but farther apart. Having long paid homage to England for planting the seeds of representative self-government across the Atlantic, some Americans could find little similarity between the two political systems.[44]

As they became more conscious of a distinct identity, Americans began to adopt the nomenclature of nationhood. They insisted on referring to the English as "foreigners," a term they had hitherto applied only to people of other nations. They also objected to the English use of the term "Anglo-American" to describe citizens of the United States, noting that a majority were descended from the Scotch, Irish, and other nations of Europe. And with many British travelers horrified by the diction of Americans, it was no wonder that some earnest patriots boldly proposed that they cease referring to the language spoken in the United States as the English language.[45]

The unanimity with which Americans responded to British criticism enabled them to forge a loose consensus even in the face of significant regional differences. When traveling Britons began to comment disapprovingly on the institution of slavery in the 1820s, Northern periodicals closed ranks with their Southern counterparts on the subject, viewing the criticism as an attack on the nation at large. Though few were willing to go so far as to defend the labor institution outright, many Northern journals did endorse certain features of the Southern rebuttal. It was not uncommon, for example, for Northern writers to blame England for establishing the institution in the thirteen colonies, or to insist that the living standards of English factory workers were inferior to that of American slaves. By the same token, Southerners were equally inclined, at least initially, to respond as patriotic Americans to British aspersions. The South Carolinian Henry Laurens Pinckney was indignant that foreign visitors were not sufficiently impressed by the recently opened Erie Canal. "Can foreign critics see nothing to admire in these wonders of improvement?" he asked in 1826. "Who among us does not rejoice in the name of American, when he reflects on the stupendous monument achieved by the industry and enterprize of New York?" Another Palmetto State native, William J. Grayson, agreed; Americans had much to be proud of. The South Carolina congressman congratulated Robert Walsh and the *North American Review* in 1828 for their efforts against "the libels of British travelers and reviewers," and called for a national campaign to properly educate Americans on the merits of their republican system.[46]

Even as slavery emerged as a highly charged political issue in the 1830s, the nation's literary journals sought to remain above the fray. Centrist by nature and anxious to appeal to subscribers nationwide, they were slow to reflect regional identities and tensions, tending to close rank whenever foreign voices were raised against the United States. Thus, many Northern literary journals could insist throughout the Jacksonian era that attacks on the plantation system were part of a broader campaign by British critics to undermine American institutions, while their Southern counterparts could even express outrage when the *Edinburgh Review* attacked the venerable poet William Channing, despite the fact that Channing's antislavery views had made him anathema to many Southern ultras. And although Frederick Marryat was one of the few British visitors of the period not repelled by the institution of slavery, his memoir won him little praise in the South. On the contrary, the *Southern Literary Messenger* published a coruscating twenty-three-page review of the book, calling the novelist "a willing instrument in the dirty work of defaming a whole people," and accused him of irresponsibly fomenting "national antipathies" at a time when caution and civility were needed most.[47]

In short, British obloquy presented educated Americans with a stark choice: they could tamely submit to such verbal hectoring, or begin to see themselves as a breed apart. Many, to be sure, still regarded British culture as the gold standard of Western civilization. Yet it was becoming increasingly difficult to express such sentiments openly; whether they wanted to or not, American intellectuals felt obliged to abandon their customary deference toward the seat of the Anglophone world. They assumed instead a defiant posture, a self-important swagger that served to shift the focus of the transatlantic debate away from republican shortcomings. Learning to accept their differences with the imperial parent, they came to embrace them. Denied the approval of Great Britain, they found sanction in its censure. If Britons ridiculed the United States' military and maritime strength, it was because they feared the rise of a potential challenger to their global dominance; if they criticized the young republic for its dearth of literary achievement, it was an effort to extinguish "the sparks of genius" before they could "kindle into a flame."

Americans had never been shy about lauding their own achievements, of course, but their chauvinism became more strident with the need to characterize British carping as "the petty spite of a faded beauty," envious of a young rival. In this manner, the protracted critique of the republic, its people and institutions, brought lasting consequences, nudging Americans along a road that led them from a deep-seated sense of cultural inferiority to a bold, if self-conscious declaration of their own exceptionalism.[48]

American Perceptions of England

Inevitably, the feud between British writers and the republic did more than put Americans on the defensive; it compelled them to look at Great Britain with new eyes. The *North American Review*, true to form, gamely insisted that the steady stream of censorious travel books and journal articles were the work of a disgruntled minority and in no way represented a barometer of British public opinion. But as each year brought new literary products from abroad that traduced the United States, its people and institutions, this sanguine view became hopelessly untenable. For a great many more Americans, condescension and censure were the only British opinions they knew.[49]

On occasion, bruised republican feelings manifested themselves in overt expressions of hostility toward British visitors. Several travelers encountered coldness from Americans, which they attributed to public resentment of foreign criticism, while others, though uncertain of the cause, also reported acts of rudeness when it was learned they hailed from the British Isles.[50] Yet such incidents were the exception rather than the norm. For the most part, Americans were content to vent their anger toward Britain as a nation, sentiments which they gladly conveyed to British travelers whenever they encountered them. Indeed, Americans seem to have felt completely at liberty to inform them that their government was "superannuated, corrupt, and profligate," and did so without the least expectation of giving offense. Several Britons reported being treated to impassioned philippics against their country by Americans who expressed no animosity toward them personally. "The real object of their ignorant wrath," one observed, "was our dreadfully despotic and tyrannical system of government."[51]

With no other country experiencing to the same degree the wrenching changes brought on by industrialization, Great Britain offered a broad target for American critics. Even as the island nation emerged victorious and unscathed from the Napoleonic Wars, its power appeared to rest on the most fragile foundations. The plight of its industrial poor, the subject of several parliamentary commissions, was given extensive coverage by the cis-Atlantic press. In the American imagination, Britain was a land of extremes, in which agrarian and industrial elites ruled over "a people ground to the dust" by poverty and taxation.[52] Americans often harped upon such themes in travel memoirs of their own, such as C. Edwards Lester's *The Glory and the Shame of England* (1841). Despite its misleading title, the book offered an irremediably bleak picture of Britain's industrial society. In Lester's urban hellscape, the factory system had made Britain a veritable sinkhole of vice and degradation, in which laborers sought refuge from their lives of grinding poverty in drug addiction and sexual depravity.[53] And since a free people would never endure such appalling social conditions, Americans could only conclude that the British lived in a totalitarian state far worse than the monarchical despotism their forefathers had fought against.[54]

The cultural preeminence of Great Britain was also fair game in the eyes of aggrieved Americans, who had never before dared to question its superiority in the *belles artes*. Citizens of the republic had confused Britain's industrial and maritime power with "true national greatness," the Southern poet William Hayne Simmons argued. The British were a nation of *poseurs*, the object of "ridicule and amusement of the rest of the world," a people laughed at on the European continent for their awkward imitation of the more refined French and Italians. Some writers accused Great Britain of resting on its cultural laurels, having not produced any great writers, historians, or philosophers in many years. The New York publisher George Palmer Putnam was so irritated by British superciliousness toward the United States that he set out to demonstrate, in an admittedly tongue-in-cheek essay, that the English were a race of "universal plagiarists" and "intellectual pickpockets," who had pilfered the best features of their literary culture from classical antiquity and the nations of Europe.[55]

American resentment of British condescension also served to reinforce the taint of moral laxity that earnest republicans had always associated with the Old World. Transatlantic cultural imports in the form of popular romantic fiction and stage comedies established for Americans the Chesterfieldian image of the British aristocrat as effete dandy and debauched libertine, unflattering stereotypes that were bolstered in the public mind whenever visitors such as Frederick Marryat behaved badly. During a visit to Baltimore, one British traveler was amused to find that an English nobleman in residence in that city was viewed as something of a local curiosity, never failing to be met by gawking onlookers when he appeared in public. "The idea which many of them entertain of an English Lord is, that he is a sort of feudal Sybarite . . . clothed in purple and fine linen, and requiring the attendance of a small army of servants," an image, the visitor noted, that had little basis in fact.[56]

By the Jacksonian era, the image of England in the American mind had been refashioned to better suit the adversarial relationship that existed between the two countries. The nation once viewed as a pastoral land of hedgerows, cathedrals, and stately manor houses had transmogrified into an industrial dystopia of wage slaves, workhouses, greedy cotton lords, and profligate noblemen. Britain was still great, but to many Americans its wealth and power masked deep-seated social problems that were slowly eating away at the grand edifice of empire from within. American Anglophiles stubbornly held fast to "Old Englandism," a nostalgic veneration for what the imperial parent once was. Increasingly, however, citizens of the republic were all too ready to jettison the memories that had long nourished the idea of Britain's august place at the head of a great transatlantic Anglophone family.[57]

Boz-mania

By the early 1840s, an entire generation of Americans had been raised to maturity with the animadversions of foreign critics ringing in its ears. But if they had long since wearied of British censure, they did not yearn any less for British praise. Patiently, pathetically, they waited for benediction. And so when it was announced that none other than Charles Dickens would be crossing the Atlantic to see the brash young republic, the accumulated resentment of decades was promptly forgotten. The United States had hosted distinguished literary types before, but Basil Hall and Frederick Marryat could hardly claim such Parnassian heights of celebrity. Dickens was, after all, the most beloved writer in the Anglophone world, and one of the first novelists in any language whose readership extended beyond the beau monde. The advent of monthly magazines, which serialized Dickens' works, had made him widely accessible to the American reading public, so much so that in 1841 crowds of anxious readers lined the wharves of New York Harbor, eager for the latest installment from London of *The Old Curiosity Shop*, to learn the fate of Little Nell.

The giddiness with which Americans prepared to embrace Dickens was due only in part to his popularity as a novelist. In Dickens Americans believed they had at last found a kindred spirit among the mob of hostile critics, an author who was uniquely suited to appreciate the virtues of their republic. Unlike so many foreign travelers whose aristocratic mien prejudiced them against the leveling spirit of American society, Dickens had grown up under humble circumstances (his father, a government clerk, had been imprisoned for debt). By the early 1840s, with working-class discontent and calls for parliamentary reform on the rise, Britain seemed to hover on the brink of civil rebellion. Dickens was no Chartist; he declined to side openly with those who were demanding universal male suffrage and representative electoral districts. Nonetheless, he was at the very least an impassioned critic of his country's social institutions, whose prose captured in vivid and often heart-rending detail the callousness of a system based on rank and privilege. Surely the great "Boz," as he was known, of all the British observers who crossed the Atlantic, would grant America and Americans a fair hearing.[58]

Certainly that was Dickens' intention. Like many reform-minded Britons, the author looked to the republic as a grand political experiment that he hoped might prove instructive as his own country navigated the currents of democratic change. Arriving in Boston in January, 1842, Dickens and his wife Catherine were mobbed by devoted fans, a scene that was repeated at subsequent stops in New York, Philadelphia, and Washington, D.C. The author seemed gratified by the welcome he received, the most lavish reception of a foreign visitor since the Marquis de Lafayette's tumultuous tour in 1824–25. At the same time, however, he was perplexed that a putatively egalitarian society could be capable of such frenzied adulation. A ball held in Dickens' honor at New York's Park Theatre, with tickets priced at an exorbitant ten dollars, was the gala event of the social season. "It was hard to open a passage where thousands were crowding to see, and . . . shake hands with him, but with great difficulty he was escorted around the room," one observer recalled years later.[59]

Not everyone was caught up in the prevailing "Boz-mania." Whenever American elites fawned over visiting British celebrities, there were critics ready to rebuke them for exhibiting such manifestly antirepublican behavior. To Philadelphia author George Lippard, it was all a terrific humbug. In The Spirit of the Times he urged his readers to take a stand against the "Boz" excitement. "It is discreditable to our city, it is derogatory to our country," he wrote, and asked that they recall the other famous British visitors who had been feted and fawned over by starstruck Americans, "before they make entire and decided judies of themselves."[60]

Such truculent voices might have been drowned out by the hosannas of an adoring public had not the British novelist made a few public relations missteps of his own. At several of the many banquets held in his honor, Dickens took the opportunity to voice his support for an international copyright law, opposing the widespread practice in the United States by which publishers pirated the works of foreign authors.

In calling for reform, Dickens was hardly alone; many American writers had made the issue a cause célèbre, arguing that they would benefit as much as foreign authors if American publishers were required by law to pay royalties on all literary works. But though Dickens' gentle admonitions on the subject of copyright were welcomed by the native literati, they were received by several Eastern papers in an altogether different light. It was one thing, evidently, for Americans to call for reform, quite another for a British author, no matter how popular, to do so. Seizing the chance to deflect the criticism that citizens of the republic were worshipers of Mammon, editorialists lambasted Dickens as a mercenary who preferred "dollars and cents to literary fame."[61] The man of the hour and the toast of high society, Dickens suddenly found himself smarting under the lash of editorial opprobrium. The cognoscenti continued to turn out in large numbers to catch a glimpse of "Boz," but the novelist returned to England thoroughly upset by his treatment by the American press.[62]

Dickens exacted his revenge a few months later with the publication of *American Notes for General Circulation*, a stinging diatribe against American institutions only slightly more charitable than Trollope's *Domestic Manners*. One day after the book arrived in New York, the *New World*, one of the city's "mammoth" weeklies, released a pirated version. Though the original London edition ran to 616 pages in two volumes, the *New World* managed to squeeze it into 46 densely-packed, quarto-sized pages. Hawked on the streets of Gotham by newsboys at 12 cents a copy, the newspaper sold 50,000 copies in forty eight hours, snatched up by Americans desperate to learn of the famous Englishman's impressions of their country.[63]

To their dismay, Americans found that they had failed to meet Dickens' great expectations. The author had clearly hoped to find, in a society in which the extremes of rich and poor were less marked than in his own country, a greater degree of solicitude toward the underprivileged. Instead, he found a distressing callousness; the famous American "go-ahead" spirit seemed to have no regard for those left behind. During a stay in New York, he had ventured off the beaten path, probing Gotham's seamy underbelly with two members of the constabulary as his guides. The author had been shocked by the slums of the Five Points, and particularly by the squalid conditions endured by the city's free black community. In Philadelphia, a visit to the East Pennsylvania Penitentiary, a much-ballyhooed model of penal reform, filled the English author with disgust, its strict rules of solitary confinement he likened to being "buried alive."[64]

The beau monde that had turned out in such numbers to honor the

English novelist was mortified. *American Notes* could not be dismissed as yet another unfair attack by an effete nobleman, a failed entrepreneur, a hack writer, or a Tory propagandist. American reviewers not only blasted the book, they were similarly critical of "those adoring parasites and sycophants" who had welcomed the English novelist to their shores.[65] Dickens' erstwhile admirers were even more upset with the release of his next novel, *Martin Chuzzlewit* (1843). Arriving in New York Harbor, Martin is asked what he thinks of the country—the universal query— even before he has disembarked. Once on American soil, he finds the young republic peopled with sharpers and scoundrels, each of whom is introduced to him as "one of the most remarkable men in the country."[66] The passage of time (and Dickens' decision to return to industrial England as the setting for his novels) enabled the author to work his way back into the good graces of Americans, and he would make a second, more pleasant visit to the United States for a lucrative readings tour after the Civil War.[67]

For all the furor generated by visiting British writers, it must be emphasized that, in aggregate, their published observations were not nearly so derogatory as Americans were inclined to believe. In addition to those who made no secret of their Tory inclinations, there were progressives, such as Frances Wright and Harriet Martineau, who ventured across the Atlantic eager to portray the republic as an egalitarian idyll. Others, such as Charles Augustus Murray and Henry Tudor, strove to take a balanced view, and took pains to refute some of the more severe indictments of their compatriots. Some, to be sure, managed to set aside their prejudices more successfully than others, but even the most uncharitable critic could deign to find something positive to say. Basil Hall had nothing but high praise for American asylums; Charles Dickens found that the factory system in Lowell, Massachusetts, compared altogether favorably with working conditions in his own country. Yet Americans were in no way content to be damned with faint praise, insisting on lavish, unequivocal encomiums of their nation and its people or none at all. They took scant notice of books that commented favorably on American life and glossed over the compliments from those whose works they judged to be unfairly critical. In the end, it was the contumelious attacks, the source of so much controversy and bitter public debate, which were burned indelibly into the national consciousness.[68]

⁌⁖⁍

It is difficult to gauge the precise impact of British censure on the republic during the first half of the nineteenth century. Certainly the verbal offensive from abroad was greatly distressing to Americans, prompting them to respond with denunciations of their own against Britain's social and political systems. But citizens of the republic were inclined to exaggerate the damage that the war of words had done to U.S.-British relations. They might work themselves into a lather with each new travel memoir or journal article that traduced the United States, but given the fact that their resentment stemmed in large part from an unrequited desire for British approval, they did not always mean what they said. The uproar over British criticism may have been a noisy affair, but it seems unlikely that it created a deep-seated animus. A few more soothing words of praise from abroad and the national snit over hostile foreign opinions could have been brought to a speedy end.[69]

Nonetheless, the rising chorus of outrage that could be heard throughout the length and breadth of the land certainly made it *seem* as if a strident Anglophobia had become inscribed into the very texture of American life. The British visitor Henry Bradshaw Fearon attributed this hostility not to foreign travel literature but to the efforts of politicians and pundits, who had instilled in Americans a reflexive hostility toward the British that existed in spite of the many ties that linked the two peoples. This shared sense of umbrage reached across regional and class boundaries. New Englanders who had opposed the recent war with Great Britain, Southerners troubled by feelings of political isolation, rural and urban Americans who were finding themselves increasingly at odds over national economic policy—all could participate in the nationwide gnashing of teeth prompted by British aspersions. Geopolitical, economic, and diplomatic crises between the two countries, to be discussed in later chapters, would galvanize specific constituencies and foster more narrowly focused anti-British sentiment. But the protracted fight against the nation's foreign detractors was a cause that Americans could rally behind, allowing them the rare opportunity to raise their voices in one collective cry of indignation.[70]

While all Americans winced under the lash of British censure, none found it more hurtful than those whose transatlantic ties ran deepest. For cosmopolitan elites, who read the latest British novels and periodicals, who opened their homes to visiting British authors, and especially for those who entertained their own dreams of literary renown, the scorn of those whom they most admired was not an easy thing to accept. Only in New England, whose people drank more deeply from the font of English culture than any other region of the country, could the current of pro-British feeling flow undisturbed. Elsewhere, however, British ridicule seems to have had a greater effect than British redcoats in dampening the innate Anglophilia of the American intellectual community.

For Charles Jared Ingersoll and other like-minded Americans, British scorn served as a call to arms, awakening them to a sense of their country's debilitating and servile attachment to transatlantic opinion. They could no longer regard with filial devotion a nation which, in assuming a posture of haughty disdain, seemed reluctant even to acknowledge paternity of its offspring. And from these feelings of resentment came a desire to free the republic once and for all from the intellectual domination of Great Britain, to establish a culture of letters that reflected a set of uniquely American values. Exactly what those values might be, and to what extent the American cognoscenti—a demographic hardly representative of the country at large—actually shared them, remained to be seen. Their dander up, the nation's public intellectuals were now ready to give the lie to Sydney Smith, to create a literature of which Americans could be proud.

3

"Who Reads an American Book?"

You steal Englishmen's books and think Englishmen's thought,
With their salt on her tail, your wild eagle is caught:
Your literature suits its each whisper and motion
To what will he thought of it over the ocean;
The cast clothes of Europe your statesmanship tries
And mumbles again the old blarney and lies;—
Forget Europe wholly, your veins throb with blood,
To which the dull current in hers is but mud;
Let her sneer, let her say your experiment fails,
In her voice there's a tremble e'en now while she rails . . .

      —James Russell Lowell, *A Fable for Critics*

Shortly after noon on the last day of August, 1837, more than two hundred past and present members of the Phi Beta Kappa chapter of Harvard College crowded into First Church, Cambridge, to hear Ralph Waldo Emerson deliver the group's annual address. It was an impressive assemblage, and a conservative one. In addition to students and faculty, the gathering included many graduates who formed the core of New England's religious, political, and intellectual elite. Some of its oldest members were diehard Federalists who had never made their peace with the boisterous democratic spirit that had come to define the political and cultural life of the nation, while its recent inductees were scarcely more progressive in outlook. Regarding with ill-concealed disdain the vulgarity of the public sphere— "a kennel in which the dirtiest dog that rolls in it, gets the most bones," sniffed Edmund Quincy, son of the university's president—Boston's Brahmins found a comforting solace in the exclusivity of their intellectual fellowship. Recent speakers at the chapter's annual gathering had decried the leveling trends in American life, sentiments that were invariably received by the group's members with appreciative applause.[1]

Emerson, the son of a Congregationalist minister, had never fully embraced this elitist tradition, and he did not flatter his audience by doing so on this occasion. Titling his address "The American Scholar," he did not lavish praise upon New England's intellectual community, issuing instead a mild rebuke for its subservience to foreign tastes. American savants tended to look for the sublime in the mists of classical antiquity, in the more recent annals of the Old World—everywhere, it seemed, but close to home. Emerson was convinced that their repudiation of the parochial was nothing more than a mark of their own cultural insecurity. He challenged his listeners to "embrace the common," and famously offered the opinion that they had "listened too long to the courtly muses of Europe." As Emerson's fame grew in the years that followed, the Phi Beta Kappa address came to be seen as a watershed moment for American letters. The poet James Russell Lowell, an undergraduate at the college in 1837, would later remark that it cut the cable that had for so long moored Americans to English thought. Oliver Wendell Holmes Sr., an alumnus also in attendance that day, echoed these sentiments, declaring the address to be nothing less than the republic's intellectual declaration of independence.[2]

This may have been giving Emerson considerably more credit than he deserved. While "The American Scholar" would gain in luster with the passage of time, in 1837 the theme of cultural autonomy was hardly a novel one. On the contrary, in recent years countless graduating classes, honor societies, and lyceum audiences throughout the country had listened patiently as earnest orators ad nauseum held forth on the need for a national literature. The topic was of all-consuming interest to American literary magazines as well. Edward Everett, a former professor of classical languages at the university, had been among the early champions of American cultural nationalism as editor of the *North American Review*. The Unitarian minister and poet, William Ellery Channing, a mentor of Emerson's, had dealt much more explicitly with this theme in an 1830 address to the American Philosophical Society in Philadelphia. Emerson himself had hinted at his unhappiness with his country's imitative tendencies in an address three years earlier, in which he conceded that all "American manners, language, and writing" were derived from British forms.[3]

Emerson was certainly no Anglophobe. Like the more conservative habitués of New England's intellectual circles, he believed that imitation was merely "the tax we pay for the splendid inheritance" of English belles lettres.[4] Nor was he a Democrat. The Jacksonians might one day cure the country of its addiction to British models, but Emerson wanted no part of it, convinced that the remedy would be worse than the disease.[5] Rather, his plea on that August afternoon was not for the emancipation of American letters from British life alone, but for the emancipation of the intellect from all forms of convention. Without flag-waving, without appealing to base emotion, he gently chided his listeners for their reflexive regard for all that was musty and archaic, for their deference to Old World traditions. He urged them to celebrate instead the newness and authenticity of their native land, to listen to their own internal muse, not the muse of another age, or of another people.

Perhaps the real significance of the address was to be found not in its message but in its venue. If Emerson's peroration seemed to James Russell Lowell and Oliver Wendell Holmes like a call to arms, it was due in part because it was uttered in the very temple of English intellectual life in North America. While the rest of American society was being buffeted by the tempests of democratic change, Harvard College remained in stasis, the guardian of an Old World cultural legacy. Like the country's other great universities, it existed in serene and cloistered isolation, its mission essentially unchanged since the institution's founding two centuries earlier. Emerson's suggestion that Europe should not be the only beacon in the search for truth might seem a radical notion to the men of Harvard College, but it was an idea that a great many Americans already took for granted.

Literary Nationalism

No group of Americans exhibited more conflicted feelings toward Great Britain than the nation's literary community—if that is the right term to describe a jumble of cliques and coteries scattered in metropolitan areas along the eastern seaboard. All could claim some degree of familiarity with that country's neoclassical literary canon, with Johnson, Dafoe, Addison, and Pope serving as the cornerstone of every formal American education. Regarding Great Britain as a veritable holy land of high culture, many American writers made pilgrimages across the Atlantic to pay dutiful homage at its most sacred sites. For these writers, the blood of England continued to course through American veins, as the poet Washington Allston declared in his poem "America to Great Britain," which concluded: "We are One."[6]

And yet most American authors, on some level at least, felt compelled to distance themselves from that which they most admired. All revered the British literary tradition, even as they longed to be free of its legacy in order to craft a uniquely national belletristic culture. On the present state of American letters there was no disagreement. Much as they took offense at Sydney Smith's sneering remark, "Who reads an American book?" native-born writers did not dispute the fact that after half a century of independence, the former colonies had done little to distinguish themselves. While staunch patriots bridled at the mimetic nature of so many aspects of American life, the underdeveloped state of belles lettres seemed especially objectionable, James Kirke Paulding complained, "because it strikes at the root of every thing we do, and say, and think, and feel."[7]

American authors faced many challenges in their efforts to create a native literature. The early decades of the nineteenth century saw nothing less than a revolution in the reading habits of Americans, as an expanding publishing industry, coupled with the growth of the nation's transportation infrastructure, made books more affordable and widely available. But well-read Americans initially exhibited little interest in the works of native-born writers, preferring instead texts that had already gained critical favor and popularity in Britain. The historical romances of Sir Walter Scott, the sentimental novels of Edward Bulwer-Lytton, the verse-tales of Lord Byron were as widely known in the United States as in their own country. British periodical literature, a reliable barometer of the latest belletristic trends, exerted enormous influence over American highbrows, despite the appearance of several home-grown magazines after the War of 1812. The editors of these new publications often perpetuated their readers' cultural inferiority complex. Reluctant to express opinions that might be at odds with the conventional wisdom that prevailed in British intellectual circles, they sometimes refrained from passing judgment on a new book—especially if the author was an American—until it had been reviewed abroad.

No career better illustrates the extent to which the republic still looked to England for its literary direction than that of Washington Irving, the first American writer to gain some measure of celebrity for his labors. Irving had dabbled in satire as a young man, co-authoring *Salmagundi* with James Kirke Paulding, but it was not until he moved to England that he enjoyed his first major critical and commercial success with a collection of short stories and essays, published in seven parts under the title *Geoffrey Crayon's Sketchbook* (1819–21). Although the work included his two best-known tales, "Rip Van Winkle" and "The Legend of Sleepy Hollow," establishing his reputation as an American writer, the remainder of the book was devoted to Irving's sentimental impressions of English life and customs, and therein lay its chief appeal to readers on both sides of the Atlantic. For seventeen years Irving lived in England, where he assiduously affected the landed gentry's habits and manners.[8]

Much of that time was spent in Birmingham, yet the ravages of industrialization over the land and its people escaped him. Instead, the author was content to wax rhapsodic on England's splendid abbeys and stately ancestral homes, its sylvan scenes of hedgerows and meadows, a picturesque world he also evoked in his second book, *Bracebridge Hall* (1822). British reviewers, who themselves seem to have preferred Irving's wistfully nostalgic England to its grimy realities, lavished praise upon the author, which was dutifully echoed by critics in the United States.[9]

Even as American intellectuals proudly embraced Washington Irving, a scion of the New World who had made good in the Old, the filial devotion they had once felt for Great Britain was being sorely tested by that country's incessant criticism of the United States. The derisive contempt with which the British highbrow periodicals regarded American belles lettres—the works of Irving and a select coterie excepted—was especially hurtful in light of the adoration the republic's literary figures had always bestowed upon their transatlantic counterparts. Resentment of British criticism in literary circles was no doubt exacerbated by the fact that the explosive growth of the domestic book market after 1815 had failed to open up new opportunities for aspiring American authors; never before had the complete monopoly of British literature over the American mind been more apparent. No longer willing to genuflect so readily at the altar of British letters, erstwhile Anglophiles responded to the attacks on the national character with a mighty howl of indignation. From every quarter of the country, editors, essayists, and academics clamored for a literature "such as Americans may be proud of, and such as British criticism may no longer ridicule or annihilate."[10]

For many American highbrows, the crusade for literary nationalism was a natural response to their irritation at British censure. Although homegrown periodicals catered largely to an Eastern readership and continued to offer a steady diet of works by British authors, almost all, with varying degrees of determination, began to take up the cause of American letters. In Philadelphia, the *Port Folio*, a staunch advocate of British models under the guidance of Jonathan Dennie, passed into new hands after the War of 1812 and was soon calling for an American literature free of British influences. Particularly prominent in the battle against an imitative literature was the *North American Review*, established in Boston in 1815. Even under the editorship of Edward Everett, a committed Anglophile who helmed the magazine during the early 1820s, the journal took a firm stand on behalf of American literary independence. The *American Quarterly Review*, edited by Robert Walsh, who continued to fight on against British cultural dominance after his *Appeal from the Judgments of Great Britain*, also adopted a firm nationalist posture, as did the *Portico* in

Baltimore. Edgar Allan Poe, who served briefly as editor of the *Southern Literary Messenger*, was too much the iconoclast and introvert to lend his voice to the patriotic hurrahs of the herd, but nonetheless believed that "there is not a more disgusting spectacle under the sun" than American subservience to British ideas.[11]

Once American writers awakened to the need for a national literary voice, they became conscious as never before of the debilitating constraints which their admiration for British letters entailed. Where Noah Webster and a few others had once grumbled at their country's excessive admiration for British literature, now a crowd of essayists stepped forward to sound the alarm. The assault on British influences compelled educated Americans to confront some troubling questions about the nature of their cherished republic. Could any nation that modeled itself after another realistically entertain any hope of achieving distinction in the arts? A colonial society, by definition, existed as a facsimile of its imperial parent, and as such seemed to present a fallow field for all forms of intellectual enterprise. A nation that derived its intellectual aliment from abroad, many argued, would forever be undernourished, incapable of producing a robust literature, or indeed anything of lasting cultural value.

The most conservative members of the cultural elite brushed off such concerns and held fast to a sentimental and reflexive Anglophilia, content to gaze across the Atlantic with a reverence that bordered on infatuation. Though, like Washington Irving, they might take umbrage at the malign invective directed at their country, the ties of culture and kinship were too strong to be eroded by petty bickering and name-calling. "We belong as a people to the English school of civilization. It is not necessary that the scene of an American work of imagination should be laid in America," huffed the poet Grenville Mellen in 1828.[12] Yet even the shrinking number of writers who remained steadfastly and publicly pro-British were obliged to concede that American intellectual life was little more than a faint echo of its parent, a state of affairs that could not be allowed to continue if the United States was to develop its full potential. The great cultural debt Americans owed Great Britain threatened to become a crushing weight; at some point they would have to think for themselves in order to create a literature worthy of a great nation. "It is a hard case for letters here," the historian William H. Prescott observed ruefully. "We have achieved only half our independence."[13]

The enthusiasm with which American writers undertook their new crusade was fired by the conviction that they were engaged in a cause the nation could ill afford to lose. In clamoring for a literature of their own, American intellectuals were not motivated simply by an emotional national pride, but by the concern that much of contemporary British literature was inappropriate reading for the citizens of a republic. The historical romances of Sir Walter Scott had won him many devoted admirers in the United States, making him in the 1820s by far the most celebrated novelist in the Anglophone world. Walt Whitman, however, found Scott's tales of courtly love undemocratic, while James Kirke Paulding complained that the British author had created an admiration for lawlessness and "the license of barbarous ages."[14] Even in the South, where a planter class liked to think it had somehow managed to preserve a cavalier, chivalric past, Scott had his detractors, South Carolina poet William Grayson complaining that Scott's fiction was "adverse to the cause of popular institutions."[15]

A more compelling target for the ire of American moralists was Edward Bulwer-Lytton. In true Chesterfieldian style, Bulwer crafted one of his most popular novels around a profligate coxcomb, in *Pelham, or, The Adventures of a Gentleman* (1828). Walt Whitman decried Bulwer's "tinsel sentimentality," while even the urbane *Knickerbocker* admitted that Bulwer's novels had "loosened a thousand moral ties, without strengthening a single moral principle." Such complaints notwithstanding, Bulwer's enormous appeal in the United States suggests that he remained for many American readers a guilty pleasure (the British traveler Harriet Martineau was probably not exaggerating when she remarked that one could not go half a day without hearing him mentioned). That such literature could still shape American notions of elegance and gentility more than half a century after the nation had achieved its political independence from Great Britain seemed to one essayist "as lamentable as it has been ridiculous."[16]

If American writers worried about the detrimental effects such "aristocratical" notions might have on the reading public, they were especially concerned about their impact on republican womanhood. During the early decades of the nineteenth century, educated, affluent American women constituted the publishing industry's biggest growth market. The proliferation of ladies' magazines and the dramatic rise of the sentimental novel created a new, gendered literary culture, which to many critics played no small part in promoting the frivolous notions of foreign gentility. William Gilmore Simms was appalled by the extent to which the ladies' literary journals regaled their readers with the prurient and sordid details of British fashionable society.[17] The *Democratic Review* blamed the "pernicious trash" of foreign novels for instilling anti-republican ideas in American women, and insisted that democratic institutions, not foreign elitist ones, alone should provide the proper training for the nation's wives and mothers.[18]

American intellectuals were no less concerned about the ill effects of English literature on the nation's youth. Great was the chagrin of one pious mother, a parenting magazine informed its readers, when she discovered that her son had clandestinely read some of Bulwer's novels. The magazine was pleased to report that the episode ended happily when she succeeded in convincing him that such putrid fiction was the work of the "arch-deceiver," and hazardous to his spiritual well-being.[19] A generation weaned on romantic novels in which the hero and heroine were scions of the titled nobility could hardly be relied upon to uphold the meritocratic values that were the underpinning of a republican society. James Kirke Paulding was only one of many writers who fretted that such effete literature would instill in male youths "an unmanly taste for effeminate frivolities," and impart "a sickly admiration" for a social system based on rank and privilege that their forefathers had fought so hard to destroy."[20]

Most proponents of literary nationalism recognized that these baneful effects could not be attributed solely to the Anglophile tastes of the American reading public. Native-born writers, too, deserved some measure of blame for the country's humiliating cultural dependency. Drawn largely from the ranks of the privileged classes, the American cognoscenti had been conspicuously slow to craft a republican aesthetic. In "seeking to write as Englishmen," Orestes Brownson maintained, native-born writers had abdicated their responsibility "to write as Americans, and as men." As members of the first generation of Americans born during the postcolonial era, the nation's writers felt keenly their obligation as inheritors of the legacy bequeathed to them by the heroes of the Revolution. To a class of Americans often criticized for their own lack of independence, the quest to redeem the nation from the sway of British influences offered a redemption of sorts—a charge worthy of that sacred trust.[21]

But no sooner had they accepted this challenge than they were daunted by the enormity of the task they had set for themselves. While all could agree that a national literature was a great desideratum, few seemed to have any idea how to create one, or what forms it should take. They fretted constantly, haunted by self-doubt, alternating between euphoria and acute despair, ready to proclaim the dawning of a new era of American letters one moment, only to bemoan the obstacles that stood in their path the next. Could a nation dedicated to the pursuit of the practical, which celebrated the common citizen and valued the utilitarian, be capable of great artistic achievement? Feelings of inadequacy ran so deep within the intellectual community that some writers were all but ready to pronounce the new republic a barren cultural desert, unfit for literary products of any kind.[22] A large part of the problem was that American and British tastes were, to a considerable degree, one and the same. Much as they wanted to write books of their own, Americans could not help but look to the British canon as the baseline for belletristic achievement. When they thought of historical romance, for example, they thought of Sir Walter Scott, unable to imagine the genre without the moated castles of his *Waverly* novels, vestiges of antiquity conspicuously absent in their own country. "Here are no gorgeous palaces and cloud-capped towers; no monuments of Gothic pride, mouldering in solitary grandeur," the *North American Review* noted glumly.[23]

Of course, in tailoring their work to foreign tastes they were engaging in the very imitativeness they abhorred. Most writers were unconscious of the paradox, and continued to emulate Britain's literary lions even as they sought to find their own voice. Maine novelist John Neal was one of the few authors who grasped the utter absurdity of an intellectual community that hoped to produce a new, national literature but refused to deviate one jot from foreign literary conventions. Why would Americans want an American Addison, he asked, when they already had the English one? The result was an "exalted" mimicry, but it was mimicry all the same.[24]

The idea took root in some quarters that Americans should seek alternative models for emulation. New England transcendentalists, notably George Ripley, Margaret Fuller, and James Freeman Clarke, looked toward the European continent in the hope that it would infuse American letters with a less worshipful regard for Great Britain. Margaret Fuller expressed the hope that the hybrid nature of American society would dilute the "excessive influence" that existed "between child and parent."[25] Having studied at the great universities of Central Europe, many transcendentalists were especially keen to see a larger role for German culture in American life. Others, too, made the case for multiculturalism. Just as the thirteen colonies sought alliances with Britain's enemies in their revolution against King George, so should the republic nurture close ties with other European nations.[26] Establishing a German literary review in the United States after the War of 1812, French-born linguist Peter de Ponceau devoted much of his energies to promoting awareness in the United States of the intellectual achievements of continental Europe. Southern novelist and essayist William Gilmore Simms agreed that the study of German and other languages would help to neutralize the English cultural hegemony that had rendered Americans "emasculated and enslaved."[27] These appeals for a greater degree of cultural pluralism in American literature failed to make much of an impact on the broader belletristic community, which was reluctant to substitute one form of imitation with another. Most literary nationalists were intent on cauterizing British influences, not diluting them with those of other countries.

Or so they liked to believe. For all its Promethean rhetoric, the crusade on behalf of an original American literature was characterized by an undercurrent of ambivalence that bespoke a continued respect for Britain's cultural life. Well-read Americans bowed low before the great figures of that country's literary pantheon, and often exhibited an unseemly infatuation with the most popular contemporary British writers. In their quest for self-determination, the nation's intellectuals seemed bent on effecting a bloodless revolution. Having been weaned on British models, they found it difficult to be militant iconoclasts. Try as they might, they could not bring themselves to tear down the temples in which they had worshiped with such devotion for so long.[28]

James Fenimore Cooper: The Rise and Fall of an American Novelist

Americans, then, sought a balance between their desire for a literature of their own and their deference to Old World tradition. In James Fenimore Cooper they would find a writer uniquely suited to bridge this transatlantic cultural divide. Rising to prominence by adapting the historical romance to the American scene, the author of the Leatherstocking Tales never quite managed to escape the long shadow of the genre's foremost practitioner, Sir Walter Scott. Nonetheless, no other American did more to lay to rest the nagging concern that the young republic was incapable of providing suitable materials for the literary imagination. Then and now, Cooper's critics have charged that his work was derivative—that his principal accomplishment was to substitute the American primeval forest for Scott's medieval England, to clothe his heroes in buckskin instead of chain mail. They have pointed, too, to his painfully stilted dialogue, tortuous prose, and baroque plot construction. But any appraisal of Cooper's career cannot be undertaken without considering the larger geocultural context in which he operated. More than just a writer of historical romances, Cooper was a public intellectual in the fullest sense of the term, a figure who spoke for the entire nation in its ongoing process of separation from Great Britain. Since both the successes and the failures of his career would be directly informed by this transatlantic relationship, they warrant a thorough examination here.

Cooper's early years gave little hint of the role that he was destined to play in the republic's campaign for cultural independence. The son of William Cooper, a high Federalist and one of the largest landholders in the state of New York, the novelist would confess that he had been born and raised among Americans who regarded England with feelings of "political, moral, and literary adoration."[29] Cooper's marriage to Susan de Lancey, whose family had been prominent Tories during the Revolutionary War, further bound him to the Anglophile subculture of the landed gentry. It was a world that would seem increasingly anachronistic as the republic entered a new century, and Cooper, like Charles Jared Ingersoll of *Inchiquin* fame, never fully embraced a fondness for England so common to his class. In the years following the War of 1812, Cooper, then a struggling gentleman farmer, would be offended by the attacks on his country from British travel writers and periodicals like the *Quarterly Review*. Not until he embarked on a literary career, however, did Cooper's nationalism take wing, following a trajectory that ascended in tandem with his celebrity.[30]

Like all aspiring American writers of the period, Cooper knew that he would first have to win favor across the Atlantic before he could be appreciated in the United States. Accordingly, the gentleman farmer's first fictional effort was a mediocre facsimile of the novels of manners then popular in England by such authors as Amelia Opie and Jane Austen. Set in the drawing rooms of the English gentry, *Precaution* (1820) chronicles the efforts of three distinguished families to arrange suitable marriages for their sons and daughters. Mindful of the Anglophile tastes of the American reading public, Cooper had the book published anonymously, in the hope that it might fare better if it were mistaken for the work of an English author.

Though *Precaution* could hardly be termed a commercial success, the novel did well enough that Cooper wrote a second, *The Spy* (1821), which proved to be the breakthrough that launched his career. This time Cooper turned his attention from the English nobility to American characters and American themes, in a tale of strife-ridden New York set during the Revolution. Yet the book could never have succeeded, on either a critical or commercial level, had Cooper written strictly for an American audience. The task for Cooper was a tricky one: how to bring the American past to life in a manner that would not offend patriotic sensibilities on either side of the Atlantic. In an effort to placate his British readers, Cooper dedicated *The Spy* to an English friend and apologized for any exhibition of "national partiality."[31] Cooper's deft, if self-conscious handling of Anglo-American conflict is evident throughout the novel. Rejecting the temptation to idealize the American cause, the author presents the Revolution less as a struggle for freedom than as a fratricidal civil war, one in which moral imperatives become almost hopelessly blurred, with duplicity and nobility evident in roughly equal measure on both sides.

Cooper returned to the Revolution in his next novel, *Lionel Lincoln* (1825), and once again refused to fashion his work to suit American patriotic feeling. The novel's titular hero is an American-born officer in General Gage's army of occupation in Boston. Despite early indications that he will desert to join the colonial cause, Lionel remains loyal to the Crown, and in the end he returns to Great Britain to become a baronet. Americans responded enthusiastically to Cooper's tales of a bygone era, which were published at a time of heightened public interest in the events that had given birth to the republic, while many British reviewers applauded the author for his efforts to do justice to their own country. In short, Cooper's early novels enjoyed success on both sides of the Atlantic, no small accomplishment given the strong emotions which the Revolution still elicited among Americans and Britons alike.[32]

Unfortunately, the American novelist would find this balancing act increasingly difficult to perform. Despite his transnational appeal, Cooper remained an essentially national figure, whose literary merit and Americanness were inextricably linked. No mere scribbler of historical romances, Cooper had become in a few short years a symbol of the country's cultural promise. Europeans read the author with great interest; here at last was the young republic's much-anticipated contribution to the world of letters. Americans, meanwhile, proudly embraced Cooper as much for the acclaim he received in Europe as for his novels; here at last was a native writer who could command the respect of foreign critics.

The burden of being the first American novelist to gain an international reputation was a heavy one, yet it was a responsibility that Cooper, with a combination of hubris and naiveté, shouldered gladly. In 1826, basking in the success of *The Last of the Mohicans*, Cooper moved with his wife and two daughters to Europe, where he found that his fame had preceded him. In France he enjoyed a reception not accorded an American since Benjamin Franklin. The New Yorker enjoyed the attention, and his early letters are filled with breathless accounts of his introduction to French society. But the novelty of rubbing shoulders with the titled nobility soon wore off, and Cooper began to adopt a more critical view of European social and political institutions. He also grew increasingly annoyed by his hosts' ignorance of the United States. That Europeans might have a dim understanding of a young nation half a world away was hardly surprising, yet Cooper seems to have agreed with those Americans who had for several years insisted that there was a more sinister explanation: a conscious and deliberate effort to traduce the United States, and thereby stifle republicanism before it could infect the peoples of Europe.[33]

A broadening of one's horizons is often a happy consequence of foreign travel; for Cooper, though, a zealous parochialism proved more than a match for his curiosity. From the outset of his European sojourn, the American transplant seemed less a man of the world than a stubborn patriot whose every experience seemed to reaffirm his devotion to his country. It may have been for this reason that the novelist abandoned his scrupulous regard for the sensibilities of his English readers and adopted an unabashedly patriotic tone in his next work, *The Red Rover* (1827), the story of an American pirate who preys on British shipping at the time of the French and Indian War. Walter Heidegger (the eponymous Red Rover) is no common criminal, but a proto-nationalist who harbors a deep seated allegiance to the American colonies and longs for their independence from the Crown. A former seaman in the Royal Navy, he is a Byronic figure whose life of piracy has noble origins, having once killed a British officer who insulted his native land. Roaming the seas as a freebooter, he exacts his revenge against the British, but would gladly abandon his life of piracy for the chance to sail under the American flag. In the book's final scene, the Red Rover achieves the redemption he has long sought, fighting for his country during the War for Independence. Mortally wounded in the battle of Yorktown, he manages to unfurl an American flag and utter with his final breath, "We have triumphed!"[34]

Yet Heidegger's dying words belied the author's own doubts that his country's independence had been won. Underlying the novel's earnest nationalism was a budding resentment toward Great Britain and its cultural hegemony over the Anglophone world. Cooper was acutely conscious of the fact that John Bull's more conservative periodicals remained lukewarm toward the new literary sensation from the former colonies. Not surprisingly, the author attributed this lack of enthusiasm to simple anti-Americanism. Convinced that he could never win their favor, Cooper instead began to adopt a more defiant stance, viewing their hostility as a badge of honor, a testament to his own patriotism.[35]

Nonetheless, a visit to Great Britain was virtually a prerequisite for any American's grand tour, and in the spring of 1828 he arrived in London for a three-month sojourn. A steady whirl of fashionable society events followed, all of which he bore with an unmistakable air of self-conscious disdain. "The Johnny Bulls have been very attentive to him," Susan Cooper wrote home, but despite the warm reception she was obliged to concede, "He does not like it much."[36]

That may have been putting it mildly. Like some of the British travel-

ers who criticized the United States, the American author seemed determined to have as disagreeable a time as possible. Manifestly incapable of
assuming the perspective of a dispassionate observer, he played the part
of the stalwart republican, maintaining a posture of stiff-necked recti-
tude in every social situation. Introduced to a dazzling array of intellectual luminaries, Cooper refused to be overawed, as though any sign
of deference would be tantamount to an admission of his country's cultural mediocrity. The author was so sensitive to insult that he mistook
compliments for condescension. It rankled him, for example, when he
overheard the comment at a ball that an American lady in attendance
danced as well as any Englishwoman. Though he recognized that Americans were not the cosmopolitan equals of their English cousins, he insisted that they be treated as such, a defensiveness that no doubt only
confirmed his hosts' suspicions of American insecurity.[37]

Increasingly, Cooper displayed a casual indifference toward the sales
of his works in Great Britain, expressing the hitherto heretical view
that an American writer must write for American audiences. He now
resolved never to pander to British tastes, even if his earning power suffered as a result. He could nearly double his income if he wrote "to suit
English feeling," he later told a friend, "but I was born and will live and
die a Yankee." In the early 1820s, Cooper had written to please readers
on both sides of the Atlantic; by the end of the decade he professed to
care little for the English book-buying public which, he was convinced,
"would greatly prefer reading abuse of us than anything else."[38]

Determined to throw down the gauntlet at the feet of the republic's
detractors, while still in Europe Cooper penned *Notions of the Americans,
Picked Up by a Travelling Bachelor* (1828). Adopting an epistolary formula
common among travel works of the time, the author presents, in a series of thirty-eight letters, the fictional travels of a Belgian visitor to the
United States. But unlike the English itinerants Cooper found so obtuse,
his visitor is soon won over by American virtues, thanks largely to the
efforts of an American traveling companion. A paean to the young republic, *Notions of the Americans* was not only intended to disabuse Europeans of their misconceptions of the United States; the author also
sought to alert his fellow Americans to the folly of harboring pro-British
sympathies, and to demonstrate the extent to which such feelings had
become engrafted upon the American mind. Thus, *Notions* did not spare
those Anglophiles who remained in thrall of British opinions and institutions. With their preference for English books, they prevented the
emergence of a national literature; with their enthusiasm for English
plays and English actors, they stymied the development of a national
drama. Yet for all their slavish imitation, Cooper saw reason for opti-

mism, allowing his fictive visitor to observe that "the time has already arrived, when America is beginning to receive with great distrust fashions and opinions from England."[39]

Cooper would soon have reason to reconsider that verdict. He had expected a severe drubbing from British reviewers, but he was not prepared for the book's lukewarm reception in the United States, where critics did not appreciate so public an exposition of their foibles from one of their own. Cooper would insist for the remainder of his life that the book ruined his career, and although this was certainly an exaggeration, there can be little doubt that *Notions* signaled the beginning of his decline as a national literary icon. Nonetheless, he vowed to continue to work to deliver Americans from foreign snares, even at the risk to his own literary career. "No sacrifice," he wrote with self-righteous resolve, "is too great to establish national independence."[40]

Cooper returned to the United States in 1833 more determined than ever to defend his country against all who disparaged it. Alas, the homecoming proved to be an unhappy one. While still abroad, the novelist had written, in quick succession, three historical romances set in the courts of Europe. Cultural conservatives, unwilling to suffer his censure in silence, fired back. The American Scott, they charged, had succumbed to the corruptions of the Old World and had adopted the sensibilities and prejudices of a European aristocrat during his years abroad. In what must have been an especially galling pill for Cooper to swallow, Washington Irving, another famous expatriate and the idolater of all things British, had arrived in New York one year earlier under very different circumstances. Having been embraced by Britain's intellectual establishment—Oxford University had awarded him an honorary degree—Irving returned to face not hostile critics but the plaudits of a grateful nation. Clearly, Americans were happy to welcome the Anglophile who brought honor to his country, but not the overzealous patriot who insisted on drawing attention to their shortcomings.

Cooper's growing sense of isolation had much to do with the fact that few Americans seemed able to meet his high standards of civic responsibility. Much as he prided himself on his immunity to Tory sentiments, he was never entirely comfortable with the strident egalitarianism that had become an increasingly prominent feature of American life during his years abroad. A democrat in principle, he remained in practice an incorrigible snob. Cooper's inability to reconcile his innate elitism with the new social order became evident soon after his return from Europe. Taking up the life of a country squire in Cooperstown, the novelist quarreled with local residents over access to a popular picnicking spot on his estate, threatening to prosecute all trespassers. The Whig press picked up the story and upbraided the author for his aristocratic conduct. The criticism stung Cooper, whose avowed faith in the wisdom of the sovereign people had always been predicated on the assumption that its views accorded with his own. Now, he was beginning to regard the general public with as much exasperation as the Anglophiles so numerous among the privileged classes. Having gone to such lengths to fashion a public identity as the first American novelist, Cooper found himself a citizen of a country he no longer seemed to recognize.[41]

Increasingly prone to feelings of persecution, he came to see himself an embattled figure, beset by enemies at home and abroad. In a fit of pique, in 1834 he announced his retirement from the world of belles lettres, having decided that Americans were "still too much under the influence of foreign theories" to accept him.[42] He soon changed his mind, and the following year released *The Monikins* (1835), a Swiftian allegory in which the transatlantic relationship is satirized in the form of two island nations of talking monkeys, the Leaphighers and Leaplowers. A series of travel books soon followed, culled from the copious notes he had taken during his years abroad. In *Gleanings in Europe: England* (1837), Cooper inveighed again against what he perceived to be that country's virulent anti-Americanism. The "history of the world," he wrote, "cannot offer another instance of prejudice in one nation against another," as that which characterized Britain's attitude toward the United States.[43] Although the book purported to be a travel memoir, Cooper could not resist admonishing his fellow citizens for their subservience, lamenting, as he had done in *Notions*, the "craven and dependent" pro-British feeling among the country's privileged classes. Cooper undoubtedly had Washington Irving in mind when he referred to the "school of sentimentalists" whom he blamed for perpetuating the national inferiority complex. This servility seemed all the more deplorable to Cooper, who regarded those of his own socioeconomic group as the guardians of national virtue—a class to whom, in the natural order of things, the rest of society looked to for moral, cultural, and political guidance.[44]

By the mid-1830s, Cooper had completely squandered the goodwill he had once enjoyed among the transatlantic literary fraternity. *The Monikins* was received not so much with unfavorable reviews as by embarrassed silence. Most journals refused to review it at all, and those that did were at a loss to describe it, dismissing the work as the product of a "warped" and deluded mind.[45] There could be no doubt as to the purpose behind his travel book on England, however. Angered by Cooper's anti-British tone, the *Quarterly Review* unleashed a full-bore personal attack on the author, questioning his talents as a writer, his integrity as a gentleman, and even his patriotism as an American. In the United

FIGURE 2.

James Fenimore Cooper, 1822, by John Wesley
Jarvis. (Fenimore Art Museum, Cooperstown, N.Y.
Photograph by Richard Walker)

States, several Whig journals reprinted the *Quarterly Review* at length,
confirming for the author what he had long suspected: that he was the
victim of a British-orchestrated plot to destroy his reputation.[46]

With his popularity at home sinking fast and his financial situation
precarious, this might have been a good time to return to more lucrative
literary endeavors. But Cooper was not done lecturing Americans on the
duties of republican citizenship. In 1838, with the release of the seafaring travel narrative *Homeward Bound*, and its sequel, *Home As Found*,
Cooper alluded, none too subtly, to his own trials in readjusting to life
in his native land. The books would spark a new round of criticism and
once again raise questions about the author's national allegiances. In the
first volume, cousins John and Edward Effingham are making their way
back to the United States after an absence of many years. Members of
the landed gentry, both men have been educated "under the influence
of the British opinions" that weigh, Cooper writes, "like an incubus on
the national interests of America."[47] *Home As Found* opens with their arrival in New York City, affording the novelist the opportunity to satirize
Gotham's Anglophile cognoscenti. In one of the few successful comedic
scenes in the Cooper oeuvre, Captain John Truck, a simple seaman, is

mistaken for a great English writer. At a dinner in his honor, all marvel at his "Byronic head" and receive his every utterance with the greatest import.[48]

Yet the author who had once relished the opportunity to single-handedly wage war against those who disparaged his country had become one of its sharpest critics. Returning to Templemore (a thinly disguised Cooperstown) in upstate New York, the Effinghams find a community much changed during their years abroad. The family becomes embroiled in a land dispute with the locals, a minor subplot mirroring the author's own legal troubles. Like Cooper himself, John Effingham discovers that the will of the majority has become a new form of tyranny, heedless of justice and fair play, prompting him to pronounce the United States "the most intolerant nation I have ever visited."[49] And though far removed from the salons of the beau monde, in rural Templemore the Effinghams find the deleterious effects of the transatlantic relationship very much in evidence. One local resident has read all the popular British authors and regards the high Tory periodicals as nothing less than sacred texts. He exists as a mere cipher, holding all things English in such high esteem that, as Eve Effingham says, he would favor polygamy if it were of English origin. But an unthinking devotion to all American cultural products, regardless of merit, was no less ridiculous than the malaise of Anglomania, Cooper believed. Thus, another Templemore neighbor proves to be so staunchly ultra-American that he is moved to declare that, in the realm of belles lettres, the United States is without peer among the nations of the world. Together the two villagers neatly encapsulate the tandem schools of thought that, in Cooper's view, had grounded the nation's efforts to achieve cultural ascendancy: one slavish in its regard for all things British, the other so obdurate in its blind chauvinism that it rendered Americans incapable of recognizing Britain's continued sway over them.[50]

American literary journals found little to praise in the Effingham saga, greeting the two novels with a greater degree of indignation than they expressed for even the most vicious of British travel memoirs. Thoroughly put out by the author's attack on American society, critics took particular exception to the way in which Cooper held up the well-traveled Effinghams as the embodiment of squirearchical gentility. In a blistering review of Home As Found, the New York Courier and Enquirer branded the author "a traitor to national pride and national character," who praised "everything that is English at the expense of everything that is American."[51]

The novelist's popularity would revive briefly in the early 1840s when, having not written a best-seller in many years and facing severe financial difficulties, he returned in *The Pathfinder* (1840) and *The Deerslayer* (1841) to the wilderness adventures that had once endeared him to the American reading public. A few critics that in recent years had tired of Cooper's didactic hectoring now welcomed his return to the cause of American letters. The author was by this time too consumed with legal battles to savor his reversal of fortune, however, and he would devote much of his energies in his final years to costly litigation against the New York Whig press and his Cooperstown neighbors.[52]

Cooper's death in 1851 provided the occasion for the literary community to reflect on his artistic legacy. In a moving but candid tribute, editor and poet William Cullen Bryant drew special attention to the novelist's efforts on behalf of cultural independence, praising Cooper for having waged a personal campaign against his country's detractors abroad and its flatterers at home. He was not the first public figure to note the extent to which British influences reigned over the mind of the republic. None, however, had shone so unremitting a spotlight on the problem, or been so zealous in laying bare the uncomfortable fact that Americans were themselves to blame for such subservience. In the end, Cooper's brutal candor won him few friends and little gratitude. The American Scott, like the prophet who can find no home in his native land, had become the American Scold. He had asked too much of his readers, insisting that they should not only be entertained by his novels, but that they should profit by them. He had insisted that they strive to become better Americans, and they could never forgive him for it.[53]

Young America and Its Critics

While the controversies that surrounded Cooper were largely of his own making, his free-fall from grace cannot be attributed solely to a prickly and overbearing temperament. If many critics found Cooper's rigid chauvinism intolerable, it was because the consensus that initially characterized American opposition toward British cultural hegemony had never been as deep as it was wide. Most members of the intellectual community could endorse the need for a "national" literature in theory, just as they could pay lip service to the idea that Americans should abandon the behaviors of their colonial past. But the enthusiasm and the seriousness of purpose with which they sought this goal was another matter. Some were sunshine patriots in the cause of literary nationalism; others still regarded Great Britain with reverent piety, and bristled at the suggestion that the republic was in any way demeaned by its transatlantic cultural ties. In short, the ongoing public debate over the existing state and future prospects of American letters, far from uniting citizens in a common cause, often had precisely the opposite effect, serving to highlight the multiple ways in which the relationship with Great Britain informed Americans' sense of nationhood.

By the late 1830s, New York City, having surpassed Philadelphia as the nation's publishing capital, emerged as the epicenter of this increasingly fractious cultural debate. While most American periodicals continued to rely on foreign reprints, Gotham's highbrow *Knickerbocker*, under the editorial control of Lewis Gaylord Clark, provided a much-needed forum for American writers. A bon vivant of Whiggish inclinations, Clark could count among his contributors such staunch Anglophiles as Washington Irving and Henry Wadsworth Longfellow. In its early years, however, the magazine exhibited a catholic cosmopolitanism, and regularly featured articles by James Kirke Paulding and other stalwart nationalists.[54]

Clark's commitment to the cause of literary autonomy would be sorely tested by the rise of a new, militant literary circle, one that was more eager than he to translate postcolonial frustrations into a coherent plan of action. In October, 1837, two months after Emerson delivered his "American Scholar" address, a twenty-three-year-old Irish American unveiled the first issue of a new journal that would become the literary voice of Jacksonian democracy. As the co-founder of the monthly *United States Magazine and Democratic Review*, John L. O'Sullivan called for nothing less than a radical exorcising of all British influence from American letters. Fired with nationalist zeal, the young editor repudiated the notion that the country was in any way beholden to the cultural traditions of the Old World. Like all well-read Americans, O'Sullivan paid the obligatory tribute to the "magnificent, venerable, splendid" character of British belles lettres, but he left his readers in no doubt that it held little practical value for the American republic. Its literary figures must pursue an altogether different course—the unabashed and unapologetic promotion of democratic values.[55] O'Sullivan would eventually expand upon this idea of the republic's special mission to argue that the surest means of achieving America's "Manifest Destiny" was through the creation of a hemispheric empire. But for now the young firebrand was content to limit his chauvinistic appeals to the dominion of the mind. The democratic principle "must be the animating spirit of our literature," he maintained. All questions pertaining to human existence would have to be reexamined from this point of view. With this bold statement of purpose, the New Yorker demanded nothing less than the politicization of the nation's cultural identity.[56]

O'Sullivan's call for a jingoistic jihad on behalf of American letters resonated powerfully with a young group of writers headed by one of his former Columbia College classmates, Evert A. Duyckinck. Like Lewis Gaylord Clark, the budding *litterateurs* were committed to providing a forum for native talent; unlike him, they believed that such work should clearly exhibit the virtues and vigor of the new nation. The group founded several literary magazines, none of which enjoyed much success, though it gained an influential mouthpiece for its views when O'Sullivan moved his *Democratic Review* from Washington to New York in 1840. Eventually christening itself "Young America," the clique hoped to succeed where James Fenimore Cooper had failed. Brimming with patriotic passion, its members were determined to lead Americans out of bondage toward a new literary promised land.[57]

With writers in other parts of the country looking to New York City as the nation's publishing mecca, Duyckinck's literary circle reached far beyond Manhattan. One eager recruit to the Young America banner was South Carolina native William Gilmore Simms, who by the early 1840s had established a reputation as a prolific novelist of Revolutionary strife and border adventures. Like James Fenimore Cooper, with whom he was often compared, Simms was a tireless defender of his country against foreign critics, and inveighed constantly against the vestiges of "colonial tyranny" which Britain continued to exercise over American intellectual life. As an essayist and editor, he devoted much of his literary labors to the theme of an independent belletristic culture. For Simms, a truly national literature was one that reflected the rich diversity of the American experience.[58] Devoted to the South and Southern institutions, he evinced more than any other writer of his generation an acute sensitivity to the folkways of a particular region (a parochialism that may have contributed to his inability to achieve a wider appeal).[59] A self-described "born Southron" and "ultra-American," Simms saw no inherent conflict in his claim to both allegiances.[60] Even as the early tremors of sectional discontent began to rumble through the Palmetto State, he remained convinced that the common cultural assumptions linking Americans would serve as a powerful antidote to disunion. For the South Carolina novelist, as for all Southern whites committed to the concept of union, the controversy over slavery would present the ultimate test of that credo in the years ahead.[61]

For a while, a respectful bonhomie governed relations between Gotham's Whiggish and Democratic literary cliques. With both the *Knickerbocker* and its more jingoistic counterparts committed to providing an outlet for native talent, Clark and Duyckinck understood that the virtual stranglehold that British literature exerted over American reading habits would have to be broken before home-grown writers of any sort could gain public favor. To that end, both cliques initially lent their support to the campaign for a federal copyright law.[62] This spirit of cultural bipartisanship was destined to be short-lived, however. As Young America found its voice, it did so with a shrillness that grated on Whiggish ears. Many conservatives had enlisted in the campaign on behalf of an independent literature more in a fit of pique than from genuine conviction, eager to sally forth against those British critics who had insulted the national honor. But wounded pride was a poor casus belli; once booted and spurred, their enthusiasm seemed to wane. The manic zeal which Young America brought to the task did little to steel their resolve. On the contrary, they were shocked by the apparent delight with which the group thumbed its nose at hallowed belletristic conventions. Continuing to hold the British literary canon in the highest esteem, traditionalists regarded any deviation from "the great English models" as intellectually irresponsible. In defying these fundamental laws, Young America exhibited a complete disregard for the natural order of things, a challenge to the status quo that threatened to disrupt the harmony of the spheres.[63]

Young America's association with O'Sullivan's *Democratic Review*, which had become an unofficial organ of the Democratic Party, also brought the broader cultural movement into disrepute in the eyes of many highbrows. They were offended by the magazine's increasingly bellicose anti-British posturing in the face of rising diplomatic tensions between the two countries. Harboring a knee-jerk Anglophilia in political matters no less than in cultural ones, conservatives dismissed such rhetoric as chauvinistic claptrap. Irritated though they may have been at British criticism, they were reluctant to lend their support to a literary movement which, in their view, seemed governed by nothing more than a spiteful and "hollow-hearted jealousy" of Great Britain.[64]

Young America was not solely responsible for this sudden change of heart among many highbrows. Duyckinck's group had simply aggravated very real doubts about literary independence which traditionalists had harbored all along. They had never really accepted the idea that a people could will into existence a fully developed literary culture. The flowering of native genius, conservatives believed, was the labor of centuries, requiring painstaking cultivation. The changing political landscape added to their growing skepticism. When the *North American Review* and similar journals first lent their support to the cause of literary nationalism after 1815, the privileged classes could readily imagine themselves as stewards of a new republic of letters. But the democratic upheaval of recent years had not only eroded their political authority, it had undermined their position as cultural arbiters as well. Thus, when Young America promised a new literature for the masses, conservatives cringed. Real genius, they believed, could never thrive in a society geared to the lowest common denominator. Here, then, was a question worthy of contemplation by Zen masters: if a writer of extraordinary gifts should emerge, would a people so lacking in sophistication even be aware of it? After all, one could not expect great art from a nation of Philistines who did not know what great art was.

Conservatives were no less contemptuous of the idea that belles lettres could play a role in strengthening the national character. Works that idealized a world of rank and privilege might well have deleterious consequences for a republican readership, they admitted. But a literature expressly designed to inculcate a sense of national pride was hardly better if it devolved into patriotic cant. Since great art was, by definition, truly universal, then a campaign to create an "American" literature, as one Whig critic noted, made as much sense as an attempt to create American science, medicine, or theology.[65] What was more, a literary culture that prized loyalty to the nation above all else could never be sure of its artistic merit. This was a problem that had occurred to some members of the Young America movement, too. A tireless booster of works he considered to be distinctly American, Evert Duyckinck was nonetheless quick to add that the nation's literary prospects would be ill served if "all the geese that should be produced on this side of the Atlantic should be called Swans."[66]

Traditionalists believed that if any native-born writers exhibited a gosling gracelessness, it was those of Young America. Lewis Gaylord Clark and others reviled the group as a "mutual admiration society" that compensated for its lack of talent by an overweening self-importance. The novelist Cornelius Mathews was a favorite target for their abuse. Whig critics dismissed his novels of the Gotham cityscape, *The Career of Puffer Hopkins* (1842) and *Big Abel and Little Manhattan* (1845), as "indescribably stupid," and consigned them to the dustbin of the American literary catalog, where they have remained to this day.[67] The nation's cultural conservatives did not limit their attacks to Young America's artistic shortcomings. In what was perhaps the unkindest cut of all, they alleged that the exponents of cultural nationalism were not nearly so national as they supposed. The group's novelists had merely taken the "cast-off garments" of British writers and given them "an American fit." Mathews' urban novels seemed to his critics shameless facsimiles of the work of Dickens, while William Gilmore Simms, like Cooper before him, came under withering fire for daring to situate the historical romances of Scott on the American frontier. Here conservatives turned the argument for an indigenous literature completely on its head, suggesting that American writers who trafficked in ostensibly national themes were merely conforming to British stereotypes and preconceptions of the rough-hewn republic. "English critics seem to expect a dash of savageness," the *North American Review* sarcastically observed; "they expect to hear the roar of Niagara, and the crash of the trees in the primeval forests" from the writers of the United States. And the American romancers had dutifully complied. In the name of a national literature, they had gone native, and in so doing pandered to the very foreigners whose views they professed to ignore.[68]

By the mid-1840s the enthusiasm for a more distinctly American literature was clearly on the wane in Whiggish intellectual circles. Not many years earlier, the nation's highbrow journals had been ready to proclaim the advent of a new era of republican letters. Now, they reminded their readers of the countless kindred associations and "ancestral memories" which tied Americans to the imperial parent. Abandoning his support for a national literature, Lewis Gaylord Clark had soured on the idea to such an extent that when Duyckinck organized a Copyright Club in 1843, the *Knickerbocker* dismissed the effort as a "humbug." Conservatives now began to close ranks, mocking the proponents of Young America as loopy millenarians, their eyes trained on the distant horizon, squinting anxiously for the dawn of a golden age that would never come.[69]

In the end, the source of American anxieties that had once given rise to the loud demand for a greater degree of cultural autonomy would also be responsible for the dissonance that now emerged among the nation's literary coteries. Editors, essayists, and novelists of every conceivable description, from meditative New England transcendentalists to the boisterous voices of Young America, had all expressed in one form or another the ardent hope that the country would one day break free of Britain's literary moorings. But to leave behind the tradition of centuries was no easy task, requiring a great leap of faith into the unknown. It was a leap the writers of Young America were only too eager to make. Independence, they were convinced, would give them wings with which to soar to everlasting fame. The old school literati, on the other hand, stood at the edge of the precipice and clung to the safety lines of custom and convention. These cherished ties to the Old World, they believed, were all that prevented the republic from tumbling into the yawning abyss of cultural anarchy.[70]

❀·❀

While American intellectuals regarded British cultural dominance to be a matter of all-absorbing interest, it was a concern the general public did not initially share. The literary magazines that provided the principal forum for all points of view on the subject were read by few outside the urban centers of the East, with even the more successful periodicals claiming at most only a few thousand subscribers. Nonetheless, the issue would ultimately engage a much wider audience than these numbers might suggest. In a country that regarded declamatory speaking as nothing less than a national pastime, the theme of cultural independence was a familiar one, a favorite subject for orators who could be found at national holiday celebrations, political rallies, civic association meetings—indeed, wherever Americans congregated.

It is also worth noting that American literary figures enjoyed a far more prominent position in the public sphere than they do today. For all its noisy populism, American political life in the early decades of the nineteenth century was not hostile to intellectual achievement. Despite a penchant for bestowing their highest honors upon military heroes, voters rewarded many politically inclined savants with elected office at the national and state level. Several writers of note won congressional seats, including the philologist George Perkins Marsh (two terms from Vermont), the essayist Charles Jared Ingersoll (five terms from Philadelphia), and the poet William J. Grayson (two terms from South Carolina). South Carolina novelist William Gilmore Simms, Massachusetts native Samuel Goodrich (of the phenomenally successful Peter Parley children's primers), and New York newspaperman John L. O'Sullivan all served in the legislatures of their respective states. A number of prominent men of letters were tapped to serve in cabinet positions. Oddly enough, the secretary of the navy during the antebellum period was not infrequently an individual of some literary merit: James Kirke Paulding served briefly in that capacity under Martin Van Buren; historian George Bancroft occupied the post in James K. Polk's cabinet; the novelist John Pendleton Kennedy held the job under Millard Fillmore. And because the literary profession was an uncertain one, even the most successful writers sought the steady income that political sinecures provided. James Fenimore Cooper and Nathaniel Hawthorne served as U.S. consuls abroad during Democratic administrations. Washington Irving, who gravitated to the Whig Party, was appointed U.S. minister to Spain in the Tyler administration.[71]

Public men, they spoke to, and spoke for, a much wider audience than their literary efforts might suggest. The crusade for cultural nationalism would thus have repercussions that would be felt far beyond the world of belles lettres. Once confined to the country's highbrow periodicals, the arcane debate over the proper role of British influences in American life soon extended beyond this rarefied forum. By that peculiar process by which ideas are transmitted, changing shape and dimension as they become more diffuse, American cultural insecurities would be passed on to the public at large, settling into the deepest pores of the national psyche. Nowhere was this osmosis of ideas more evident than in the realm of commercial entertainment, the focus of the next chapter.

4

"America Rules England Tonight, by Jesus"

Fashion, a Comedy—I'll go—but stay—
Now I read farther, 'tis a native play!
Bah! homemade calicoes are well enough,
But homemade dramas must be stupid stuff;
Had it the London stamp 'twould do—but then,
For plays we lack and the manners and the men!

— Ann Cora Mowatt, *Fashion, A Comedy*

During the early decades of the nineteenth century, no American theater enjoyed greater prestige or influence than New York City's Park Theatre. Under the management of Edmund Simpson, an Englishman, and his American partner, Stephen Price, the Park served as the entertainment venue of choice for Gotham's beau monde, a position of cultural dominance it held by virtue of its connections to the London stage. The two impresarios initially recruited English stars for their own productions, and over time expanded their activities to serve as talent agents for the country's burgeoning entertainment industry. Under what came to be known as the "star system," Simpson and Price lured the best foreign actors for lengthy engagements at the Park, which were then followed by extended national tours. In most cases, a visiting performer would remain in the United States for the entire theatrical season, with the two managers handling bookings, publicity, and other arrangements. They had little difficulty recruiting major stars, for the republic was fast becoming a rich field of opportunity that the celebrated players of Drury Lane and other foreign entertainers could ill afford to ignore.

In 1810, the two managers brought the acclaimed English actor George Frederick Cooke to the United States. Although stateside audiences were familiar with Cooke's triumphs on the London stage, the star arrived under less than auspicious circumstances. Relations between the two countries had deteriorated in recent years, and would continue to do so as the United States became drawn into the contest between Great Britain and France then raging in Europe. British maritime policies, which included the seizure of U.S. ships and the impressment of American seamen into service in the Royal Navy, had greatly inflamed public opinion. Despite rising transatlantic tensions, however, Americans accorded Cooke a hero's welcome. Hungry for English cultural products, cosmopolitan elites refused to allow national antipathies to spoil an evening's entertainment, and jammed theaters wherever Cooke appeared on the playbill.[1]

Sadly, they did not see a great actor at the height of his powers. An alcoholic who frequently flubbed his lines and was often too drunk to perform, Cooke was a physical wreck. Onstage, his performances were disappointing; offstage, his behavior was bizarre. Insulting all who encountered him, Cooke referred to the American people as "rebels" and even claimed, falsely, that he had fought against them at Bunker Hill. Upon learning that President Madison wished to attend one of his performances, he declared that he had appeared before George III and would not stoop to entertain "the contemptible King of the Yankee Doodles." Simpson and Price were horrified. Fearful that Cooke might antagonize Americans at a time when the two countries were on the verge of war, they made every effort to keep him in line, assigning a staff member to watch over their besotted star.

Remarkably, Cooke's erratic conduct had no appreciable impact on his box office appeal. Night after night, he was received by enthusiastic audiences. Theater critics, too, chose to ignore his onstage bouts of delirium tremens and lavished plaudits upon the visiting star. Even after Congress declared war against Britain in June 1812, the American love fest with Cooke continued unabated. It did not end until the actor succumbed to the ravages of his affliction, dying in New York City three months later.[2]

After the war, Simpson and Price resumed their practice of luring British performers across the Atlantic. While the star system continued to work successfully for the Park management, there were signs that urban audiences were beginning to shed their easy-to-please provincialism. When an English vocalist in 1817 refused requests for an encore, a melee broke out inside the theater. The management called for the watch, which made several arrests. But the singer was applauded warmly by the Park's patrons at his next performance, suggesting that a desire to get their money's worth, not national antipathies, had been the cause of the affair. Americans might not be so ready to forgive the snubs of visiting actors, but they were still eager to catch the latest Drury Lane sensation. They still wanted to be entertained.[3]

In 1820 Simpson and Price scored their biggest coup, signing Edmund Kean, the most renowned Shakespearean actor of his day, for the upcoming season. At first, the tour exceeded the two impresarios' expectations. Arriving in November, Kean opened at the Park to a tumultuous reception, universally hailed by critics as the greatest actor to grace the boards of an American theater. After several sold-out performances, a triumphant tour of Eastern cities followed. On opening night in Philadelphia, the crush of the crowd was so great that many female theatergoers stayed home; in Boston, the theater sold its choicest box seats by public auction. The tour proved so lucrative that Kean began to make plans to remain in the United States to repeat his success the next season. Knowing that the summer heat would soon force theaters to close their doors, the British star decided to return to Boston for a final string of performances.[4]

Kean had misjudged his popularity with American audiences. Poor ticket sales on opening night left little doubt that public interest in the English star had already peaked. On the second night, Kean peered through the stage curtains before he was scheduled to go on and saw a half empty house. Furious, he refused to perform, later informing the theater manager that "my professional reputation must not be trifled with."[5] Kean's tantrum caused an uproar in the local press, which denounced the actor for this affront to the people of the Bay State. The negative publicity followed him to New York City, where he issued a statement defending his conduct—but no apology. Recognizing that the British actor had lost the goodwill of his audience, Simpson and Price advised against any further engagements. Kean beat a hasty retreat to England.

Kean might not have returned to the United States had he not experienced a sharp reversal of fortune a few years later. In 1824, the actor found himself embroiled in scandal, the result of a longtime affair with the wife of a London city alderman. Charged with adultery, the actor was forced to endure a sensational trial, in which his letters to the woman were entered as evidence. Facing severe financial difficulties and anxious to escape the London press, Kean looked once more across the Atlantic, signing on with Simpson and Price for another tour of Eastern cities. Surely, he must have thought, American audiences had forgotten the incident that had sent him packing four years earlier.[6]

It proved to be a forlorn hope. Always eager for news from abroad, Americans had followed the Kean affair with a good deal of prurient interest. To make matters worse, the actor's letters to the woman contained disparaging references to the United States, further souring the public against him. Ominous rumblings of disapproval in the press greeted the hapless Kean upon his arrival in New York in November, 1825. Despite the urging of some critics to boycott his Park engagement, the public frenzy generated by the British tragedian was so great that an enormous crowd began assembling at the theater three hours before his performance of Richard III. When the curtain rose, Kean came forward to address the audience, but his remarks were drowned out by a cacophony of catcalls and hisses. Throughout the performance hostile audience members continued to voice their disapproval and bombarded the actors with assorted fruits and vegetables. Kean was not without his supporters, however. Two days later, he performed Othello to a much more appreciative house, and his remaining nine appearances at the Park also went off without incident.[7]

In December, Kean returned to Boston, the scene of his 1821 transgression. Anxious to avoid a repeat of his opening night fiasco in New York, the actor published a letter offering a contrite if belated apology. But the temper of the crowd was as inhospitable as it had been in Gotham. Making another before-curtain appearance, the hapless actor found his efforts at atonement rebuffed by the audience. The disturbances continued throughout the first act, at the end of which Kean, fearing for his safety, left the theater. As in New York, a fierce battle raged between the supporters and enemies of the English actor, sending law-abiding theater-goers heading for the exits. Patrons on the second floor, finding the stairways blocked by the surging crowd, were obliged to scramble out the windows onto ledges, from which they managed to jump to the pavement below. Although the worst of the protests were over, the threat of violence dogged the British tragedian for the remainder of his tour.[8]

The demonstrations against Kean signaled a new spirit of contrariness on the part of Americans. For the next quarter of a century, urban theater-goers would continue to pack playhouses to see British performers, often receiving them with rapturous enthusiasm. But their adoration could vanish in an instant should it be rumored that a visiting actor had in some way insulted his hosts. New York City alone would experience half a dozen major *émuetes* during this period, as well as numerous disturbances that either temporarily disrupted or brought a premature end to an evening's entertainment.[9] Every Eastern city with a permanent theater company also saw occasional protests directed against British actors. While only a handful of players had the unpleasant experience of being threatened by an angry mob, virtually all major stars of the London stage (and a great many lesser-known ones), were obliged to defend themselves against charges of misconduct. Clearly, the forbearance that citizens of the republic had once so gladly extended to George Frederick Cooke was a thing of the past.

Anatomy of a Theater Riot

Why had American audiences accorded such different receptions to the two visiting stars? The answer can be found in the fact that public tastes and expectations were changing in ways that even the Park's managers, Simpson and Price, may not have fully understood. In the first decade of the nineteenth century, American audiences not only tolerated, but insisted upon entertainment that carried the British seal of approval. Catering to an Anglophile urban elite, the playhouses of New York, Philadelphia, and other Eastern cities differed little from provincial theaters in the British Isles. Most were owned and/or operated by English managers, whose companies were composed largely of actors who had immigrated to the United States.[10] Their repertoire ranged from the Shakespearean canon to plays that had only recently made their London debut. Theater managers felt little pressure to include the works of American dramatists, since the upper classes who filled the most expensive seats shared their disdain for the work of native talent. So strong was the prejudice against local authors, in fact, that in 1812 a Philadelphia theater presented a play written by an American as a British work.[11] In such a climate, American audiences could hardly be expected to find fault with visiting actors; indeed, their very presence in the United States was seen as evidence of the country's cultural maturity. Far from taking offense at Cooke's behavior, the cognoscenti crowed that the star's American tour signaled a newfound sophistication on the part of republican audiences, "incontestable proof," one newspaper gushed, of their city's "taste [and] refinement."[12]

By the time Kean arrived a decade later, American theater-goers were less inclined to take their stage directions from abroad. Gone were the days when even a dissipated star like Cooke could expect an enthusiastic reception. At the Park, the beau monde still formed the theater's core constituency, but the Kean riots offered an early indication that it could no longer take its position as the arbiter of public taste for granted. After the country's second war with Great Britain, Americans wore their nationalism self-consciously on their sleeve, and the theater seemed to many citizens an especially obnoxious symbol of foreign cultural hegemony. "The whole atmosphere of our Theatres is essentially English," complained one New York pundit. "All the plays present English scenes, English characters, English thoughts, delivered in English accents."[13]

Theater owners who sought to accommodate the Anglophile tastes of the privileged classes would have to tread carefully, lest they arouse the prickly patriotism of the general public. To satisfy both constituencies would be no easy task, requiring management to locate a middle ground that would only become less well-defined in the years ahead.

Audience protests during the early nineteenth century took many forms and varied widely in intensity and scope. The full-fledged riot—involving large numbers of city dwellers, multiple arrests, damage to theater property, and injury—was a relatively rare occurrence, while only one, the Astor Place Riot in 1849, resulted in loss of life. Planned and sometimes even publicly announced days prior to a performance, such events represented the most extreme form of audience disapprobation. Most theatrical disturbances, on the other hand, consisted of individuals or small groups acting spontaneously, attracted little attention from the press, and were resolved as quickly as they had begun. More often than not, patrons who hissed during a performance or made an actor the target of a well-aimed piece of fruit or other projectile did not plan their actions well in advance, or intend them to lead to further disorder.

No comment was too trivial, no slight too absurd to raise the patriotic hackles of American audiences. When William Charles Macready became angry at a Baltimore theater property man who had failed to provide him with a suitable arrow for the play *William Tell*, his outburst provoked so much resentment that he was obliged to issue a formal apology.[14] The tide of public opinion proved fickle indeed, and could turn against even the most popular English actors. While out riding with a companion in Washington, D.C., the celebrated actress Fanny Kemble made a disparaging remark about American horses, sparking an uproar that quickly became the talk of the nation's capital. Reports of the incident followed her to Philadelphia, where handbills calling upon the community to protest the insult were posted throughout the city. During one performance, a group of angry theater-goers in the upper tiers showered the handbills onto the audience seated in the parquet below, briefly bringing the play to a halt.[15]

Obviously, such trifling matters by themselves were not enough to send audiences into fits of rage, but acted as triggers for deeper currents of resentment. American hostility to Great Britain took many forms, and needed little prodding to rise to the surface. Political and economic disputes between the two countries undoubtedly figured in the calculus of opposition against British actors, as did the literary works of critical British travelers. Some actors, following the lead of Hall and Trollope, wrote their own uncharitable memoirs, which seemed to Americans particularly galling in view of the profits which they reaped from transatlantic tours. As highly visible ambassadors of British culture, members of the dramatic profession often bore the brunt of American unhappiness with the way in which the United States was portrayed across the Atlantic. For theater audiences, the hissing of a British actor, or an organized effort to drive one from the stage, was proper payment for the insults they had long borne at the hands of British authors.[16]

Crowd protests also had roots in class antagonisms within the urban community. Resentful of upper-class pretensions, urban laborers took part in theater demonstrations not only to express their dissatisfaction with arrogant British actors, but with the cosmopolitan nabobs who fawned over them. The most serious theatrical disturbances took on the character of open class warfare, pitting artisans and mechanics against the "kid glove aristocracy." Venting their hostility at a foreign target had its advantages for working-class audience members. While disruptive behavior could never be tolerated by the authorities, it enjoyed some measure of legitimacy among the general public when exercised in defense of the nation's honor. Unruly patrons justified their actions as a civic obligation—indeed, as a patriotic duty. Elites who deplored the violence and called for the punishment of rioters, on the other hand, could be cast as the sycophants of a foreign power. Invariably, it was the rowdies who prevailed—at least until the watch arrived.

Still, class conflict can only go so far in explaining the theater disturbances that sometimes erupted. The American beau monde toasted celebrities from other countries too (such as the Austrian ballerina Fanny Ellsler and the Swedish singer Jenny Lind), all of whom managed to tour the United States without creating an international incident. And it should be noted that American audiences seemed just as eager to punish journeymen performers from the British Isles—though they could hardly be deemed adequate symbols of aristocratic privilege—as the most celebrated Drury Lane stars. In Albany, New York, a little-known English actor was denounced in handbills posted throughout the city after remarking that Americans were "a parcel of ignoramuses." In separate incidents in Providence, Rhode Island, not long after the Kean demonstrations, the public rose up against two English-born members of the stock company who had made derogatory remarks about American institutions, forcing their dismissal.[17] Urban crowds did not, therefore, lash out indiscriminately at symbols of privilege. They understood that the British theatrical community and the upper classes each bore some measure of responsibility for the neocolonial character of the American stage. Working-class hostility toward local elites may have fueled such disturbances, but it cannot be easily separated from the geopolitical context in which it occurred.

Native-born theater personnel often assumed a key role in the process by which these broad feelings of frustration mutated into acts of civil disobedience. Resentful of British dominance of their profession, American actors were instrumental in bringing quarrels among the *corps dramatique* to the public's attention. "The bloody Englishmen have got possession of our best theatres," fumed actor Harry Watkins. "I am actually driven out of my native city by Englishmen."[18] In disputes between American and British performers, the majority of theater-goers sided unhesitatingly and loudly with their countrymen. The dancer Julia Turnbull precipitated a disturbance in August, 1848, when she announced to the audience at the Bowery Theatre that an English performer would not dance with her because she was an American. A popular figure among the denizens of the Bowery pit, Turnbull must have known what effect this statement would have on her admirers. The "cry for native talent rang through the theatre," the *New York Herald* reported, and a "general tearing up of the seats" began.[19] Rumors that the friends of American actresses Naomi Vincent and Josephine Clifton were preparing to hiss Fanny Kemble dogged the British actress during her 1832–33 tour, while Edwin Forrest, who will be discussed in detail later in this chapter, made every effort to characterize his professional rivalry with William Charles Macready as a cultural contest between the two countries.[20]

Disgruntled American actors found willing allies in a jingoistic urban press. By the 1830s, as competition among big city newspapers increased, editors began to acquire a taste for the sensational, and did not hesitate to exploit controversies involving British actors. Exerting an influence far beyond theatrical circles, the mass circulation dailies were an indispensable ingredient of every major disturbance, fueling public outrage, and at times even goading readers into acts of protest. The *New York Sun* averred that such demonstrations were justified, "when the character of our country is assailed by foreigners." It added: "This will teach English play actors a lesson they will long remember."[21] In the aftermath of a riot, editors reverted to their roles as respectable pillars of social order, deploring the violence with an air of surprise and indignation. There could be no escaping the fact, however, that their breathless reporting and inflammatory editorials incited many citizens to act.

In short, the theater disturbance served as a locus for a combustible mix of geopolitical conflict, socioeconomic tensions, and petty grudges. Yet it should be added that the trivial allegations of impropriety that served as catalysts for crowd anger were not always pretexts for other concerns. When British actors misbehaved, they provided Americans with a rare opportunity to compensate for the indignity they felt as citizens of a nation that had yet to fully secure its cultural independence.

Americans were obliged to concede their lack of refinement, but such an admission still rankled. As a result, they insisted that dramatic talent alone was not enough to win public favor. For a British actor to be well-received in the United States, he would have to be judged by other standards as well, and demonstrate his willingness to adhere to an "American" code of behavior.

American theater-goers took their role as enforcers of this code very seriously indeed. Not only were British actors expected to keep anti-American opinions to themselves; they were required to behave as model republicans during their stay in the United States. Evidence of aristocratic pretensions invited severe public censure, as Charles J. Mathews, a well-known British comedian, and his wife, the renowned singer Madame Vestris, discovered when they arrived late one evening at a Poughkeepsie resort. Finding a dance in progress, the fatigued celebrities declined an invitation to attend the affair and asked to be shown immediately to their rooms. The other patrons resented the slight, and the incident was reported in the New York press. The negative publicity could not have come at a worse time for the couple. Having long been linked romantically, they had married only a few weeks before their American tour, reportedly at the urging of the Park management. Boycotted by polite society, Mathews and Vestris decided to cancel their remaining engagements, returning to England after only two months.[22] Other British actors faced similar charges of moral turpitude. The opposition of the American press toward Edmund Kean's ill-fated second tour owed perhaps as much to his trial for adultery as to his earlier snubbing of a Boston audience. Mocked with cries of "Hurra for the seducer!" when he appeared at the Park in 1825, Kean seemed to personify the laxity of morals that Americans associated with a decadent Old World.[23]

British actors suspected of behaving from purely mercenary motives were also likely to incur the ire of American theater-goers. Stung by the widely held British perception that citizens of the republic worshipped the dollar, audiences were quick to take offense when actors from across the Atlantic demonstrated similar tendencies. Edmund Kean was only one of many visiting English stars scolded for putting financial concerns above their responsibility to the theater-going public. The celebrated actor William Charles Macready commanded ticket prices of up to one dollar during his 1844 American tour, prompting severe public criticism and a short-lived farce entitled *Macgreedy*. The Irish actor Tyrone Power, renowned for his aristocratic demeanor, also refused to perform to a meager house at Albany's Old Pearl Street Theatre, enraging the local citizenry. The following night a much larger, more hostile audience greeted Power. The actor made an attempt at an apology, but his voice could hardly be heard above the din, which continued throughout the performance.[24]

Male stars who behaved incourteously toward women were likewise hauled before the bar of public opinion. Upbraided by Trollope et al. for their bad manners, American men seized any opportunity to instruct British actors when they exhibited a lack of gallantry. The celebrated singer Joseph Wood demonstrated an especially obtuse disregard for American sensibilities when, on a tour of the Eastern states with his wife in 1835–36, he refused to perform at the benefit of a popular but lesser-known English singer, Mrs. Conduit. Although both stars in question were foreign-born, it was Wood's nationality, not Mrs. Conduit's, that attracted the attention of the New York press. The *Courier and Enquirer* rushed to Mrs. Conduit's defense and rebuked Wood for his ungenerous conduct. That night the British singer was greeted with "groans and hisses" from the audience, and was obliged to come forward to insist that the newspaper's statements were groundless before the show could go on. Unsatisfied by Woods's explanation of the affair, the *Courier and Enquirer* editorialized that the actor should "be taught his place" and called upon its readers to express their displeasure. Accordingly, at the next appearance of the British couple, an assortment of missiles, including a six-foot-long piece of a bench, rained down upon the stage. The performers stood mute until they were pelted off.[25]

Quick to punish, the theater audience could also show clemency toward British actors who violated republican norms. But first an act of atonement was required, usually in the form of an apologetic open letter published in the press, followed by a humbling before-curtain speech. In some cases an extravagant and heartfelt mea culpa was enough to still crowd passions and prevent a disturbance from escalating into a full-scale riot. Audiences could also spring to the defense of an actor they believed had been wrongfully accused. One such episode occurred at Philadelphia's Chestnut Street Theatre in the aftermath of the Kean demonstrations. Anxious to placate his patriotic audience, the American stage manager took the liberty of deleting all references to the nationality of an English character, offending British actor Francis Wemyss, who refused to read the new lines. The flap soon became the talk of Philadelphia's theater-going community. The audience hissed Wemyss at his next performance, but the actor came forward to address his critics, and was allowed to continue.[26] George Vandenhoff found himself in a similar predicament during an engagement in New Orleans in 1843, after a dispute with a stagehand. The next day, Vandenhoff discovered that "thousands" of handbills had been posted throughout the city denouncing him as an "aristocratical hypocrite." Prior to that evening's performance, a deputation of citizens called upon Vandenhoff to learn his version of the affair. Evidently, the actor's explanation proved satisfactory, for the play went on without incident.[27]

In the end, it mattered little whether an actor was welcomed back into favor or hooted from the stage. Whatever the outcome, the audience had made its point, acting to redress feelings of impotence in the face of vaunted British power. Pitting a riotous crowd against a solitary, hapless thespian, the theater disturbance offered participants a risk-free form of retribution, a lopsided contest in which the outcome was never in doubt. Sitting in judgment over offending Britons and meting out summary punishment, American audiences found themselves in a unique position of authority. They did not hesitate to exercise it, demanding a public apology no matter how insignificant the transgression. By this humbling, humiliating act of expiation, the wrongdoer atoned not only for his own crimes and misdemeanors, but for the nation he represented.

Thomas Hamblin and the Bowery Theatre

By the early 1830s, the Park's reign as New York's preeminent theater was slowly drawing to a close. Although it was still the venue of choice for the city's fashionable set, the Park now found itself locked in fierce competition with a host of newer playhouses, all of which were more eager to accommodate the changing tastes of Gotham's increasingly diverse theater-going community. New York and other Eastern cities were in the throes of a population boom, serving as magnets of opportunity for a steady stream of European immigrants and a young generation of Americans facing diminishing prospects in nearby rural communities. As a result, the theater was no longer a haven for urban highbrows, but a contested space in which various constituencies jostled for dominance. In this fractious and turbulent environment, the potential for conflict was always present.[28]

In October 1831 the Park again became a battleground with the arrival in New York of the English actor/singer Joshua Anderson. Anderson had reportedly been an obnoxious passenger on the transatlantic voyage, quarreling with other passengers and the crew and making comments insulting to the national character.[29] Whatever the merit of the charges, they sparked a chain of events that by now had become almost routine for New York's theater community. Anderson's opening performance was disrupted by angry patrons, who shouted "Off! Off! Go back to England!! Tell them the Yankees sent you back!" Anderson published a letter in the newspapers the following day in which he denied speaking disrespectfully of the American people, but the apology had no effect. At his next performance, on October 15, theater-goers once again refused to allow Anderson to go on, while a large crowd outside began pelting the building with rocks. Tensions mounted when it was noticed that a pair of American eagles that once adorned the two gas lampposts in front of the theater had been removed. The rioters eventually dispersed, but returned the following day. By that time, Price and Simpson had taken appropriate measures, having draped the building with American flags and patriotic bunting. The managers even felt compelled to issue a statement regarding the missing eagles, which, they explained, had been damaged and were being repaired.[30]

The difficulties at the Park could not have been unwelcome news to the management of its principal rival, the Bowery Theatre. Earlier that year Thomas Hamblin, an English actor of some repute, had assumed full control of the theater and was busily engaged in making it the most popular entertainment venue in the city. Like the upscale Park, the Bowery still put on Shakespearean tragedies and the most popular London plays, but it also offered a repertory designed to appeal to a cross-section of New Yorkers. Burlesques, spectacular "blood and thunder" melodramas, circuses, minstrelsy, and equestrian shows—all provided at low ticket prices—attracted working-class citizens to the Bowery in large numbers.

Always looking to gain an edge over the competition, Hamblin seized the opportunity to exploit the visceral nationalism of Gotham's theatergoers. Henceforth, he announced in the days following the riot, his establishment would be known as the American Theater, Bowery. The name change drew a round of criticism from the press; even the *Evening Post*, a Democratic paper, admonished Hamblin for capitalizing on the Park's misfortunes, and for his shameless and cynical efforts to promote the Bowery as a "pseudo American theatre." Undeterred, Hamblin also ordered a large eagle to adorn the façade of the building, which he unveiled with much fanfare a month later.[31]

Hamblin's efforts to establish a playhouse more attuned to the patriotic sensibilities of his audience were not purely cosmetic. The enterprising manager worked to reduce British influences over the American stage by commissioning plays from aspiring American dramatists. Moreover, he rejected the star system pioneered by Price and Simpson in favor of homegrown—and considerably cheaper—native talent. In the face of vigorous competition from the Bowery, the once-venerable Park soon fell into disfavor with all but the upper echelons of New York society. Showing little inclination to dispel its stodgy reputation as a purveyor of highbrow culture, Simpson and Price continued to book costly

European stars at a time when a large segment of the public preferred homegrown talent.[32]

Ironically, the trend toward a more nationalistic theater culture did not have the effect of preventing audience demonstrations; indeed it may have actually helped encourage them. In years past, urban elites formed the theater's primary constituency, and assumed responsibility for enforcing certain standards of decorum within it. While these standards had broken down on occasion, they remained largely intact until the 1830s, when theaters like the Bowery for the first time began to cater to the tastes of the general public. Unlike the well-to-do, for whom the theater was the venue for an evening's divertissement, working-class patrons expected a far greater degree of audience engagement. Like the modern spectator sporting event, the theater often became an arena of frenzied competition, pitting rival actors and their legions of avid followers against each other. Whereas crowd disturbances at the Park had been isolated events, stemming from a set of specific, abnormal circumstances, during the heyday of the Bowery they were manifestations of a more raucous theater culture. By deliberately encouraging national rivalries, theater managers like Hamblin fostered an environment in which actors were recognized less for their dramatic ability than for their roles as competitors in a geocultural arena. In so doing, they created a commercial entertainment space in which male bonds of belonging could be forged, aggressive behaviors tolerated.[33]

As hard as Hamblin tried to curry favor with New York's working class, even the Bowery could never entirely shed the stigma of being British-owned and operated. In the summer of 1834, a local butcher alleged that he had been assaulted by George Farren, Hamblin's British stage manager. According to the complaint, Farren had "cursed the Yankees" during the fracas, calling them "jackasses."[34] Given the touchiness of Gotham theater-goers, this was certainly grounds for a disturbance. But as in so many incidents of this kind, public hostility toward a British actor drew from other, seemingly unrelated sources. One year earlier, Great Britain had passed the Emancipation Act, signaling the end of slavery in its West Indian possessions. The decision had galvanized American antislavery groups, whose activities were met with fierce opposition. In early July, the city experienced a rash of anti-abolition disturbances, stoked by the summer heat and the patriotic passions generated by the Independence Day observances. In this volatile climate, all Englishmen, regardless of their feelings toward slavery, fell under suspicion.

As bad luck would have it, a benefit for Farren had been scheduled for July 9, the same day an abolitionist meeting was to be held at the nearby Chatham Street Chapel. That evening, an angry crowd converged on the

FIGURE 3.
Thomas S. Hamblin. Photograph by Mathew Brady. (Courtesy Library of Congress, Prints & Photographs Division, LC-
USZ62-109998)

chapel to disrupt the gathering, only to find that it had been cancelled. Instantaneously, the anti-abolition mob metamorphosed into an anti-British one, and a "shout was made for the Bowery Theatre."[35] The mass of protesters grew in size as it surged up the street, and upon reaching the theater, merged with a smaller crowd that had gathered in opposition to Farren. The throng poured inside, where it found an up-and-coming American actor, Edwin Forrest, onstage performing *Metamora*. Hamblin appeared before the audience, waving an American flag like a "talisman," according to one theater-goer, but the magical power that it traditionally exerted over the crowd failed on this occasion, and he was compelled to retreat under a withering barrage of missiles. As the situation continued to deteriorate, the crowd called for "the American Forrest." At length, Forrest appeared to announce that Farren had been dismissed. The rioters remained in control of the theater until police arrived and forced them out into the street. Then, once again reverting back to its anti-abolitionist character, the crowd marched on the house of antislavery leader Lewis Tappan and, finding him not at home, ransacked the residence. Sporadic violence against abolitionists and free blacks continued for the next five days.[36]

More than any other major theater disturbance of the period, the

Farren riot revealed the fluid nature of crowd aggression. By all accounts, the mob that descended upon the Chatham Street Chapel had
no interest in the Farren affair, seizing upon it only when its search for
a suitable symbol of the abolition movement failed. No doubt its readiness to switch targets can be attributed to the fact that its ranks included
many who, to borrow the vernacular of the Bowery B'hoys, were looking
for a "muss" of any kind. Be that as it may, the actions of the crowd were
neither random nor capricious. Although the two issues were ostensibly
unrelated, New Yorkers saw both as evidence of the nation's continuing
subservience to Great Britain. Whether lashing out at imperious actors
or antislavery agitators, Gotham's residents understood that they were
directing their energies against emblems of authority that bore a foreign
stamp.

Chastened by the experience, Hamblin redoubled his efforts to establish the Bowery as a distinctly American place of entertainment. One
month after the episode, the management announced that it intended
to "pursue more diligently than ever" the promotion of native talent.[37]
Two years later, the *New York Mirror*, a strong supporter of the Bowery,
praised Hamblin for helping to create a thoroughly "national" theater,
suggesting that his establishment may have finally managed to immu-
nize itself from the taint of anti-Americanism. The Bowery's success was
not due to "English money, for Hamblin took it an impoverished man;
not English patronage, for its attractions, name, and company, are all
American; not English talent, for it has profited wholly by the native
genius of our soil," the *Mirror* observed. Rather, Hamblin's success could
be traced entirely to his refusal to bend to the English tastes of New York
nabobs. By dint of his own service to the cause of cultural nationalism,
Hamblin had become an honorary American.[38]

Constructing a National Theater Culture

The overwhelming majority of theater patrons, of course, took no part
in disturbances of any kind. Yet those of less obstreperous temperament
also managed to voice their opposition to British hegemony in meaningful if less dramatic ways. Demonstrations of audience discontent were,
after all, momentary eruptions of a much deeper undercurrent of public
opposition to British dominance. Far from being passive recipients of
foreign culture, American audiences managed to put their own unique
imprint on the popular entertainment of the period. While the latest
London hit continued to draw the fashionable set to the theater, by the
1830s most Americans had ceased to view with disfavor the works of native dramatists. Their willingness to accept local playwrights was in part

a reflection of changing tastes: with their growing appetite for the sensational and the exotic, audiences now preferred melodramas and romantic adventure—genres in which American dramatists excelled—to the Shakespearean canon and the drawing-room comedies of contemporary British playwrights.[39]

As native-born dramatists began to find an audience for their work, they began to shape American theater culture in subtle yet substantive ways. American playwrights dealt cautiously with geopolitical themes, since their livelihood depended on the patronage of British-run theater companies. Nonetheless, by the Jacksonian period American audiences frequently saw plays that satirized Great Britain or otherwise depicted its citizens in an unfavorable light. Native plays offered no shortage of unflattering British stereotypes; particularly popular was the foppish aristocrat, a familiar stage figure since the Restoration comedies of William Congreve. Such caricatures were readily incorporated into the broad humor employed by American comic actors, but unlike the stage Yankee, Bowery b'hoy, or Western backwoodsman—characters that gently poked fun at regional stereotypes—the shallow English aristocrat possessed few if any redeeming qualities. When one British visitor attended a farce at the Park Theatre in 1832, he noted disapprovingly that the main character was "a pompous old baronet," who "is the laughing stock of the piece. Insult and ridicule follow him in every scene; he is kicked and cuffed to the hearty content of the audience, who return home full of contempt for the English aristocracy, and chuckling at the thought that there are no baronets in America."[40]

While theater-goers on both sides of the Atlantic preferred plays that came with a hefty dose of moral instruction, American audiences insisted on a uniquely republican version of virtue triumphant. The dissolute character of the effete, dandified English nobleman offered an irresistible comedic vehicle for native playwrights, and served as a foil that could be juxtaposed against the simple, stout-hearted virtues of Americans. Frequently the aristocrat was not an aristocrat at all, but a swindler and poseur in search of money, sex, or both, whose false claim to nobility was revealed in the last act. James Kirke Paulding's *Lion of the West* (1832) and Joseph S. Jones's *The Green Mountain Boy* (1833) feature almost identical English peers, who seek to woo guileless American daughters away from their true, native-born loves, but who are ultimately unmasked as unscrupulous fortune-hunters.

American playwright Samuel Woodworth created one of the most odious British characters in the popular *The Forest Rose* (1825), a farce that owed its enormous popularity in large part to its deft coupling of American postcolonial and racial anxieties. Bellamy, a Londoner and self-styled "sportsman" in matters of the heart, arrives in a rural American village and is immediately smitten by Harriet, a simple but virtuous milkmaid. Determined to carry her off to New York City and, in the words of one villager, "initiate her into a life of vice and infamy," Bellamy arranges a secret rendezvous prior to their departure. His plans are foiled by the rustics, who send Rose, an ugly and malodorous black servant, in Harriet's stead. With her identity hidden by a veil, Rose meets and embraces Bellamy, whose humiliation is the cause of great merriment among the villagers when he discovers the deception in the final scene. In this comedic denouement of mistaken identity, Negrophobia and Anglophobia are employed in tandem to provide a morally satisfying resolution for theater audiences. The hapless Bellamy can only vow as he departs, "I will not fail to notice you all when I publish my Three Months in America."[41]

Bellamy's threat would have been a familiar one to American theater patrons, the English traveler with literary ambitions being a popular fixture of the American stage. Countless comedies and burlesques written by native-born playwrights lampooned British critics of American society. Basil Hall appeared as Sir Croesus Mushroom, "a pretended English baronet on his travels"—yet another Briton masquerading as an aristocrat—in The Times, or Life in New York (1829), while Fanny Kemble was satirized in The Bugs (1835) after she penned a memoir critical of the United States. Frances Trollope became the most frequent target of American satirists, caricatured as Madame Truelip in Woodworth's Foundling of the Sea (1833), as "a well-bred lady of foreign distraction" in Life in New York (1834), and, in her most famous stage incarnation, as Mrs. Wollope in Paulding's The Lion of the West.[42]

American playwrights sometimes used the role of the British tourist as a vehicle with which to plead for reconciliation between the two countries. William Dunlap good-naturedly satirized the prejudices of English visitors in A Trip to Niagara (1829), in which two British characters attempt to disabuse a third of his anti-American sentiments. The trio encounter several representative American characters along the way, and by the end of the piece the misguided Englishman sees clearly the error of his ways. "When the film of prejudice is removed from the eye," he declares, "man sees in his fellow man in every clime a brother."[43] Freeman, the aptly named central character in Paulding's Lion of the West, expresses similar sentiments, believing that the affinity between the two Anglophone peoples must surely triumph over "the petty fires of dissension."[44] Even plays that concluded on a conciliatory note, however, may have only reinforced the notion that Americans were capable of behaving magnanimously in the face of British condescension. Theater audiences knew from experience that most English visitors did not return home with a better appreciation of America, its people and institutions, but with their Old World prejudices firmly intact.

Dramas glorifying the nation's martial past also served to reinforce in the public mind the long-standing adversarial relationship between the two countries. Even at the Park Theatre, national holidays had for many years provided a respite from the steady diet of English productions. On the Fourth of July and other national holidays, Americans insisted on more patriotic fare. William Dunlap's *The Glory of Columbia* (1803) and Mordecai M. Noah's *She Would be a Soldier* (1819), two plays set during the Revolution, were the first patriotic dramas to gain wide popularity with American audiences. The Jacksonian era saw the proliferation of patriotic extravaganzas by native-born playwrights, such as Richard Penn Smith's *The Eighth of January* (1829), Stephen Glover's *The Cradle of Liberty* (1832), and Nathaniel Bannister's *Putnam, Iron Son of '76* (1844). Theater-goers could not fail to miss the frequent gibes directed at the British which these plays contained; indeed, playwrights often appear to have made a calculated effort to win the favor of the audience by appealing to national prejudices at key dramatic moments. In the Bowery staging of the spectacular melodrama *Lafitte, Pirate of the Gulf* (1836), for example, the patriotic buccaneer's decision to reject overtures from the British to join with them against the Americans brought the play to a temporary halt, "so repeated and enthusiastic were the shouts of national pride and pleasure."[45]

Clearly, the epic staging of historical conflicts with Great Britain did more than reaffirm for Americans their national creation myth. Playwright and audience alike strove in a conscious and deliberate manner to invest historical melodrama with a contemporary relevance. Such plays served to revivify "all the ancient animosities," between Great Britain and the United States, feelings that belied the close commercial relations and natural cultural affinities that bound the two countries.[46]

The intense *amor patriae* of American theater-goers frequently led to the blurring of boundaries that delineated audience and performers. At various intervals during the evening, the orchestra entertained the audience with a repertoire that consisted largely of patriotic music accompanied by patrons who sang and stomped their feet. Attending a Fourth of July extravaganza at the Park in 1832, one British visitor counted no less than two encores for both "Yankee Doodle" and "Sons of Freedom," as well as renditions of "Washington's March," "General Spicer's March," "Hail, Columbia," and the "Star-Spangled Banner." Throughout the evening, the audience sang and cheered with such boisterous enthusiasm that he could scarcely hear the music.[47] Frances Trollope observed much the same conduct at a Cincinnati theater: "When a patriotic fit seized them, and 'Yankee Doodle' was called for; every man seemed to think his reputation as a citizen depended on the noise he made."[48] Members of the audience also insisted on the right to make impromptu changes in the musical program as their mood dictated. At Hamblin's Bowery, the male patrons in the pit were known to call upon the orchestra to strike up "Yankee Doodle," the perennial favorite, when they were displeased with the overture.[49]

Of course, manifestations of patriotic ardor did not necessarily spring, ipso facto, from hostility toward Great Britain. Anglophiles could sing just as energetically as Anglophobes when the orchestra struck up "Yankee Doodle" and other patriotic airs. Yet the role that Great Britain played in fashioning a national identity was not lost on American audiences. Although the patriotic enthusiasm encouraged by theater managers like Hamblin was bereft of any explicit anti-British content, audience members clearly used demonstrations of hostility toward Great Britain as a standard by which their national allegiance could be measured. The linkage of Anglophobia and expressions of national solidarity represented a vital part of the theatrical experience, and, if one German visitor to New York can be believed, the most important part. "Not a creature pays the least attention to what is passing on the stage," she observed, "unless when an American actor comes forward, or some sarcastic *bon mot* is uttered against the English; and then the thundering stamp of heels expresses the universal applause."[50]

Theater managers took elaborate pains to create an entertainment space that nourished their audiences' patriotic ardor. As if to give the lie to the nation's cultural subservience to Great Britain, the Jacksonian playhouse was a temple of national pride. In Philadelphia's Walnut Street Theatre, each tier of boxes was adorned with paintings representing major battles from the Revolutionary period and the War of 1812; large painted medallions of the heads of all the presidents were placed around the dress circle, around the second and third tiers the heads of famous generals and naval commanders. At the Bowery, ever the bastion of patriotic correctness, a painting of George Washington gazed down upon the audience from the top of the stage. Drop curtains, too, depicted historical events; the Chatham had a painting of the 1812 naval battle between the *Constitution* and the *Guerriere*, while Philadelphia's Chestnut Street Theatre portrayed Washington crossing the Delaware. By contrast, the upscale Park Theatre displayed around its dress circle the portraits of English playwrights and, on the second and third tiers, scenes from Shakespeare's life and plays.[51]

The pervasiveness of nationalist iconography in the realm of commercial entertainment is indicative of the profound insecurities with which Americans, for all their chauvinistic bravado, viewed themselves and their republic. Americans wrapped themselves in the trappings of nationhood in an almost desperate effort to assert a sovereignty which they sensed they did not possess. The eagle and the flag offered reassuring reminders of independence, protection against the alien influences that confronted them in their cultural space, as it did in their everyday lives on a regular basis. The crowds that became enraged over the removal of the lamppost eagles outside the Park during the Anderson Riot, and pacified when the theater was later draped with patriotic bunting, invested these objects with sacramental significance. It was a lesson not lost on Thomas Hamblin, who tried to placate angry Gothamites by waving American flags as he sought a hearing in the midst of the Farren disturbance. Such totemic symbols served as tangible manifestations of their national sovereignty, thereby mitigating—at least temporarily—the nation's inferior position in the transatlantic relationship.

Dueling Dramatists: The Astor Place Riot

Few Americans felt this sense of cultural inferiority more acutely, or steeled themselves against it with the armor of a self-conscious nationalism more deliberately, than Edwin Forrest. After making his New York debut in 1826, the Philadelphia-born actor emerged by the mid-1830s as the preeminent tragedian of the American theater. A man of considerable physical strength, Forrest brought to his Shakespearean roles a vigorous athleticism that contrasted starkly with the nuanced interpretations of his English rivals. While traditionalists found such histrionics coarse and unrefined, his acting style had an electrifying effect on his admirers. One British visitor to the United States was not favorably impressed with the American tragedian, and still less by the republican rabble who flocked to the Bowery to see him perform. The actor's every flourish was greeted with "louder thunders from box, pit, and gallery, till it sometimes became a matter of serious calculation, how much longer one's tympanum could stand the crash."[52] The *New York Mirror* defended Forrest against the charge of overacting, but conceded that "many think he has been distinguished as much by the partiality of his countrymen as by his intrinsic worth."[53]

Yearning for British acceptance even as he deeply resented it, Edwin Forrest personified the fundamental quandary that the American republic faced in its quest for legitimacy. In this regard Forrest's career offers many significant parallels with that of James Fenimore Cooper, another American artist who had recently vaulted to national attention. Like

Cooper, Forrest spurned the "servile and degraded spirit" of the nation's cultural nabobs.[54] Like Cooper, he sought validation on his own terms, identifying with the democratic forces that repudiated English models. The cause of cultural independence became for both men nothing less than a crusade, an indelible feature of their public personae. But whereas Cooper alienated the reading public with patronizing lectures on the duties of citizenship, the Philadelphia actor made no such demands on his audience. Casting himself in the role of the people's champion, Forrest allied himself so openly with the party of Jackson that in 1838 New York Democrats begged him in vain to accept their nomination as a candidate for Congress (thus becoming the first American entertainer whose talents seemed to qualify him for high public office).

But the acclaim of working-class Americans was not enough; to reach the pinnacle of his craft and win the unconditional respect of critics in the United States, Forrest would first have to conquer England. Accordingly, the actor announced plans in 1836 for a European tour. In a remarkable public announcement issued before his departure, Forrest insisted disingenuously that it was not his idea to go to England at all; he had only undertaken the tour at the urging of British and American friends. Were the decision up to him, he would not make the trip, his ambition being "satisfied with the applause of my own countrymen."[55] Forrest need not have worried how the tour would be perceived at home. Most of his supporters cheered his decision to beard the British lion. Whether they were willing to admit it or not, they were no less anxious to see him pass muster with London critics.

The tour proved to be a great success on several levels. A hit with critics and the general public, Forrest won rave reviews, which were reprinted throughout the United States, making the Philadelphia actor a source of enormous national pride. At the same time, he managed to cement his ties to the British theatrical community by courting and marrying Catherine Sinclair, the daughter of a popular singer. As a cultural representative from the former colonies who had won the acclaim of British highbrows, it seemed that the "American Tragedian" had succeeded where the "American Scott" had failed.[56]

But the nation's first great actor—again, like its first great novelist—found the burden of an entire nation's need for validation a heavy one to bear. Temperamentally unsuited to the task, Forrest shared Cooper's outsider worldview. He never managed to abandon the suspicion that the theatrical establishment in England, and the "English clique" that exerted such influence in the United States, were in league against him. Just as Cooper raged against the New York Whig press, which he believed was taking its cues from British periodicals, Forrest spied a transatlantic cabal bent on thwarting his career. After his successful tour abroad, he fully expected all doors to be open to him at home, to be greeted by the hosannas of American highbrows. The favorable notices he received abroad did indeed add luster to his reputation, and he could now command top billing at the Park. Yet the beau monde was not prepared to abandon its preference for English talent, making it necessary for him to secure engagements at the Bowery and other less-prestigious theaters.[57]

Similarly, London's theatrical community was prepared to embrace Forrest, but only up to a point. While it had received the American courteously in 1836, none believed he was the equal of Britain's reigning tragedian, William Charles Macready. Renowned for an introspective, cerebral acting technique, Macready could not have been more different from the robust muscularity of his American rival, who was twenty years his junior. The contrasting styles of the two actors inevitably invited comparisons of their respective nations. As Forrest began to emerge as a serious challenger to the British tragedian, the budding rivalry seemed to suggest a much broader conflict, pitting the cultural elitism of the Old World against the bumptious democratic spirit of the New. "In Macready," wrote one American, theater-goers "beheld the pet of princes and nobles," while in Forrest, they saw "the representative of the people."[58]

Public interest was therefore high when Macready announced plans for an American tour in 1844. Enterprising theater managers were quick to exploit the dramatic duel, and though Forrest and Macready remained on ostensibly cordial terms, the competition inevitably bred suspicion and a mutual dislike between the two actors. Before returning to England, Macready embarked on a nationwide tour. Forrest followed him much of the way, as if to dramatize the point that Americans no longer needed to look across the Atlantic for theatrical talent. The nation's urban newspapers gave the contest considerable coverage, publishing not only reviews of each actor's performance, but box office totals, a more accurate barometer of public approval.

No sooner had Macready returned home than Forrest, eager to keep the rivalry before the public, made arrangements for a second tour of Great Britain the following year. Determined to take what had become—in his own mind, at least—a war for dominance into the enemy's camp, he would find the London theater establishment in a similarly combative mood. Lukewarm reviews convinced him that Macready was orchestrating a plot to sabotage his tour. Matters came to a head when the American actor attended a performance of *Hamlet* starring his rival in Edinburgh. In the middle of Act III, there arose "a long, sustained hiss" from a member of the audience, "like the sound of a steam engine." The culprit proved to be none other than Forrest himself. Far from disavowing the act, Forrest defiantly insisted on his right to express his disapprobation as a member of the audience. Apoplectic with rage, Macready would later write in his diary: "No Englishman would have done a thing so base. . . . The low-minded ruffian!"[59]

The news of Forrest's ill-fated second British tour caused a sensation in the United States. While the Whig press upbraided Forrest for his incivility toward Macready, the American tragedian's supporters regarded the episode as a perfectly reasonable response to the unfair panning he had received at the hands of London reviewers. Convinced that Britain's drama critics were governed by ulterior motives, they did not lack for theories to explain this gross affront to their champion. Some pundits attributed Forrest's poor reviews to the fact that several states, including the actor's home state of Pennsylvania, had recently defaulted on their debt obligations to British banks. Others pointed to deteriorating relations between the two countries over the Oregon boundary, as well as U.S. territorial ambitions in Texas and California. According to still another theory, Forrest's poor reviews was payback for the unfavorable publicity surrounding the American tour of Charles Dickens, who, it will be recalled, had been roundly criticized for his comments on behalf of a federal copyright law.[60]

For his part, Forrest did everything he could to encourage such conspiratorial thinking. Driven by feelings of persecution, the American actor was convinced that the cognoscenti on both sides of the Atlantic were in league against him. When a group of his New York friends hosted a homecoming banquet for the actor, Forrest used the occasion to denounce "the machinations of theatrical *cliques*" in England.[61] The American actor also labored assiduously to promote his feud with Macready, characterizing it as part of the nation's struggle for cultural independence.

A day of reckoning was inevitable, and it was not long in coming. Macready returned to the United States in 1848, reigniting the feud between the two dramatists. The British actor's engagements in New York and Boston passed without incident, but a much chillier reception awaited him in Forrest's native Philadelphia, where hecklers tried to disrupt Macready's opening night performance. Two days later, Forrest published a blistering personal attack on the actor, accusing him of attempting to undermine his last British tour. Macready fired back with the threat of a libel suit, then set off on a tour of the Southern and Western states. Even in the American hinterlands, the controversy followed him. During a performance in Cincinnati, for reasons unknown—and perhaps best left that way—a patron threw the carcass of half a sheep onto the stage.[62]

FIGURE 4.
Edwin Forrest. Photograph by Mathew Brady. (Courtesy Library of Congress, Prints & Photographs Division, LC-USZ62-109868)

In late April, Macready returned to New York City for his farewell engagement. The British actor was scheduled to perform at the Astor Place Opera House, which had recently opened to cater to the city's fashionable set (the Park having burned down in 1848). Forrest, still intent on feeding the public frenzy, was already in New York, where he issued another public letter against his rival. No sooner did Macready make it known that he would be performing Macbeth on May 7 than Forrest announced he would perform the same role that night at the Broadway Theatre.

The stage was now set for what the *New York Herald* characterized, without hyperbole, as a "Theatrical Prize-Fight."[63] By this time, however, the affair no longer engaged the theater-going community alone, but had seized the attention of all of Gotham. This was due in no small part to the active involvement of individuals uniquely poised to mobilize the city's working poor. Eager to capitalize on the controversy was Isaiah Rynders, a saloon keeper and Tammany Hall boss of the Sixth Ward, who had evidently become acquainted with Forrest through the latter's association with the New York Democratic Party. In his capacity as a Democratic Party operative, Rynders in recent years had played a key role in recruiting newly arrived Irish immigrants to the Tammany machine.[64] Enjoying an equally devoted grassroots following was the Protestant Irishman, Mike Walsh, a working-class pol who headed the Spartan Association, a Bowery workingmen's club. Although Walsh had clashed with Tammany Hall, he shared Rynders's fierce hostility toward Great Britain, and in the mid-1840s had cobbled together a disparate working-class constituency opposed to British interference in Texas.[65] Another dedicated Anglophobe active in the days leading up to Macready's engagement was E. C. Z. Judson. A journalist and dime novelist of adventure yarns, better known by his pen name, Ned Buntline, Judson published an eponymous scandal sheet, *Ned Buntline's Own*, that railed against a seemingly endless array of British threats against the United States. No less important, finally, was the active participation of Forrest himself. One of the actor's closest associates would later admit that Forrest had lent his tacit support to a behind-the-scenes campaign against Macready, by which tickets had been bought up and distributed to volunteer fire companies and other working-class groups throughout the city to disrupt the British actor's performance.[66]

Incredibly, though it had been widely reported that Forrest's supporters intended to cause a disturbance at Astor Place, Macready seems to have been unaware of the full extent of the opposition that had been raised against him. When he made his entrance in Act I, he initially mistook the roar of the crowd for tumultuous applause. But there could be no mistaking the purpose behind the shower of potatoes and rotten eggs that followed. For fifteen minutes, the play had to be stopped. The chaos did not subside with the opening of Act II. When Macready intoned, "Is this a dagger which I see before me, / Its handle towards my hand?" a patron replied by tossing a chair from the upper tier, shouting when it crashed onto the stage, "No, you miserable John Bull! It's a chair, and be d——d to you!" A roar of hisses and catcalls followed. Theater rowdies heaved more chairs onto the stage in Act III, and the curtain was rung down. A shaken Macready returned to his hotel room, relieved to have made his escape "safe and unharmed."[67]

Meanwhile, at the Broadway Theatre, Edwin Forrest was enjoying a very different reception, playing to a crowded house of loyal supporters. When Macbeth declares in Act IV, "What rhubarb, senna, or what purgative drug / Would scour these English hence?" the audience leaped to its feet and cheered lustily.[68]

Macready's initial reaction was to cancel his engagement and sail immediately for England. But a delegation of the city's beau monde begged him to reconsider. A formal letter signed by Washington Irving and

forty-six other prominent New Yorkers condemned the Astor Place rioters and implored Macready to perform Macbeth again on Thursday, May
10.[69] In rallying around the beleaguered British actor, the city's cultural
elite added a new element to the tense situation, stirring pent-up resentment among laboring classes toward Gotham's "kid glove aristocracy." It
seems to have further antagonized the embittered Forrest, who, having
never enjoyed the respect of the cultural establishment that he believed
he deserved, regarded the pro-Macready letter as a personal insult.
The rumor that the crew of a British vessel intended to make a show of
support for Macready at his next performance further inflamed public
opinion. By Thursday morning, the working-class neighborhoods of the
city were plastered with handbills designed to fuel both anti-British and
class antagonisms:

WORKING MEN,

SHALL

AMERICANS

OR

ENGLISH RULE

IN THIS CITY?

The crew of the British steamer have

Threatened all Americans who shall dare to

express their opinions this night, at the

ENGLISH ARISTOCRATIC OPERA HOUSE!

We advocate no violence, but a free expression of

opinion to all public men!

WORKINGMEN! FREEMEN!

Stand By Your

LAWFUL RIGHTS!

AMERICAN COMMITTEE[70]

The identity of the American Committee was never revealed, but a New
York City policeman who later investigated the case traced the handbills
back to the headquarters of Isaiah Rynders's Empire Club.[71] The mood in
the city was now so ominous that Forrest's associates urged him to issue
a public appeal for calm. The actor refused.

Macready's performance of Macbeth on May 10 went much as it had
three days earlier, with the actor's entrance in Act I the signal for a general melee. Outside the theater, newspaperman E. C. Z. Judson, waving
a sword, exhorted the crowds that had gathered to stone the building.
The windows, which had been boarded up after the previous disturbance, withstood the onslaught for a few minutes, then gave way, the

sound of breaking glass causing panic inside the theater. As the violence increased, a division of the state militia and a battalion of the National Guard arrived. Meeting a barrage of paving stones and other missiles, the troops fired a volley into the air, then fired directly into the crowd, killing 22 and wounding 36. It would be the deadliest night of violence the city would experience until the draft riots of 1863.[72]

The following day, a crowd estimated at more than twenty thousand gathered in City Hall Park to hear Isaiah Rynders, Mike Walsh, and others defend the actions of the rioters. "Why was this murder perpetrated?" Rynders asked the crowd, and gave the following answer: "To please an aristocratic Englishman, backed by a few sycophantic Americans." He added: "I was not hostile to Mr. Macready because he was an Englishman, but because he was full of his country's prejudices."[73]

During the weeks that followed, New Yorkers endlessly debated the causes of the riot. Most analysts in the press placed the blame for the tragedy squarely on the city's working poor, though exactly what had prompted the denizens of Gotham's lower wards to flout the rule of law was a matter of some disagreement. Most pundits pointed to the lower orders' deepening resentment toward the city's *bon ton*, while some blamed the severity of the disturbance on the Irish, who in recent years had poured into the city by the thousands. The *Courier and Enquirer* and

FIGURE 5.
"Great riot at the Astor Place Opera House, New York." (Courtesy Library of Congress, Prints & Photographs Division, LC-USZ62-42326)

other Whig papers, always critical of Forrest, also faulted the actor and his supporters for inciting the public.[74]

After the Astor Place Riot, the two actors stayed on their respective sides of the Atlantic. Macready retired two years later, while the younger Forrest would not exit the stage until the early 1870s. Forrest remained a crowd favorite, but rumors of his role in the events at Astor Place dogged him for the rest of his career, making him a pariah to the country's cultural elite. Not long after the riot, Forrest would again serve as a lightning rod for class and national antipathies. His marriage to the Englishwoman Catherine Sinclair was already on the rocks in 1849, and the following year she sued for divorce on the grounds of adultery. The case became the nation's first celebrity scandal, complete with allegations of infidelity leveled by both sides. During the course of the month-long trial, Forrest's attorney—John Van Buren, son of the former president—characterized his client as an American innocent, misled by the wiles of a foreign siren. Unconvinced, the jury ruled against Forrest, ordering him to pay a whopping three thousand dollars annually to his ex-wife. Forrest's supporters rallied to his defense. When the tragedian made his next appearance in New York after the trial, his engagement ran an astonishing sixty-nine performances, shattering all attendance records. On opening night, a tumultuous crowd cheered their champion and tossed small American flags and bouquets onto the stage. A larger flag that hung from the balcony proclaimed: "This is our verdict!"[75]

It is common in any study of crowd violence to focus on underlying community tensions, and certainly there is abundant evidence of such in New York and other Eastern cities during this period. Class conflict and anti-abolitionist hysteria were both part of the calculus of theater unrest, reflecting two of the more ominous fault lines in American life. Geopolitical tensions too, stemming from specific diplomatic contretemps with Great Britain or a broader unhappiness with that country's economic and cultural influence, could also erupt at a moment's notice. And for many participants, no doubt, a British actor's behavior allowed them to tap into a reservoir of anger that was murky and deep, the precise sources of which even they may have not fully understood.

But perhaps it is a mistake to examine only those factors that speak to an urban population's discontent. There was, after all, something empowering about a theater disturbance, allowing audience members to participate—whether as instigators or as passive onlookers—in a shared community experience. This is not to minimize class divisions, since elites who were most likely to defend an actor's conduct also became targets of public hostility. But within the rioting crowd, all other class and ethno-cultural divisions were subordinated to a larger, ostensibly national, cause. Anti-British sentiment thus acted as an adhesive for crowd action, binding together city dwellers of different backgrounds who may have been motivated by a welter of concerns and agendas. Outbursts of popular protest exploded, albeit temporarily, the stark gradations of urban life, allowing all involved to express themselves as patriots, as Americans.

"America rules England to-night, by Jesus," one man in the crowd outside the Astor Place Opera House was reported to have cried.[76] It was a sentiment that had echoes in other theater disturbances, and indeed in many aspects of American life. The humbling of a British actor represented, in one triumphantly cathartic moment, the humbling of Great Britain, a symbolic corrective to the manifold wrongs and indignities Americans believed they had suffered at the hands of the imperial parent. At the same time, by directing their aggression at the very public representative of a foreign power, citizens of the young republic reinforced and lent clarity to the meaning of citizenship. In a country of disparate, even divergent parts, such urban demonstrations gave a crude but forceful resonance to the discourse of national identity. In so doing, they helped point the way as the republic moved toward a sense of self-definition.

5

The Politics of Anglophobia

American mechanics, John, will never sell their votes,
For Mint Drops or for Treasury Bills, or even British coats;
They want no English coaches, John, white servants they forego,
For their country is of Yankee stamp, John C. Calhoun, my Jo.

—Whig campaign song, 1844

They tried when Hickory had the field,
These bankites and their creatures,
With British gold to sand our eyes,
And coonefy our features . . .
Then rouse ye freemen of the land,
Awake the bugle's calling,
And give these British Whigs a touch,
Of good old Yankee malling.

—Democratic campaign song, 1844

I n the political sphere, as in the cultural one, geopolitical fault lines often had the effect of dividing Americans. Just as members of the beau monde were reproached for their Anglophile tastes, Americans with aspirations to high public office who expressed a fondness for Great Britain did so at their peril. It was a lesson Federalist leaders had learned the hard way. Drawn largely from the ranks of the seaboard gentry, most had never abandoned their deep affection for the imperial parent and its people. Even during the tumult of revolution, they had tended to view the contest in purely political terms, as a crisis provoked by the despotic policies of the Crown. Any enmity generated by the war, moreover, was offset to no small degree by the cataclysm of the French Revolution that soon followed, cooling the republican ardor of American conservatives, who had little desire to see the fever of Jacobinism take hold on their side of the Atlantic.

The Federalists' pro-British sympathies became more evident by the turn of the century. As an expanding Jeffersonian majority secured its grip on the levers of power in the nation's capital, Federalist disaffection with their republican system grew. The war for maritime supremacy that erupted between France and Britain following the French Revolution drove Federalist New England even more firmly into the British embrace. By the time Congress declared war against Britain in 1812, the secessionist sympathies of many prominent Federalists, including Gouverneur Morris, who had helped craft the blueprint for a stronger national government in 1787, were a matter of public knowledge. New England became such a hotbed of antiwar activity that when naval commander Stephen Decatur attempted to run the British blockade at New London, Connecticut, he claimed that blue lanterns at the harbor mouth had been lit to alert the Royal Navy. The story took hold in the public mind, making the term "blue light Federalist" an expression of opprobrium applied to all who did not support the war effort.[1]

Federalist opposition to the war came to a head in late 1814, when twenty-six delegates from the New England states assembled in Hartford, Connecticut. The resolutions drafted by the Hartford Convention were designed to reclaim the political stature New England had lost in recent years to the South and the West, agricultural regions of the country solidly in the Jeffersonian camp. The convention proposed seven constitutional amendments, one calling for a two-thirds majority of both houses for the admission of new states, another for the repeal of the Three-Fifths Rule, by which the South received increased congressional representation based on its slave population. Finally, the delegates expressed their intention to convene again should their resolutions be rebuffed, "with such powers and instructions as the exigency of a crisis so momentous may require."

In a case of monumentally poor timing, the convention's deliberations became public just as the nation learned of Jackson's smashing victory at New Orleans. In the orgy of congratulatory jingoism that followed, the delegates at Hartford seemed wholly out of step with the rest of the nation. While the resolutions did not contain the threat of secession, many Jeffersonians, deeply resentful of New England's anti-war stance, believed that such was the Federalists' intention had the government refused to accede to their demands. Upon learning of the deliberations at Hartford, Andrew Jackson remarked that he would have hanged the ringleaders as monarchists. The meeting proved to be a public relations fiasco for the ailing Federalist Party, which managed to carry only four states in the presidential contest the following year. By 1820, unable to put forward a presidential candidate, it had all but disappeared.[2]

The nation's first political party faded quietly away, but the memory of its last secessionist throes would linger in the American consciousness, an unwelcome reminder that citizens of the republic were by no means committed to a uniform set of republican ideals. Although the politics of consensus that characterized the postwar years temporarily dampened such concerns, the return of partisan rancor in the mid-1820s brought with it fresh allegations that pro-British elements were plotting the country's demise. The Federalist Party had not disappeared, but rather had simply changed its name in order to commit "new crimes and impostures."[3] In the years that followed, the episode remained vivid in the minds of Jeffersonians and their ideological descendants, who routinely sought to remind voters of the treason at Hartford and to stigmatize their adversaries as Tories.[4] On his deathbed three decades later, Andrew Jackson was still warning of John Bull's homegrown collaborators, the "Hartford convention men" and "Blue light federalists," whom he regarded not just as political adversaries, but as enemies of the state. One New York Whig expressed amazement that, a generation after the party's demise, the Federalist label remained a term of reproach, even though Americans were "as ignorant of its meaning [as] they are of the Talmud."[5]

Why did the Hartford Convention enjoy such a long shelf life in American public memory? To a certain extent, its symbolic resonance for later generations was a simple matter of political expediency; the most effective way to discredit campaign adversaries was to link them to familiar foes, to recast in contemporary terms the earlier crises in which the republic had been threatened by subversive elements. The Connecticut conclave proved especially useful in this regard for Southern Democrats, who would remind voters of New England's suspect loyalties when the region emerged in later years as a hotbed of antislavery sentiment.

At the same time, however, the dredging up of old political disputes could not have occurred had it not spoken to Americans' concerns about the fragility of their republic. Long after the delegates to the Connecticut meeting had passed from the scene, the Hartford Convention was still being invoked as a symbolic shorthand to remind voters of the dangers that a fifth column could pose to the American way of life. Even as the nation matured in the decades following the War of 1812, its political culture continued to be influenced in myriad ways by past conflicts with Great Britain. Americans may have believed that their independence was secure, but they remained on their guard, and their vigilance was directed not toward the nation's traditional enemy alone. Rather, they frequently spied a more insidious threat—those eager collaborators who, like the Hartford delegates, stood alongside Great Britain, ready to undermine the republic from within.

Andrew Jackson and the Memory of Revolution

The bitter partisan strife between Federalists and Democratic-Republicans during the early national period had made it difficult for Americans to agree on the meaning of their struggle for independence. But with the total eclipse of the party of Hamilton and Adams in the years after the War of 1812, a unifying historical narrative began to emerge. As the rising tide of Jeffersonianism engulfed its critics, the nation's first political party came to be seen as something of an aberration. Tarred by the brush of Toryism, the Federalists seemed a querulous minority who had failed to sign on to the true goals of the Revolution. Gradually, some of the principal architects of the American republic were all but expunged from the national memory, while others, like Alexander Hamilton, who once proclaimed the British government "the best model the world ever produced," were held up as turncoats who would have liked nothing more than to return the nation to British rule.[6]

One Federalist, however, remained immune from accusations of republican declension. During the early decades of the nineteenth century, George Washington occupied a transcendent position in the national memory, revered by all Americans. To be sure, Washington's luster as commander of the Continental Army had dimmed somewhat as a result of his two terms as president, in which he exhibited a strong willingness to expand the powers of the national government. Jeffersonians had been deeply disappointed by his decision to endorse Hamilton's plan to charter a national bank modeled after the Bank of England, and aghast when he personally led an army into western Pennsylvania to crush a farmers' revolt against the excise tax on whiskey. But no sooner had Washington vacated the presidential chair than his reputation was miraculously restored, and his death in 1799 was the occasion for an outpouring of national grief undiminished by partisan rancor. For the fact was that Washington's value as a national symbol far outweighed any criticism he may have endured as a political leader. As the central figure in the American creation myth, he could not be maligned without disparaging the Revolutionary cause itself.[7]

Accordingly, nineteenth-century Americans were obliged to refashion Washington's persona, to deemphasize the ideology of patrician conservatism that guided the first president during his eight years in office. The rewriting of Washington's legacy following his death devoted con-

FIGURE 6.

"The Hartford Convention or Leap no Leap." In 1815, New England Federalists met at Hartford, Connecticut, in opposition to the war with Great Britain. In this cartoon, they are seen leaping into the arms of John Bull. Unfavorable public reaction to the Hartford Convention hastened the demise of the Federalist Party. (Courtesy Library of Congress, Prints & Photographs Division, LC-DIG-ppmsca-10755)

siderable attention to the Revolutionary hero's professed belief that the United States should remain aloof from European conflicts. Although Washington was by no means a rigid isolationist, and his famous Farewell Address was intended to single out the dangers to the republic of French intrigue, nineteenth-century Americans applied his admonition against "the insidious wiles of foreign influence" to Great Britain. Read at all Washington birthday celebrations, the Farewell Address became a ringing endorsement of Jeffersonian Anglophobia. Thus, while other prominent Federalists were being stricken from the historical record, Washington retained his exalted station as iconic paterfamilias, a figure who, as Gustave de Beaumont observed in 1835, "is not a man but a god."[8]

Americans were generally oblivious to the irony of such rank hero worship. Despite their commitment to democratic precepts, they continued to view political contests in intensely personal terms, placing their trust in those who seemed to embody the virtues of the republican polity. Policies and personality were braided tightly together in the public mind, with an unswerving dedication to a set of principles seen as evidence of the constancy and firmness voters looked for in candidates for higher office. Issues may have mattered to the American electorate, but a voter's party affiliation was rarely decided simply in terms of his own self-interest. As many historians of the period have noted, ethnic and cultural factors were all part of the calculus of party membership. Less studied—perhaps because it defies precise measurement—is the visceral connection voters established with the candidate of their choice. This preoccupation with public figures was hardly an American phenomenon, and was in some respects a transatlantic extension of the European Romantics' fascination with "great men" and individual genius. Adapting to the emerging democratic culture of the United States, the cult of personality lent a crude homogeneity to the patchwork of American politics, allowing for the emergence of broad-based national parties that could embrace widely divergent constituencies. Voters with little in common, from Eastern wage laborers to hardscrabble Western farmers to Southern slaveholders, could all participate in the political process through their identification with public men whom they believed to be their true representatives.

No individual symbolized the electorate's fascination with those at the very top of the political hierarchy better than Andrew Jackson, a personality so dominant that his name has been appropriated by many historians to define the age itself. Even so, Jackson eludes precise categorization. Some scholars have portrayed him as an agrarian populist, while others have emphasized his role as a champion of urban labor. Seeking to situate Jackson in the context of a rapidly changing economy, some have viewed him as a reactionary figure who spoke to Americans' fears in an increasingly complex, volatile marketplace, while others have pegged him as the forward-looking symbol of unfettered capitalism. No doubt these divergent perspectives can be attributed in large part to the fact that the many constituencies that coalesced around the Democratic banner in the 1820s each saw Jackson in their own way, according to their own economic, cultural, and regional orientation.[9]

In one respect, however, all shared a common view of the Tennessee general, seeing him as a vital link to their revolutionary past. It was certainly no accident that at a time when Americans were becoming acutely aware of their history and the need to preserve it, a majority of the electorate turned to a military chieftain who had bested Great Britain on the battlefield. By the middle of the decade Americans were in the grip of a patriotic mania, occasioned by the approaching fiftieth anniversary of the nation's independence. In 1824 the Marquis de Lafayette, who had served as Washington's aide-de-camp, crossed the Atlantic at the invitation of President Monroe for a year-long tour of the country he had helped to create. While Lafayette's visit does not seem to have occasioned a resurgence of anti-British feeling, the adulation that greeted the war hero wherever he went signaled a renewed interest in the national creation narrative among citizens of the republic, and a longing to reconnect with their idealized past.[10]

Underlying the frenzied jubilation that accompanied the seventy-year-old Frenchman's visit was the melancholy realization that the Revolutionary generation was passing from the scene. It had long been a tradition at Fourth of July celebrations to honor the gray-haired, wizened patriots who had faced British muskets in the struggle for independence. But as their ranks thinned with each passing year, Americans were left with little tangible evidence of the sacrifices that had helped forge a nation. For all the boisterous enthusiasm with which its citizens celebrated Independence Day, some wondered if the nation was beginning to take its liberty for granted. Earnest patriots noted ruefully the complacent attitude of the younger generation, and predicted dark days ahead for a republic which no longer understood the true meaning of its conflict with Great Britain. The national holiday, they complained, had become a drunken revel, the principles on which the nation had been founded little more than the "idle theme of boyish declamation."[11]

The cult of personality that grew up around Andrew Jackson drew heavily from this swelling tide of patriotic emotion. When the Hero of New Orleans made his first presidential bid in 1824, Americans sensed that an era in their nation's brief history was drawing to a close. Four candidates took the field in the chaotic presidential campaign, each claiming to be the rightful heir to the Revolutionary tradition. None, however, worked harder to identify himself with the public memory of independence than the senator from Tennessee. Noting that the incumbent, James Monroe, was among "the last of that immortal band of patriots," Jackson's supporters reminded voters that their candidate had also fought against the British during the Revolution. This was a bit of a stretch; in crafting their candidate's image for the electorate, Jackson's campaign operatives made much of the fact that as a youth of fourteen, he and a brother had been taken prisoner by the British after the Battle of Camden, and that during his incarceration he had received a scar on his hand when he refused to shine a British officer's boots. The Tennessean carried emotional scars as well, his campaign biographers suggested. The fierce struggle for control of South Carolina had claimed the lives of his mother and both brothers, leaving him an orphan (his father had died the year he was born). Trumpeting their candidate's Revolutionary experiences hardly seemed necessary. Jackson could, after all, claim more meaningful clashes with the imperial parent as an adult. But the image of the young Andrew standing his ground against a British officer resonated powerfully with an electorate waxing nostalgic for its Revolutionary past, and promptly became a conspicuous feature of the protean Jackson myth.

The need for a unifying candidate seemed especially important in light of the fact that the broad consensus that had characterized American politics at the national level for a decade was beginning to unravel. With the tariff and other economic issues creating a sudden burst of sectional rancor, the 1824 campaign formally marked the end of the so-called "Era of Good Feeling."[12] Voters warmed to a candidate unbound by parochial limitations, whose life from youth to adulthood could be identified with some of the most memorable moments of the national experience. In the *Letters of Wyoming*, a widely distributed Jackson election tract, campaign manager John Eaton adroitly played on the electorate's desire for a candidate who could assume the mantle of the nation's Revolutionary heroes, extolling Jackson as "the last of these valiant establishers of liberty" who had fought and bled to create a nation.[13] It did not hurt that Old Hickory's public career seemed to mirror that of George Washington, the very personification of national unity. Like Washington, Jackson had saved the republic from the British, and then, inviting allusions to the Roman general Cincinnatus, had spurned the laurels of victory, expressing no greater ambition than to return to the life of a simple farmer. In addition, Eaton played skillfully on the cultural isolationism linked to Washington by virtue of his Farewell Address. "In manners, dress, and language we are imitators, and borrowers from abroad," Eaton wrote, echoing the language of the legions of social critics who bemoaned the national reliance on British norms.[14] On the tariff, Jackson presented himself as a candidate who would protect the nation from British commerce, just as he had defended it against British troops (though when pressed he equivocated on the issue, attempting to navigate a middle course acceptable both to protectionists and free traders).[15] But it was the theme of historical continuity that the Tennessee leader's supporters stressed above all else. A Jackson victory, they argued, would maintain the line of Revolutionary leaders in the White House unbroken for at least another four years.[16]

The Jackson machine was still exploiting the nation's Revolutionary nostalgia in the famously vicious rematch against John Quincy Adams in 1828. The public declarations calling upon the Tennessee general to throw his hat into the ring were replete with historical allusions, reminding voters that their candidate had been "rocked in the cradle" of the Revolution, and touting him as "*one of the few remaining soldiers*" in the struggle that had given birth to the nation. As in 1824, the Jack-

son campaign characterized their candidate as both a symbol of republican renewal and a man who could drive the Revolution forward into a
new golden age.[17] By contrast, the current occupant of the White House
was characterized by the Tennessean's adherents as a throwback to the
Anglophile, anti-republican tendencies of the Federalist era. Despite a
brilliant diplomatic career, John Quincy Adams would discover that his
years spent abroad were a major political liability among an electorate
that harbored a deeply rooted antipathy toward the Old World. The Jackson campaign charged that Adams had been educated among the sons of
British nabobs at Eton (although he had spent only a few months at the
school), and made much of the fact that his wife Louisa had been born
in England. Most damning of all, the Jackson campaign linked the president to the Federalist administration of Adams *père*, which had passed
the highly unpopular Alien and Sedition Acts of 1798. Making the case
for guilt by association, Jackson's supporters linked the president to the
political blunders of a party that had vanished a decade earlier, insisting
that "those who fell with the first Adams, rise with the second."[18]

Adams' supporters made every effort to dispel the notion that
he harbored a fond regard for the imperial parent. Like their Jackson
counterparts, they strove to impress upon voters that their candidate's
anti-British sentiments were deeply ingrained, manifesting themselves
even in his youth. According to one campaign biographer, John Quincy
had spurned an opportunity to return to England when his father was
appointed U.S. minister to the Court of St. James's in 1785. "He had
learned to hate the British; and resisting the temptations of London
pleasures, he chose to come home to America rather than go to England."[19] (A disdain for the effete luxury of the British metropolis actually had little to do with his decision; Adams had simply returned to the
United States to complete his education and pursue a career in the law.)
Although Adams had been abroad during the years prior to the second
war with Great Britain, serving as U.S. minister to Russia, his supporters
nonetheless represented him as a vigorous war hawk, who, "with manly
firmness," had opposed British suppression of American commerce and
the impressment of U.S. seamen.[20]

Try as they might to burnish the portly Adams' heroic image and
anti-British credentials, his supporters were well aware that their candidate's reputation as defender of the nation paled beside that of the man
who had routed Pakenham's army at New Orleans. Employing tactics
that smacked of desperation, they endeavored to tar the general with
the brush of Toryism. In one of the most scurrilous accusations of the
1828 campaign, the *Cincinnati Gazette* charged that Jackson's mother had
been an English prostitute, brought over to the colonies by British sol-

diers.[21] National Republicans also sought to draw upon the wellspring of American anger toward British condescension in their attempt to characterize Jackson as a semi-literate frontiersman. One anti-Jackson tract wondered what the highbrow British periodicals, which have "defamed even the best writings of our countrymen," would say of a man who could not spell *one word in four.* Since it seems unlikely that Jackson's supporters would have been bothered by the suggestion that they had placed their trust in an orthographically challenged candidate, such campaign tactics probably backfired, serving only to alert voters to the weight foreign journals carried in National Republican circles.[22]

In other ways, too, the Adams camp sought to neutralize Jackson's vote-getting appeal, characterizing the Tennessean as a brutal leader whose megalomania threatened to undermine republicanism and reinstate the tyranny Americans had known under British rule. Again and again they returned to the theme that the military chieftain was a martinet whose imperious behavior endangered the sovereignty of a free people. Jackson's enemies likened him to a parade of putatively despotic figures—Caesar, Napoleon, and others—but it was the comparison to British tyrants that they stressed most often, linking Jackson to the very monarchical authoritarianism Americans had fought two wars to end. Citing the British government as a striking example of the danger to be apprehended from an increase of executive power, one orator declared in 1828, "If the influence of the King has changed the British constitution, may not executive influence produce the same result here?" While such charges did not link Jackson directly to British influence, they served as a counterweight to the populist hero-myth of a candidate who had rescued the country from British aggression.[23]

The victory in the 1828 election of an individual whose principal claim to voters' affections rested largely on his defiance of Britain's military power did not augur well for U.S. relations with that country. To the surprise of observers on both sides of the Atlantic, however, Jackson's lifelong antipathy to Great Britain did not prove to be a significant factor in his conduct of American foreign policy. The new president, whose struggles with domestic political enemies often revealed a combative and vengeful nature, was guided not by prejudice but by a pragmatic policy of constructive engagement in his negotiations with Whitehall. Moving quickly to resolve outstanding grievances between the two nations, Jackson scored one of his most impressive diplomatic achievements early in his administration, convincing Great Britain to reopen its West Indies ports to American trade, which had been closed to U.S. vessels since 1793.[24] Preoccupied with domestic policy concerns in 1833, Jackson did not protest when the Royal Navy took control of the Falkland

Islands. Jackson got along so well with British leaders, praising them extravagantly in his annual messages to Congress, that Aaron Vail, the U.S. chargé d'affaires to the Court of St. James's, could exult: "Jackson is decidedly the most popular President in England we ever had."[25]

A suspicious nature was nonetheless part of Jackson's genetic code, and he remained ever alert to any effort on the part of Great Britain to involve itself directly or indirectly in the affairs of the republic. When resentment of protective duties prompted South Carolina to defy Washington and claim the right to nullify federal law, the president initially believed the crisis to be the handiwork of British agents. Jackson believed, too, that Great Britain would stop at nothing to check the republic's dominance of the North American continent. The president's Indian removal policy was grounded in the knowledge that for the past half century the Indian depredations that had plagued white settlers in the southeastern states had been sponsored—overtly in time of war, covertly in time of peace—by their British allies. Though Jackson's public statements on removal invariably employed the language of a compassionate father, his brand of paternalism masked a deep concern that Native Americans, goaded by the British, remained a serious threat to national security.[26] And when a revolution erupted in Mexican-held Texas as his second term drew to a close, Jackson feared that Britain might exploit the volatile situation, an idea that would grow into a monomania and consume him in his final years (discussed more fully in chapters 9 and 10).

The policy issue which, perhaps more than any other, came to define Jackson's presidency and his confrontational brand of leadership, his decision to dismantle the Bank of the United States, spoke to a more insidious threat—the extent to which British influences were corrupting the very fabric of American life. Like many Americans, the rough-hewn president regarded a national bank as an institution of alien origin, antithetical to sturdy republican values. Though himself a member of the planter elite, Jackson viewed Eastern monied interests with suspicion and disdain. Democratic pundits routinely compared the president's efforts to destroy the bank with his famous battle at New Orleans, and exhorted Democrats to rally around the president in language that recalled the sacrifices of the Revolutionary generation.[27] As a military leader, Jackson had "pushed back the English bayonets," one Democrat politician declared. As president, he now sought to destroy the "English influence which seeks to enslave you."[28]

It would be a mistake to dismiss such rhetoric as political gasconade intended merely for popular consumption. A man of fiery and combative temperament, Jackson himself tended to approach every policy battle as a fight to the finish, with no quarter given or received. Wholly ill-suited to the art of compromise, the president had a habit of turning political contretemps into epic struggles, with the result that an atmosphere of crisis pervaded much of his eight years in office. Historians have sometimes looked for psychological motives to explain Jackson's inflexible behavior, volcanic temperament, and his almost obsessive desire to crush his political enemies.[29] Yet the president cannot be fully understood without recognizing that many Americans in the early decades of the nineteenth century still viewed the republic as a fragile thing, to be zealously protected from those who wished to destroy it. To his stalwart followers, Jackson met each challenge with the fixity of purpose the occasion demanded. Like them, he genuinely believed the very future of the nation was at stake.

This sense of precariousness, which modern Americans accustomed to the United States' subsequent position of untrammeled global power have often failed to appreciate, lay at the root of Jackson's unyielding Anglophobia. His tireless vigilance toward Great Britain and other enemies of the republic—which to later, more secure generations might seem irrational, even paranoid—goes far to explain his charismatic appeal. Regarding Jackson as a vital link to their past at the outset of his presidency, his supporters tended to view him even more clearly as a bulwark against Great Britain in the years that followed. As Americans fumed over British criticism, and as the extent of British influence over American arts and letters and public policy became ever more apparent, many saw Jackson as a symbol of an ongoing process of separation. For Massachusetts Democratic congressman Robert Rantoul, there was one great name in each of the three distinct epochs in the nation's path toward complete independence. Washington had thrown off "the yoke of British power," Jefferson had broken "the charm of British precedents, and British authority," while Jackson had swept away the remaining vestiges "of British institutions, and British policy." Jackson's popular appeal, Rantoul believed, stemmed from his unyielding determination to fight against the Tory interests in the United States which Great Britain had arrayed against him.[30] Reflecting on the Jacksonian legacy in a similar vein, another Massachusetts Democrat, the historian George Bancroft, declared that the Tennessee general had come to the White House with one goal in mind: to lift the republic "out of the forms of English legislation."[31] At a time when many political elites, by virtue of their economic and social positions, were vulnerable to the charge of Toryism, Jackson remained immune, a paragon of patriotic probity. He had never yielded to British power, or truckled to British opinion. To an electorate increasingly self-conscious about its subordinate relationship to the imperial parent, this was no small achievement.

The Second Party System

By the end of Jackson's second term the structures of a new, two-party system were firmly in place. As state governments expanded the franchise to include the entire adult white male population, mobilizing the electorate became the key to success at the ballot box. Democrats and the newly formed Whig Party adapted to the changing political realities by creating highly efficient and sophisticated organizations to foster intense partisan loyalty and encourage public engagement. Mass rallies, torchlight parades, and other forms of electioneering all became part of the new political culture that would see the highest voter turnouts in the nation's history.

Anti-British expression would find a conspicuous place in these party contests. Although the U.S. relationship with Great Britain was not the most important issue confronting the American electorate, Anglophobia nonetheless managed to insinuate itself into many of the major policy debates of the period. As public discourse began to assume an increasingly emotionalized, call-and-response character, both parties played to the crowd, larding their rhetoric with the language of liberation that invoked memories of past struggles against tyrannical foes. Bearding the British lion offered decided advantages in an era when both organizations were trying to bring divergent national constituencies into their respective tents. On the campaign stump and in legislative chambers across the country, officeholders did not hesitate to exploit anti-British feeling for political advantage. Party members might disagree over slavery or the proper role of the federal government in conducting the nation's economic affairs, but on the subject of their hostility to England they found common ground.

By attaching a British label to any policies they opposed, American political leaders also helped to fuel Anglophobic feeling. With economic issues such as banking and the tariff at the forefront of the national political agenda during the Jacksonian period, issues that must have seemed impossibly arcane to the average voter, Anglophobia allowed the two parties the means to explain their respective agendas in ways the electorate could readily understand. Since it was widely assumed that British and American interests were mutually exclusive, both parties found it a relatively simple matter to attack the opposition's economic policies by insisting that they benefited Great Britain. In this manner, Whigs condemned Democrats' free trade doctrines as a boon to foreign manufacturers, while Democrats excoriated the Whigs' defense of a national banking system as a sign of their unnatural and anti-republican attachment to British principles of political economy.

In addition to reducing complex issues to familiar and readily digestible form, Anglophobia enabled both parties to play to the electorate's deepest resentments and fears, thereby raising the stakes of partisan conflict in the all-important drive to mobilize their constituents. By branding the political opposition a Tory "fifth column" bent on subverting the republic from within, party propagandists infused election contests with a dramatic sense of urgency, in which the very survival of the nation seemed to hinge on the outcome. Allegations that an opponent had fallen under the sway of British interests or had been bribed by British gold were particularly likely to surface in the weeks before an election, as both parties sought to rally the faithful and get them to the polls. Party battles thus became Manichean contests, with both sides characterizing their opponents as either dupes or willing agents of a sinister conspiracy headquartered in London. Though "latent and unseen," one Democratic news organ warned its readers in 1840, British influence over the Whig Party "is tremendously powerful, and is every day acquiring new energies."[32] Whig leaders often said the same thing about the Democrats. That same year, a Whig congressman complained that Americans were wholly unaware of the extent to which funds from abroad had poured into Democratic coffers, declaring that there were "a thousand secret channels through which this subtle poison" had been injected into the electoral process to promote British interests.[33]

Unlike American novelists and actors, who required the sanction of Britain's cultural arbiters to win highbrow approval at home, American political leaders did not seek foreign praise. The opinions of the British press were followed closely by the two parties, not for validation but as ammunition to be used against their opponents. London editorials praising the Democrats' campaign pledge to reduce duties on British-made goods quickly found their way into Whig campaign speeches; commentary that congratulated Whigs on their support of a federal banking system, meanwhile, instantly became fodder for the Democrats. Conversely, American politicians wasted no time in proudly calling attention to any critiques leveled against them by the British press. A scathing editorial from the *London Times* was displayed as a badge of honor, proof positive that the recipient was an upstanding defender of the republican weal. Upon learning that the *Times* found Tyler's 1843 annual message "ludicrous" for its tone of bombastic nationalism, the *Daily Madisonian* retorted: "If a thick-headed Tory Englishman" could not understand the American political system, it was hardly the president's fault.[34]

Anti-British rhetoric continued to intrude upon the political process after an election, offering a ready excuse for the losing party to explain its repudiation at the polls. In both local and national campaigns, party leaders often attributed defeat to foreign interference, claiming that "British gold" had been used to fund campaign literature, organize rallies and parades, and even to buy votes. Despite their victory in the 1832 presidential contest, Philadelphia Democrats fared poorly in local elections, an outcome they attributed to British subterfuge. The party news organ complained that "hundreds, almost thousands, of tory Englishmen" had been "hunted up and naturalized" on the eve of the election, to defeat the Democratic mayoral candidate.[35] Whigs, too, pointed an accusing finger at the British when election results did not go their way. "We cannot always fight the *Loco Focos* when they are backed by British gold," one Whig editor remarked after the party lost the Maine statehouse to the Democrats in 1838.[36]

While both parties incorporated Anglophobia into their political catechism, it was an especially prominent element of the Democratic liturgy. Taking their cues in such matters from their patron saint, Andrew Jackson, most party leaders regarded hostility to Great Britain as an article of faith, one of the eternal verities upon which they based their claim as guardians of the public trust. After his death in 1845, Democrats continued to invoke the Tennessee general's name as they strove to follow his example of unflinching resolve in the face of new contretemps with Great Britain. "England's threats were idle tales to him," declared one Missouri congressman in urging his colleagues to oppose British claims to the Pacific Northwest.[37]

Although the campaign rhetoric of both parties drew heavily from historical precedent, Democratic leaders reaffirmed their patriotic ardor by recasting the struggle for independence in contemporary terms.[38] Whenever Washington and Whitehall found themselves at loggerheads, Democrats invariably sought to shame those who advocated a conciliatory course by reminding them that Americans were not in the habit of kowtowing to Great Britain. "This is truly a degenerate age," intoned one congressman during the Oregon boundary crisis, "when the roll of the British drums" was enough to intimidate the descendants of the sons of '76.[39] Nowhere did anti-British expression reach more frenzied levels than among the Democratic leaders of the Western states, whose constituents harbored vivid memories of British-sponsored Indian depredations. William Allen, two-term senator from Ohio and chairman of the

Foreign Relations Committee in the early 1840s, was known to pound on his desk with such vehemence during his harangues against the British that his hands bled, while Michigan senator Lewis Cass could "hardly think or speak of [England]," observed one British traveler after a visit to the gallery, "without verging on apoplexy."[40]

Such rabid Anglophobia was rare among Whig Party leaders. On the stump and in party news organs, Whig spokesmen often railed against British economic power in urging tradesmen and mechanics to embrace the doctrine of protectionism, and never tired of reminding voters of the conspicuous role party standard-bearers had played in the last war against the British.[41] But their anti-British rhetoric was prompted more by expediency than principle and, unlike their Democratic counterparts, rarely found expression in their private correspondence. Drawn largely from the ranks of the nation's privileged, Whig Party leaders were much more inclined than other Americans to regard the imperial parent as the touchstone of standards of good taste and gentility. This was especially true in the industrial/commercial centers of the North and the Mid-Atlantic states, where Whig elites enjoyed close business contacts with British banks and mercantile interests.

In New England, where the Whigs enjoyed a solid majority in several states, a strong current of pro-British sentiment militated against the use of Anglophobic rhetoric as an electioneering device. Even disputes over boundaries in Maine and the commercially valuable Pacific Northwest failed to generate much anti-British feeling (causing Massachusetts politicians Caleb Cushing and Alexander Everett, both unyielding in their defense of American territorial ambitions, to bolt to the Democratic ranks in the 1840s). While most Whig Anglophiles tended to keep such sentiments to themselves, a few prominent party leaders made no secret of their deep veneration for the imperial parent. Massachusetts senator Daniel Webster decorated the foyer of his Washington, D.C., home with portraits of the British nobility and yearned to be appointed U.S. minister to the Court of St. James's. As the Whig Party's greatest orator, the "Godlike Daniel" never failed to attract huge, enthusiastic crowds wherever he spoke. Yet for all his charisma, Webster remained a controversial figure whose unabashed Anglophilia proved to be an embarrassing liability for a party accused by its opponents of being the spawn of Tory Federalism. An equivocal stance in the War of 1812 dogged the Massachusetts senator throughout his career, while his financial connections with the House of Baring—he served openly as an agent of the London banking house in Washington—also provoked unfavorable public comment.[42] Certainly Webster's unwavering Anglophilia doomed any presidential ambitions he may have entertained. When his name surfaced as a possible candidate to head the Whig ticket in 1848, the *New York Herald* dismissed him as a Federalist whose "sympathy and partiality for every thing English—English laws, English principles of government, English nobility, English policy, and English ascendancy," was such that he had become thoroughly "anti-Americanized."[43]

The English Coach of Martin Van Buren

Aspirants to public office did not need to advance policies that favored British interests to be accused of having fallen under the sway of British influence. As often as not, such ad hominem attacks focused on personal traits that could be loosely construed as inimical to sound republican precepts. By these vague standards, virtually any transgressive behavior could be deemed "aristocratical," and thus pro-British. Accusations of cronyism and elitism were especially likely to be leveled by political enemies in this newly democratic, ostensibly egalitarian age. While socially prominent Whigs naturally came under intense fire from Jacksonian propagandists, Democrats lacking a humble pedigree were likewise vulnerable to such attacks. In the no-holds-barred arena of American politics, both parties endeavored to whip up popular resentment against candidates who seemed to lack the necessary republican credentials.

Perhaps no party leader was subject to more ridicule on these grounds than Andrew Jackson's hand-picked successor, Martin Van Buren. As the architect of the Democratic organization in the all-important state of New York, Van Buren commanded a strong base of support, but his rise to prominence had not been without controversy. Incurring the deep resentment of others who hoped to succeed Jackson, most notably John C. Calhoun, Van Buren had faced withering intraparty criticism long before he became the Democrats' presidential nominee in 1836. To his enemies, Van Buren seemed the embodiment of the self-aggrandizing, professional politician. He had not been an early supporter of the Tennessee general, but quickly tacked to the prevailing political winds, causing his rivals for presidential favor to grumble that his sycophantic devotion to Jackson had more to do with personal ambition than principle. A backroom dealmaker who had built a party machine in his home state on the distribution of patronage, Van Buren was likened by critics to Sir Robert Walpole, the British exemplar of corruption and venality.[44]

The contours of the New Yorker's unfavorable public image would grow more distinct as he moved out of Jackson's shadow into the national spotlight. Wholly lacking the alpha male attributes of his predecessor, Van Buren could claim no battlefield laurels, having been an obscure state senator during the War of 1812. At the same time, the diminutive, urbane Van Buren was associated with a cosmopolitan culture that many rural Americans regarded with suspicion as effete and anti-democratic. Although raised under modest circumstances as the son of a village tavern keeper, Van Buren was nonetheless characterized by Whig propagandists as a "lavender dandy," a man so vain he wore corsets and perfumed his whiskers.[45] Having identified Jackson with the brutal despotism of Britain's monarchy, the Whigs sought to link his successor with the unmanly excesses of its aristocracy. Van Buren had served a brief stint as U.S. minister to the Court of St. James's in 1831–32, and although his tenure was cut short after only six months when his nomination was rejected by the Senate, the appointment proved a boon to his political enemies. For Whig pundits, Van Buren's image as a Jackson toady morphed easily into a new persona: the fawning courtier. They contended that during the brief time he had spent in London, Van Buren had enjoyed himself far too much, and circulated the story—hotly denied by Democrats—that he had had an elaborately gilded coach and carriage harness made there and shipped home. The opposition lampooned the New Yorker for affecting British habits and manners, and claimed to have seen the vice president reclining in his stately coach as it careened through the streets of Washington, splattering lowly pedestrians with mud.[46]

Whigs continued to harp upon Van Buren's ambiguous masculinity during his four years in the White House. Embroiled in a number of crises with Great Britain over the Maine boundary and rebellions in Canada, the administration took a conciliatory course, winning bipartisan support from Congress. This did not stop the opposition press, however, from charging the administration with being "soft" on the nation's imperial adversary during the next presidential campaign. Van Buren's non-confrontational diplomacy, moreover, seemed to complement the president's aristocratic proclivities. Whig critics had a field day when the president dispatched his son John to the coronation of Queen Victoria in 1838, going so far as to claim that "Prince John," as he was thereafter known, was intent on wooing the young monarch in the hopes of establishing a union between the Van Burens and the House of Hanover![47] The president again played unwittingly into the hands of his detractors by asking Congress for appropriations to refurbish the White House. Predictably, critics seized upon the budget item—a relatively modest $3,600—deriding the lavish lifestyle of the chief executive who, they claimed, had turned the President's House into a regal palace, replete with fine British carpets and new wallpaper (the latter expenditure being necessary because the existing wallpaper had recently gone out of fashion in London high society).[48]

By the time Van Buren ran for reelection in 1840, the nation was firmly in the grip of a severe depression, hardly favorable conditions for a politician whose reputation for elegant urbanity was already firmly etched in voters' minds. To make matters worse for the Little Magician, the opposing party fielded a challenger whose military career underscored Van Buren's cosmopolitan image. In nominating William Henry Harrison, the putative "hero of Tippecanoe," the Whigs skillfully presented voters with two antipodal constructions of masculine identity. Although Harrison was an Ohio gentleman farmer and scion of one of Virginia's most prominent families, Whig mythmakers portrayed their candidate as a backwoods rustic who lived in a log cabin. In a presidential campaign notable for its electioneering buncombe and carnival atmosphere, the Whigs offered the electorate few specifics on substantive issues, devoting their energies to fanning voters' visceral resentment of an Eastern cosmopolitan culture that aped British mores, an especially effective motif during hard economic times. In the hands of Whig propagandists, Van Buren's "English coach" became as emblematic of the president's aristocratic pretensions as Harrison's log cabin was illustrative of Old Tippecanoe's yeoman simplicity. "In English coaches he's no rider," the Harrison clubs sang of their party nominee, "but he could fight and drink hard cider."[49]

The success with which the Whigs appropriated traditionally Jacksonian themes in the 1840 campaign posed problems for the Democrats. Party news organs denounced the Whig nominee as a former Federalist, and sought to turn one of Harrison's strengths—his deliberately vague stand on the issues—to their advantage. If Harrison was a blank canvas, Democrats offered voters a detailed portrait of their own, one that painted the Whig nominee not only as the tool of party power brokers, but of sinister forces headquartered overseas.[50] While Harrison would have much preferred to remain silent on the subject of slavery, this became impossible when a handful of Whigs publicly endorsed the World Anti-Slavery Convention held that summer in London. Mainstream Whigs promptly distanced themselves and their candidate from the London meeting, declaring their staunch and unyielding support for the right of Southerners to own slaves. This did not, of course, prevent the Democratic press from linking Harrison to abolitionism on an almost daily basis. Placed in the awkward position of having to denounce the international anti-slavery movement but not their party brethren who endorsed it, many Whigs condemned the convention as a British ploy to promote sectional discord.[51]

With the country in the throes of a depression that had begun at the start of Van Buren's presidency, the Democrats' need to find foreign

FIGURE 7.

The Working Man's Advocate, October 15, 1840. In this and other cartoons, Democrats in 1840 mocked their opponents' "log cabin campaign" and urged voters not to barter their liberties for "English gold." (The Library Company of Philadelphia)

scapegoats was especially acute. Taking the offensive in an effort to pre-empt the opposition's assault on Democratic fiscal policies, the Van Burenites laid the blame for the crisis at the door of British banking houses, and insisted that a Harrison victory would extend their stranglehold on the American economy.[52] Allegations of collusion between British "fund mongers" and the Whig Party seemed all the more plausible in view of the seemingly limitless financial resources the Whigs had at their disposal to stage rallies and parades. As enthusiastic citizens turned out in droves for Harrison mass meetings, anxious Democrats wondered aloud how the Whigs had managed to pay for such an elaborate campaign. The only possible explanation, they alleged, was that British financiers were bankrolling the Whigs' "log cabin pageantry." Democrats could not contain their delight when it was learned that many of the Tippecanoe handkerchiefs, log-cabin breastpins, and other forms of campaign paraphernalia distributed by the thousands at Whig rallies had been made in Sheffield. While the news was hardly evidence of British financial collusion, it was at the very least an embarrassing revelation for a party that favored a high protective tariff to protect American labor. As the election drew near, the *Washington Globe* began to charge that "British agents and funds" had been dispatched by London banking houses to the United States to ensure a Whig victory.[53]

So pervasive were allegations that British gold had been brought to bear to influence the outcome of the election that Democrats turned naturally to this scenario when they were crushed by the Whig juggernaut in November. Some of the party's most senior spokesmen attributed the electoral disaster not to the depression or to savvy Whig electioneering, but to the financial backing their opponents had allegedly received from the titans of Lombard and Threadneedle Streets. In his post-mortem analysis of the party's defeat, Thomas Hart Benton sputtered that the election was a violation of the popular will, dismissing the outcome as "a stock jobbing operation on the London exchange." Called upon by Whig colleagues to provide evidence of his sensational charges, the Missouri senator could do little more than offer the hardly controversial observation that British banking houses had favored a Harrison victory.[54]

1844

In the early 1840s, the Democratic Party was an organization in disarray. The Jacksonian economic agenda had lost much of its resonance with the electorate, particularly in the wake of the Panic of 1837, leaving many party loyalists "sick of the old subjects of discussion."[55] The economic downturn had raised serious doubts about the wisdom of Democrats' fiscal policies, while party leaders in key manufacturing states were beginning to break rank and side with their Whig opponents on the issue of a protective tariff. Most troubling of all was the slavery question, which was becoming a potentially divisive party issue now that slaveholders had begun to clamor loudly for the annexation of Texas, an objective that many Northerners, most notably party standard-bearer Martin Van Buren, viewed with little enthusiasm.

As the 1844 campaign approached, some party leaders came to regard expansion of the national domain as a means to both rally the party's base and neutralize antislavery as a disruptive political force. This new crusade aimed to isolate the antislavery minority by emphasizing the advantages of a broad-based program of territorial growth, a policy opposed by Great Britain, which was eager to thwart the emergence of a formidable rival on the North American continent. Although the expansionist appetites of Southern whites had always been larger than those of their Northern brethren, this could be offset, to some degree, by aggressively asserting U.S. claims in the Pacific Northwest. Recognizing that a defiant posture against Great Britain was a policy with broad, nationwide appeal, James Buchanan expressed the view of many Democrats that every region of the country had just cause to complain of its "all-pervading arrogance and injustice." Though he professed a desire to see these disputes resolved amicably, the Pennsylvania senator was not unmindful of the fact that "we shall be a united people" should hostilities result.[56]

Since American expansionism and the Texas question will be examined in some detail in subsequent chapters, it is enough to say here that antislavery Whigs in Congress had managed to block Southern efforts to acquire the Lone Star Republic following its separation from Mexico in 1836, but that support for the measure had been growing steadily ever since. Despite fierce antislavery opposition, annexation was not strictly a Southern issue. Fueled by reports of British meddling in Texas affairs, annexation also drew support from the West and the Mid-Atlantic states, having been touted by expansionists as a national security measure. In the spring of 1844, arguing that the Lone Star Republic was in danger of becoming a satellite of Great Britain, President Tyler concluded a treaty of annexation with Texas diplomats and sent it on to the Senate for ratification, forcing members of both parties to take a stand on the issue as the campaign season approached.

The pending Texas treaty was an unwelcome development for the two presumptive nominees, Henry Clay and Martin Van Buren, neither of whom wished to roil the political waters over the expansion of slavery. Both men issued carefully worded policy statements opposing the annexation offer, which were seen as position papers for their respective parties in the fall campaign.[57] At the same time, the two candidates were not unmindful of the electorate's concerns regarding British activities in Texas, and sought to reassure anxious voters that they would act resolutely to combat outside interference in the American Southwest if elected.[58] Such caveats notwithstanding, their statements on annexation left both Clay and Van Buren vulnerable to the charge of weakness in the face of possible British aggrandizement. Although Clay won his party's nomination by acclamation, he had clearly misjudged the depth of public support for annexation in the South, and he would spend much of the fall campaign trying to clarify his position. Van Buren's equivocal stand enraged Democratic expansionists, who had been disappointed with the New Yorker's performance in the last election and now lobbied to keep him off the party ticket. Should Van Buren receive the nomination, one Virginia editorialist raged, the "lone star" would soon be found "twinkling luridly, under the flaming Red Cross of St. George," and would henceforth be known as "BRITISH TEXAS!"[59]

Michigan senator Lewis Cass seemed the likely party leader to capitalize on this sudden rebellion in the Democratic ranks. A former governor of the Michigan territory for 18 years, he had frequently locked horns with British officials in Canada over neutrality rights on the Great Lakes. Later, as U.S. minister to France, he had objected strongly to Britain's searching of American vessels to enforce the ban on the slave trade. Cass's highly publicized opposition to British maritime policies won him high marks among Southern Democrats, but made him anathema to British leaders, who accused him of political grandstanding.[60] On the eve of the party convention, political allies in his home state urged him to come out boldly in favor of annexation, one congressman suggesting that Cass issue a "short, forceful, patriotic, anti-British letter (such as you know how to write)," and downplaying the issue as one of concern to the South alone.[61] The eager candidate had in fact already written such a letter, pointing out the manifest advantages of a union of the two republics and leaving no doubt that the danger of British interference in Texas's affairs was the most salient reason to revive the annexation issue.[62]

At the party convention in Baltimore, the Michigan senator's quest for the presidential nomination foundered in the face of determined opposition from the Van Burenites, who swung their support on the ninth ballot to a compromise candidate, a Tennessean, James K. Polk. Nonetheless, the convention represented a complete victory for the party's expansionist wing. In Polk, a protégé of Andrew Jackson, it had secured the nomination of a Western candidate who embodied his section's historical animus toward Great Britain, and who was convinced that Her Majesty's government was determined to foreclose all future territorial growth by the United States.

In the first election in which U.S. foreign policy played a central role, the Democrats' called for the immediate annexation of the Lone Star Republic and the repudiation of British claims to the Oregon Territory. The party had always accused Whig challengers of harboring British ideas and opinions. In the fall campaign, however, the Democrats accorded Great Britain a more conspicuous role than ever, raising the specter of a foreign enemy eager to thwart American interests, both in the South and the Pacific Northwest. Portraying their Whig opponents as weak on the issue of national defense, they argued that only the disciples of Andrew Jackson possessed the credentials and the mettle to stand up to the British lion.[63]

The Whigs responded with what had become a familiar staple in national politics—ad hominem attacks designed to cast doubt on their opponent's loyalty to the nation. Polk was accused of having "dodged a draft" in the War of 1812, a lack of patriotism he had presumably inherited from his grandfather. Ezekiel Polk, Whigs claimed, had been a Loyalist who collaborated with the British during the Revolution.[64] Their campaign literature even compared him to Benedict Arnold, going so far as to suggest that British capital was now being funneled to the Polk campaign in exchange for the services rendered by Polk's grandfather seventy-five years earlier. Wild as these charges might seem today, the attacks against Ezekiel were not taken lightly by the Democrats. Campaign tracts that testified to the patriotism of the nominee's grandfather were promptly issued, reproducing his captain's commission in the North Carolina militia and the Mecklenburg Declaration of Independence (the first of its kind in the thirteen colonies), which Ezekiel had signed in May 1775.[65]

As usual, a protective tariff remained for the Whigs their most potent election issue. Fearful that a Democratic victory would undo the Tariff of 1842, the only significant domestic achievement of the ill-fated Tyler administration, the Whigs argued that a Polk victory would result in a deluge of cheap foreign imports, branding the Democratic candidate as the paid agent of British industry. There may have been some truth in reports that more than $400,000 had been raised in Great Britain to circulate free trade pamphlets in the United States, but Whig campaign literature led voters to believe that such subscriptions had gone directly into the coffers of the Democratic Party.[66] In what would become a popular Whig metaphor for the campaign, Senator John Clayton of Delaware compared the party slates to two wagons. The Whig vehicle was made in America; the one driven by Democrats was of foreign manufacture. Of the Polk/Dallas conveyance, Clayton observed: "The very wood of which it is made, is of foreign growth—even the horse-shoes were made by English blacksmiths; the harness is all manufactured out of English leather by English harness makers; all the wheel tire[s], the axle trees,

FIGURE 8.

"British Gold to Buy!!" In 1844, Democratic presidential nominee
James K. Polk promised to reduce tariff rates, prompting Whigs to
counter that he had been bribed by British manufacturing interests.
(The Western Reserve Historical Society, Cleveland, Ohio)

and even the bridle bits, were imported from Liverpool. No American
laborer, whether native or naturalized, was allowed to drive a nail into
the wagon."[67]

Thus, the campaign of 1844 presented American voters with a clear
choice: a Democratic candidate who promised to defend the nation
against British territorial ambitions in Texas and Oregon, and a Whig
candidate who vowed to protect American economic interests from Brit-

ish commercial penetration. Although both appeals resonated powerfully with their respective constituencies, the Whig focus on pocketbook
issues lacked the novelty and the visceral jingoism of the Democrats' territorial agenda, and did little to help the party in the South, where Texas
annexation was the overriding issue. This time, it was the Whig's turn to
blame the outcome on Great Britain. "Our opponents have succeeded
with the banner of a foreign land as their Emblem, and by the aid and
influence of British interests, and British capital," one Illinois resident
fumed in a letter of condolence to the Whig nominee.[68]

Great Britain occupied a unique place in American political culture.
When Washington and Whitehall clashed over territory or commercial
policy, leaders of the two major parties had little difficulty rousing the
electorate against the nation's longtime antagonist. More commonly,
though, Great Britain tended to play an auxiliary role. As a one-size-fits-
all bête noire, the imperial parent was invoked by Democrats and Whigs
alike to articulate a wide range of concerns, even those that seemed to
have little to do with U.S.-British relations. In the hands of party propagandists, anti-British feeling proved to be an exceedingly facile material
which could be molded to suit virtually any contingency. Concerns over
the preservation of republican rule; the rise of an effete, cosmopolitan
culture; a volatile economic climate; antislavery; the restriction of territorial growth—all could be laid, to varying degrees, at the door of Great
Britain. The figure of John Bull intruded upon the American electoral
process because of its singular ability to assume a seemingly limitless
number of threatening guises—tyrannical monarch, simpering aristocrat, shady moneylender, brass-knuckled commercial rival, antislavery
agitator—which party leaders could employ to demonize their political
opponents.

This is not to suggest that Anglophobia was merely adventitious,
a false phantom tacked cynically onto a particular issue by campaign
operatives to rally the party faithful. When the British visitor George
Warburton expressed concern at the intense hostility that Americans exhibited toward his country, he was told that they condemned the empire
out of habit, not from any genuine, deeply rooted animus. Warburton
was not convinced. If anti-British opinions were uttered often enough,
he believed, at some point they would acquire a life of their own, for
"the habit of speaking becomes a habit of thinking, and thinking, sooner
or later will become acting."[69] American politicians might exploit Anglophobia on the stump, but after a while they came to believe and act upon
their own rhetoric. Believing it to be their sacred duty to cross swords

with Great Britain, just as earlier generations had done, they helped to keep anti-British sentiment alive. Their denunciations of John Bull could not be simply dismissed after an election, however. American political leaders may have initially cast domestic issues in terms of a wider transatlantic threat for reasons of expediency, but at some point the rhetoric itself became part of the rationale, and assumed a self-fulfilling role in shaping public policy. Thus, anti-British feeling did not drive the domestic political agenda, but it did help to frame responses to important policy questions. The republic's symbiotic economic relationship with Great Britain, for example, proved to be a matter of no small importance in what were surely the most controversial issues for the two major parties during the Jacksonian era: trade and banking. How the transatlantic relationship informed their responses to these challenges will be examined in the two chapters that follow.

☙ 6 ☙

"Politically Free, Commercial Slaves"

Our plough and spades,
Our looms and trades,
Will keep our country free.
John Bull may growl,
And swear 'tis foul,
But a Tariff there must be.
—Whig campaign song, 1844

The return of peace after the Napoleonic Wars marked the onset of a new era in the commercial relationship between Great Britain and the United States. Always a large consumer of foreign manufactures, the American republic soon found itself inundated by imports from that country, as British merchants seized the opportunity to empty overstocked warehouses and unload their inventory on the American market. The glut of foreign items was compounded by the auction system, by which British exporters sold their goods in American port cities through wholesale agents, accepting lower prices in exchange for reduced operating costs and quick returns. The system proved so successful that it continued even after the immediate postwar appetite for British products had been satisfied. American importers were soon deeply in debt, having borrowed heavily to take full advantage of the boom. British exporters, meanwhile, found themselves similarly overextended when the cost of credit began to rise in early 1816. With importer and exporter alike in dire need of ready cash, both turned to auction sales for relief, dumping British goods on the American market at almost any price.[1]

The sudden availability of British imports was a boon to consumers but a disaster for American manufacturers, who had prospered since the outbreak of war in Europe. With transatlantic commerce choked off by the naval duel between France and Britain, manufacturers of dry goods, such as cotton and woolen textiles, enjoyed a virtual monopoly over the home market. The return of peace brought the republic's economic isolation to an abrupt end, spelling ruin for the stripling manufacturing sector just as it was beginning to find its legs. Predictably, factory owners clamored for relief.

Democratic-Republicans had traditionally been deaf to such entreaties. During the Federalist era of the 1790s, the party of Jefferson had vigorously opposed any efforts by Washington to interfere in the nation's economic affairs. When treasury secretary Alexander Hamilton proposed higher tariffs to nurture infant industries, the idea failed to win congressional approval, rejected by Jeffersonians as a Federalist ploy to promote industry at the expense of agriculture. By the early 1800s, however, as the country began to develop a manufacturing base of its own, many Jeffersonians expressed a cautious willingness to use the tariff to promote economic development. After the war, a cohort of influential economists and pamphleteers, such as Irish-born Matthew Carey and German-born Friedrich List, argued that the laissez-faire doctrines that had hitherto framed the Jeffersonian ideology were no longer adequate to deal with changing economic realities. Reflecting the nationalist fervor of the postwar period, they were committed to the belief that a government responsive to the well-being of its people had an obligation to promote national wealth and economic security. A protective tariff, they maintained, was not a sop to special interests, but a mechanism that would enable the republic to reach its full commercial potential.[2]

No American would do more to raise public awareness of the tariff question than Hezekiah Niles, editor of the eponymous *Niles' Weekly Register*. Founding the paper in 1811, Niles was one of the country's most influential publishers until his retirement in 1836. Unlike most newspapers of the time, the *Register* accepted no advertisements or financial support from either political party, making a modest profit through subscriptions alone. As a result, the paper enjoyed both a national readership and a reputation for independence all but unknown among its competitors. Although the *Register* reprinted items from other papers to keep its readers abreast of breaking news at home and abroad, Niles kept a strict rein over editorial content. The Baltimore newspaperman did not shrink from sounding off on a wide range of important issues, and when it came to the tariff the message was loud and clear. An early disciple of the protectionist cause, Niles treated his readers to a regular barrage of editorials on the manifold benefits of higher duties, devoting more space in the *Register* to this issue than any other. Eschewing abstract theory and dry statistics, he wrote for the layman, distilling his argument to a few central points, which he never grew tired of repeating. With the *Register* as his bully pulpit, Niles preached the protectionist gospel with an unwavering, evangelical fervor during the course of his twenty-five-year career.[3]

Niles's commitment to higher duties was rooted in the belief that protection was nothing less than a magic key to national prosperity, a boon that would bestow unimagined benefits on all Americans. With a little help from the federal government, he maintained, the United States would soon be in a position to challenge the imperial parent as the workshop of the world. A tireless booster for homegrown manufactures, Niles filled the pages of his newspaper with success stories of domestic industry, crowing loudly when American products found an overseas market. The Baltimore editor was no paid propagandist for American business; a staunch Jeffersonian, he had no interest in serving as an advocate for an elite constituency.[4] To be sure, American manufacturers would reap substantial rewards from a policy that gave them an advantage over foreign competitors. But Niles was no less convinced that agriculture would gain equally by a protective system. A thriving textile industry would, in time, absorb most of the wool and cotton produced in the United States, while a growing urban population would increase the demand for domestic foodstuffs, eliminating farmers' dependence on volatile foreign markets. The beauty of protection, Niles believed, was that it would create a system of interdependent economic units, in which the prosperity of one was inextricably linked to the prosperity of all.

Not all Americans were won over by Niles's populist protectionism. Many had misgivings about a commercial policy designed to promote domestic manufacturing, anxious to avoid the blighting effects of the British factory system. In the South, the planter class feared that domestic trade barriers might jeopardize the market for agricultural staples overseas. Niles had little patience with these critics. He dismissed as so much nervous hand-wringing the predictions that industrialization would impoverish the American worker. A healthy republican system, he argued, would act as a check against the social inequality so evident in Great Britain, and ensure a broader distribution of wealth and power. Niles was equally disdainful of complaints from the planter class, loath to concede that any section of the country was disadvantaged by higher duties. If poor market conditions existed for cotton growers, he insisted, U.S. trade policy was not to blame.[5]

For the Baltimore newspaperman, protectionism was heavily freighted with geopolitical implications, a position reinforced by his lifelong and deeply held Anglophobia. Born to Quaker parents in 1777 as

British and colonial forces converged on the rolling hills outside Philadelphia, Niles took great pride in having entered the world amid the
tumult of the American Revolution. He was particularly fond of relating
the family story that his pregnant mother, only days before the battle
of Brandywine, had almost been run through with a bayonet by a British grenadier intent on killing "two rebels at once."[6] Whatever the truth
of the story, Niles reached adulthood with one guiding conviction: that
Great Britain posed the single most serious threat to the prosperity and
the security of the United States.

For Niles, the stakes in this economic contest could not have been
higher; indeed, he argued, nothing less than the future of the republic
hung in the balance. Much earlier than many of his contemporaries, the
Baltimore editor grasped the consequences for the developing world of
the industrial dominance of Great Britain, a nation whose goal was "to
make all the world her *tributaries*, through the consumption of her manufactures."[7] In the new global marketplace, national greatness would be
measured as much by industrial productivity as by military strength. A
protective tariff was the country's first line of defense against British imperialism. More to the point, a nation that served as a source of raw materials for Britain's factories would always occupy a subordinate position
in the transatlantic equation, an unacceptable prospect for the patriotic
Niles, who declared, "The people of the United States will not 'play a
second fiddle' to any other people."[8]

After 1815, many Americans came to share this view. In an era of
rising nationalism, it was hardly surprising that some citizens should
embrace a brand of political economy that promised to transform the
United States from an agrarian republic into a manufacturing power-
house capable of rivaling Great Britain. Such a policy would, of course,
involve a conspicuous retreat from the conventional Jeffersonian wisdom
that an industrial, urban society was incompatible with republicanism.
Its proponents, however, insisted that real, meaningful independence
could not be achieved without it. Henry Clay, who would make protection one of the guiding principles of his political career, noted ruefully,
"The truth is, and it is in vain to disguise it," that almost half a century
after the Revolution, the United States remained little more than "independent colonies of England—*politically free, commercial slaves*."[9]

The Ideology of Protection

Although the tariff question would ultimately devolve into a bitter contest between competing economic and sectional interests, organized opposition to protection was slow to develop. The recent war had made

FIGURE 9.
Hezekiah Niles, by John Wesley Jarvis. (Courtesy of The
Maryland Historical Society)

Americans acutely aware of the extent to which they remained vulnerable to British power, prompting many to see the issue as a national security measure.[10] Advocates of higher duties based their appeals on the
need for a strong manufacturing sector that would better prepare the
nation for the next war with Great Britain. For this reason, the 1816 tariff bill specifically targeted defense-related products for protection, such
as lumber, iron, and hemp (a staple for rope and cordage in the shipping
industry). The 14th Congress drafted a tariff bill that imposed duties
ranging from 20 to 30 percent on such items as rolled and hammered
iron and cotton goods, products dominated by British manufacturers.
South Carolina congressman John C. Calhoun, then an ardent nationalist, regarded the protection of American manufacturing as "a new and
most powerful cement," bonding the sections of the country together
in mutual dependence and commercial intercourse. Many of his Southern colleagues disagreed, finding little in the new schedule to benefit

their plantation economy. They favored instead an across-the-board ad valorem tariff, the costs of which would be borne equally by all sections. None, however, questioned the constitutionality of protection, an issue that would become paramount for proponents of free trade in the years ahead.[11]

Advocates of protection also played skillfully upon the nation's cultural insecurities, co-opting the language of those who decried the persistence of British influences in American life. Just as the nation's patriotic literati aimed to correct the American prejudice against homegrown novels and plays, protectionists upbraided their fellow citizens for preferring imported calicoes and pocket handkerchiefs. In the economic sphere as in the cultural one, nationalists pointed to the country's unseemly reliance on foreign ideas and attitudes.[12] Advocates of higher duties reminded their fellow citizens that the Revolutionary generation had refused to bow to Britain's economic aggression, and liked to refer to Lord Chatham's famous sneer that the colonies would never be allowed to make a "hobnail boot" for the British home market. Contemporary British statesmen expressed a similar contempt for American industry, Lord Henry Brougham calling upon Parliament to "stifle in the cradle" the manufacturing system in the United States, which, "contrary to the natural order of things," had emerged during the recent war.[13] Just as Sydney Smith's query, "Who reads an American book?" served as a spur to American writers, such statements infuriated those who hoped to see their country rival Britain in the economic sphere.

With the onset of the Panic of 1819, the drumbeat on behalf of a protective duty system began in earnest. Auction sales rose sharply in the wake of the economic downturn. Congress responded the following year, when the newly created House Committee on Manufactures drafted a bill calling for an increase in tariff rates to an average of 33 percent ad valorem, with a 10 percent tax on auction sales. As author of the committee report, chairman Henry Baldwin of Pennsylvania defended the proposed tariff revisions as a necessary counterweight to British protectionism, pointing to the prohibitive duties imposed by Parliament on American grain. In an effort to gain Southern support for the bill, Baldwin predicted that American cotton growers would face similarly ruinous restrictions should British textile manufacturers ever be able to rely on an ample source of supply from India. The struggle for economic independence, he reminded his colleagues, had its roots in the Revolutionary conflict, when patriotic Americans had renounced British cotton fabrics in favor of homespun woolens. It was a line of reasoning that would become a familiar refrain among protectionists every time Congress turned to the tariff issue during the next quarter of a century.[14]

Many Southern congressmen were in no way persuaded by Baldwin's appeal to historical precedent, or his argument that their section would one day fall victim to British exclusionary trade practices. They correctly sensed that the bill signaled a marked shift in U.S. commercial policy: a tariff schedule not simply designed to enhance the competitiveness of American manufacturers, but to guarantee their complete dominance of the home market. So radical a measure could not be effected without tampering with the very federal system itself, investing the national government with the formidable authority to oversee, direct, and ultimately determine the course of the republic's economic future. Baldwin had hinted at such an expanded role for Washington in his committee report, decrying the fact that no other country "studiously leaves her great concerns to regulate themselves."[15] Where Baldwin saw the promotion of American manufacturing competitiveness as a challenge that only the national government could meet, many Southerners saw a Rubicon that, once crossed, would irrevocably upset the delicate balance between federal and state sovereignty. Closing ranks, Southern leaders managed to defeat the bill, though just barely, the measure failing to win passage by a single Senate vote.

Even as some Americans considered following Britain's protectionist lead, in Parliament a very different debate over commercial policy was taking shape. For two and a half centuries the island kingdom had adhered to mercantilist principles—hoarding its wealth, acquiring new sources of raw materials, and reducing imports in an unending quest for self-sufficiency. American merchants grumbled that the lucrative commerce of the West Indies remained closed to U.S. shipping. American farmers, too, were denied access to markets in Britain, where powerful landed interests had secured in 1815 passage of the Corn Laws, which imposed price supports on domestic grains. But as British manufacturers sought new markets around the globe, pressure began to build for the dismantling of these trade barriers. Free trade economists called for reduced duties on a wide range of goods and advocated a sliding scale to regulate the duty on agricultural products. Richard Cobden and others touted the doctrine of open markets as a "grand panacea" that would distribute the benefits of capitalism throughout the globe. In their more exuberant moments, they predicted that free trade would usher in a new age of peace and prosperity, eliminating any reason for conflict between nations. Such lofty goals would not compromise Britain's economic interests, free traders argued, but would actually serve to promote them. In rejecting the parochialism of protection, they envisioned a system in which peripheral economies would supply mechanized ones with the materials needed to satisfy the world's appetite for manufactured goods—a blueprint, in essence, for the perpetuation of the status quo, and Britain's unrivalled dominance.[16]

American manufacturers regarded Parliament's newfound enthusiasm for free trade principles with considerable skepticism. They had long argued that Britain's economic success was due in no small part to the practice of shielding its producers from foreign competition. The apparent readiness of some members of Parliament to end this policy struck cynics as a transparent ploy to pressure other nations to forswear the very practices that had made Britain the world's industrial leader. Since American manufacturers were a long way from being competitive in British markets, they saw little benefit in a policy that would give their foreign counterparts unfettered access to American consumers. As a young nation, the United States needed a government that would aggressively encourage and foster economic growth. That British leaders were now converting to the gospel of free trade, they insisted, proved that the higher duties of the Tariff of 1816 were beginning to show results. With continued assistance from the federal government, fledgling American industries would soon be in a position to compete successfully with their British rivals.

With the country slow to recover from the Panic of 1819, the tariff issue became the focus of heated activity, as legislators came under increasing pressure from a host of new societies created for the encouragement of domestic manufactures. Henry Clay, the Speaker of the House and a contender for the presidency, would lead the drive for an upward revision of the tariff. Clay sought a tariff schedule higher than that proposed earlier by Baldwin, imposing duties of 33⅓ percent on cotton and woolen goods. In an effort to broaden the bill's regional appeal, Clay offered protection to a number of industries, such as hemp manufacturing and cotton bagging, that had gained a foothold in western states, including his native Kentucky. Touted by its supporters as the key to national self-sufficiency, a measure explicitly designed to "counteract the policy of foreigners," the 1824 tariff bill became the centerpiece of Clay's so-called "American System." Despite having bested Great Britain on the battlefield, the young republic would ever remain what "the policy of England had made us," so long as Americans allowed British manufacturers to dominate the home market.[17]

Yet so formidable was Britain's economic position that the former War Hawk could not refrain from holding it up as an example the United States would do well to follow. The Kentucky congressman claimed to be "no eulogist of England," but that did not prevent him from waxing enthusiastic on the "wonderful prosperity" which, he believed, had been the key to its victory over Napoleonic France. Unlike the United States,

Great Britain would never find itself reliant upon another nation for the materials of war. "Self-poised, resting upon her own internal resources, possessing a home market carefully cherished and guarded, she is ever prepared for any emergency."[18]

Clay had hoped that his program of economic nationalism would carry him into the White House. But the tariff issue had become a lightning rod for partisan and sectional rancor, scuttling his bid for the presidency in 1824. As the political clout of manufacturing interests increased, so did resentment among those who saw no benefit from higher duties. In the Northeast, mercantile interests were wary of any measure that threatened to curtail the transatlantic trade. New England's opposition to higher duties was modest compared to that of the South, which saw the bill as a federal subsidy for manufacturers that would drive up the price of consumer goods. Even more important, the planter class feared Britain would retaliate with higher duties on cotton, or seek new sources of supply if denied access to American markets. Opponents reproached the Speaker for praising the very system that was the source of the republic's recent economic distress. The inequities inherent in British society were simply too well known for that country to be regarded as a model worthy of emulation. Clay's American System, they charged, was in reality a blueprint for the modern industrial state—a British system in disguise.[19]

"An Ally in the Centre of the American Line"

The passage of the 1824 tariff stilled, but did not silence, the drive for higher duties. The woolens industry, in particular, complained that it could not compete with British imports, and soon mounted an aggressive campaign to pressure Congress to grant it further protection. In the spring of 1827, tariff meetings were held in several Northern states, which were a prelude to a tariff convention to be held in Harrisburg, Pennsylvania that summer.

Roused to action, the South responded with anti-tariff meetings of its own. Opposition was strongest in South Carolina, where the planter class, to an even greater degree than in other Southern states, dominated the political culture. One of the prime movers of the Palmetto State's fierce resentment of federal tariff policy was Thomas Cooper, president of South Carolina College. An English-born free-thinker, Cooper was no stranger to controversy. His radical views had made him unwelcome in Britain and France, prompting his emigration to the United States in the 1790s. Throwing himself into local politics, he would spend six months in jail for violating the Sedition Act. Now, in the mid-1820s, his interest in political economy would gain the septuagenarian a new lease on notoriety. The university president's writings on the subject, a melding of the Manchester school's free trade principles and the doctrines of American classical republicanism, were not in themselves provocative. The same could not be said, however, for the political solution he proposed. Lacking the native son's visceral patriotism, the British expatriate warned that state residents should prepare themselves for the possibility of secession if the federal government did not eschew trade policies injurious to Southern interests.[20] In a speech to an anti-tariff meeting at Columbia in July 1827, Cooper famously declared that the time was not far distant when Palmetto State residents would have to "calculate the value of our union." Ominously, he asked: "What use to us is this unequal alliance?"[21]

Despite growing frustration over the tariff, many South Carolinians were unwilling to endorse so defiant a stance as the one the college president now advocated. Moderate public leaders, anxious to quash rising popular support for a more radical approach to the tariff controversy, attributed the agitation to a British-backed free trade cabal, with the foreign-born Cooper at its head. Having become an American citizen more than thirty years earlier, Cooper could hardly be characterized as a foreign interloper. Indeed, as a longtime critic of British policies and traditions (he had been an especially vocal critic of American reliance on English common law), he was something of an Anglophobe himself. Nonetheless, the *Charleston City Gazette*, edited by a young William Gilmore Simms, whose stalwart defense of a national literature lay some years in the future, vigorously attacked Cooper's incendiary speech. It was bad enough for a native American to harbor disunionist views, one reader argued in a letter to the paper, "but in a foreigner, whether naturalized or not, it is insufferable."[22]

Congress paid little attention to the rumblings of discontent in the Palmetto State and tackled the tariff issue again in the midst of the presidential campaign season of 1828. The resulting legislation imposed the highest tariff schedule in the nation's history, with average duties higher even than the Depression-era's unpopular Hawley-Smoot Tariff of 1930.[23] Promptly dubbed the "Tariff of Abominations" by its opponents, the act galvanized the fledgling anti-tariff movement. In South Carolina, angry planters had begun to question Washington's trade policy on constitutional grounds. Bowing to the clamor, Vice President John C. Calhoun distanced himself from his earlier support for modest protection, anonymously authoring a state legislative report sharply critical of the new tariff. Known as the *Exposition and Protest*, the report advanced the radical doctrine of nullification, a state's inherent right to nullify federal law. Calhoun believed his constitutional argument offered a "peaceful remedy" to the controversy; others regarded it as a dangerous formula for disunion.

In the protectionist Mid-Atlantic states, the full implications of South Carolina's defiance of the new tariff now became clear. Following the lead of the Palmetto State's unionist press, Northern newspapers focused their ire on the English-born president of South Carolina College. But Cooper, an aging and somewhat eccentric academic, was an unlikely ringleader, wholly lacking the political skills to transform public resentment of federal tariff policy into a cohesive movement. While his views continued to influence the planter class, leadership of the anti-tariff agitation had already passed to some of the state's most prominent public figures, such as Governor James Hamilton and Beaufort congressman George McDuffie. The mere fact that South Carolina natives were now heading the nullification groundswell did not dampen fears of foreign interference, however. The *Niles' Register* was especially inclined to see Britain's free trade fingerprints on any challenge to protectionist policy. To the Baltimore editor, it seemed inconceivable that loyal Americans could oppose a measure so clearly in the national interest. There could be but one explanation: citizens of the Palmetto State had been duped by a foreign enemy. Limning the contours of a full-blown plot to divide the union, Niles insisted that British agents were funding the free trade press, buying votes, influencing elections, and in other ways aiding and abetting states' rights ultras and their "Carolina doctrines." Allowing his Anglophobic imagination free rein, Niles maintained that the British government was determined to foment open rebellion in the Southern states, and stood ready to supply its radical leaders with "English muskets free of charge."[24]

The British press did little to quell rumors in the United States that the crisis had been engineered in Whitehall. Many newspapers and journals applauded South Carolina's position, and their editorials were widely reprinted across the Atlantic as evidence of the intentions of the British government.[25] Occasionally, new, unsubstantiated reports surfaced of a British free trade connection in the nullification controversy, all of it duly printed by the Eastern press. According to one account, a Palmetto State agent had arrived in London in July, 1830, to assess the situation with parliamentary leaders; still another claimed that a plan had been hatched in Whitehall to exploit the American tariff controversy, with the goal of bringing about a separation of the union within five years.[26]

Palmetto State radicals had been emboldened by the belief that President Jackson, as a Southern planter, shared their views on the tariff.

In the recent presidential campaign, the Tennessean had advocated a modest tariff schedule, with duties only high enough to provide revenue for the federal government. But if the new president saw no need to protect American manufacturers, he was not willing to go along with states' rights extremists who called for the nullification of federal law. Angered by talk of disunion (as well as by the knowledge that his vice president, John C. Calhoun, was actively involved in the agitation), Jackson made his disapproval known in his first major policy statement on the question, a public letter which was read at a Charleston Fourth of July celebration in 1831. Echoing the concerns of many state unionists, the president predicted that South Carolina would become a vassal state of the British empire should it persist in its reckless course.[27]

As time passed, the absence of concrete evidence made allegations of a foreign plot impossible to sustain. Whitehall remained conspicuously aloof from the controversy, and though its support for open markets was a matter of public record, this was a slender reed on which to hang a conspiracy theory of transatlantic dimensions. Hezekiah Niles, not surprisingly, would cling longer than most to the fiction that "the *moving power* of the present excitement is located in Great Britain." As agitation against the 1828 tariff continued, however, even stalwart Anglophobes were obliged to concede that British influence alone could not account for the Palmetto State's deep hostility toward federal tariff policies.[28]

Be that as it may, the habit of blaming external enemies for internal problems was a hard one for Americans to break. Genuine apprehensions of foreign interference may have ceased to figure prominently in the dispute over the tariff, but anti-British sentiment was too deeply ingrained in American political culture to disappear entirely. One reason was tradition: nullifiers and unionists alike saw the conflict in terms of a broader historical narrative in which each claimed to be the authentic standard-bearer of the nation's Revolutionary legacy. Nullifiers staged elaborate July 4th dinners and other celebrations that deftly fused past and present, conflating New England and Old England as symbols of oppression. A toast delivered by George McDuffie at an Edgefield anti-tariff dinner may serve as a typical example: "The stamp act of 1765, and the Tariff of 1828—kindred acts of despotism."[29] Not to be outdone, unionists formed the Washington Society, which held meetings across the state to drum up opposition to the nullification groundswell. Harangues against "the degenerate and corrupt government of Old England" were standard fare at such gatherings, invariably accompanied by a reading of Washington's familiar admonition to beware of foreign influences.[30] The group called upon citizens of the Palmetto State to reaffirm their patriotic ardor by carrying on the great work bequeathed to them by their forebears. "The spirit of our fathers would, from the grave, rebuke our madness" should South Carolina humble itself before its historic enemy, declared one unionist state senator.[31]

Claiming legitimacy on the basis of past struggles with Great Britain was only one way in which both sides employed Anglophobia in the nullification debate. As in so many political battles, the imperial parent was a multipurpose bête noire. For states' rights stalwarts, the need to reference a foreign threat was simple enough. Allusions to the specter of British power served to raise the stakes in their confrontation with Washington, investing the crisis with the hint of greater menace. As early as the summer of 1828, leading nullifiers freely broached the possibility of a war with Great Britain should Washington attempt to blockade the port of Charleston.[32] Hinting that the Royal Navy might intervene in the event of an armed struggle between South Carolina and the federal government, they warned that the state would have no choice but to turn to England for aid.[33]

FIGURE 10.

"The Union Pie." Great Britain was widely accused of supporting nullification as a means to undermine the American republic. In this cartoon, John Bull has taken a slice of South Carolina, and remarks: "If I cannot eat all now, I'll see it divide!" (Negative no. 35159, Collection of The New-York Historical Society)

Palmetto State unionists had their own reasons for keeping the specter of British interference alive. From the outset, the group struggled to
present an effective alternative to nullification. An unwieldy coalition of
Upcountry Jacksonians and Tidewater neo-Federalists, the faction could
claim little socioeconomic or ideological cohesiveness. Indeed, the
group actually shared with the nullifiers a deep aversion to protectionism, taking issue only with the drastic remedy they proposed.[34] The task
for this disparate group, then, was a tricky one: to somehow find a middle ground between nullifiers and the pro-tariff North, presenting itself
as an effective champion of Palmetto State interests on the one hand,
while simultaneously appealing to South Carolinians' national loyalties
on the other. Little wonder that the group welcomed the opportunity
to cast the controversy in geopolitical terms. States' rights ultras could
inveigh against "federal usurpation" all they wanted, moderates argued,
but their reckless course of action would ultimately force South Carolina
to seek an alliance with Great Britain, which alone possessed the military and financial resources to guarantee its sovereignty. Unionists not
only disputed the nullifiers' contention that the state could stand alone,
but predicted that Britain would make Charleston a free trade entrepôt
from which to inundate the United States with foreign goods, giving it
"an ally in the centre of the American line" and bringing the commerce
of every other port city to a standstill.[35]

The unionists' rhetorical arsenal also included generic arguments
familiar to all Americans: leading nullifiers, they claimed, had fallen
under the spell of British opinion. Long after it became clear that the
British government had played no role in fomenting the crisis, unionists continued to insist that their opponents were swayed by an anti-
republican ideology propagated by British periodicals, and by literature
disseminated by British manufacturers to "deceive, divide, and, if possible, destroy the American people."[36] The effects of this propaganda campaign could be seen in the conduct of such leading nullifiers as South
Carolina senator Robert Hayne, who was said to be "too full of imported
notions" to weigh the merits of protection objectively.[37] The language of
cultural imitativeness allowed unionists to mock the nullifiers as fawning Anglophiles, whose leaders were more inclined to deliver "elaborate
panegyrics on the literature and genius" of Great Britain than stand firm
as bulwarks of American republican institutions.[38] Stung by the accusa-
tion that they were "submissionists" eager to do Washington's bidding,
the anti-nullifiers replied that it was their opponents, in fact, who were
the real submissionists, craven supplicants for British favor who would
have South Carolina "throw herself into the arms of her old step mother,
beg forgiveness and promise to be a good child."[39]

Finally, it should be added that Great Britain played on the minds of South Carolina citizens on both sides of the issue for another reason, one that had little to do with the tariff itself. In recent years the British antislavery movement had emerged as one of the dominant forces in parliamentary politics, and in the early 1830s was on the verge of achieving its long-sought objective: the emancipation of 800,000 West Indian slaves. Historian William Freehling has argued that the rising antislavery clamor in the United States provided an important backstory to the nullification crisis. States' rights ultras, he maintains, were prepared to defy Washington over the tariff because they saw the controversy as a test of the federal government's indifference to Southern concerns. Robert Turnbull, for example, an early propagandist for the nullifier cause, warned in a series of essays in 1827 that the same arguments used to broaden federal authority on matters of trade could also be used to attack the institution of slavery.[40]

Yet Palmetto State radicals who flirted with the idea of secession were well aware that such a drastic step would not inoculate them from the antislavery virus. Indeed, some slaveholders wondered if South Carolina might be more susceptible to antislavery pressures as an independent nation. As Parliament inched closer toward emancipation, speculation that Great Britain would compel the Palmetto State to free its own slaves as the price of its intercession became a familiar argument in the anti-nullification campaign. Here was yet another reason to fear the British, unionists insisted. Far from safeguarding slavery, secession would actually threaten it, resulting in the "servile war and desolation" that Southern whites dreaded most.[41]

In Washington, meanwhile, tensions over the tariff were ramped up by the approaching 1832 election. The congressional debates over the issue revealed the extent to which a political culture now firmly planted in the public sphere had transformed the debate over the nation's tariff policy. Protectionist leaders scrupulously avoided any praise of "the British example," preferring to thunder against foreign interference in American affairs. Anxious to establish their Anglophobic bona fides, they accused Great Britain of waging a "war of extermination" against domestic manufacturing, denouncing free trade as a plot designed "to exhaust our resources and swell her wealth."[42] Echoing the concerns of Southern moderates, Northern statesmen painted a grim picture of the British lion ready to pounce at the first signs of disunity exhibited by the United States.[43] Having learned from experience that it was politically unwise to defend protection by pointing to Britain's economic achievements, Henry Clay sought to burnish his credentials as a stalwart Anglophobe. Arguing that Britain's self-aggrandizing policies had changed little since the pre-Revolutionary period, Clay maintained that it was the unswerving and unalterable policy of the British government to reduce the republic to a state of colonial vassalage. "It is not free trade that they are recommending," he argued in defense of higher duties, but a policy that would lead "to the recolonization of these States, under the commercial dominion of Great Britain."[44]

South Carolina nullifiers regarded the 1832 tariff as little better than the one passed four years earlier. With no remedy in sight, Governor James Hamilton and his supporters now took matters into their own hands. Having built a formidable grassroots political organization, the nullifiers routed Palmetto unionists in the October elections to the state legislature. Hamilton promptly called a nullification convention to meet the following month. While the Washington Society continued to hold rallies to express its opposition to the proceedings in Columbia, the contest now shifted to a showdown between the nullifiers and the Jackson administration. As expected, the nullification convention took the fateful step states' rights hotspurs had been demanding since the outset, and declared the recent tariffs to be null and void. Fearing retaliation from Washington, the convention called for a volunteer army to be mustered in Charleston. The president, who had been monitoring events in South Carolina closely, wasted no time answering this challenge, and in January issued his famous Nullification Proclamation, declaring unequivocally his belief that no state had the right to usurp the sovereignty of the federal government. Warning against "a vile dependence on a foreign power," the president again urged the state's voters to reject disunion, making it clear that he regarded any attempt by South Carolina to defy federal law as an act of treason. Congress agreed, passing a "Force Bill" authorizing him to use whatever means necessary to break the Palmetto State's resistance.[45]

With the prospect of armed conflict looming, both sides suddenly began to cast about for a face-saving solution to the impasse. Clay and Calhoun (both now serving in the Senate), hastily brokered a compromise tariff. The new schedule offered only modest reductions initially, with the promise of more substantial cuts, to a 20 percent flat rate, within a decade. It hardly represented a victory for free trade principles, but the nullifiers were ready to grasp the congressional olive branch, preferring it to the executive sword. The Nullification Crisis, the first serious threat to the integrity of the Union, had come to an anticlimactic end.

Historians have tended to focus, understandably enough, on the Palmetto State controversy as a harbinger of the conflict that would rend the Union in 1861. In both cases, Great Britain, tied to the planter class by virtue of its insatiable appetite for raw cotton, lurked on the wings of the political stage, never playing a central role but always informing the thinking and arguments of the actors involved. During the Nullification Crisis, John Bull loomed especially large to a country that had yet to emerge as a continental power. Many Americans were quick to assume that Great Britain had a hand in provoking the crisis, or at the very least intended to profit from it by exploiting sectional tensions. Even when it became clear that these suspicions were unfounded, nullifiers and unionists alike continued to invoke the specter of foreign interference. They did so not only out of habit or for rhetorical effect; theirs was a relatively weak nation that still felt the gravitational pull of Britain's empire. Fifty years after the founding of the republic, Americans still looked to external factors to make sense of internal crises.

Free Trade Prevails

When the nation in 1837 plunged into a depression more severe and protracted than the one in 1819, a rash of factory closings and a sudden shortfall in federal revenues as a result of lower tariff receipts inevitably prompted renewed calls for higher duties. Whigs once again couched their appeals in terms of economic self determination. "Shall we madly cut asunder the great link of national independence forged by our protective policy, and place ourselves in a condition to be humbled . . . [by] the mandate of British power?" asked one Whig congressman.[46] Increasingly, Whig protectionists found allies among Democrats in the Mid-Atlantic states, most notably in Pennsylvania, where powerful coal and iron interests clamored loudly for legislative relief. President Tyler proved less helpful, twice vetoing tariff bills passed by the Whig-controlled Congress. In August 1842, however, the president reluctantly signed legislation that returned duties roughly to the levels established by the Tariff of 1832.

Protectionists had little time to savor the fruits of their victory. The Democrats would retake the White House two years later, electing a devout free-trader, James K. Polk. During the 1844 campaign, the candidate made a transparent effort to mollify protection-minded Democrats in the Northern states, issuing a public statement in which he took a deliberately vague stand in favor of a "judicious" tariff. But the Tennessean had no interest in bolstering the country's competitiveness in the manufacturing sector. Once in office, Polk called for sweeping reductions in the tariff schedule, a task he entrusted to treasury secretary Robert J. Walker. By year's end, Walker submitted his sweeping report on the tariff, which declared flatly: "Agriculture is our chief employment."[47]

Polk's commitment to lower duties was rooted in a Jeffersonian agrarian philosophy, but support for the measure increasingly had less to do with the virtues of a self-reliant yeomanry than with the changing dynamics of the international marketplace. By the 1840s, Western grain producers had taken note of the Anti-Corn Law League's efforts to end Parliament's hoary tradition of agricultural protection. The political pressure in London had come largely from manufacturers, who saw a twofold benefit to free trade. Repeal of the Corn Laws would reduce the cost of food for their workers at home, allowing them to keep wages low. Eyeing lucrative American markets, they also aimed to give Washington an incentive to relax its own tariff schedule. Food shortages brought on by the Irish potato famine lent a dramatic urgency to the repeal campaign, and in the spring of 1846 the Peel government abandoned the Corn Laws and opened up Britain's agricultural markets to foreign producers. Fortuitously, news of the historic decision reached Washington three days before debate on Walker's tariff bill began.[48]

Repeal of the Corn Laws did little to allay protectionist sentiment in the Northern states, however, and the bill embodying Walker's proposals elicited a predictable chorus of indignation from the Whig ranks. Eliminating protective duties would devastate the American economy, they maintained, just as the nation was recovering from the recent depression. It would deal a body blow to the nation's manufacturers, impoverish its workers, and send the bulk of its hard currency across the Atlantic to pay for British exports. In addition to these economic arguments, there were the usual objections that a low tariff would return Americans to a state of "colonial dependence" and dishonor the memory of their Revolutionary forbears. Whig leaders mocked "Sir Robert" Walker for his "spaniel-like" devotion to British interests and charged the Polk administration of colluding with Whitehall. The Democrats, they alleged, had entered into a secret agreement with the Peel government, offering a free trade tariff as its price to obtain British support for a resolution of territorial disputes, specifically the two nations' competing claims to the Pacific Northwest.[49]

More troubling from the Polk administration's standpoint was the increasingly vocal opposition of Northern Democrats. In the minds of many, the president had reneged on his campaign promise to support a "judicious" tariff. Their resentment was exacerbated by the fact that in recent months they had dutifully followed the party line on the administration's foreign policy agenda, and they grumbled that their loyalty had availed them nothing. The controversy over the tariff bill caused a rift within Polk's own cabinet. Vice President George Mifflin Dallas and Secretary of State James Buchanan were both Pennsylvanians, and believed their leadership of the Keystone State Democracy would be jeopardized by the administration's zealous pursuit of lower duties.

After countless modifications and some last-minute arm-twisting, the administration mustered barely enough votes for passage. In its final form the so-called Walker Tariff slashed duties on two of the most politically sensitive product groups, rail iron and cotton goods, from roughly 70 percent under the 1842 tariff, to 30 percent and 25 percent, respectively. The measure was not the free trade victory its critics claimed, for it imposed duties well above the generally recognized 20 percent minimum required to meet federal expenditures. Nonetheless, the bill marked a signal defeat for the advocates of protection, bringing to a close a three-decades-old trend toward higher duties.[50]

In the early nineteenth century, the campaign for a protective tariff derived much of its momentum from the widespread belief that economic independence from Great Britain had not yet been achieved. Although manufacturing interests certainly exploited this argument for their own advantage, there was nothing cynical about Hezekiah Niles's commitment to the goal of economic self-sufficiency. Before the republic could be a truly sovereign nation, he and other protectionists maintained, Americans would have to wean themselves away from their addiction to British-made goods, just as they would have to be cured of their penchant for British literature. That so many citizens, especially Southerners, were unable to see what protectionists took for granted—that the nation was impoverished by its commercial relationship with Great Britain—only bolstered their contention that Americans remained imprisoned by a colonial mindset.

And yet any policy that aimed to achieve parity with Britain was handicapped politically by the fact that protection carried with it the taint of emulation. It mattered not at all that Niles and other exponents of higher duties couched their arguments in explicitly anti-British terms. To vie with Britain in the global marketplace was to play by its rules, to compete in an arena it had designed. To critics, this was a posture which could only be seen as an admission of American inferiority. The argument that Clay's American System was in reality a British system in disguise spoke to a basic shibboleth of American political life: the need to repudiate any policy that bore the imprint of Great Britain.

Reflecting upon the achievements of his administration as his term of office drew to a close, James K. Polk in his last annual message to Congress ventured an opinion on the competing economic philosophies which had been the source of so much bitter partisan strife for more than a quarter of a century. The salutary condition of the American economy, the president averred, was due in no small part to the fact that he and others of his party had rejected British models. He then proceeded to pronounce the demise of the American System, whose architects, he maintained, had for so long sought to keep political and economic power in the hands of a privileged few. The Tennessean left no doubt that he was happy to leave office having thwarted those who sought to reconstruct American society "upon the European plan."[51]

Polk's autopsy would prove to be premature. Lying moribund for the next twelve years, the doctrines of economic nationalism would be exhumed by the Republican Party in 1860. Lincoln's victory would signal the onset of a new era of protectionism, one that would continue unchecked until the early 1900s. But while the tariff issue would periodically reemerge as a source of political discord, it would never again take on the character of a battle royal as it had during the Jacksonian era. No doubt the passions that the tariff initially aroused stemmed in part from Southern anxieties of encroaching federal power. At the same time, however, Americans on both sides of the debate during the early decades of the nineteenth century did not see the tariff strictly as an economic matter, or a constitutional one. Rather, the tariff issue spoke directly to a fundamental question, as yet unresolved. Should the republic strive to imitate the economic systems of the nation that had given birth to it, or pursue a wholly different course?

Americans would have many more opportunities to ask themselves that question. The Walker Tariff had dealt a major blow to the principle of protection, but the reduction of duties could not arrest the pace of industrial and urban growth in the United States. Their agrarian world was fast receding, giving way to a more mechanized and increasingly impersonal marketplace. Regardless of the policy directives emanating from Washington, the nation with each passing year seemed to be moving inexorably along a path that very much resembled the one marked out by Great Britain.

❖ 7 ❖

The Money Power of England

Hard times, hard times, is all the cry,
The country's in confusion,
The banks have stopped—but still they try
To mystify delusion.
They give us trash, and keep their cash,
To send across the waters,
To pay for things they've bought of kings
To gull our sons and daughters.
— Democratic campaign song, 1844

When Hezekiah Niles and other economic nationalists offered the hopeful prediction that the United States would one day rival Britain as an industrial giant, they described a future that some Americans could only regard with unmixed horror. To old school Jeffersonians, the republic owed its success to its self-reliant yeomanry, who tilled the land, harvested their crops, and sought no assistance from the government. In their view, the republican nation-state had been conceived, born, and nurtured in a pastoral world; it could not properly thrive in any other environment. An industrial society might compete with Great Britain in the global marketplace, but at an unacceptable cost: the concentration of wealth in the hands of a few. Only a nation devoted exclusively to agricultural pursuits could foster the broad distribution of economic and political power that was the sine qua non of republican government.

In time, most Jeffersonian republicans managed to make their peace with the new economic order. Even Jefferson himself came to appreciate the value of domestic industry, as did his successor in the presidential chair, James Madison. Both men, too, having opposed Federalist efforts to strengthen the national government as leaders of the minority party, took a decidedly more flexible position on the issue of federal power once in office. But a cohort of doctrinaires refused to give ground on either point, branding as heresy any deviation from the principles of classical republicanism. Even as the party of Jefferson dominated the political landscape after 1800, a group of Republican ultras continued to sound the alarm against encroaching federal authority.

One of the more articulate voices of this laissez-faire philosophy was John Taylor of Caroline. Born in Caroline County, Virginia, in 1753, Taylor was a successful lawyer and gentleman farmer. An intellectual who had little taste for the rough-and-tumble world of politics, he served only one term in the U.S. Senate, though he would later consent to return to that chamber for two brief stints to complete the terms of incumbents who had died in office. Reluctant to give up the comfort and tranquility of Hazenwood, his tobacco plantation on the banks of the Rappahannock River, Taylor nonetheless kept a watchful eye on the goings-on in the nation's capital. An active correspondent and essayist, he would produce a sizable and influential body of work, all of it premised on a central theme: that a weak national government was the key to a strong republic.[1]

Like many of his generation, Taylor looked across the Atlantic and saw a world of inequality, decadence, and corruption. In Britain, a landed nobility historically held sway over Parliament, although in recent years its power had been challenged by manufacturers, who too sought the favor of the national government. Over time, the privileges accorded both groups had become woven into the fabric of the political order, perpetuated and protected by Parliament itself. Private interests had become indistinguishable from the public trust, rendering the government, in Taylor's view, little more than a plutocracy dedicated to the fleecing of the people.[2]

This gloomy scene stood in stark contrast to the Edenic wholesomeness of Taylor's beloved republic. But though an ocean separated the two nations, the Virginia patrician remained vigilant, ever fearful that the New World might succumb to the vices of the Old. Echoing the views of American writers in the belles lettres who insisted that the United States must free itself from all British forms and traditions, Taylor warned that political independence alone could not guarantee the success of the republican experiment, for there were many Americans who had never reconciled themselves to a separation from the Crown.[3] Fiercely opposed to efforts to broaden the powers of the national government, Taylor regarded the Federalists as little more than monarchists still loyal to the colonial ancien regime, men committed to the goal of secretly subverting the republican ideal. Even their eclipse after 1815 offered little comfort to Taylor, who regarded the party's disappearance following the Hartford Convention as a tactical retreat for the party of Hamilton and Adams, rather than its final demise.[4]

Despite the broad political consensus that seemed to characterize the "Era of Good Feeling," the postwar years were unhappy ones for Taylor. Especially troubling was the ascendancy of a manufacturing interest closely resembling that of Great Britain. Taylor insisted that he was not opposed to non-agricultural wealth per se, but to business leaders' unceasing demands for privileges and concessions. Since these were special favors that only the nation's lawmakers could provide, their greed would set in motion a process that would inevitably result in the steady expansion of federal power.[5] Not surprisingly, this republican of the old school regarded with no little anxiety the rising clamor for higher tariffs to protect infant industries. Alarmed by the congressional debates over the 1819 Baldwin Bill, Taylor took pen in hand to write *Tyranny Unmasked* (1822), one of the most important treatises of the strict constructionist gospel. The brief volume chided the bill's supporters for their desire to perpetuate a British system of political economy, in which the interests of public and private power had become one and the same. Although pro-tariff lawmakers claimed to hold no fondness for British opinions, Taylor argued that in advocating protection for manufactures they were recommending nothing less than "an imitation of the British nation."[6]

Regarding his republic as unspoiled and pure, Taylor was deeply troubled that Americans might succumb to foreign snares, a fear that found frequent expression in metaphors of sexual violation. The efforts of a monied elite to recharter the national bank, Taylor insisted in 1814, constituted "an invasion of the national chastity." On the subject of the tariff, the Virginian believed that the advocates of protection had become so infatuated with the British system, so smitten by Parliament's ability to produce revenue by burdening its people with crushing taxes, that they were willing to divorce "the healthy and chaste country girl" in favor of a diseased, "painted courtezan." The gendered language Taylor employed to convey the image of a feminine republic in peril bespoke his belief in the exceedingly fragile, vulnerable nature of American institutions. Emphasizing the danger of insidious, vestigial British influences, rather than a direct threat from Great Britain itself, Taylor's apprehensions were heightened by the unhappy realization that the purity of republican values had to some extent already been compromised. The young republic was being seduced by the corrupting temptations of the new economic order; once deflowered, its virtue could never be redeemed.[7]

Taylor's concerns had no place in the future envisioned by Baltimore

newspaperman Hezekiah Niles, who had spent his career as the cheer-
leader for domestic manufacturing. His brand of republicanism was
rooted in the agrarian culture of the eighteenth century; Niles, by contrast, never doubted that the Jeffersonian ideology could adapt and thrive
in a modern economic environment. And yet the two men shared one
organizing principle: both viewed Great Britain and its lingering influence over its former colonies as the great bane of the American republic.
It was a danger they perceived in diametrically opposite ways. For the
bourgeois newspaperman, the nation required only the protective armor of high tariffs to compete successfully against British manufactures
and create prosperity for all. Taylor, on the other hand, saw in a policy of
higher duties a massive concession to the manufacturing interest, which
would lead to the rise of a corrupt, British system of government. And
while Niles saw the principal threat to the nation in the rapacious policies of Parliament, Taylor feared a more insidious danger: the corrosive
Tory doctrines of old, which would continue to weaken the body politic
from within.

One might be tempted to dismiss Taylor as a rigid antiquarian, out
of step and largely irrelevant to changing times, and so he was regarded
by many of his contemporaries. And yet, obdurate reactionary though
he was, Taylor possessed the acuity of an observer who, standing still as
others rush madly by, grasped the larger implications of the forces his
nation was experiencing. Taylor sensed far better than most Americans
that the rise of an industrial economy would alter profoundly the delicate balance that existed between public and private power. Augment-
ing the Virginia planter's sense of foreboding was his belief that such a
future would have especially dire consequences for the South. For while
Hezekiel Niles confidently predicted the emergence of an economic giant that would produce untold wealth for every American citizen, Taylor
saw the destruction of the American pastoral idyll, the only world he
knew.

Wealth and Avarice in the New Marketplace

One did not need to subscribe to Taylor's brand of paleo-republicanism
to be concerned by the scope and speed of economic change. The nation
was clearly moving into uncharted terrain as a more complex capitalist
economy shifted into high gear. Rapid urbanization, the factory system,
and a transportation network of canals and roads connecting Western
farms with Eastern markets were all part of a new economic order that
left many Americans disoriented and longing for a less frenetic pace of
life. "This world is going on too fast," observed the New York merchant

Philip Hone. "Railroads, steamers, packets, race against time and beat it hollow. . . . Oh, for the good old days of heavy post-coaches and speed at the rate of six miles an hour!"[8] Inevitably, these modernizing trends brought social dislocations in their wake. And, just as inevitably, they gave rise to new concerns that the nation was following a pattern of economic development already well-established across the Atlantic. Left untended, the American Eden would soon be overrun by noxious weeds of foreign genus.

One of the most distressing aspects of the new economic order was the spirit of acquisitiveness that permeated every segment of American society. For a nation founded on the principles of civic virtue, it was no easy matter coming to grips with the fact that Americans en masse seemed to be abandoning their responsibilities as citizens in favor of their own self-interest. Nonetheless, they deeply resented the reputation for crass materialism given to them by British observers, convinced that the "anxious pursuit of gain" stemmed from the national tendency to copy the behaviors of their transatlantic cousins. If Americans were a superficial people, given to ostentatious displays of wealth, then their "miserable and servile imitation of the English" was the cause. William Gilmore Simms decried "this wretched love of show, this absence of plain living," which seemed to be "hurrying us on, with gamester phrenzy," tempting Americans with new and false desires.[9]

If the contagion of avarice seemed to infect all classes, the emergence of an urban oligarchy brought home to Americans with special force the realization that the arcadian world they had known was slipping away. It was one of the ironies of the Jacksonian period that at a time in which white society embraced the principles of economic democracy and the rise of the so-called "common man," the gap between rich and poor grew visibly wider. Rapid economic expansion had created a new aristocracy, an urban upper class that seemed oblivious to the obligations of its social position. To many Americans, the new rich seemed to exhibit all the characteristics of Britain's titled nobility, aping its manners and demonstrating a like contempt for the laboring classes.[10]

Americans who felt the twinge of class resentment did not merely draw comparisons between the socioeconomic elites of the two countries. As earnest republicans, they hewed to the belief that aristocracy in all its forms was a foreign institution. The existence of a cosmopolitan beau monde was evidence that "a *regal* fungus" bearing all the hallmarks of an Old World ruling class had taken hold and was slowly eroding the principles upon which the country had been founded.[11] The disparity of wealth and income was nothing less than "a germ of English growth transplanted here by some foreign monarchists," Jacksonians maintained.[12] Contributing to these suspicions was the widely held belief that American commercial and financial elites were in league with monopolists and fund-mongers across the Atlantic. British banking and mercantile firms all had agents in the United States who had grown rich through their overseas business connections. Unseemly displays of luxury and affectation by the titans of commerce and banking would have rankled republican sensibilities under any circumstances. But such behavior seemed all the more deplorable because it bore the unmistakable imprint of British collusion, of wealth attained by dishonest means. In the minds of many stalwart democrats, the nation's traditional enemy had, in effect, subsidized a new ruling elite, which did not share the true interests and sympathies of Americans.[13]

No segment of the workforce felt more threatened by the currents of economic change than the artisan class. As much a part of the republican tradition as the yeoman farmer who tilled the soil, the skilled laborer took pride in his status as an independent producer. He also found satisfaction in the fellowship of his craft, a well-ordered world in which masters, journeymen, and apprentices worked and lived together in an atmosphere of respectful familiarity. With the advent of a more competitive marketplace, however, these preindustrial traditions quickly dissolved, to be replaced by a more impersonal set of employer-employee relations. As masters with access to capital became entrepreneurs, they began to see the labor of their workers as a commodity and implemented new technologies and production techniques that would reduce journeymen to semi-skilled or unskilled wage-earners. Faced with lower wages and declining status, journeymen sought protection in craft unions, as well as in short-lived political parties that hovered at the margins of the two-party system. And, like all citizens of the republic, they saw themselves as the heirs of the Sons of '76. Tailoring the language of liberation to the labor struggle, American workers stood ready to "claim by the blood of our fathers, shed on the battlefields in the war of the revolution, the rights of American freemen."[14]

It should be stressed that the early American labor movement did not seek legitimacy on the basis of its patriotic credentials alone. With so many disaffected artisans on the other side of the Atlantic, it was only natural that workingmen's groups should see their struggle in broader, international terms. Indeed, the push for workers' rights in American cities was not unlike other social and cultural movements that took their cues from abroad. Several of the most prominent leaders in Eastern cities were British expatriates. Some, infused with the radical free thought ideology of the Enlightenment, enshrined Tom Paine as the movement's patron saint and commingled with an assortment of British reformers, including Frances Wright and Robert Owen. Working-class newspapers in Eastern cities reprinted articles from their transatlantic counterparts, such as the *Northern Star*, keeping their readers abreast of trade union developments and the campaign for greater political representation in Britain.[15]

These overseas connections did not prevent American workers from invoking historic rivalries when it suited their purposes, however. Such was the case when two Philadelphia laborers were fired by a lamp manufacturer for refusing to sign a no-strike agreement in 1834. The pair appealed to the local Democratic Party for redress, which promptly issued a list of resolves to rebuke the employer for his "English principles." The manufacturer's labor policies, party ward leaders averred, were more akin to "British factory habits" than American ones.[16] Labor disputes inevitably acquired a geopolitical dimension if the employer had the misfortune to be foreign-born. When Bowery theater manager Thomas Hamblin dismissed an American member of his company, D. D. McKinney, in 1833, the journeyman actor took his case to Tammany Hall, which publicly denounced Hamblin's "despotic, aristocratic and unprincipled" conduct as "degrading" to the American character. Hamblin refused to reconsider his decision, and McKinney was obliged to find employment at the rival Park Theatre. (The American actor may have won a belated revenge; when the riot against British stage manager George Farren erupted the following summer, McKinney was rumored to be a ringleader.)[17]

Employers, not surprisingly, were just as quick to geopoliticize class tensions. In casting blame for labor unrest on the foreign-born, they aimed to brand working-class discontent as un-American, accusing strikers of "aping the degenerate practices of English operatives."[18] When a series of strikes gripped New York City in 1836, a worried Gotham business community attributed the trouble to militant tradesmen newly arrived from England. Following a walkout by local tailors that led to the arrest on conspiracy charges of twenty journeymen, the presiding judge offered the opinion that labor combinations were organized by and for the benefit of foreigners, despite the fact that most of the defendants in the case were Americans. That same year, a Gotham newspaper publisher complained that a typesetters' strike had been orchestrated by British immigrants; even the native-born workers who had taken part in the work stoppage, he maintained, had been "led astray by the wicked English radical spirit which stimulated them to mischief."[19]

The most potent symbol of the new economic order, though it affected the lives of few Americans directly, was the factory system. This, too, was for Americans a distinctly foreign import. In recent years the

British factory had become the source of endless commentary in the United States, with newspapers publishing with undisguised satisfaction the findings of the Sadler Commission and other exposés into the oppressive conditions of Britain's factory operatives. Bristling at foreign criticism of their own country, citizens of the republic could at least take comfort from the fact that Britain's position as the workshop of the world had come at no small social cost.

Such views were so widely held that even some of the earliest pioneers of American manufacturing regarded Britain's industrial experience less as a "splendid example" than as a cautionary one. When Francis Cabot Lowell and his cousin, Nathan Appleton, opened the nation's first textile factory in Waltham, Massachusetts, in 1813, they set about to create a work environment unlike anything seen in Britain. Both men had recently crossed the Atlantic on fact-finding tours of the textile industry, and were appalled by the human misery they observed in Lancashire's mill towns. Appleton blamed not only the factory system but the inequality rooted in British society, which he would later describe as "the most stupendous and ingeniously devised system of fraud and oppression ever invented," a system made all the more abhorrent because it was conducted under the "guise of freedom."[20] The two Massachusetts entrepreneurs devised a new approach to industrial labor, which relied on farm girls as factory operatives, who signed short-term labor contracts and were housed in clean, well-run boarding houses.

Sadly, the Lowell experiment proved to be not only unique, but short-lived.[21] Working conditions at the Waltham mills soon deteriorated, and the factory towns that dotted the New England landscape eventually came to resemble their European counterparts. By the 1830s, handloom weavers from the British Isles began to replace the mill girls of Lowell. Native-born textile workers resented the new arrivals, whom they regarded as too uneducated to stand up for their rights, too eager to submit to the demands of management. Labor leaders complained that the local press was happy to join in the general condemnation of the British industrial system, never failing to publish heart-rending accounts of its squalid factories, but turned a blind eye to the deteriorating conditions in the New England mills. By the mid-1840s, delegates to the General Trades' Union's national convention would report that the workers at Lowell had been reduced to a state of "wretchedness, disease and misery" identical to that of Britain's factory operatives.[22]

The situation was somewhat different in Philadelphia, where a burgeoning complex of manufactories had been attracting immigrants from the British Isles since the 1820s. Textile entrepreneurs exhibited considerably less anxiety than Appleton and Lowell about modeling the British experience, and by the end of the decade the area along the Schuylkill River a few miles north of the city was being hailed by local boosters as "the Manchester of Manayunk." Mill workers would certainly have found the comparison an appropriate one, though for different reasons. Already familiar with the human costs of the factory system, having been displaced by technological innovation at home, they encountered a work environment little better than the one they had left behind. Although Pennsylvania mill operatives received higher wages than in Britain, they worked more hours and under more oppressive conditions, especially after Parliament passed the Factory Acts of 1833 and 1844. As in the craft labor movement, some of the more prominent organizers of Philadelphia's factory workers were recent transplants from the British Isles, products of a well-established tradition of working-class radicalism. As a result, labor unrest in the area bore a marked resemblance to the kind of working-class agitation long seen in the industrial centers of Britain. Anger over wage reductions led to strikes that shut down the Schuylkill River textile mills in 1833 and 1834, followed by an area-wide general strike in 1835, in which 20,000 wage earners demanded a ten-hour workday. Though still in its infancy, the American industrial experience was well on its way to replicating Britain's "dark satanic mills."[23]

Thus, the stirrings of an early American labor movement operated on two distinct planes, one rooted in the republicanism of independent producers, the other in a proletarian mentality nourished in the mill towns of the Midlands. Looming large in both strains of thought was Great Britain, a reference point that allowed skilled artisans and factory operatives alike to measure their own sense of economic alienation. Whether casting employers as imperious aristocrats or drawing attention to the abominable working conditions of the factory, American wage-earners looked to Britain for an organizing trope that could be used to give meaning to a wide array of anxieties. Simply put, it was impossible to think of the challenges labor faced in the new economic order without thinking of the nation that had come to symbolize the inequality between rich and poor. The American working class was far too disparate a group to think or act with any semblance of solidarity, but on one point there existed complete agreement: that an "English system with English misery and English degradation" should never be allowed to take root in the United States.[24]

Banks and Capital

Whatever citizens of the republic may have thought about the breakneck pace of economic development during the early national period, there could be no denying that the engine that drove American commerce was British capital. In recent years a handful of merchant banks headquartered in London and Liverpool had come to dominate the transatlantic economy, creating a vast, sophisticated financial network that made the mercantile relationships of the colonial era seem primitive by comparison. Baring Brothers and half a dozen other British firms provided the credit and financial services that enabled American agricultural producers to find a ready market for their crops in Europe. With agents in cities along the Atlantic and Gulf coasts, they purchased cotton from factorage houses or on consignment for sale in Liverpool. On occasion, they operated as commodities traders, speculating in cotton, wheat, and other goods on their own account. They served as purchasing agents for American importing firms, buying not only British textiles but goods from the European continent and Asia for the American market. The solid reputation for probity which these merchant banks enjoyed was such that their bills of exchange served as legal tender in any port in North America (and, for that matter, the world). Nor were their functions limited strictly to mercantile transactions. By the 1830s, British banking houses saw in the United States a highly attractive area for long-term capital investment. The success of New York's Erie Canal had sparked a transportation boom, creating a demand for capital that far exceeded the resources of American financial institutions. British bankers were only too happy to step into the breach, underwriting bond issues for states eager to begin their own turnpike, canal, and railway construction projects. In addition to marketing these securities to investors in Britain and Europe, they also invested directly in American corporations engaged in building the young republic's transportation infrastructure. Washington politicians might argue bitterly over the federal government's proper role in the marketplace, but the most important decisions determining the pace of American economic growth had already been made, not in the nation's capital but in the banking houses of London.[25]

Americans' easy access to British capital was not without its drawbacks. While foreign merchant banks did much to stimulate economic development, interruptions in the availability of credit during times of uncertainty often had ruinous consequences for American borrowers. This in turn contributed to a boom-and-bust business cycle in which periods of boundless optimism were invariably followed by periods of acute despair. By extending easy credit terms to American importers, British merchant banks helped to create a serious trade deficit (averaging $26 million annually during the 1830s), owed in specie.[26] Critics grumbled, too, that the expansion of credit only served to stimulate the American appetite for British goods, turning simple republicans into avid consumers of "foreign gewgaws."[27] Some argued that the ease with which British goods could be purchased on credit acted as a far greater impediment to fledgling American industries than lower tariffs. What was more, the expansion of the paper money supply drove up prices, making American products less desirable on the foreign market. Perhaps the most serious problem stemming from the availability of British capital was the spending frenzy it generated among state governments, which were eager to approve even the most dubious transportation schemes. The profligate spending of several states left them deeply in debt, a situation that would have serious repercussions when the economy stalled in the late 1830s.[28]

No less important than these very real problems was the visceral unease which many Americans felt toward the international banking system. In the span of a few short years it had come to completely dominate the global economic landscape, a vast, complex machine that determined the price of goods and the cost of credit and influenced the livelihoods of untold millions. Yet it was a machine that most Americans only dimly understood, and as a result offered a ready target for those who regarded with growing concern the market forces that were rapidly reshaping American life. In bad economic times, hostility toward England's "money power" bordered on hysteria. Indeed, there were few crises either at home or abroad that could not be traced to London banks, whose lack of transparency fueled wild speculation regarding their ability to control events. New York editor and essayist Parke Godwin raged at the thought of a "handful of men, gathered in a back parlor of the Bank of England," with the power to "paralyze the industry of millions."[29] Missouri senator Thomas Hart Benton was no less fervent in denouncing the British lords of finance, whom he regarded as a cabal that had caused "rahjahs and sultans" to tumble "from their thrones."[30] In this regard, the political debates on the banking question took on an even more frenzied tone than those over the tariff. The determined zeal of free-traders and protectionists notwithstanding, the debate over import duties was a simple one, the merits of which could be readily understood and argued by manufacturers, laborers, and consumers alike. Opposition to the international banking system, on the other hand, was often infused with an exaggerated sense of menace that owed much to the fact that it was for many Americans an inscrutable institution, its Rosicrucian mysteries hidden to all but a select few.

Dominating the international securities market, Great Britain figured prominently in the protracted debate over centralized banking in the United States. To what extent the federal government should involve itself in the fiscal affairs of the nation—or whether it should do so at all—was arguably the most polarizing political question of the early republic period. When Alexander Hamilton first broached the idea of a national bank in 1791, he sparked a debate over federal monetary policy that would not be resolved with any degree of permanence until the Polk administration more than half a century later. Although Thomas Jefferson, the institution's most formidable early critic, was eventually persuaded by his secretary of the treasury, Albert Gallatin, that a national bank could serve a useful purpose, republican reservations persisted. This was due in part to the fact that the institution's privately held stock (approximately four-fifths of its total capital) gradually passed from American into foreign (primarily British) hands. Although the charter for the Bank of the United States prohibited foreign stockholders from exercising the same privileges as Americans, such as voting for the institution's board of directors, critics remained dubious that the Bank was free of foreign influence. So great was the authority of Threadneedle and Lombard Streets in American banking circles, they argued, that it would be a simple matter to secure the appointment to the board of "tories, or monarchists" to serve as the pliant tools of the British financial world.[31]

Despite being rechartered after the War of 1812, the Bank remained unpopular in many quarters. Republicans of the old school, like John Taylor of Caroline, were rabidly opposed to any institution that blurred the line between the private sector and federal authority. State banking interests, meanwhile, deeply resented the Bank's regulatory functions and the competitive advantages which it enjoyed as the nation's most powerful financial institution. Western land speculators disapproved of the Bank's tight-fisted credit policies, which they blamed for the collapse of land prices in 1819, precipitating a nationwide depression. But whether this hostility stemmed from political conviction, self-interest, or a combination of these and other factors, the Bank's foreign associations called into question the very Americanness of the institution. Although British interference in its operations did not constitute the only indictment against the Bank, it was an issue around which all critics of the institution could unite.

Opponents of the B.U.S drew from a wealth of literature to buttress their argument that its continued existence was detrimental to sound republican principles. Among the most influential were the writings of hard-money proponent William Gouge, who viewed with distrust not just the Bank of the United States but all banks. In *A Short History of Paper Money*, Gouge argued that the credit-based economy was unreliable and of benefit only to a monied aristocracy. In granting exclusive privileges to banks and other corporations, the government created a ruling class no less avaricious and powerful than the titled nobility of the Old

World. With every passing year, Gouge warned, such a system would en-
rich the few while impoverishing the many, creating a social order that
would ultimately be indistinguishable from that which existed in Great
Britain.[32]

The controversy over the Bank would come to a head during the
Jackson administration. Exactly when the president turned against the
Bank, and, more importantly, why he did so, is by no means clear. Wary
of banks to begin with, having lost a fortune of his own in the 1790s,
Jackson early in his presidency expressed doubts about the constitutionality of the Bank and misgivings about its political influence. In the summer of 1830, the director of the Bank's regional office in Nashville met
with the president and found him "well satisfied" with the management
of the institution, though Jackson expressed concern that so much of
its stock was held by foreigners.[33] During his first term, Jackson seems
to have entertained the possibility of reforming the Bank, but his opposition stiffened when its president, Nicholas Biddle, applied for an
early renewal of its charter in 1832, an election year. With the backing
of presidential hopeful Henry Clay, Biddle intended to make recharter
an issue in the upcoming campaign. Jackson's early reservations about
the Bank now gave way to a fierce determination to crush the institution completely. Clearly, political motives as much as fiscal ones guided
Jackson's decision. For the combative president, the contest quickly took
on the character of a titanic struggle, in which he saw himself as the
people's champion doing battle against powerful monied interests.

Although Biddle had substantial support in Congress, the more important battle—the one for public opinion—would ultimately be won
by the administration. Like the rough-hewn president, many Americans
were already inclined to regard the Philadelphia bank as a symbol of
aristocratic privilege. The Jacksonians skillfully exploited these suspicions, and to this end made much of the Bank's British connections.
During the course of the recharter debates in Congress, Thomas Hart
Benton introduced a motion to exclude foreigners from holding stock
in the Bank, and begged his Senate colleagues to consider whether they
wished to surrender the finances of the government to a group of "Lords
and ladies . . . knights and barons; military officers; reverend clergymen
and country squires."[34] Could anyone doubt, Benton asked, that such
individuals could be indifferent to the outcome of the pending presidential election, when the incumbent was the very man whose victory
at New Orleans in 1815 represented "the most signal defeat the arms of
England ever sustained?"[35] The fact that the stockholders of the B.U.S.—
a public institution—remained anonymous, unknown even to members
of Congress, only fueled unfavorable speculation about the Bank's ac-

tivities, prompting Jacksonians to draw the inevitable parallels with the Revolutionary generation's struggle against earlier forms of tyranny and "foreign thralldom."[36]

All this seemed perfectly ludicrous to the Bank's many supporters, who responded with patriotic bravado of their own. "If we are not afraid of an Englishman with a loaded musket," declared one pro-Bank citizens' group, "we will hardly fear him with his pockets full of money."[37] They were especially vigorous in rejecting the argument that British stockholders were in any position to manipulate the B.U.S. For all the rhetoric that British influence would again reduce the country to colonial status, foreign investment in the institution had actually declined since 1811—from three-fourths of the first Bank's capital to approximately one-fifth during the Jackson administration two decades later. To some scholars, this fact is reason enough to accuse Jackson of mounting a deliberate campaign of misinformation. Economic historian Bray Hammond, for example, has judged the president's veto message "absurd," deriding its anti-British tenor as an attempt "to impress the ignorant."[38]

Yet Jackson's apprehensions were nothing if not consistent with a deeply ingrained Anglophobia that had been an ever-present feature of his public career. In railing against foreign influence, Jackson was repeating the mantras of his forebears, nostrums that resonated all the more powerfully as the nation experienced wrenching social changes that neither the president nor his supporters seemed to fully comprehend. No doubt the recent furor over nullification, and the widespread accusations that British influence had been brought to bear on the hotspurs of South Carolina, contributed to the president's perception that the Bank of the United States had indeed been shanghaied by the lords of Lombard and Threadneedle Streets. Jackson's opposition to a central bank on the grounds that it might fall under the sway of foreign stockholders was hardly cynical fear-mongering. Rather, it revealed his almost pathological suspicion of British power, and his willingness to believe that other Americans—namely, those who opposed him—could be swayed to act on its behalf. "Never was a man so beset with plots and conspiracies as our venerable ex-president," one senator snickered, soon after Old Hickory left office. But if Jackson was susceptible to exaggerated and imaginary dangers, it was a mindset he shared with a great many Americans.[39]

In the summer of 1832, Congress defied the administration and voted to extend the institution's charter, prompting Jackson to veto the bill, on the grounds that the Bank was unconstitutional. The president's veto message, generally attributed to the pen of Jackson confidante Amos

Kendall, revisited familiar fears of British influence. Kendall's initial veto message was peppered with anti-British rhetoric, although subsequent drafts of the state paper replaced specific references to the British with the more ambiguous "foreigner," which appeared no less than fourteen times. Whatever cognomen Jackson employed, there was little doubt in the president's mind that British stockholders exercised undue influence, either directly or indirectly, over the institution. "Controlling our currency, receiving our public moneys, and holding thousands of our citizens in dependence," a national bank, he argued, would be more formidable and more dangerous than Britain's military power. "If we must have a bank with private stockholders," the president urged, let it be "*purely American.*"[40]

Despite the president's veto and subsequent victory in the 1832 campaign, the Bank's contract had not yet expired, and it continued to conduct business more or less as usual. Worried that the next Congress might override his veto, Jackson resolved to bring down the Bank without further delay, striking at the very heart of the institution's power by removing the funds of the federal government. Henceforth, federal revenues would be deposited at selected state banks, while existing deposits would be withdrawn from the B.U.S. as needed to meet the government's expenditures. As the Bank's currency reserves dwindled, a desperate Biddle began to call in outstanding loans and negotiate new lines of credit with British banking houses. His efforts only served to incense his critics, who pointed to the actions of the B.U.S. as evidence that the institution did indeed exercise an unhealthy degree of control over the nation's economy. The president's point man on the House Ways and Means Committee, James K. Polk, was especially shocked to learn that Biddle, unable to cover a sudden and unexpected withdrawal of funds by the federal government, had dispatched a "secret agent" to London to negotiate a special loan with a British banking house. The transaction had been made without the knowledge of the Treasury Department— proof positive, Polk claimed, of the Bank's utter disregard for the charter under which it operated.[41]

The president's victory proved to be a Pyrrhic one. Although the "Bank War" was over, the Jacksonians' feud with Biddle would simmer for several more years. The Philadelphia banker promptly applied for a new banking charter in his home state, and in 1836 resumed banking operations as president of the United States' Bank of Pennsylvania. Democrats seethed as Biddle not only refused to cancel the outstanding B.U.S. notes in circulation, but continued to reissue the original institution's paper long after its banking privileges had been revoked. The new bank proceeded to establish branch banks in other states, quickly taking on the monopolistic character that had made the old B.U.S. a Jacksonian bête noire.

More importantly, Jackson and his supporters failed to understand that Biddle's financial institution was only a symbol of the larger market forces they feared. In what would prove to be a supreme irony, the Democrats had eliminated the one institution in the United States with the ability to help finance the growing demand for canals, railroads, and other improvements. State governments in need of credit were now obliged to market their securities with the assistance of Baring Brothers and other foreign lenders. Jackson may have killed Biddle's "monster," but the country remained more dependent on capital from abroad than ever before.

Hard Times: 1837–1843

As Andrew Jackson stepped down from office in the spring of 1837, Eastern cities began to experience a rash of bank failures and factory closings, which would soon escalate into the most serious economic crisis the nation had yet faced. In the months that followed, the full extent of American dependence on foreign capital would become apparent.[42] Although historians differ as to what impact the fiscal policies of the Jackson administration may have played in the Panic of 1837, there is general agreement that the principal catalyst of the so-called "derangement" of the nation's finances was to be found abroad. In the summer of 1836, the Bank of England, alarmed by the depletion of its gold reserves, twice raised its discount rate and restricted credit to British banks doing business in the United States.[43] The republic had enjoyed unprecedented economic growth throughout the decade, a boom that was financed largely by the expansion of foreign credit. The effects of the sudden contraction of the specie supply were severe and immediate. The price of cotton, the lynchpin of the American economy, fell 25 percent in a matter of weeks, spelling ruin for merchants and brokers in New Orleans and New York. Banks in those cities suspended specie payments, and financial institutions across the country quickly followed suit. This in turn led to a drop in factory orders, resulting in widespread unemployment in Eastern cities.[44]

At first, the panic appeared to be only a momentary economic downturn. Once its specie reserves had been replenished, the Bank of England restored liberal credit terms to merchant banking houses in that country, which did the same with their customers across the Atlantic. The American economy quickly revived, allowing state banks to once again resume specie payments. But in 1839 the hard times returned with a vengeance. A bad wheat harvest in Britain necessitated an increase in grain imports, causing the Bank of England to once again restrict credit to stanch the flow of capital out of the country. This, combined with a drop in cotton prices owing to a bumper crop in the United States, spelled disaster for all who had borrowed money on the assumption that the price for the commodity would continue to rise, as it had done for several years. Once again, banks refused to redeem their notes in specie. In the absence of additional foreign capital, the long-term construction projects authorized by several states ground to a halt.

The Whigs seized on the crisis as evidence of the folly of the Democrats' fiscal policies in general, and the recent campaign to destroy the Bank of the United States in particular. This time, however, it was clear they had learned a valuable lesson from the bruising B.U.S. recharter battle. In order to deflect the charge that they were colleagued with British capitalists, they cast Nicholas Biddle's institution as a bulwark of American financial independence, the destruction of which had surrendered the nation to the avaricious clutches of British imperialism. Co-opting the Jacksonian demonology that had become so familiar to Americans, Henry Clay pointed to the Bank of England as the real hydra of corruption, insisting that it was actually the Democrats who had "thrown us into the jaws of a foreign monster which we can neither cage nor control." He declared: "You tore from us our best shield against the Bank of England, and now profess to be surprised at the influence which it exercises upon our interests."[45] A national bank would not only foster economic independence, Whigs argued, but would provide the credit American business interests needed to compete successfully in the global marketplace, without which the "great bulk of the commerce of the world would fall at once into the arms, and its profits into the lap, of our great rival."[46]

At first the Democrats turned to a ready and familiar target, heaping no small measure of abuse on Nicholas Biddle as the principal culprit for the collapse. The standoff between Jackson and Biddle was still fresh in the public mind, and the B.U.S. had been singled out for blame during sudden contractions of the money supply in the past. Though not everyone in the administration was hostile to Biddle—he had close friends within Van Buren's cabinet—the party propaganda machine soon settled into its customary role of "appealing to public prejudice against the Bank."[47] The *Washington Globe* kept up a withering attack against the institution, accusing its president of manipulating the crisis to win popular support in an effort to regain its position as the official bank of the federal government.[48]

But it soon became clear that the financial panics of the late 1830s, so plainly rooted in the disruption of international specie flows, could not be laid at the door of Biddle's Chestnut Street bank alone. From the outset, even hard-money Democrats took a more wide-ranging view of the crisis, placing much of the blame on the extensive transatlantic financial network of which Biddle and his institution were only a part. The utter and abrupt prostration of the American economy following each decision by the Bank of England to raise its discount rate bore witness to that institution's awesome power, which had "crushed our whole banking system, depreciated our currency, and paralysed our trade, foreign and domestic."[49] In mass meetings and conventions held in response to the distress, Biddle was characterized more often as a co-conspirator in the crisis than as its mastermind, who aimed to render the country "a tributary to British insolence and corruption."[50] Speaking to a standing-room-only crowd in New York's Masonic Hall, the peripatetic English radical Frances Wright denounced the Philadelphia bank as "a conjurer's trick . . . with a secret door leading into the Bank of England."[51]

The full extent of the crisis became dramatically apparent as the decade drew to a close, when the Panic claimed its biggest victim, Biddle's own United States' Bank of Pennsylvania. Biddle had resigned as chairman of the bank early in 1839, but remained active in the institution's affairs. The suspension of specie payments again in the fall of that year sparked a bitter power struggle between Biddle and the board of directors. The board was compelled to implement the measure a third time, in February 1841, whereupon all public confidence in the bank evaporated, forcing it to cease operations. When Charles Dickens visited Philadelphia later that year he was struck by the "mournful, ghost-like" appearance of the neoclassical marble building that had only recently been the epicenter of the American financial world. Now, the desolate building stood in silent witness to the nation's economic collapse, a "Tomb of many fortunes," its doors shut tight.[52]

The failure of Biddle's bank did not deter Democrats in their search for homegrown scapegoats. Some chided the American people for their appetite for luxury goods, which had contributed to a swollen foreign debt, leaving the nation at the mercy of British creditors. More often, however, Democratic pundits invoked the old nostrums of their political faith, attributing the malaise to unseen cabals working to undermine the republic from within. Even as the very symbols of monopoly and privilege were being swept away, Jacksonians still managed to see a sinister design in recent events. In the view of one writer for the *Democratic Review*, it was all part of a plot that could be traced back to the 1790s, when Robert Morris and Alexander Hamilton—both advocates of "the

British order of things"—had planted the seeds of a monied aristocracy that would poison the fruits of the Revolution. Evidence that the plot had succeeded could be found in the fact that, despite wholly disparate political institutions, the United States was imitating the social institutions of Great Britain, with its extremes of wealth and poor. Instead of exercising vigilance in the face of clear and present dangers to the republic, Americans had been blind to the "moral canker" in their very midst.[53]

The collapse came at an especially inconvenient time in U.S.-British relations, already severely strained as a result of unrest along the Canadian border. Separatist revolts in Upper and Lower Canada had received the active support of Americans in the northern states, and the Van Buren administration was trying to dampen a growing war fever when a new problem arose. Several states had been especially profligate consumers of British capital in recent years and now found it difficult to meet their obligations. Facing sullen taxpayers who were in no mood to carry a heavier burden to maintain fiscal solvency, eight state legislatures defaulted on their interest payments to British banks. With British investors in U.S. securities facing ruinous losses, the Tory press—invariably hostile to Brother Jonathan in the best of times—stepped up its abuse of the United States, which in turn provoked angry jingoistic screeds stateside.[54]

Rather than draw back from Jackson's hard-money policies, Van Buren now prepared to take them a bold step further. From the outset of the crisis in 1837 the administration had pointed to the credit system itself as the underlying cause of the malaise. The solution, Van Buren believed—or at least a partial one, for the evil was too far advanced to be eliminated entirely—was a plan far more drastic than anything Andrew Jackson had envisioned: the restructuring of the credit system itself. The independent treasury system, as it would come to be known, would require government agencies that collected revenue, such as customs houses and land offices, to retain these funds until they were needed to meet the government's expenses, rather than deposit them in private banks. By denying banks access to federal funds, the plan would sharply restrict the paper money in circulation. This would in turn result in a reduction in prices, thereby mitigating the current distress. And, with paper money in shorter supply, American merchants would be obliged to pay for imported goods in hard currency, which would dramatically reduce, if not end altogether, the port-city auctions that since 1815 had been used to inundate the U.S. market with cheap British manufactures. In one stroke, the United States could reduce its indebtedness to Great Britain and wean itself away from its taste for foreign goods. Only by curtailing the influence which the British hegemon exerted over its former colonies, hard-money theorists argued, could the republic establish, once and for all, its financial independence.[55]

Congress initially balked at the independent treasury idea, but support for the plan grew as the economic outlook became more dire following the return of hard times in the fall of 1839.[56] In his December message to Congress, the president revisited the proposal, offering a candid if dispiriting assessment of the country's utter dependence on the financial resources of a foreign power. Whereas Andrew Jackson had once railed against the monopolistic practices of a single banking institution, Van Buren argued that systemic problems lay at the root of the current crisis. Lured by the prospect of greater profits, all financial institutions, large and small, had allowed themselves to be seduced by the credit system, and in so doing had become bound by a "chain of dependence," in which the distress of one inevitably led to the distress of others. A paper currency might suffice for domestic business transactions, Van Buren conceded, but it was of little use to pay the loans borrowed from Europe, which were owed in hard currency. And it was here, in the American financial relationship to London banking houses, that the real cause of the crisis could be found. American indebtedness to Great Britain had become so serious that a bank in even the most remote village of the republic operated "within the influence of the money power in England." Neither the creation of new, private banks nor the reestablishment of a national one could arrest the problem, the president argued. To do so would only create more debt, and bind the nation ever closer to the caprices of "a foreign moneyed interest."[57]

Defeated twice in 1839, Van Buren's independent treasury bill finally secured enough votes for passage when it came up again the following year. Though never a wildly popular measure among Democrats, the sub-treasury system appealed to a wide range of party constituencies. Rooted in the conviction that monopolies of all kinds were dangerous to the well-being of a republic, the measure drew support from hard-money doctrinaires who favored a drastic reduction in the powers of banks and a return to a specie basis for all loans. Working-class Locofocos resentful of aristocracy stood squarely behind the bill, as did many Southern Democrats, with their ingrained hostility to federal authority in any form. All could endorse a plan that promised to bring a speedy end to the fiscal enslavement that rendered Americans impoverished, "while ship loads of gold and silver," as Thomas Hart Benton put it, "are dispatched to our masters in England." Billed as a second declaration of independence, the Independent Treasury Act was signed into law by Van Buren on July 4, 1840.[58]

With the country still firmly in the grip of a depression as the 1840 election approached, incumbent Democrats found themselves on the defensive. Looking desperately for a silver lining amid the despair that enveloped the nation, Jacksonians gamely pointed out that the crisis had at least served to weaken the chains of credit and indebtedness that bound the republic to Great Britain. And they reminded voters that should the Whigs triumph in November, those chains would be fastened upon the republic even more firmly than before. The B.U.S. would be revived, inundating the country with commercial paper, a problem made even more serious by the surplus revenues the government would receive from a higher tariff, all of which would fuel a new round of inflation and speculation. A Whig administration might also assume the debts of the states, creating new financial obligations for the federal government and necessitating even higher import duties to pay for them.[59]

While these arguments could not prevent a Harrison victory in November, the president's death soon after the inauguration doomed Whig efforts to reverse the Jacksonians' hard-money course. The 27th Congress repealed Van Buren's Independent Treasury Act and drafted a proposal for a new "Fiscal Bank," a central banking system that would serve as a counterweight to the enormous clout of the Bank of England. Threadneedle Street's influence over the United States would never be corrected until the republic established a similar institution with like powers, Henry Clay maintained. But Harrison's successor, states' rights stalwart John Tyler, disagreed, and twice vetoed the measure on constitutional grounds.[60]

By 1843, the depression had largely run its course, and with the return of prosperity the furious debate over the federal government's proper role in banking lost much of its urgency. With Polk's election the following year, the Democrats revived the independent treasury plan. Unlike its earlier incarnation, the measure passed with little difficulty. As in the tariff controversy, the long-running debate over the nation's fiscal institutions would be cut short by the economic boom of the mid- to late 1840s. Washington would not create an institutional mechanism to regulate the nation's banking system until the Federal Reserve Act seventy years later.

Perhaps no other issue brought into sharper focus American feelings of insecurity toward Great Britain than the debtor-creditor relationship that existed between the two countries. By any measure, the United States had experienced astonishing growth in the years since 1815, a fact that Americans regarded with no small amount of pride. But material progress had not brought the country any closer to economic independence. The collapse of 1837–43 brought with it the jarring realization that American prosperity hinged to a considerable extent on decisions made in Great Britain. Even as the tide of westward migration rolled forward, into the Mississippi River Valley and beyond; even as the wharves of Eastern port cities filled with the produce of American farms and plantations—the nation seemed drawn ever more deeply into a web of dependence spun by British banking houses.

❖·❖

Bitterly divisive, the economic issues of the Jacksonian era opened up multiple chasms of contention between parties, classes, and sections. A vibrant Anglophobia fueled these concerns, spurred by the deeply held suspicion that Britain's vast commercial and financial empire aimed to keep the North American republic in a state of vassalage. But Americans did not simply differ over issues of trade and banking. On a more fundamental level, the partisan economic battles that occupied center stage for much of the period hinged upon two antithetical concepts of political economy, one rooted in an agrarian republicanism that was becoming increasingly anachronistic in a rapidly changing marketplace, the other characterized by a desire to emulate the British economic model. Mainstream Whigs generally took the view that the United States must be always on its guard, ever vigilant against foreign aggrandizement. Yet few begrudged Britain the right to pursue its own interests, and they tended to agree that its policies constituted a "manly, open, undisguised exertion of every honest form of power," even when they ran counter to the United States.[61] For all their grumbling about British economic dominance, they longed for a day when the two Anglo-Saxon nations would occupy positions of relative parity and mutual respect. For orthodox Jacksonians, on the other hand, there was little that was open or undisguised about Britain's economic policy. Much less comfortable with the global marketplace and their place in it than their Whig rivals, they tended to look upon the world's leading economic power with profound distrust. Fearing what they did not fully comprehend, they saw across the Atlantic a sinister plot in which the British government was conspiring with British banking and commercial interests to destroy the union.

In the contest between these two competing ideologies, Jacksonians had a distinct advantage. Ignorant though party leaders may have been of modern market forces, they embraced a brand of economic obscurantism that struck a chord in an electorate wary of change, and especially change that bore a foreign stamp. Like many societies that would emerge from long periods of colonial rule, the American republic harbored an innate distrust of any policy associated with the imperial parent. Democrats skillfully managed to exploit these sentiments, portraying partisan rivals as entrenched elites loyal to the norms and models of the ancien regime. Whig leaders, try as they might to present their economic message in the language of liberation, were unable to disguise their innate Anglophilia. It was largely for this reason that Henry Clay's American System could never be evaluated on its merits. In the end, the mere fact that an economic program appeared to mimic the policies in place in Britain was reason enough for many voters to oppose it. John C. Calhoun needed only to link the Kentucky statesman to Britain's most conservative political interests to bring the program into disrepute in the eyes of many Americans. "The tory party are the patrons of corporate monopolies; *and are not you?* They are advocates of a high tariff; *and are not you? They* are the supporters of a national bank; *and are not you?*"[62]

While the country's attention was focused on the bruising partisan slugfests over banks and tariffs, the new economic order was also helping to aggravate even more dangerous sectional discord. In the face of rising antislavery criticism, white Southerners retreated behind a nostalgic view of their way of life as a pastoral idyll of benevolent masters and contented slaves, a world far removed from emergent industrialization. Below the Mason-Dixon Line, civic leaders expressed profound misgivings about the newly mechanized world of the "Spinning Jenney, Steam and Rail Roads."[63] In drawing attention to the blighting effects of urbanization in the North, the planter class naturally emphasized the similarities between that section and Great Britain. With each passing year, the North seemed to more closely resemble the British industrial state, a veritable Babylon whose inhabitants had become addicted to luxury and consumed by avarice.[64] When these sons of the South directed their gaze toward Northern cities, they beheld a world of Dickensian horrors. Industrialization had become "the evil of the age," and in the reckless pursuit of wealth and progress, England had served as "our great example."[65] White Southerners suspected that the new economic order was a virus that could not be contained, threatening to contaminate the agrarian world they knew. Though the factory system was still confined largely to the Northern states, they saw a new ethos of immorality that was slowly percolating into the most distant corners of the republic. The engine of progress would soon transform the entire nation, creating a new economic order in which slavery would have no place, in which "my peculiar section, and the peculiar institution existing in it," South Carolina congressman Francis Pickens lamented, "will be overwhelmed."[66]

As Southern concerns grew, many recalled the earlier warnings of old republicans like John Taylor of Caroline. When *Tyranny Unmasked* was published in 1822, the perils of consolidation that so alarmed Taylor seemed remote to most Americans, and indeed a great many Southerners. In the face of a broad consensus that favored a much looser construction of federal power, Taylor's anti-government ideology receded. The hoary doctrine of a disgruntled Southern minority, his brand of republicanism seemed destined to become little more than a quaint relic of the past. But the passage of time had given fresh meaning to Taylor's warnings. As the American republic came to resemble the nation that had given birth to it, many Southern leaders blamed those in the North who had never managed to break free of the "old prejudices" of the colonial mind. These neo-Federalists had "taken their examples from England—from English institutions—English principles and customs" and "attempted to apply them to us—a people totally different in every respect."[67] And in their eagerness to emulate a foreign system of governance, Southerners insisted, they had succeeded only too well, creating one that no longer resembled the polity the Framers had envisioned. By the 1830s, many of the South's leading statesmen had abandoned their initial enthusiasm for a program of economic nationalism and put their shoulders to the wheel of the strict constructionist cause. But their campaign to check the advance of centralized authority was unavailing; the region's growing political isolation during the Jacksonian period would be a testament to their futile efforts to arrest the trend toward consolidation. Taylor's prediction that the republic was in danger of imitating the English model had proven all too true. His diseased, "painted courtezan" had come hideously to life.

"An Army of Fanatics"

Ye negroes of the colonies, who know emancipation—
On your marrow bones, ye vagabonds,
And thank the British nation.
Observe how it regards you as the factory children's betters,
Since it cuts in twain your galling chains,
But leaves untouched their fetters . . .
Thank God your children's skins are black—their hair is crisp and curly;
So they at least shall not be seized
And doomed to death so early.
　　　　　—"British Emancipation," in *The John Donkey,* 1848

In the early 1830s American antislavery was a reform movement hardly deserving of the name. Elsewhere in North America, the so-called peculiar institution was crumbling. Mexico had abolished slavery in 1829; the British government would bow to popular pressure and begin the process of emancipating its Caribbean slave population four years later. In the United States, however, the most conspicuous antislavery organization was the hopelessly ineffectual American Colonization Society. Founded in 1816, over the years the organization had developed what can only be described as a serious identity crisis, its members holding widely divergent views as to its long-term goals. Some members were philanthropists who genuinely believed the ACS would pave the way for the gradual abolition of slavery. Colonization, they reasoned, would offer an acceptable alternative for Southern planters, who might otherwise be reluctant to emancipate their slaves for fear of creating a large free black population they could not control. Yet others seem to have been attracted to the organization for wholly different motives. Uninterested in the goal of emancipation, they saw the colonization effort as a means of ridding the South of troublesome free blacks, which would strengthen, not weaken the institution of slavery. The results, not surprisingly, were unimpressive. In its first fifteen years of operation, the ACS managed to relocate just 1,722 free blacks on the West African coast.[1]

The colonization effort held scant appeal for most free blacks in any case. Together with a small contingent of white antislavery militants, they called for more energetic measures to hasten the demise of the peculiar institution. But support for what would loosely come to be known as immediatism had thus far failed to gain much traction in the North. The federal system allowed indifferent Northerners to ignore the issue, on the grounds that they had no right to interfere in Southern affairs. Many feared emancipation would inundate Eastern cities with cheap black labor. Northern politicians, meanwhile, had little interest in broaching a subject that had the potential to destroy the delicate bi-regional balance so essential to the stability of both parties. Once in a while, questions pertaining to the institution of slavery required the attention of Congress, but for the most part, mainstream political leaders had managed to keep a tight lid on the issue, well aware of its radioactive properties.[2]

No American felt a greater sense of outrage at this conspiracy of silence than William Lloyd Garrison. Briefly a member of the ACS, Garrison had come to believe that the organization was a fraud perpetrated by slaveholders to promote their interests under the guise of philanthropy. Brimming with sulfurous indignation, on January 1, 1831, the twenty-five-year-old newspaper editor delivered his historic challenge to the ACS and all Americans who either supported or gave their tacit consent to the peculiar institution. Demanding the immediate abolition of slavery, the young militant famously promised his readers, "I will not retreat a single inch—and I will be heard!"[3]

For the next two years, few Americans listened. The newspaper did manage to achieve a certain notoriety in the South when it refused to condemn the 1831 Nat Turner insurrection, prompting some slaveholders to call for its suppression. But most Northerners were unaware of the Liberator's existence, its principal readership consisting of free blacks in the New England area. By 1833, the Boston editor decided that he could speak more loudly from across the Atlantic. In May, Garrison sailed to England, ostensibly to solicit funds for a Negro school. The abolitionist's real purpose, however, was to woo British reformers to his cause. In the antislavery crusade, as in so many spheres of endeavor, it helped to have the British stamp of approval. To win hearts and minds at home, it was first necessary to win hearts and minds abroad.[4]

Garrison was not the only American antislavery activist seeking to obtain the sanction of his British counterparts. The American Colonization Society already had its own representative on the ground in England, a Philadelphia Quaker named Elliot Cresson. Unlike some of the more conservative elements of his organization, Cresson seems to have been genuinely committed to the doctrine of gradual emancipation. In the summer of 1833, however, with antislavery leaders in Parliament hammering out the final details of the Emancipation Act, he was finding the colonization message a hard sell across the Atlantic. Emboldened by this stunning success, most British reformers proved much more receptive to Garrison's plea for radical action.

Abandoning all pretense of school fundraising soon after he arrived, the Boston newspaperman launched a full-bore attack on American colonizationists. Garrison hounded the hapless Cresson throughout the summer, repeatedly challenging the Philadelphia merchant to a debate. When Cresson refused, Garrison denounced the ACS in open letters to English newspapers and in a series of engagements on the antislavery circuit. His mission accomplished, Garrison returned to the United States with a cache of abolitionist tracts and pledges of future support from British antislavery groups. Most valuable of all was a letter repudiating the ACS signed by the movement's most influential leaders, including— in what was deemed a major coup—no less a figure than William Wilberforce, the éminence grise of British reform.[5]

A firestorm greeted Garrison upon his arrival in New York City in October. Angry ACS members had published excerpts of Garrison's British speeches in the press, in which he had denounced not only Southern slaveholders but all Americans for tolerating an un-Christian and immoral labor system.[6] Garrison's enemies did not merely condemn him for a want of patriotism; they sought to link the abolitionist to the British censure that had so wounded American pride in recent years. Coming on the heels of the furor sparked by Frances Trollope's *Domestic Manners of the Americans* and other travel memoirs, Garrison's overseas visit was characterized as but another indication of the British propensity to denigrate and possibly undermine the institutions of the United States. Furious that one of their fellow citizens would seek to "bring the American Nation before the bar of British opinion," Garrison's critics viewed the Boston abolitionist as a pawn who had allowed himself to be manipulated by "our ancient enemies." Adding to the public frenzy, Gotham's own antislavery activists, led by merchants Arthur and Lewis Tappan, had been greatly encouraged by the news from England and decided the time had come to establish a New York antislavery society. Roused to anger, Tammany gangs roamed the streets in a vain search for the Tappans and the "lunatic Garrison."[7]

The ACS continued its campaign against Garrison in the weeks and months that followed, alleging, among other things, that he had wheedled the Wilberforce letter from the venerable reformer when he was near death and no longer of sound mind.[8] But the damage to the organization had been done. Utterly discredited by Cresson's humiliation in England, the ACS never recovered its prestige as the nation's preeminent antislavery organization. Some of its most prominent members publicly repudiated the group and its goals. Donations soon dried up, and within a year it had all but collapsed in several Northern states. Those hostile to slavery ceased to view the ACS as an acceptable alternative to emancipation, no longer willing to put their faith in an organization Wilberforce held in such low esteem.

Not that Northern antislavery opinion was ready to embrace Garrisonian immediatism. The Boston firebrand stood well outside the antislavery mainstream, and there he would remain, an unapologetic *enragé* who had no use for half-measures that would perpetuate the sin of slavery. There were other, more moderate voices raised against the institution during this period, and even those who shared Garrison's immediatist views would later part ways with him over his commitment to women's rights and his rejection of political activism. Whereas William Wilberforce served as the towering figure of the British antislavery movement, in the United States the Boston editor was content to play the role of agent provocateur. Firing angry philippics at the South, he would leave others to grapple with the political crises of a divided union.

Even so, Garrison's transatlantic journey produced a sea change in the movement to abolish slavery in the United States. Rising from virtual obscurity to be acclaimed by the most renowned figures of Britain's emancipation crusade, the Boston editor vaulted to the front rank of the American antislavery leadership. The movement's center of gravity now shifted as the enfeebled gradualism of the ACS retreated before the growing clamor for immediate action. Once again, as in the great debates over tariffs and banking, the slavery crisis would remind Americans of the extent to which developments across the Atlantic shaped events at home. And, once again, Americans would find themselves divided over whether to follow in the footsteps of the imperial parent.

The "British Example"

With Americans blaming Great Britain for a wide range of troublesome domestic issues, it was little wonder that they instinctively turned a suspicious eye across the Atlantic as they sought to come to terms with the problem of slavery. Indeed, they had held Britain responsible for the institution since before the Revolution, when some Southern colonies petitioned the Crown to end the slave trade. Humanitarianism was not the issue; planters with an adequate supply of slaves feared further imports would reduce the value of their existing labor force. Parliament ignored their entreaties and continued the lucrative traffic, prompting Thomas Jefferson to include this complaint in the list of indictments against the King in an initial draft of the Declaration of Independence. Not all Southern delegates to the Continental Congress opposed the traffic, however, and the issue was deleted from the document in its final form.[9]

For the South, the Crown's connection with North American slavery was hardly a matter of arcane historical interest. In both its wars against Americans, Britain had attempted to weaponize the plantation labor force, and was thus linked inextricably to Southern whites' darkest and most terrifying fears of race war. In 1775, several hundred slaves heeded Virginia governor Lord Dunmore's promise of freedom and rose up in rebellion, only to be routed with their British allies at the Battle of Great Bridge. Later in the conflict, the British recruited freedmen and runaways to form the Black Carolina Corps, which was eventually incorporated into British regiments in the West Indies. The Royal Army's use of black troops had also been the source of considerable alarm for Southern whites in the War of 1812. About one thousand black soldiers from Jamaica, Barbados, and the Bahamas—their ranks swelled by American slaves who had escaped to British lines—were part of the force that landed in Louisiana and fought in the Battle of New Orleans. For their service in these contests, the British government evacuated several thousand black loyalists to Canada and the West Indies.[10]

Such wartime experiences caused Southern blacks to link British power with the prospect of emancipation in the years that followed. Within the slave community along the Chesapeake and the Gulf Coast, an oral tradition emerged that the British would one day return to complete the task of liberation and "massacre all the white people." Amid the confusion and hysteria that gripped the Lower Chesapeake region in the early days of the Nat Turner rebellion in the summer of 1831, rumors quickly spread that Virginia slaves had been incited to act by British authorities. Area whites were in such a state of anxiety that when an Englishman named Robinson was heard to remark that the slaves were entitled to their freedom and ought to be emancipated, he was dragged from his house by an angry mob, stripped naked, whipped, and drummed out of town.[11]

For a brief period in the early nineteenth century it seemed as if the two nations' attempts to deal with the issue of slavery were moving along parallel lines. Britain abolished the slave trade in 1807, the United States a year later—political actions that were widely hailed at the time as the death knell of the institution in the western hemisphere. But even as humanitarian reformers on both sides of the Atlantic celebrated their achievement, economic forces were conspiring to bring this hopeful synergy to an end. Industrialization transformed British society, giving rise to a new middle class that embraced the values of liberalism and Christian benevolence. Serendipitously, the rising wealth and political power of this class coincided with a gradual decline of the West Indian sugar colonies, assuring its ultimate triumph over planter interests in Parliament. But while Britain's new industrial order fostered a moral climate and bourgeois sensibility that denounced slavery, its textile mills required a steady diet of cotton that only the American South could provide. Thus, as Britons joined in the clamor against the institution, a great many Americans found it increasingly hard to imagine their world without it.

British reformers had always assumed that the institution would wither and die once the traffic in human cargo ceased. According to conventional wisdom, mortality rates on the plantations of the West Indies were so high that the population could not sustain itself through natural increase. This fallacy became evident after Britain abolished the trade, and in 1823 Wilberforce and other antislavery leaders launched a new campaign dedicated to the complete eradication of the institution in the empire's Caribbean possessions. Perfecting the techniques its leaders had used in the battle against the slave trade, the British Anti-Slavery Society worked to mobilize public opinion on a grand and unprecedented scale, holding mass meetings, blanketing the country with antislavery tract literature, and inundating Parliament with petitions calling for an end to the practice.

With the peculiar institution in the West Indies a matter of all-absorbing interest to Britons, those who visited the United States were naturally curious about the plantation system as it existed in the American South. Although white Southerners liked to point out that conditions for slave labor were far better in the United States than in the Caribbean islands, this mattered little to British observers, who seized the opportunity to expose the hypocrisy of the new country's much-ballyhooed freedoms. Henry Bradshaw Fearon described with disgust the whipping of a fourteen-year-old boy in Kentucky; he was no less disturbed by the degradation and discrimination of free blacks he witnessed in the Northern states.[12] An especially gruesome indictment of the institution came from the pen of William Faux, whose *Memorable Days in America* described the training of dogs to hunt runaways, and the whipping deaths of two South Carolina slaves, the body of one left unburied for the dogs to eat.[13]

In the early decades of the nineteenth century, citizens of the republic responded to these attacks in much the same way as they had to other forms of foreign censure: not as members of a particular region, but as Americans. Southern whites were predictably outraged, and quickly crafted a set of arguments to defend the institution and discredit its opponents. While Northerners were generally unwilling to justify slavery on moral grounds, many nonetheless regarded the antislavery critique as but one of the many unjust indictments of their country at the hands of carping foreigners. The standard explanation that the institution had been forced on reluctant North American colonies by the Crown solely for the benefit of British slave-traders was repeated so often and in so many quarters that it may well have been the only thing on which proslavery and antislavery advocates agreed.[14] Those who raised their voices against British criticism, such as Charles Jared Ingersoll, Robert Walsh, and James Kirke Paulding, all reiterated the charge that Great Britain deserved responsibility for establishing the institution on American soil. Even in New England, British attacks on slavery did not go unchallenged. In an angry 1824 rejoinder to Faux's memoir, the *North American Review*, hardly a defender of the peculiar institution, nonetheless felt compelled to declare, "Slavery in America is a British institution, established by British laws, for the benefit of British traders." The Boston journal even went so far as to insist that British efforts to ameliorate the condition of West Indian slaves was due to the example already set by the benevolent slave masters of North America.[15]

What appeared to the American public as the intolerably smug self-righteousness of Britain's reformers seemed even more galling in view of Parliament's less than enlightened conduct toward its millions of other oppressed subjects. Britain's own social problems took on special significance in the campaign to discredit the antislavery critique from abroad. Critics charged that the Royal Navy was still engaged in its own form of slavery by forcibly impressing Britons into its service. They pointed, too, to Britain's long-standing history of oppression in Ireland. Above all, they upbraided overseas critics for having the temerity to condemn American labor practices in view of the vice and misery entailed upon the people of England by a brutal factory system.[16] Though *New York Evening Post* editor William Leggett opposed slavery, he had little patience for the putative humanitarianism of the British, who "sought to quiet their consciences, for oppressing one colour, by becoming the advocates of the freedom of the other."[17] "How dare you talk to us before the world of slavery?" raged South Carolina governor James Henry Hammond. Referring to Britain's laboring population, he declared: "Raise them from the condition of brutes, to the level of human beings—of American slaves, at least."[18] It was a view shared by many Americans, Hammond's proslavery extremism notwithstanding. "Thousands and millions of *slaves* exist in the confines of that kingdom," a young Walt Whitman declared in the *Brooklyn Daily Eagle*, "to whose lot the condition of the South Carolinian negro is paradise."[19]

Making Britain's hypocrisy on the slavery issue all the more objectionable was the belief that ulterior motives lay behind that country's newfound humanitarianism. Having profited from the slave trade more than any other country, its sudden pangs of conscience at the close of the eighteenth century seemed more than a little suspicious to many Americans. Great Britain's insistence on the right to search vessels suspected of slave-trading, they argued, was merely a pretext to obstruct the commerce of its maritime competitors. The subsequent crusade against the institution of slavery itself also appeared to be a policy designed to capitalize on the decline of the plantation economy in its own colonial possessions. That Britain was at the very same time calling for open markets worldwide while keeping its Corn Laws in effect at home only lent credence to charges of a double standard. Whether the issue was free trade or antislavery, few Americans doubted that Great Britain was pursuing policies with its own self-interest in mind.[20]

All the while, the abolitionist tide rolled inexorably forward across the Atlantic, gaining strength and momentum until it finally crested during Garrison's visit to England in 1833. Britain's antislavery organizations flooded Parliament with memorials and petitions expressing support for their cause. Hundreds of petitions were regularly laid before the House of Commons and House of Lords, each bearing thousands of signatures. During Garrison's stay in London the Ladies' Anti-Slavery Society submitted a petition to the lower house signed by 187,000 British citizens.[21] Political developments also worked to undermine the interests of West Indian planters. In 1832 Parliament expanded the size of the electorate with the historic Reform Bill, which not only gave traditionally antislavery constituencies in the urban and industrialized regions a greater voice in the House of Commons, but also abolished many seats that had traditionally supported planters' interests. Eight months later, Parliament passed the Emancipation Act, which in its final form would allocate £20 million to compensate West Indian slave owners to phase in the new policy by the end of the decade. All slaves under the age of six would be freed when the act went into effect the following year; the bulk of the slave population was to receive its freedom after serving a

FIGURE 11.

"British Warfare in 1812, 1837–38." Having aided and abetted Native Americans in the War of 1812, Great Britain was widely believed to be a source of antislavery agitation after Parliament passed the Emancipation Act in 1833. (Courtesy American Antiquarian Society)

period of "apprenticeship." When it became clear that the apprentice system greatly augmented the sufferings of West Indian laborers, Parliament granted all slaves their freedom on August 1, 1838.[22]

Still, American Anglophobes remained skeptical of British motives, and pointed to loopholes in the new law. Critics called attention to the fact that the act did not apply to the human cargo seized from slave ships by the Royal Navy. Instead of being immediately emancipated, these slaves were often apprenticed to West Indian sugar plantations or impressed into military service. The act said nothing about the brutal treatment of laborers elsewhere in the British empire, such as South Africa, and explicitly excluded any territories in the possession of the East India Company. To many Americans, it was all a humbug designed to allow Great Britain to cloak itself in the guise of humanitarianism while continuing its ruthless campaign of global oppression. Even John Quincy Adams, one of the earliest and most impassioned enemies of the expansion of slavery in the United States, harbored few illusions that Her Majesty's government was genuinely committed to improving the well-being of the African slave.[23]

"Our Country Is the World"

While most white Americans raged at what they perceived to be the transparent hypocrisy of Britain, there would always be some who felt the sting of the imperial parent's reproach. From the earliest days of the antislavery controversy, Americans seeking to curtail the institution pointed to Great Britain as a model worthy of emulation. When Illinois petitioned for statehood in 1818, New York congressman James Tallmadge, mindful of foreign visitors who derided the slaveholding republic for its claims as the freest nation in the world, called upon members of the House to prohibit slavery there. Although Tallmadge blamed Parliament for committing the "original sin" of planting slavery in the thirteen colonies, he did not believe the federal government should compound the offense by expanding it. He urged Congress to capture the high moral ground by containing the institution within its existing boundaries. Congress rejected the idea, and the following year Tallmadge famously proposed a similar resolution that would formally proscribe the institution in Missouri. In the heated debates that followed, Tallmadge noted that Great Britain, unlike the United States, had endeavored in recent years to atone for its guilt by meliorating the condition of its colonial slave population. Southern leaders seethed with indignation at the comparison. If England has "ceased to enslave men," Senator William Smith of South Carolina retorted, it was only because it had "found it more profitable to enslave nations."[24]

The British example resonated with special force in certain quarters of the Northern religious community. Whereas the nation's literati endeavored, with mixed results, to tear itself away from British moorings, many American evangelicals saw no reason to try. Unrepentantly transatlantic in outlook, their strong ties to England had not been severed by political independence, or diminished by the Anglophobic feeling of many of their fellow citizens. The best known British evangelicals could claim a ministry that spanned the Atlantic world (William Wilberforce's *Practical Views of the Prevailing Religious System*, the unofficial handbook of Anglophone evangelicalism, would go through twenty-five editions in the United States). American spiritual leaders were not only moved by jeremiads against the decline of religion and morality, they were also inspired to copy their overseas counterparts' charitable activities. When British reformers established benevolent societies to found Sunday schools, distribute Bibles and religious tract literature, and promote other forms of Christian uplift, American religious groups promptly followed suit.[25]

The campaign to eradicate slavery in the western hemisphere would prove to be the ultimate test of the American evangelical community's readiness to follow the path blazed by their British coadjutors. Slavery was an evil far removed for most Britons; in the United States, on the other hand, it had become woven into the fabric of life for millions of its citizens. Unwilling to antagonize Southern members, the dominant Protestant churches shied away from taking a stand on the slavery issue for several years. Yet the moral beacon of Great Britain proved for Northern evangelicals impossible to ignore. American Quakers, who had worked with the Society of Friends in Britain to build public opposition against the slave trade in the eighteenth century, made sure that British antislavery writings received wide distribution in the Northeast. Aiding in this cause were the Unitarians, a nonconformist sect of Presbyterianism that had taken root across the Atlantic in the liberal wing of the Congregational Church. By the 1820s the sect could claim one hundred churches in the Boston area, whose leaders echoed the fervent antislavery sentiments of their British brethren.[26]

For the scions of well-established New England families, who were conspicuous among the ranks of the early antislavery leaders, admiration for Britain's place in the van of the emancipation movement was accompanied by deep feelings of cultural kinship. While ardent nationalists decried the extent of British influences in American life, Anglophile New Englanders gloried in the melding of the two cultures. The "sentiments and feelings of the British nation on this subject cannot fail to be diffused among us," the New England Anti-Slavery Society predicted optimistically in its fourth annual meeting, "their literature being intimately blended with our own."[27] Steeped in an intellectual and cultural tradition that remained deeply indebted to Great Britain, American abolitionists operated under the assumption that as the view of slavery changed on the other side of the Atlantic, it could not fail to do so at home.

Prominent women in the antislavery cause likewise enjoyed a bond with their counterparts across the Atlantic. American Quakers Lucretia Mott and Amy Post were profoundly influenced by Elizabeth Pease, a towering figure in British antislavery reform.[28] Maria Weston Chapman, one of the principal organizers of the Boston Female Antislavery Society, had been educated in England and coveted the "sympathy and prayers" of her friends abroad, many of whom sent goods to be sold for the fundraising efforts at the anti-slavery fairs she organized in the Bay State. Like so many abolitionists, it seemed to her inconceivable that the British example would not inspire the people of Massachusetts, who were, after all, "of pure English descent."[29]

If the British Isles served as a beacon of liberty for New Englanders, it shone with special brilliance for African Americans. "The English are the best friends the coloured people have upon earth," declared David Walker in his famous incendiary *Appeal*, published in 1829. Exhorting African Americans in bondage in the Southern states to rebel against their masters, Walker asserted that the English "have done one hundred times more for the melioration of our condition, than all the other nations of the earth put together."[30] To an even greater degree than their white counterparts, black leaders paid homage to the pioneers of British emancipation. William Wilberforce assumed almost mythical, messianic status in the African American pantheon, universally regarded, one British visitor observed, as "the great saviour of their race."[31]

In short, for American reformers the emancipation of Britain's West Indian slaves was nothing less than a clarion call to arms. Passage of the act sparked a flurry of activity, with antislavery activists fired with a new sense of purpose, giddy with enthusiasm for the great task ahead. As noted earlier, the Tappans formed the New York Anti-Slavery Society immediately upon learning the news; with Garrison's help a national organization was formed in December. When William IV signed his name to the Emancipation Act, "he signed the death warrant of slavery throughout the civilized world," the New England Anti-Slavery Society announced in its first annual report.[32] Emancipation in the West Indies, exulted one antislavery periodical, had made "abolition in our country imperative and unavoidable."[33]

The burst of breathless enthusiasm among antislavery militants in the United States occasioned by the Emancipation Act brought into stark relief Americans' disparate views of Great Britain. Here, once again, a group of Americans enjoined the nation to follow in the footsteps of the British, seemingly oblivious to the hostile, knee-jerk reaction such entreaties often elicited from the public at large. "Let us imitate our British brethren and open the flood gates of light upon this dark subject," declared Joshua Leavitt's *New York Evangelist*, an immediatist newspaper.[34] Immune to the anti-British sentiment that so often colored American cultural and political life, the early disciples of the abolitionist crusade were steeped in an Anglophile tradition that regarded Great Britain as the apogee of Western civilization. In their more naive moments, they seem to have genuinely believed that the British example would alone be sufficient to awaken the nation to the sin of slavery. Stressing the familial ties that bound the two nations, antislavery militants urged Americans to pay Britain the deference owed a wise and venerable parent. Surely, they believed, it was only a matter of time before the scales would fall from America's eyes and its people would be able to see clearly the moral imperative of emancipation.[35]

For this reason, then, New England's moral crusaders did not share the nation's sense of umbrage at the censure of foreign journals and travel writers. In their view, it mattered little whether Americans received British criticism grudgingly or gratefully, so long as they profited by it.[36] They alone saw a silver lining in Britain's reproach, for it would show Americans the folly of their ways, and in so doing, "rouse the nation, as one *man*, to imitate the people of our fatherland."[37] Some of the more patrician abolitionists exhibited the same kind of snobbery so widespread among highbrow *litterateurs*. Just as the cognoscenti was known to prefer foreign cultural productions, turning up its nose at American plays and books, members of the reform community often took the view that moral instruction was a tonic best administered from abroad. Harvard-educated Wendell Phillips believed that Northern antislavery appeals fell on deaf ears in the South, whereas "*your* appeals sink deep," he wrote to the Scottish abolitionist George Thompson. Americans did not appreciate being scolded by Americans; only their famous sensitivity to foreign censure, Phillips insisted, could shame them into action.[38]

As for William Lloyd Garrison, like most middle-class Americans, he held conflicted feelings toward Great Britain. He was not blind to its faults, believing the empire to be perched precariously upon a volcano that could erupt in social chaos at any moment, yet this assessment was far outweighed by the sense of marvel he felt at that country's deep commitment to abolitionism.[39] For all its manifest defects, England seemed to him a benevolent idyll of universal fellowship and biracial fraternity. He was amazed, naively perhaps, at the reception accorded black delegates at the World Anti-Slavery Convention in 1840. "Surely," he wrote home, "if dukes, lords, duchesses and the like, are not ashamed to eat, sit, walk and talk with colored Americans, the *democrats* of our country need not deem it a vulgar or odious thing to do likewise."[40]

Garrison's transatlantic orientation left him unmoved by allegations that he was a traitor to his country. Stubbornly self-righteous, he made no attempt to deny the charge and unapologetically pleaded guilty to having condemned the republic for its shameful history of abuse of African Americans during his visit to Great Britain.[41] Like so many public figures, he drew comparisons between his own struggles and those of Revolutionary heroes, and regarded the Declaration of Independence as a sacred text that guaranteed liberty to all Americans. But he revered the core beliefs on which the nation had been founded, not the nation-state itself. His was an evangelical worldview in which God's law reigned above all secular concerns. And because the ideals enshrined in the Declaration were universal and divinely inspired, he could in good conscience declare: "We love the land of our nativity, only as we love all other lands."[42] In an age of rampant nationalism, this was a view that few Americans shared. Many were appalled when the New Englander publicly burned a copy of the Constitution, and no less so when he insisted on celebrating August 1st, the date the Emancipation Act went into effect, instead of the Fourth of July. The overwhelming majority of the republic's citizens saw no inherent conflict in their religious and civic obligations. But for Garrison the sin of slavery was so great an offense to a divine plan that it had to be rooted out, whatever the cost to national harmony. If that meant forging alliances with the nation's traditional adversaries, so be it. In 1840, he wrote home from England, "In attempting to put away the evil that is in the world, we must forget all national distinctions and geographical boundaries, and remember that we are indeed members of one family, to whom there is nothing foreign, nothing remote."[43]

Garrison and other immediatists, then, not only differed from most Americans in their view of the slavery question. By their worshipful admiration of Great Britain, they saw the transatlantic relationship differently, too. While Garrison famously eschewed any involvement in domestic politics—an issue that would cause a split within the movement by 1840—his insistence that the holy war against slavery transcended loyalty to the nation allowed critics to assert that larger and more powerful geopolitical forces were at work. Whether they genuinely believed Garrison was colluding with foreign enemies or not, anti-abolitionists took full advantage of the opportunity to discredit antislavery militancy as a movement with transatlantic roots. It was an allegation that Garrison—who proudly emblazoned the masthead of the *Liberator* with the epigraph: "Our country is the world and our countrymen all mankind"— did little to refute.[44]

This is not to suggest that a constructive and reasoned national conversation over slavery could have occurred had the issue been viewed strictly as a domestic matter. Any discussion of abolition, whatever the source, was enough to induce apoplexy among proslavery Americans. But in playing midwife to the antislavery movement in the United States, British reformers had made the republic's greatest challenge an even more intractable and polarizing one. Garrison's reception in London had ensured the early primacy of the most militant brand of immediatism, muffling for the present more moderate antislavery voices. What was more, the immediatists' transatlantic connections allowed their opponents to level a charge all too familiar to Americans: the charge of foreign influence. Just how far British antislavery leaders were willing to go to support the fledgling movement would soon become apparent.

Emissaries from Foreign Parts

The triumph of Britain's antislavery reformers in the 1830s brought a marked shift in that country's attitudes toward slavery in the United States. British visitors to North America no longer had any reason to exercise restraint in censuring their republican cousins for their stubborn defense of the institution, and their criticism of slavery now assumed a more unequivocal and strident tone. Virtually every British traveler felt obliged to include at least one slaveholding state on their itinerary, in order to view the institution firsthand and record his or her impressions for readers at home.[45]

In the South, whites had followed the parliamentary debates leading up to passage of the Emancipation Act with growing trepidation. Already on edge as a result of the Nat Turner Rebellion and the Jamaican Christmas Revolt in 1831, some predicted a racial bloodbath between master and slave. Others, perhaps in an effort to quiet their own fears, assumed a whistling-past-the-graveyard insouciance, as if the liberation of almost a million slaves in the Caribbean was a matter of little consequence to American slaveholders. "We have nothing to do with England," the *Charleston Courier* asserted bravely in July 1833, adding, a few weeks later, that the South need only maintain "peace and tranquility at home."[46] Southern whites, of course, were anything but indifferent to British emancipation. In their view, the fate of slavery in the West Indian colonies offered troubling portents for the institution in the United States. Liverpool's sugar merchants and Jamaica's planter class had once enjoyed broad support in Parliament, secure in the belief that the institution remained safe from antislavery agitation. Yet for all their political influence, these defenders of the status quo in the West Indies had been utterly routed by a cohort of "fanatics," whose propaganda had created a great clamor for abolition among a general public long indifferent to the plight of colonial slaves. If a determined minority could effect such a radical shift in popular attitudes in Great Britain, American slaveholders asked themselves, might such a frightening scenario occur just as easily in the Northern states?[47]

Southern apprehensions about the political influence of a nascent, homegrown abolitionist movement were soon accompanied by more pressing concerns, as British reformers, flush from their West Indian triumph, now turned their attention to new horizons. British antislavery leaders had never made a secret of their desire to undertake the eradication of the institution throughout the western hemisphere, and they looked to the American South as their next great challenge. "Why are the Emancipation Societies of England still organized, and in full operation?" asked one Southern editor. The answer did not appear to be in doubt: British philanthropy had undertaken as its new goal to "reform the world."[48]

Hard evidence of British cooperation in the American antislavery movement was not long in coming. In May 1834, Charles Stuart, an early British critic of colonization, embarked upon a lengthy speaking tour of the Northern and Western states on behalf of the newly formed American Anti-Slavery Society. A retired captain of the East India Company, Stuart often encountered fierce hostility and, occasionally, physical abuse from Americans, who resented not only the immediatist message but the foreign messenger. In Middletown, Connecticut, a mob disrupted a meeting at which he was speaking and pelted him with eggs. Some months later, the Quaker reformer was mobbed while touring western New York and knocked senseless by a brickbat.[49]

Stuart's modest efforts on behalf of the antislavery cause would soon be eclipsed by the arrival of a far more conspicuous, far more militant traveling ambassador. During his visit to Great Britain the previous year, William Lloyd Garrison had been dazzled by the fiery oratory of the Scottish abolitionist George Thompson, and convinced him to undertake a speaking tour in the United States. During the campaign for West Indian emancipation, Thompson had been a vigorous opponent of compromise with the planter class over compensation and the apprenticeship system. A member of the Agency Committee, Thompson belonged to a group of young radicals within the British antislavery movement which, after 1833, declared American slavery to be its top priority. Several moderate British antislavery leaders worried that Thompson's impassioned zeal might make him ill-suited for the task of carrying the emancipation message to the United States. For Garrison, however, the Scottish abolitionist's great virtue lay in his implacable hatred of the peculiar institution. Thompson, he believed, was just the sort of firebrand to shake Americans from their moral lethargy and alert them to the crime of slavery.

Concerns that Thompson might antagonize Americans rather than convert them to the antislavery cause proved well founded. The abolitionist's transatlantic errand attracted considerable public attention; even before he disembarked in New York, the American anti-abolition press had branded Thompson a dangerous foreign interloper who had no business meddling in the republic's domestic affairs. The Scotsman and his family soon repaired to the more hospitable environment of New England, where the fledgling abolitionist community accorded him a hero's welcome. New Englanders soon got a taste of the Agency Committee orator's inflammatory invective. Thompson excoriated not only those who participated directly in the crime of slavery, but all who lacked the moral courage to demand its immediate dissolution. Quoted as having declared that every slave had the right "to cut the throat of his master"—a statement he denied making—Thompson soon faced a veritable tidal wave of anti-abolition sentiment not seen in New England before his arrival.[50] In towns across Massachusetts anti-abolitionists disrupted his speaking engagements, distributing handbills calculated to inflame Anglophobic feeling (much as other groups had done in protest against British actors). "Shall Lowell be the first place to suffer an Englishman to disturb the peace and harmony of our country?" one broadside asked. "Do you wish instruction from an Englishman?" In Concord, New Hampshire, a large crowd forced Thompson to flee in disguise and burned him in effigy, sending the Scottish orator into hiding for the next two weeks.[51]

Even on those occasions when Thompson did not encounter brickbats and surly mobs, he was harried by hecklers who persistently questioned his right to lecture Americans on their institutions. In cities and towns throughout the Northeast, citizens' groups held anti-abolition meetings and drafted resolutions reaffirming their commitment to defend Southern rights, declaring their "deep indignation" at the interference of "foreign emissaries."[52] In New York City, Governor William Marcy presided over a meeting at City Park that drew a crowd of five thousand citizens in opposition to Thompson and his American supporters. Even those who may have sympathized with the antislavery cause had little patience for the immediatists' inflammatory rhetoric. What were Americans to think of a foreigner whose every action in the United States seemed "calculated to divide our churches, produce insubordination in our theological and literary institutions, and prostrate our political union?" asked the president of Wesleyan College.[53] The *Boston Recorder*, a nondenominational Christian weekly with strong antislavery sentiments, deplored mob violence but believed that Garrison and his followers deserved at least some of the blame, suggesting that they were deliberately trying to incite hostility in an attempt to win public favor. They would do well, the *Recorder* advised, to sever their association with British agents.[54]

Northern disapproval notwithstanding, Southern whites viewed these turbulent events with no small degree of alarm. In the nation's capital, Southern congressmen condemned Thompson as a "miscreant foreigner" who was "recruiting his army of fanatics in the North."[55] President Jackson also entered the public debate, applauding in his December 1835 annual message the "strong and impressive" response of Northerners against "emissaries from foreign parts" who had "dared to interfere" in a domestic controversy.[56] Throughout the South, the public furor generated by Thompson's visit prompted widespread rumors of other British-inspired acts of sedition among the slave population. According to one news account, a mob hanged an itinerant English bookseller in October 1835 for inciting slave unrest in the area of Lynchburg, Virginia.[57]

Public indignation over Thompson's visit at last came to a head in Boston in October 1835. A handbill distributed throughout the city exhorted citizens to take matters into their own hands: "That infamous foreign scoundrel THOMPSON, will hold forth this afternoon, at the Liberator office, No. 48, Washington street. The present is a fair opportunity to snake Thompson out!"[58] A crowd gathered at the appointed time, but Thompson was nowhere to be found, having reportedly fled the building in disguise. Garrison also attempted to make his escape, but was soon apprehended and led through the streets at the end of a rope as thousands cheered. In their own accounts of the event, Garrison and his supporters downplayed public resentment of the foreign abolitionist, casting the struggle as an outrage against a native-born citizen. The evidence suggests, however, that the mob had indeed formed to prevent Thompson from speaking, angered that yet another foreigner had the temerity to lecture Americans on their institutions. The chauvinistic mood of the crowd may have actually saved Garrison's life. As the *Liberator* publisher was being led through the streets, according to some reports, cries of "He is an American!" stilled the passions of the mob and saved him from more serious harm.[59]

Thompson departed for home soon afterward. Despite the public furor that accompanied the tour from the outset, and the sour note on which it ended, American immediatists seemed well-pleased with the affair, crediting the Scotsman with "waking up our country."[60] Certainly Thompson had brought the immediatist cause a considerable amount of publicity, which may well have been Garrison's principal objective. Whether the tour had actually won new disciples to the immediatist cause was another matter, though Thompson's oratory netted at least one notable convert: Angelina Grimké, who with her sister Sarah would assume a leadership role in the women's antislavery movement, joined the cause after seeing him speak in Philadelphia.[61]

More moderate antislavery leaders, on the other hand, mindful of the nationalist passions Thompson's tour had provoked, would now seek to maintain a cautious distance from the British emancipation crusade. Reluctant to indulge in unqualified praise of Britain's humanitarian endeavors for fear of giving the appearance of truckling to foreign interests, they lambasted Britain for the social ills that beset the empire, a posture that allowed them to assume common ground with Southern moderates. While applauding emancipation in the West Indies, less radical antislavery leaders felt compelled to add that Great Britain, with its repression of Ireland, starving laboring classes, and "bloated aristocracy," remained a far from perfect example of benevolence.[62] When the Boston Unitarian minister William Ellery Channing held up Great Britain as a model of Christian charity in a much-publicized 1837 open letter to Henry Clay, he was vehemently attacked in the proslavery press for his Anglophile musings. In an effort to clarify his views, the New England cleric issued a subsequent antislavery tract, insisting that he had not meant to single out the American slaveholder for condemnation. Despite the Emancipation Act, he averred, Great Britain remained a country of "boundless luxury, and unthinkable wretchedness."[63]

Northern anti-abolitionists, meanwhile, used Thompson's visit to draw attention to the antislavery movement's British connections and to call for a new spirit of interregional solidarity. One Philadelphia editor downplayed sectional divisions, noting that the Scotsman's speaking tour had produced "a *national* pride, which will frown with just indignation" at all attempts to infringe upon the rights of the South.[64] But while some insisted that the North had risen to the challenge from abroad, not all who condoned slavery were so sure that their section had withstood its trial unscathed. For the author James Kirke Paulding, who understood better than most Americans the extent to which British opinions shaped the postcolonial mind, George Thompson's tour signaled an ominous new phase of Britain's condescension toward its North American offspring. While foreign visitors had long poked fun at the crudities of a bumptious republic, never before had they deliberately engaged in a campaign to set one section of the country against another. Even more worrisome was the fact that this new crop of British visitors was no longer content to simply disparage American institutions, but brazenly called upon citizens of the republic to overthrow them. The attack on slavery, Paulding believed, revealed for the first time a darker purpose: a concrete, well-laid plan to dissolve the Union. Harboring no fondness for slavery, the New Yorker nonetheless believed that even the most objectionable of American institutions had to be defended in the face of British aspersions. The obsequiousness with which Americans bowed to British mores could no longer be lightly dismissed as a sign of immaturity in the young nation. While he continued to ridicule American mimicry of everything British, he left little doubt that the stakes were now immeasurably higher. British blandishments, if allowed to take root, could actually threaten the union itself.[65]

In the South, moderates fearful of rising sectional tensions also

FIGURE 12.

"The Abolition Garrison in Danger and the Narrow Escape of the Scotch Ambassador." In 1834, Scottish abolitionist George Thompson arrived in the United States on a speaking tour arranged by William Lloyd Garrison. In October 1835, a Boston mob ransacked the *Liberator* office. Unable to find Thompson, who had reportedly fled disguised as a woman (*see far right*), the crowd manhandled Garrison, leading him through town with a rope around his neck. (The Library Company of Philadelphia)

clung to the belief that Northern extremism was the product of British subterfuge. Preferring to pillory foreign agitators rather than home-grown ones, they took note of the money and literature that had poured into the country from English abolitionist organizations and wondered if Americans were not playing into British hands by quarreling among themselves.[66] Yet many Southerners were unwilling to place the blame for the turmoil solely upon British reformers. Anger at Northern anti-slavery agitation had been rising before Thompson arrived, and his tour offered compelling evidence that the threat to their way of life was even more serious than they had previously imagined. That a British-inspired abolitionist movement should emerge in New England came as little surprise to the white South, which had harbored doubts about the region's national allegiances since the Hartford Convention. South Carolina congressman William Preston was one of many Southerners troubled by the Anglophilia of the North, and attributed the recent turmoil in part to the fact that its inhabitants had more in common with the British than their Southern brethren. Great Britain, he believed, exercised "a vast power" over American public opinion, especially in the Northeast. "An intense and immediate sympathy bind them together."[67]

A steady stream of British antislavery missionaries followed in Thompson's wake, and though none provoked the same kind of public outrage, their presence continued to stir controversy. When American Methodists held their quadrennial General Conference in May 1836, in Cincinnati, Ohio, Britain's Wesleyans dispatched the Reverend William Lord, bearing antislavery memorials from prominent church leaders. Lord addressed the conference to offer his organization's "fatherly counsel" on the slavery question, thus forcing the nation's Methodist clerics to address the issue for the first time. Despite Methodism's long-standing opposition to the institution in principle, the conference's conservative majority resented foreign meddling. They respectfully pointed to the many differences between slavery as formerly practiced in the British West Indies and slavery in the United States before voting overwhelmingly to condemn abolition. Then, for good measure, they censured those delegates who had supported the British remonstrances.[68]

The debate within the conference had important repercussions for Cincinnati itself, long a tinderbox of racial tensions. The city was home to a sizable free black population, which included a large number of manumitted slaves from nearby Kentucky and Virginia. The antislavery reform movement in the area included several prominent British immigrants, three of whom served on the Ohio Anti-Slavery Society's executive committee. At the same time, the town was an important entrepôt for commerce with the Upper South, and many conservative business leaders were fiercely opposed to any activity that might jeopardize its economic position. These simmering animosities and the recent Methodist Conference both seem to have fueled the anti-abolitionist demonstrations that rocked the city that summer. In a rare spirit of bipartisanship, the Democratic and Whig newspapers blamed foreign agitators for the unrest, the latter enjoining its readers not to "permit a band of fanatics, led on by an English emissary, to make this city the theatre of their operations, from whence they may throw fire-brands in the slave states."[69] The unrest culminated in the destruction of the *Philanthropist* editor James Birney's printing press and attacks on the town's black residents. "When we examine into the character of these men, and enquire from what land they spring, the majority of them will be found *Englishmen!*" declared one Western editor after the rioting.[70]

Tensions in the Queen City on the slavery question remained quiescent for the next few years, but when they resurfaced in the early 1840s, a British citizen once again provided a lightning rod for anti-abolition sentiment. In September, 1841, allegations that Cornelius Burnett, a British-born baker and prominent antislavery advocate, was giving shelter to runaway slaves from Kentucky led to two days of rioting that destroyed Burnett's bakery. Two years later, the abduction by local abolitionists of a slave girl owned by a citizen of New Orleans again brought angry mobs onto the streets of Cincinnati. This time, Burnett seems to have taken no role in the affair, though both the Whig and Democratic papers again pointed to him as one of the city's most notorious abolitionist ringleaders. For two nights Burnett's bakery was the focus of anti-abolition anger, but authorities on this occasion managed to keep at bay a proslavery crowd intent on ransacking the establishment.[71]

Of course, anti-abolition mobs did not target Stuart, Thompson, Burnett, and other British antislavery activists simply because of their foreign birth, but because they fanned to a white heat Northern fears of social chaos and racial amalgamation. British critics of slavery, whether itinerant lecturers or longtime residents of the United States, temporarily shared, but never seized the spotlight from native-born champions of the antislavery movement, who were also targets of anti-abolition fury. Yet nationality played an important part in galvanizing urban crowds hostile to abolitionism, much as it had done in the *émeutes* that periodically disrupted the theatrical scene in Eastern cities. Even when expressions of popular unrest occurred without evidence of British agents, anti-abolitionists continued to employ nativist feeling to whip up popular outrage. When rioting broke out in Alton, Illinois, in November 1837, culminating in the death of abolitionism's first martyr, Elijah Lovejoy, proslavery leaders justified their actions by calling upon citizens to resist "foreign dictation."[72] Exhibitions of public anger, whatever their source, generally drew their energy from a sense of powerlessness and a desire to humble symbols of authority. British agents proved a natural target, for nothing characterized these anxieties more clearly than the American relationship with Great Britain. Like the urban-dwellers who protested visiting English actors, anti-abolition mobs skillfully co-opted an anti-imperialist discourse that was an ever-present feature of republican political culture. That British visitors and residents often *did* play a significant and visible role in the antislavery cause made the task of demonizing antislavery as an assault on national institutions that much easier.

Within the next few years, rising public support for abolition in the Northeast would make it possible for antislavery emissaries to undertake speaking tours without risk of physical harm, though Americans never warmed to the idea of being lectured to by itinerant foreigners. James S. Buckingham declined to address a Boston audience in 1838, having experienced among Americans an unwillingness to give a fair hearing to foreigners whose views disagreed with their own.[73] Yet antislavery activists John Scoble and Joseph Sturge crossed the Atlantic on separate tours soon afterward and found Northern audiences much more receptive to their message. One Englishman Sturge encountered in upstate New York informed him that he had been mobbed by the local townsfolk for speaking out against slavery on no less than four separate occasions since moving there in the 1830s, but that the subject could now be discussed in open forum without incident.[74]

The anti-abolitionist hysteria that gripped Northern cities proved to be short-lived, but its reverberations would be felt long afterward. White Southerners tried to take what comfort they could from the fact that the early immediatists had been roughly treated in many Northern communities. But all the public demonstrations and strongly worded resolutions against "fanatical" agitators could do little to deter the antislavery movement, and thus failed to soothe jangled Southern nerves. Slave owners demanded direct, proactive measures to silence immediate abolitionism, measures the North seemed unable, or unwilling, to provide.

The World Anti-Slavery Convention, 1840

Having rallied a sizable minority of Northerners in opposition to the labor practices of the South, the American antislavery movement now turned its sights on Washington in an effort to bring pressure to bear on the nation's lawmakers. Once again, it drew inspiration and guidance from abroad, calling for a massive petition campaign like the one that had enjoyed such success in Britain. In 1835 the American Anti-Slavery Society laid the first of these petitions before Congress, and two years later the AAS announced plans for a major nationwide petition drive. A handful of Northern representatives, led by John Quincy Adams, began to present petitions from constituents to demand a range of legislative action that included the abolition of slavery and the slave trade in the nation's capital and a ban on the admission of new slave states. The petition drives initially showed signs of becoming the kind of grassroots phenomenon seen in Britain, with an estimated 415,000 signatures collected by the American Anti-Slavery Society in 1838.

It soon became evident, however, that there were limits to how far Americans could go in following the British example. The petition drives that had proved so successful in bringing pressure to bear on Britain's national government were not well-suited to a decentralized federal system in which states exercised considerable autonomy. Proslavery leaders argued that the citizens of one state had no authority to petition the national government for the redress of grievances in another. Antislavery proponents, meanwhile, pointed to the fact that the right of petition was guaranteed to all citizens by the First Amendment. Some, seeking a more august legal basis, traced the right of petition back to the Magna Carta, an argument that prompted the inevitable accusations of Anglophile imitativeness.[75] After much heated debate, Southern members managed to push through the famous "gag" rule, by which all antislavery memorials would be received by the House and then tabled without further discussion. Thereafter, the petitions ceased to be the principal tool for mobilizing antislavery sentiment, although Adams and other committed partisans courted Southern fury and presented them anyway.[76]

Never achieving the cohesion of its British counterpart, the American antislavery movement soon began to fragment over strategies and goals. By the late 1830s, the American Anti-Slavery Society had all but collapsed amid bitter disagreements between the Garrisonians and the more moderate New York faction led by Arthur and Lewis Tappan. Angered by the Boston editor's unyielding opposition to political activism and his insistence that women be given positions of authority within the movement, the moderates in 1840 bolted the group they had helped create.[77]

Predictably, the schism set off a new scramble among American antislavery leaders for British support. By chance, a World Anti-Slavery Convention had been in the planning stages for several months, to be held in London in June. In a scenario reminiscent of the Cresson-Garrison duel seven years earlier, both sides not only sent delegates to attend the meeting, but lobbied heavily to align themselves with a new generation of reformers that had recently assumed leadership of Britain's antislavery crusade. Though ostensibly international in character and purpose, the convention was to a large extent a binational body of American and British abolitionists devoted to the cause of emancipation in the American South.[78] Hosted by the newly formed British and Foreign Antislavery Society, the meeting aimed to establish a formal alliance between the two countries' antislavery movements, a goal that was stymied by the schism within the American ranks. Garrison had dispatched a representative some months earlier to enlist support for the New England faction, but Britain's reformers were decidedly hostile to the group's calls for gender equality.[79] The Tappanites, meanwhile, were also at work to establish close ties with the British organization—in a nod to their British coadjutors, they had named their splinter group the American and Foreign Antislavery Society—and arrived in London to a much warmer reception. The organizing committee refused to seat the six women members of the American delegation, all Garrisonians, a group that included Lucretia Mott and Maria Weston Chapman. Garrison himself arrived too late to take part in the seating controversy. Relinquishing his own seat in protest, he watched the proceedings in angry silence from the gallery.[80]

Despite the contretemps over the seating of female delegates, the meeting did little to discredit the widely held view in the United States that British reformers were actively engaged in fomenting American abolitionist sentiment, prompting critics to rage anew at British meddling in their affairs. That a meeting to discuss the elimination of Southern slavery could even be held on foreign soil was preposterous, they claimed, as egregious an affront to national sovereignty as if Americans had held a conference to support the democratic Chartist movement in the British Isles. What was more, the conference revealed the extent to which the loftiest circles of British society had involved themselves in the American slavery question. While stateside abolitionists could be dismissed as "mere cyphers," the World Anti-Slavery Convention demonstrated that the British movement was a highly sophisticated, well-funded organization consisting of peers of the realm, members of Parliament, captains of industry and commerce. Americans were especially shocked to learn that Prince Albert, the husband of Queen Victoria, had chaired one of the sessions.[81] No less ominously, as far as proslavery advocates were concerned, the deliberations furnished fresh and compelling evidence that a small group of American activists was working hand in glove with the British reform movement. Composed largely of Tappanites, the U.S. delegation had assumed a prominent role in the proceedings, with James Birney serving as one of the vice-chairmen of the conference. After the meeting adjourned, several members embarked on speaking tours to lecture British audiences on the evils of Southern slavery, eliciting much unfavorable comment in the anti-abolition press at home.[82]

Convening as the presidential campaign in the United States was getting underway, the London meeting helped to fix the slavery question firmly in the national spotlight, much to the dismay of mainstream political leaders. Moderates of both parties had managed to prevent the issue from disturbing the 1836 presidential contest, but by 1840, as Washington solons quarreled over the gag rule and the possible annexation of slaveholding Texas, the two parties' customary evasion on the subject had become all but impossible. Although moderate Northern Whigs tried to distance themselves from the goings-on in London, a small cohort of antislavery activists praised the conference and its goals. In a move calculated to inflame Southern leaders, John Quincy Adams even invited conference organizers Lord Morpeth and Joseph Sturge to sit in the House gallery when they visited the capital eighteen months later. The gesture had the desired effect. Henry Wise, a thirty-five-year-old Whig congressman from Virginia, was so infuriated by the presence of the two abolitionists that he held the floor for two days, excoriating Adams and his antislavery colleagues as full-fledged members of an "English party." In a voice "so fitful and unsteady" that much of what he said was lost to the House reporter, Wise accused Adams of aiding and abetting the British government in a plot to destroy slavery throughout the hemisphere. As in other heated partisan battles, when tempers flared, charges of treason—and, more precisely, collusion with British enemies—inevitably followed.[83]

❧

In the decade since William Lloyd Garrison first called for the abolition of the slave empire, the doctrine of immediatism seemed to have made little headway as a national reform issue. Public support for the cause remained limited, and its leading adherents had parted ways, bitterly at odds over tactics and goals. Yet radical abolitionism could best be judged not by its substantive achievements, but by its ability to generate fear within the slaveholding community, and in that regard its success had been nothing short of spectacular. It did not, of course, take much to fan the flames of Southern hysteria. Slaveholders had always been alert to even the most remote peril to their institution, and as the chorus of opposition grew louder, they became ever more eager to view such threats in apocalyptic terms. For this reason, it seemed hard to believe that something as ominous as antislavery extremism was the work of meddling reformers. Southerners had once been willing to allow, albeit grudgingly, that humanitarian concerns had prompted Wilberforce and others to campaign against the slave trade. Now they wondered whether more insidious forces were at work, suspecting that Christian benevolence was being exploited by British leaders "as a cloak for their designs on America."[84]

As has been seen in earlier chapters, Americans during the Jacksonian period routinely indulged in transatlantic scapegoating. They believed that British travel writers had been dispatched by their government to discredit democratic institutions and quash the stirrings of popular sovereignty at home. They believed that Parliament was seeking to flood the American market with cheaply made factory goods in order to thwart the emergence of the United States as a manufacturing rival. They believed, too, that the British government was using the Bank of England as an instrument to bring the American financial system under its control. Little wonder, then, that Americans readily accepted the proposition that the British government had co-opted antislavery reform for the express purpose of sowing seeds of discord in the United States, to pit one section against the other under the guise of philanthropy.

Just as they had done in the controversy over the tariff, Americans looked instinctively to Great Britain at the first sign of antislavery agitation. Anti-abolitionist leaders had discerned the broad outlines of a sinister conspiracy hatched in Whitehall when William Lloyd Garrison returned from England in 1833.[85] The subsequent arrival of British antislavery lecturers and the petition campaigns modeled after those which had proved so successful in Britain lent credence to such a plot, convincing American Anglophobes that the transatlantic antislavery campaign had its roots in the larger geopolitical rivalry between Great Britain and the republic.[86] In their most frenzied—and self-involved—moments, some Southerners could even declare that Parliament had passed the Emancipation Act with the American South foremost in mind. The 1840 antislavery conference, in which parliamentary leaders made clear their eagerness to export their program of emancipation, served to buttress the suspicion that antislavery reform was part of a larger transatlantic conspiracy conceived and directed by the British government.[87]

Anxious slaveholders did not, of course, minimize the role played by Americans in the rapid rise of abolitionist sentiment. But in the alternate universe that is the peculiar domain of the conspiratorially minded, the unfamiliar, external threat often serves to complement and reinforce the threat that exists close at hand. Americans had always pointed an accusing finger across the Atlantic in times of domestic crisis, and as the abolition movement gathered momentum they continued to do so. In a political culture that had long been saturated by rumors of British intrigue, it took little imagination to arrive at the conclusion that antislavery agitation was part of a preexisting conspiratorial trope "with branches on both sides of the Atlantic."[88] This was not the view of an excitable minority. The most sober-minded citizens also subscribed to the theory that larger, transatlantic forces were at work; indeed, they may have been even more susceptible to such phantoms. Better to believe that Great Britain was plotting "the downfall of our country," than that Americans would do so on their own.[89]

⊰ 9 ⊱

Breaking the "Iron Hoop"

We are marching on to Madawask,
To fight the trespassers;
We'll teach the British how to walk
And come off conquerors.
We'll have our land, right good and clear,
For all the English say;
They shall not cut another log,
Nor stay another day.

—Aroostook war song, 1838

I t is tempting to regard the diplomatic relations between Great Britain and the United States immediately after the War of 1812 as an extension of the harmony often associated with American domestic politics—a transatlantic "Era of Good Feeling." The Treaty of Ghent ending the war had proved so popular that the Senate had ratified it without a single dissenting vote. Substantive agreements on other thorny issues soon followed. The 1817 Rush-Bagot Treaty provided for the naval disarmament of the Great Lakes (although both sides continued to build land fortifications along the border). The Convention of 1818 fixed the U.S.-Canadian boundary at the 49th parallel and stipulated that the two countries would, for the time being, respect each other's claim to the Oregon Territory.[1] To be sure, conflicts sometimes arose, prompting strongly worded notes of protest to course through diplomatic channels. On the whole, however, the dialogue between the two capitals during the early decades of the nineteenth century was characterized by a tone of gentlemanly civility, with like-minded elites representing like-minded nations.

Yet beneath the surface calm of diplomatic decorum lay the shared memory of two generations of violent conflict. Convinced that Great

Britain would remain alert to any sign of weakness on the part of the United States, Americans believed their republic was most vulnerable at the margins. Lingering fears that peace had not brought the end of Britain's campaign to destabilize the republic's frontier were reinforced by postwar developments in Florida. There, a political vacuum existed as Spain's overseas empire collapsed. In recent years the area had become a volatile sanctuary for runaway slaves, maroons, and refugee Creeks, who had been decisively defeated in 1814 by Andrew Jackson at the Battle of Horseshoe Bend. All mixed freely with indigenous Seminoles to form a polyglot population of the dispossessed. The Pensacola region had served as a staging area for British troops during the recent war, from which Sir Edward Pakenham launched his offensive against Louisiana that would end so disastrously at the Battle of New Orleans. Although British forces evacuated the Florida panhandle in compliance with the Treaty of Ghent, they left behind a well-stocked fort on the Apalachicola River, twenty-five miles from the Gulf of Mexico, occupied by several hundred blacks, many still in British uniform. Adding to American concerns, British merchants and sundry adventurers continued to drift in and out of the area from the Bahamas, trading with the Indians and nourishing their hopes of renewed British military aid. When Spanish authorities proved powerless to comply with Washington's requests to subjugate the fort—now renamed Negro Fort but still flying the British flag—the United States dispatched an expedition to destroy the stronghold.[2]

The border strife between Indians and settlers in Georgia and Alabama persisted, however, and in 1818 Washington ordered General Andrew Jackson, the nation's new military champion, to deal with the Seminole threat. Jackson's instructions were vague—by design, according to some historians, who have argued that the Monroe administration was looking for a pretext to seize Florida. Monroe had alerted Jackson to the unwelcome intelligence that Britain was believed to be cooperating fully with Spain to gain control of the area, a rumor which, if true, would threaten the security of the Southeastern states.[3] Whatever the president's intentions, Jackson was soon barging across the border, convinced that the Seminole depredations against American settlers were the handiwork of British agent provocateurs. As the army moved south, it distributed handbills urging the Indians to cease their attacks, informing them that they had been misled and betrayed by "the people beyond the sea."[4]

Jackson soon found evidence to confirm his suspicions of British agitation. The army captured Robert Ambrister, a former officer in the Royal Marines, at the head of an armed company of non-whites. Shortly afterward, Alexander Arbuthnot, a Scottish merchant with a reputation as an outspoken advocate of British protection of Indian rights, was arrested and his schooner seized. Although Ambrister's filibustering activities do not appear to have been sanctioned by his government, and the evidence that Arbuthnot had aided the Indians in their attacks against Americans was circumstantial at best, Jackson ordered both men executed after a brief military trial. Seemingly oblivious to the fact that he had caused a major international incident by invading the soil of a sovereign nation and executing citizens of a country with which the United States was not at war, Jackson crossed back into Alabama, well-pleased at having rid the area of "foreign influence" and "foreign agents" and having brought at last a sense of security to the Southeastern states.[5]

The incursion and subsequent execution of Arbuthnot and Ambrister have often been attributed to Jackson's legendary hotheadedness. Yet it should be added that, in this instance at least, the frontier general's ingrained Anglophobia was also a reason for his intemperate conduct. Like many border-dwelling Americans, Jackson was never more alive to the danger of Indian depredations as when he believed they were being sponsored by the British. For the Tennessee general and other settlers living on the fringes of the republic, a sense of security had always proved elusive, and would remain so as long as Britain claimed a foothold on the continent.[6]

Jackson's apprehensions were shared by many Americans after 1815. While the war had finally put to rest the fear that Great Britain might reconquer its errant colonies, Washington continued to regard its commanding presence in the western hemisphere with no little concern. With its standard planted firmly in Canada and the Caribbean, Britain was still in a position to threaten the United States. These encirclement anxieties would only grow more acute in the years ahead, as the British empire became more formidable, its geopolitical ambitions in the western hemisphere more obtrusive. Westward-looking Americans, as well as those whose mercantile orientation made them more aware of the republic's place in a global marketplace, both took the view that Great Britain was the greatest single obstacle to their ambitions.

The *North American Review* articulated the concerns of many citizens when it noted in 1828 that Great Britain was uniquely situated to frustrate both the territorial and commercial aspirations of Americans by virtue of its "perfect line of military stations" extending from the Windward Islands in the Caribbean to Halifax, Nova Scotia; from Eastport, Maine, to the mouth of the Columbia River in Oregon.[7] As the nation began to push beyond its existing limits, as it began to define its strategic and economic interests in terms that extended beyond its own borders, the North American republic would confront the myriad ways in which its imperial parent could potentially check its growth. Americans may have been secure in their Independence, but they still chafed at the cords of British power, which after 1815 seemed to grip more tightly than ever before.[8]

The Power to the North

Much like Southern planters who saw evidence of foreign agency at the root of slave unrest, citizens on the margins of the republic tended to regard threats to public safety in a wider, transatlantic context. This was particularly true in the Old Northwest, where the Crown's alliances with the Native American tribes had been successful in impeding white settlement since the end of the Revolution. These alliances were at best uneasy ones. At times the Indians acted at the behest of, or in concert with, their British sponsors; at times they pursued a political agenda of their own, wholly independent of royal authority. Regardless of the precise nature of Indian allegiances at any given moment, there could be no doubt that the arming and outfitting of Native Americans by British officials had contributed greatly to the havoc visited on white settlements west of the Appalachians in the years since independence. During the late war, the British had lent their support to Native American efforts to create a tribal confederacy in the West extending from the Great Lakes to the Gulf of Mexico, a goal that ended with the death of the Shawnee chief Tecumseh at the Battle of the Thames in 1813. After the Treaty of Ghent, Britain abandoned its claim to the Old Northwest and withdrew above the 49th parallel, a fundamental shift in its North America policy that signaled its grudging acceptance of U.S. sovereignty. Nonetheless, the history of British-sponsored Indian depredations was a long one that would remain imprinted in the collective psyche of Western settlers for many years to come.

Although Jackson's foray into Florida put an end to American fears of British-Indian collusion in the Southeast, the informal alliance continued to be a concern for federal and state authorities in the Great Lakes region. From their forts in Canada, British officials and independent traders continued to lavish gifts upon the Indians, as they had always done, winning favor through the distribution of food, blankets, clothing, iron implements, and, most importantly, guns and ammunition. To counteract British influence in the Great Lakes, the federal government had established trading posts, providing merchandise to the Indians in exchange for furs. A variety of obstacles—underfunding by Congress, the opposition of private American fur companies, and the preference of the Indians for British-made goods—contributed to the abandonment of the system in 1822.[9] With area settlers lacking the resources to assume the trade on their own, Native Americans continued to maintain close relations with the British in Canada, visiting each summer Drummond Island on Lake Huron, and Fort Malden on the Detroit River.[10] Lewis Cass, then serving as governor of the Michigan Territory, informed the War Department that in "nine cases out of ten," depredations against white settlers in the Michigan Territory were committed by Indians returning from outposts in Canada, "carrying with them British presents & British counsels." Echoing the sentiments of Americans who regarded British antislavery humanitarianism as a sham, Cass maintained that it was "perfectly farcical" to assume that British gifting practices stemmed from philanthropic motives; rather, they were designed to prejudice the Western tribes against white Americans.[11]

The protection of the Northwestern frontier was a high priority for the Monroe administration. Under the energetic leadership of John C. Calhoun, the War Department authorized a series of expeditions to explore the region from the Great Lakes to the Rocky Mountains. The purpose of these expeditions was twofold: to establish military outposts to keep a watchful eye on British activities, and to protect the American fur trade from the Hudson's Bay Company and Northwest Company, which were believed to be operating south of the 49th parallel. In addition, Washington lawmakers approved an extensive Western road-building program, hoping to protect the northern frontier by encouraging settlement.[12]

Fears that Britain might renew its efforts to pit the North American tribes against white settlers would lend considerable weight to the argument that Native peoples should be relocated west of the Mississippi. Thomas Jefferson, who at least flirted with the idea of coexistence, abandoned his hopes for the cultural assimilation of Native Americans after the War of 1812, noting that the "unprincipled policy of England has defeated all our labors for the salvation of these unfortunate people."[13] The prospect of a renewed Indian-British alliance was still an issue when Washington turned aggressively to a policy of tribal removal under Andrew Jackson. As Jackson's secretary of war, Lewis Cass cited national security concerns as a reason for relocation, concerns that seemed fully justified to Western settlers with the outbreak of the Black Hawk War.[14] Following passage of the Indian Removal Bill in 1829, federal authorities ordered the Sauk and Fox tribes to abandon their lands in northern Illinois and move west of the Mississippi River into Iowa. Bowing to the inevitable, most villages submitted to federal authority, save for a group known as the "British band," led by Black Hawk, a Sauk war chief and a veteran of the War of 1812. Black Hawk had continued to maintain strong ties with Canadian officials, making annual visits each summer to receive presents from the British at Fort Malden.[15] Cherishing a "deep rooted infatuation towards England," the Sauks had heard rumors, reportedly spread by "foreign agents," that a war between Great Britain and the United States was imminent. Believing, like the Seminoles fifteen years earlier, that British aid would be forthcoming, Black Hawk crossed the Mississippi in 1831 in search of food and to reclaim tribal lands. Returning again the following year, Black Hawk and his followers were crushed by a combined force of federal troops and state militia at the Battle of the Bad Axe River.[16]

After the Black Hawk War, the War Department continued to worry that Native Americans in the Old Northwest would be encouraged to harass white settlements by their allies to the north. The northern tribes could only be effectively neutralized as a security threat, the advocates of removal argued, if they were situated far from Canadian trading posts. Acting on these fears, the Bureau of Indian Affairs in 1841 unveiled a plan to create a 30-million-acre Indian Territory encompassing parts of northern Iowa, southern Minnesota, and the eastern regions of North and South Dakota. The Tyler administration lacked sufficient support in Congress to implement the policy, however, and the plan was shelved.[17]

Meanwhile, a new flashpoint for smoldering tensions between Great Britain and the United States had erupted along the Canadian border. In 1837 rebellions flared in both Upper and Lower Canada in opposition to the British colonial government. Lacking effective coordination, the insurrections stood little chance of success, and the end of the year found the rebels in disarray, many having fled south into the United States. There they found not only sympathy but strong public support for their cause. As Americans rushed to their aid, the insurrections soon became less a struggle for home rule than a frenzy of filibusterism that created havoc along the border and threatened to provoke a third war between Great Britain and the United States. Lured by the prospect of profit and adventure in the midst of hard economic times, young men from the Northern states joined a network of secret societies known as the Hunters' Lodges to wrest Canada from British control.[18]

In December 1837, a band of American filibusters seized a Canadian island in the Niagara River and hired a vessel, the *Caroline*, to ferry supplies from the American side. In response, a Canadian force crossed the river and seized the ship, killing one crew member and torching the vessel before setting it adrift. The ship sank before it reached the Falls, though initial reports that the *Caroline* had plummeted to its destruction with all hands aboard further inflamed American public opinion. The jingoistic press called for war. The Van Buren administration prudently demurred, mindful of the fact that the incursions of American filibusters into Canada had provoked British officials to act in the first place.[19]

The following year would see the most serious clash of arms between Britons and Americans since the War of 1812, with the Lodges and their Canadian allies launching a series of uncoordinated attacks along a 1,000-mile border from Maine to Michigan. Shouting "Remember the *Caroline!*" American filibusters avenged the destruction of the U.S. vessel in late May by burning a Canadian steamer, the *Sir Robert Peel.* In November, an invasion force of three hundred attempted to take Fort Wellington near the town of Prescott on the St. Lawrence River, but surrendered after a four-day siege. An attack on Windsor the following month again resulted in the routing of American adventurers, and by 1840 the filibusters had dispersed.[20]

As the activities of the Hunters' Lodges subsided, another crisis was brewing in the Northeast over the Maine boundary. The border between the state of Maine and the Canadian province of New Brunswick had been a source of contention since the close of the War for Independence, with each side basing their claim on differing interpretations of the 1783 Treaty of Paris. The dispute became more acrimonious following Maine statehood in 1820, when the new legislature, determined to gain control of the richly forested Aroostook River Valley, began issuing land titles to settlers in defiance of British claims. Tensions flared during the winter of 1838–39 when Canadian lumberjacks entered the disputed area, prompting Maine to call out its state militia. The harried Van Buren administration dispatched General Winfield Scott to the northern border to arrange a truce before the "Aroostook War" could claim any lives. Anxious to avoid hostilities, Washington and Whitehall agreed to submit their claims to a boundary commission.[21]

Competing territorial claims on the opposite side of the North American continent were another source of transatlantic disagreement. Since the late eighteenth century both countries had laid claim to the Pacific Northwest, where trading companies vied for the lucrative fur trade, buying pelts from the Indians that were then shipped to Asia. By far the most successful of these operations was the British Hudson's Bay Company, which built a fort at the mouth of the Columbia River and a chain of outposts throughout the Pacific Northwest. In 1818 British and American diplomats agreed to the joint occupation of the region, an agreement that was renewed in 1827. With Americans largely ignorant of the potential attractions of Oregon, however, the Hudson's Bay Company enjoyed virtual control over the area, a situation that changed in 1834 when American missionaries settled in the fertile Willamette Valley.

Due largely to their promotional efforts, hundreds of land-hungry set-tlers were soon making their way along the Oregon Trail, and by the end of the decade some 5,000 emigrants had made the arduous trek across the continent. American mercantile interests, meanwhile, increasingly frustrated by Britain's Corn Laws and other commercial barriers, had begun to look westward for new markets, regarding the Puget Sound as an attractive gateway to Asian commerce.[22]

Leading the charge in the House of Representatives for an aggressive assertion of American claims to the Oregon Territory was Caleb Cush-ing, a young Whig maverick from Massachusetts. The heir to a shipping fortune, Cushing's interest in Oregon had much to do with his desire to see the nation acquire deep-water harbors on the Pacific coast, although he often echoed the rhetoric of Western Democrats in calling for Brit-ain's expulsion from the Northwest to ensure the safety of the Anglo-American frontier.[23] Accusing the British of arming the Indian tribes in preparation for a third war with the United States, the Massachusetts congressman alleged that the Hudson's Bay Company was no harmless commercial enterprise, but a power unto itself, much like the East India Company. Although its relations with the American settlers who trick-led into the area were generally more helpful than menacing, Cushing characterized the operation as an ominous instrument of British imperi-alism that waited only for the word from London to strike at defenseless American settlements. A fervent Anglophobe, Cushing "thought that inflammatory declamation against England upon all possible topics was the shortcut to popularity," the crusty John Quincy Adams noted in his diary, "and he speechified accordingly."[24]

Britain and the Latin American Republics

Vigilant toward British territorial aggrandizement in the western hemi-sphere, U.S. policymakers were no less disturbed by the informal network of financial and commercial arrangements that advanced Whitehall's strategic and geopolitical interests. After the Napoleonic Wars, a new British empire had emerged, more formidable in its sweep and reach than the mercantile colonial system of old, combining the island's tradi-tional strength, its mastery of the seas, with its new role as the world's preeminent, (and indeed, for a time the *only*) industrialized nation. In the 1820s, both Great Britain and the United States speedily recognized the fledgling Latin American republics that had been created following the collapse of Spain's colonial empire, excited by the prospect of new markets that had long been closed to them by the Bourbon's strict mer-cantilistic policies. It soon became apparent that monarchical Britain, with its cheap manufactured goods and abundant investment capital, not the sister republic to the north, was better positioned to win favor with creole elites. British investors poured money into Latin America, and although these ventures failed to yield the bonanza they had hoped for, the extensive business connections that resulted from them brought the new regimes firmly within the economic orbit of the British empire. The goodwill British capitalists enjoyed in Latin America caused profound jealousy in Washington, so much so that when Spain sought to reimpose its colonial rule, Foreign Secretary George Canning's suggestion that the two governments issue a joint declaration of protest was promptly scotched by Secretary of State John Quincy Adams. Determined that the United States not be seen as "a cock boat in the wake of the British man-of-war," Adams urged President Monroe to issue a non-colonization statement of his own.[25]

This spirited if empty gesture of independence, known to later generations as the Monroe Doctrine, could do nothing to stem British commercial penetration of Latin America. While the two countries' mercantile interests jockeyed for the carrying trade, the United States could not compete with Britain as a source of manufactures or investment capital, any more than it could supply the wants of Native Americans in the Old Northwest. U.S. diplomats chafed at the special favors accorded British commercial agents, which they communicated in plaintive dispatches to the State Department. In Buenos Aires, the U.S. consul wrote that he could scarcely find "any gentleman of rank" who was not "directly or indirectly subservient to British influence." Recognizing that capital constituted a new form of geopolitical power, he marveled at how Britain enjoyed "all the advantages of colonial dependence without the expense of civil or military administration."[26]

The challenges the United States faced in its competition with Britain to win the favor of hemispheric neighbors were not strictly economic. Wedded to the principle of isolationism and the strictures of limited government, Washington saw little need for a professional foreign service, and as a consequence each administration tended to rely on party loyalists to fill the ranks of the diplomatic corps, the vast majority of whom were utterly lacking in experience abroad. Such parochialism contrasted sharply with the global vision of the Foreign Office, whose career diplomats served not only as emissaries of their government but as de facto agents of British economic power. In this capacity, they collected data for cartographers and provided valuable, highly detailed information regarding their host country's potential for commercial penetration, colonization, and financial investment. Their findings often reached a wide audience at home as travel memoirs and emigrant guides, feeding

Britons' insatiable appetite for practical knowledge as they set about the task of empire-building. American envoys, by contrast, were generally oblivious to these wider national constituencies, and tended to confine their efforts within the narrow range of diplomatic duties prescribed by the State Department.

Britain's relationship with the Mexican republic presented the most serious and long-standing irritant for those seeking to advance U.S. interests in Latin America. In the mid-1820s Mexico borrowed £6,400,000 through the sale of interest-bearing bonds, a transaction that borrower and creditor alike would soon regret. By 1827, its economy still reeling from the War for Independence against Spain, Mexico defaulted on the debt, unable to pay even the dividends due the bondholders. British investors had little choice but to reschedule the loan, in what would prove to be only the first of many failed efforts to help Mexico meet its debt obligations. As dividend arrears accumulated, the principal rose to £10,000,000 by mid-century, a crippling financial burden for a nation emerging from three centuries of colonial rule.[27] A poor investment, the loans nonetheless gave Whitehall considerable leverage over a succession of Mexican governments, much to the chagrin of the U.S. legation. The suspicion and distrust with which American representatives regarded their British counterparts on occasion devolved into unseemly ministerial feuds. Joel Poinsett, the United States' first minister to Mexico, became so resentful of his British rival, Henry George Ward, and the influence Ward enjoyed over the conservative government of Lucas Alamán, that he allied himself openly with the opposition party in the nation's capital. Despite a fluency in Spanish, Poinsett found himself thoroughly outmaneuvered by Ward, an effective lobbyist for British mining interests and the author of a two-volume treatise on Mexico's mineral wealth. The Alamán government eventually collapsed, but Poinsett's efforts to bring about a more pro-American regime had created so much ill will that the new government was obliged to request his recall in 1829.[28]

As Washington became increasingly aware of the desirability of gaining ports on the Pacific, Mexico's indebtedness took on a more worrisome aspect. In 1839, with the publication of Alexander Forbes's *California*, Americans first became alarmed that Great Britain might seek to add the harbors of California to its global commercial empire. A British merchant and consular official in Mexico, Forbes waxed rhapsodic about the region's virtues as a colony for English settlers, and speculated openly about the possibility that Britain might cancel its debt to Mexico in exchange for the cession of the territory. In the years that followed, the American press would periodically catch wind of fresh rumors that an insolvent Mexico had decided to cede California to Great Britain in exchange for the assumption of its debt obligations, sparking a flurry of calls to extend American aegis to the Pacific.[29]

In October 1842, in an episode weirdly reminiscent of Andrew Jackson's unauthorized raid into Florida a quarter of a century earlier, an overzealous U.S. naval commander, Commodore Thomas ap Catesby Jones, acting on the erroneous belief that Mexico, backed by Great Britain, had declared war against the United States, briefly seized Monterey, California. Training his cannon on the fort guarding the harbor, Jones issued a proclamation claiming the entire area for the United States, while the bewildered Californios looked on. Only after local authorities showed him the most recent copies of Mexico City newspapers, which said nothing about war between the two countries, did Jones realize his mistake and sheepishly lower his flag. Officially, the administration had no choice but to disavow Jones's impetuosity, although no disciplinary action against him was taken. But once again, the rash conduct of American military commanders, acting seemingly on their own initiative, revealed the deeper anxieties of a republic that felt straitjacketed by British power.[30]

The South Endangered: The Caribbean Basin

The Caribbean Basin represented another vital pressure point that could be exploited by Great Britain, many U.S. policymakers believed. Although the economic value of its sugar plantations had declined in recent years, Britain remained the dominant presence in the region, having over the course of two centuries amassed a collection of colonies anchored by Jamaica, the Bahamas, and the Leeward and Windward Islands. In addition, Britain claimed footholds in Central America (Honduras), and on South America's northeastern coast (British Guiana). After 1815 it added St. Lucia, Trinidad, and Tobago to its crop of sugar colonies in the West Indies, and was widely rumored to covet Cuba and Puerto Rico, still nominally held by Spain.[31] Britain's broad swath of island and coastal possessions gave it enormous strategic advantages in the mid-Atlantic rim, providing ports of call for the Royal Navy, which stood poised to blockade the American South in the event of war. But it was not just Britain's naval supremacy in the region that gave Americans pause. As the plantation system expanded across the Lower South, whites saw with no little alarm the potential for British troublemaking. With its population of two million slaves, the South increasingly came to be seen as the American republic's Achilles' heel.

It was one of the great ironies of American slavery that Southern whites feared the peculiar institution even as they vowed to defend it at all costs, and nowhere did they fear it more than in areas beyond their control. While Southerners were thrown into absolute panic by the occasional slave revolts that occurred within their own borders, the much larger and destructive insurrections that periodically gripped the sugar plantations of the Caribbean also served to remind them that they had fashioned their world out of combustible materials. The Haitian Revolution in 1802, which resulted in the virtual annihilation of the French colony's planter class, had been the hemisphere's bloodiest racial conflagration, and, more recently, violence had engulfed the British colonies as well. Some 13,000 slaves revolted in Demerara (eastern British Guiana) in 1823, and as many as 60,000 took part in the so-called Christmas Rebellion in Jamaica in 1831 (the same year as the Nat Turner Revolt). In short, Southern whites regarded the Caribbean as a giant tinderbox, one spark from which would set their world aflame.[32]

The Emancipation Act of 1833 ensured that the Caribbean would continue to be an area of utmost concern to Americans. The liberation of 800,000 slaves in its sugar colonies represented for Britain a great leap into the unknown, a social experiment on a grand scale that could not help but have a profound impact on the slavery debate in the United States. Southerners, not surprisingly, predicted that the islands would descend into anarchy, igniting a racial bloodbath between master and slave. Such nightmarish scenarios proved unwarranted, although emancipation did have important economic repercussions. Having ceased to be a cornerstone of Britain's wealth, the colonies had been in decline for some time, a trend that accelerated following the elimination of the apprentice system in 1838.[33]

Proslavery and antislavery groups both endeavored to put their own spin on the situation in the West Indies in an effort to influence public opinion in the United States. The first indication that emancipation would have deleterious consequences for the sugar economy came from Robert M. Harrison, U.S. consul to Kingston, Jamaica. A slaveholder who believed the Afro-Caribbean population unfit for emancipation, Harrison was hardly the most objective analyst. He was also a staunch Anglophobe, who harbored no doubt that ulterior motives were behind British philanthropy. Nonetheless, the American merchant had been at his post since the Jackson administration, and his opinions carried considerable weight in Washington. The businessman enjoyed especially close contacts with John C. Calhoun and members of his inner circle, who lost no time feeding his reports of economic chaos to the Southern press. By the early 1840s, the verdict was in, at least as far as Southern slaveholders were concerned. Britain's great experiment, they declared, had been an economic disaster.[34]

Why the British government, so omnipotent, so zealous in its pursuit of its own self-interest, had allowed this to occur was a matter of considerable speculation in the United States. Some conspiracy theorists posited that the West Indian sugar trade had actually been undermined by other commercial interests within the empire, specifically East Indian planters and merchants who stood to profit from its demise. Whatever the reason, Southern slaveholders, for whom the glass always seemed to be half empty rather than half full, took little comfort from reports of the British West Indies' economic difficulties. Instead, they grimly spied a new threat to their way of life. Now that emancipation had failed, they believed, Britain would seek to impose the same system of free labor on its rivals to regain its economic competitiveness in tropical agriculture.[35]

The first signs that the British government was seeking to promote antislavery among its neighbors appeared in Cuba, once the diadem of Spain's colonial empire. In 1840, Foreign Secretary Lord Palmerston appointed David Turnbull, a well-known antislavery activist, as British consul to Havana. The diplomat wasted little time antagonizing Cuba's planters, who demanded his immediate recall. Whitehall bowed to pressure from Spanish officials and in 1842 removed Turnbull from office, but not before the zealous abolitionist attempted to liberate several hundred slaves who had been shipped to Cuba from the Bahamas. Spanish authorities, their patience at an end, ordered his arrest and expelled him from the island. Sent by the Foreign Office to a new post in Jamaica, Turnbull was allegedly still plotting to liberate slaves in the Spanish colony two years later.[36]

Faced with evidence that Great Britain was seeking to incite slave insurrections in Cuba, American slaveholders believed that it might do the same against the Southern states. This was hardly wild-eyed alarmism, Southern whites having not forgotten Pakenham's use of black troops in his invasion of Louisiana a quarter of a century earlier. By 1840, Harrison in Kingston was sending disturbing notes to Washington, warning of British plans to "*spy out all our defenses*" in anticipation of an invasion of the Lower South. The U.S. consul was especially exercised by the idea that this could be accomplished covertly, with elite black forces that could infiltrate the South, train slaves in the use of firearms, and lead them in revolt. The British press could not resist stoking the flames of Southern hysteria. Declaring that a war with the United States would be "a blessing to mankind," an 1841 editorial in *Fraser's Magazine*, widely quoted in American newspapers, suggested that the dissolution of the union could be easily effected by sending Jamaican troops to foment rebellion.[37] The prospect of servile insurrection launched from the British West Indies held for Southern political leaders like John C. Calhoun all the horrors of a racial Armageddon:

> To this continent the blow would be calamitous beyond description. . . . It would not end there; but would in all probability extend, by example, the war of races over all of South America, including Mexico, and extending to the Indian, as well as to the African race; and make the whole one scene of blood and devastation.[38]

While most Northerners did not share Calhoun's sense of apocalyptic foreboding, the idea that the British government intended to use West Indian emancipation to agitate the slavery question in the United States enjoyed wide credence. Even Boston's *North American Review* argued for increased naval preparedness in the Gulf of Mexico, fearing that the South would be the most obvious target of a British invasion.[39] With the exception of antislavery immediatists, Americans by the 1840s generally viewed emancipation as a component of Britain's imperial policy, one of the more frightening weapons in its arsenal, which could be used to bring down rival nation-states. It "has been the great mover in the hellish plot against our welfare," declared the *Louisville Democrat* of Britain's role in the growing antislavery crisis. "She has warmed the viper into life, and cast it among us, to poison us with insidious stings, the quiet of our firesides, the peace of our domestic circles."[40]

The South Endangered: Texas

Southern conspiracy fears were also being driven by events closer to home. Mexican-held Texas had long been viewed as a potential area for development by Southern whites, who were fond of claiming, on the flimsiest of evidence, that the region had actually been acquired by the United States in the Louisiana Purchase in 1803. American filibusters considered the sparsely populated region ripe with opportunity, launching occasional forays into the area. In an effort to put an end to expansionist pressures from the United States, Mexico in the 1820s initiated an immigration program to settle the region. To its dismay, it found that few Mexicans or Europeans were prepared to take advantage of the offer. Instead, the policy touched off a land rush among Anglo-Americans in the Lower Mississippi Valley, who constituted Texas's dominant ethnic group within a few years.

American interest in Texas soon attracted the notice of Whitehall, which worried that these developments might undermine the territorial integrity and political stability of its closest Latin American ally. British diplomats warned the Mexican government that more stringent measures were needed to curtail the influx of American settlers. But having opened the door to U.S. immigration, Mexico would now find it impossible to close. British leaders became even more concerned when two presidents, John Quincy Adams and Andrew Jackson, tried to purchase Texas. The Mexican government needed no prodding from Whitehall to reject these overtures, but some British leaders were sufficiently worried by evidence of American expansionist appetites to state publicly that their government would not allow the United States to extend its domain at the expense of Mexico.[41]

For their part, U.S. policymakers were no less wary of British influence in the region. In the 1820s, the slavery controversy had yet to fully grab the nation's attention, and there existed a bipartisan and biregional consensus that Mexico's indebtedness to British bondholders could well be injurious to American long-term geopolitical objectives. With unrestricted access to the Gulf of Mexico viewed as essential not only to American commerce but also American national security, the prospect of British dominion over Texas was an unsettling one. And as hopes for stable republican government in Mexico faded amid a series of military coups, a British satellite on the southern boundary of the United States seemed less and less like a remote possibility. Soon after his arrival in Texas, Sam Houston, who would later gain fame at the Battle of San Jacinto, alerted his mentor Andrew Jackson to the danger of British interference in the area, observing that if the United States did not acquire it, "England will most assuredly obtain it by some means."[42]

Fifteen years after Mexico opened Texas to foreign settlement, British concerns that Americans might try to wrest the land from its control were realized. The pretext for revolt came in 1834, when Mexican president Antonio López de Santa Anna, in an effort to consolidate his political power, abrogated the federalist Constitution of 1824. A wave of rebellions and resistance followed throughout the country. Above the Rio Grande, Tejanos and Anglo-Texans initially joined in common cause against Santa Anna's centralist rule. But the Texas rebellion soon proved altogether different than the uprisings in other provinces. What began as a struggle to reassert Texas's autonomy within the Mexican state quickly became a war for independence, as thousands of Anglo-American volunteers poured across the Sabine River, lured by the prospect of adventure and land bounties.

The crisis unfolding in Texas was watched with genuine trepidation by a growing band of antislavery militants in the United States. John

Quincy Adams, once an enthusiastic booster of U.S. acquisition, now balked at the prospect of annexing any territory that would enlarge the slave empire. Although Mexico had abolished the institution in 1829, it had not enforced the ban in Texas, which was home to some 5,000 slaves brought by American settlers to open up the area to the cultivation of cotton. As part of the United States, Texas would greatly increase the economic and political power of the Southern slavocracy. As an independent republic in the Southwest, it could revive the slave trade and become an entrepôt for Caribbean slaves, who could then be smuggled into the Southern states. Either way, the secession of Texas could have only one result: the westward march of slavery, prolonging indefinitely the life of the peculiar institution on the North American continent.

American abolitionists clung briefly to the far-fetched idea that Great Britain, as the champion of universal emancipation, might consider intervening in the crisis on the side of Mexico, possibly in exchange for the cession of Texas.[43] This hope was dashed when, less than seven months after the outbreak of the rebellion, a force of Texans and volunteers from the United States routed the Mexican army at the Battle of San Jacinto in April 1836. Still, few observers could ponder the future of Texas without taking into account the possibility of British intervention. In the months following the disastrous Texas campaign, the Mexican Congress discussed the possibility of ceding the region to Great Britain to keep it from falling into the hands of the United States. Rumors of British interposition were also taken seriously in the South. Apprehensive that Whitehall might attempt to exploit the fluid political situation, just as it had done in Florida two decades earlier, Southern leaders urged Washington to promptly recognize Texas as a sovereign nation. But Americans and Mexicans alike seem to have exaggerated the ability and overestimated the desire of the British government to arrest the course of events half a world away. Reluctant to intervene directly in North American affairs, Parliament evinced no desire whatsoever to intrude in the contest over Texas.[44]

The rebellion was over, but a new struggle for control of the land west of the Sabine River was just beginning. With Southern expansionists boldly declaring that Texas would soon be incorporated into the union, antislavery advocates immediately launched a proactive effort to discredit the secessionist movement. At the head of this campaign was Benjamin Lundy, a Philadelphia Quaker and newspaper editor whom Southern whites had denounced as a tool of the British for his antislavery activities as early as the 1820s.[45] Disregarding genuine points of disagreement between Anglo-Texas settlers (as well as many Tejanos) and Mexico's centralist government, Lundy argued that the rebellion had been engineered by a cabal of Southern slave merchants and Northern land speculators. In doing so, he raised the specter of a "slave power" engaged in a scheme to extend the territorial limits and political clout of the South, a conspiracy theory that would gain credibility among Northerners in the years ahead.[46]

Of course, allegations that the Texas Revolution had been a plot engineered by slaveholders could hardly be expected to galvanize a Northern public that in 1836 remained largely indifferent to the expansion of the plantation system. To bolster its case, the antislavery movement emphasized not only moral reasons for rejecting Texas, but practical ones as well. Annexation would not mean war with Mexico alone, Lundy argued, hinting that Great Britain might intervene to block the expansion of the United States. Lundy's apprehensions were soon echoed in the nation's capital by John Quincy Adams. With the florid hyperbole that came with passionate conviction, the aging congressman warned his slaveholding colleagues that Great Britain "will carry abolition and emancipation with her in every fold of her flag; while your stars, as they increase in numbers, will be overcast with the murky vapors of oppression, and the only portion of your banners visible to the eye, will be the blood-stained stripes of the taskmaster."[47]

Such warnings proved to be self-fulfilling prophecy. A few weeks after Adams delivered his remarks, the House of Commons took up the Texas question to determine the consequences to British interests if the United States annexed Texas, with several members quoting the former U.S. president as an authority on the matter. A union of the two slaveholding North American republics, some members argued, would only whet the appetite of American expansionists, reconfiguring the balance of power in the western hemisphere.[48] If such discussions hardly amounted to the threat of war, American antislavery leaders happily included them in their litany of arguments against the possible U.S. acquisition of Texas.

A showdown in Washington over the expansion of slavery became inevitable when Texas voters approved an annexation referendum by an overwhelming margin in the fall of 1836. Antislavery societies inundated Congress with petitions opposing the measure. Increasingly, their protests gained a hearing in the North, where moderates of both parties began to balk at the prospect of dramatically increasing the political power of the Southern slavocracy.[49] At the forefront of this campaign was the geriatric but indefatigable Adams. In the summer of 1838 the congressman from Braintree, Massachusetts, staged a twenty-two-day filibuster to prevent a resolution calling for the immediate annexation of Texas from coming to a vote, and the 25th Congress adjourned without taking any action on the matter. The message to the Van Buren administration was clear: any attempt to revive the issue could expect fierce opposition from antislavery groups, who would resort to any means necessary to block the peculiar institution's westward growth. Unwilling to hazard such a political firestorm, the Van Buren administration notified Texas diplomats that it would not pursue the measure in the next session.

The defeat of annexation was a stunning coup for the antislavery lobby, still a numerically insignificant force in Congress. Its leaders had just cause to celebrate their victory, but their strategy to compel Washington to curb its expansionist appetite proved in the long run to be a serious miscalculation. In adverting to the possible danger of British interference, Lundy, Adams, and others clearly hoped to dampen enthusiasm for annexation. Instead, they only served to confirm the growing suspicion that some in the North were conspiring with a foreign government to destroy their institution. Far from chastening the South, antislavery warnings of a foreign threat appear to have had precisely the opposite effect. In the years that followed, Southern expansionists would redouble their efforts to shepherd Texas into the Union, fearful that it could indeed become a satellite of the British empire.

The Birth of Manifest Destiny

By a happy coincidence, a change of government on both sides of the Atlantic in 1841 brought about an easing of tensions between the two countries. The Whig victory of William Henry Harrison brought arch-Anglophile Daniel Webster into the State Department, while in London Sir Robert Peel formed a new Tory government, appointing Lord George-Hamilton Gordon, Fourth Earl of Aberdeen, to serve as Foreign Secretary. A complaisant adversary, Aberdeen had little enthusiasm for the aggressive saber-rattling of his predecessor, Lord Palmerston, and the following year he would dispatch a special envoy, Lord Ashburton, to resolve some of the outstanding disputes between the two nations. During a hot Washington summer, Ashburton and Webster managed to hammer out agreements on a wide range of bothersome issues. The resulting treaty fixed the Maine boundary at the St. John's River and established the boundary line of Minnesota, giving the United States 7,000 square miles of disputed territory. The British offered a backhanded apology for the *Caroline* incident, conceding that a violation of U.S. territorial sovereignty had occurred when the vessel was seized. Britain's determination to enforce the ban on the slave trade was another source of contention between the two governments. To placate Southern leaders, Webster refused to permit the Royal Navy to board American vessels, though the administration agreed to station U.S. ships off the African coast in an effort to detect Americans engaging in the practice.[50]

By all outward appearances, the Webster-Ashburton Treaty marked an historic moment in U.S.-British relations, yet another emblem of the fraternal feeling that existed between the two Anglophone nations. Once again, however, appearances were deceiving. The Democrats viewed the treaty as a total capitulation to British interests. In the Western states, Ashburton's refusal to discuss the Oregon boundary question infuriated many Jacksonians. In the Northeast, the news that the Foreign Office had had in its possession a map showing that a portion of the land ceded to the British government rightfully belonged to Maine raised questions of bad faith.[51] Southerners, meanwhile, still bridled at Britain's aggressive role in enforcing the slave trade ban.[52]

In the final analysis, Webster could claim a number of significant achievements, the inevitable partisan griping notwithstanding. What the treaty could not resolve, however, was the frustration many Americans felt at the seemingly ubiquitous British presence on the North American continent. Expansionists still saw the threat of British encroachment everywhere they turned: in Oregon and California to the west, in Cuba and Texas to the south. With Great Britain poised to capture lands vital to American economic growth and security if the federal government failed to act, many demanded a more aggressive policy of territorial acquisition. In the years following the Webster-Ashburton Treaty, Washington policymakers began to exhibit an almost manic desire to increase the national domain. The result, in a span of less than five remarkable years, would be the extension of U.S. sovereignty over Oregon and all of Mexico's northern provinces, from Texas to California.

It is common to view this period of rapid territorial growth as a time of jingoistic bombast, a period in which Americans became giddy with the seemingly boundless potential of their republican empire. Patriotic pundits, like *Democratic Review* editor John L. O'Sullivan and other members of the Young America movement, vied to outdo each other in effusions of rodomontade, characterizing the surge westward as the inexorable march of a muscular nation on the rise. In their more hyperbolic moments—which were not infrequent—they saw the republic standing at the vanguard of civilization, cloaked in the glowing nimbus of a Divine Providence. "We are the nation of human progress," O'Sullivan exulted, "and who will, what can, set limits to our onward march?"[53] In Washington, the halls of Congress rang with patriotic froth, as the American eagle ranged "over every foot of soil from Tierra del Fuego to the North Pole."[54] One British visitor, amused by all the soaring rhetoric, dismissed such ornithological musings as mere flights of fancy, and had this to say of the national emblem:

> How often have I heard an excited orator conjure him up in all his inflated dimensions, and with expanded wing send him sweeping over the length and breadth of the continent which he proudly claimed as his own! On how many lofty rocks is he not daily made to perch! What imperial panoramas are not constantly stretched beneath his feet! How he is made to soar above all other eagles . . . and how the poor earth-bound British lion is made to tremble at the very shadow of his flight! The poor o'erlaboured bird![33]

In the summer of 1845, an article widely credited to O'Sullivan appeared in the *Democratic Review* that claimed for the nation a "manifest destiny" to extend its dominion across the continent.[56] The euphony of the term enthralled pundits of the mid-1840s and quickly entered the national lexicon. It has since exerted a similarly seductive resonance for generations of historians who, writing in an age when the nation enjoyed world power status, have tended to view the republic's expansionist tendencies as inexorable, employing it as a metonymic device to define the era. Yet it is only in retrospect that the self-conscious bravado of Manifest Destiny has assumed the swagger of inevitability. Americans liked to boast of their battlefield triumphs in the two wars for independence, and often called for a new day of reckoning between the two nations, boldly predicting that republican institutions would prevail. But such gasconade could not disguise pervasive feelings of vulnerability. If politicians and pundits often invoked the imagery of a soaring eagle as they described an American empire which, they hoped, would soon extend from sea to sea and pole to pole, they were equally prone to conjure up images of a British imperial behemoth, red in tooth and claw. Americans had not overcome their insecurities or their fear of British encirclement; they had simply become more adept at hiding them, to themselves and to others.[57]

Nor did Americans of the period have a particularly well-defined sense of what their "manifest destiny" entailed. At best, O'Sullivan's catchphrase was an opaque term, the potency of which lay in its ambiguity. There was never a consensus as to what territory the nation should acquire, or what means it should employ to acquire it. Americans had always exhibited a strong pioneering impulse, gravitating to the westernmost fringes of the republic and, in increasing numbers, becoming expatriates as they abandoned the nation in search of cheap and abundant arable lands elsewhere. Washington, on the other hand, had been slow to embrace the expansionist zeal of so many of its westering citizens. True, overeager military commanders acting on their own initiative (e.g., Andrew Jackson and Thomas ap Catesby Jones) occasionally revealed a more aggressive side, not to mention a willingness to resort to extralegal means to acquire territorial objectives. For the most part, however, it had managed to hold these impulses in check. When American leaders pined for an enlarged national domain, they generally did so within normal diplomatic channels, and demonstrated a consistent if sometimes grudging respect for the sovereignty of neighboring states. They could afford to do so, convinced that coveted Western lands would fall like ripe fruit into the lap of the United States when they were ready.

During the 1840s, this complacence abruptly gave way to an almost manic desire to increase the national domain. Although a number of factors contributed to American settlement of the West—population growth, the opening up to white settlement of Indian lands, the advent of new transportation technologies, to name only a few—the land fever exhibited by Washington during this period stemmed from geopolitical considerations. Specifically, U.S. policymakers saw Great Britain poised to capture territories vital to American economic growth and security. "Now or never" became the watchwords of the age ("now or sooner," according to Manifest Destiny's critics), inscribing the expansionist impulse with a special sense of urgency unknown to previous generations. Only now did Washington begin to match the cormorant territorial appetites so long exhibited at the grassroots level. Only now did the fitful process of gradual expansion give way to a new, aggressive doctrine of continentalism, in which questions of title were dismissed as legal quibbling, in which the long-standing territorial claims of other nations could be seen as affronts to the national honor. Only now did a subdued interest in an enlarged dominion morph into an unbridled rapaciousness, with the acquisition of new lands whetting the desire for more.

This determination to stand firm in the face of British hemispheric power did not stem entirely from encirclement anxieties alone. Undergirding American resolve was a quarter century of abuse from British journals and travel writers, which in aggregate had created the perception abroad of the United States as a benighted land, a view that stood in jarring and humiliating contrast to the American self-image as a progressive beacon of republican liberty. The recent financial embarrassments of several states had prompted the British press to add defalcation to the long list of republican shortcomings, while transatlantic condemnation of American slavery had grown louder and more supercilious since the 1833 Emancipation Act. For Charles Jared Ingersoll—who in 1810 had struck one of the first blows against transatlantic carping with his fictional *Inchiquin, the Jesuit's Letters*—a determined stand against the British offered the best opportunity to erase the catalog of indignities which the imperial parent had visited upon its offspring since the War for Independence. Now chairman of the House Foreign Affairs Committee, Ingersoll was one of Washington's most strident Anglophobes, refusing even to speak to the British minister to the United States on social occasions.[58] In a speech calling on the House to force a resolution of the Oregon boundary question, Ingersoll complained of the "ribald vituperation" which citizens of the republic had been forced to endure, "of late more than ever." The Pennsylvania congressman made it clear that in demanding the extension of U.S. sovereignty over the entire Pacific Northwest, he was guided not only by the question of legal title as by his profound irritation at Great Britain, a nation that persisted in calling attention to "American knavery, American vanity, American meanness, American vulgarity, American slavery, American lawlessness and blackguardism."[59]

For Ingersoll and other like-minded patriots, the controversy over territorial limits was a natural extension of the protracted and wide-ranging debate over the nation's susceptibility to British influences. Any American statesman who dared suggest that the enlargement of the national domain might jeopardize U.S.-British relations left himself open to the charge of harboring sentiments "tinctured with British feeling."[60] Echoing the concerns of cultural and economic nationalists, expansionists insisted that the core principles of the republic were being vitiated by those who looked across the Atlantic "for all they deem worthy of imitation."[61] Indeed, it was this very absence of intellectual independence, expansionists argued, that made the opponents of Manifest Destiny insensible to the dangers British encirclement posed to U.S. interests.[62]

And yet, as was so often the case when Americans sought to redefine the power relations that existed between the two countries, the charge of emulation cut both ways. Critics of expansion did not fail to notice that the process of American empire-building appeared distressingly similar to the policies of their transatlantic cousins. Unfazed, the apostles of Manifest Destiny had a ready answer for those who likened the nation's westward march to British imperialism. Accustomed to walking a fine line between association and repudiation of British norms, Americans who championed a policy of aggressive territorial expansion—like those who called for a new direction in arts and letters—often credited British antecedents even as they proudly espoused defiance of the imperial parent. The *American Review*, not one of the more jingoistic journals of the period, conceded in 1846 that Americans inherited their passion for extended dominion from their English forebears. Unlike them, however, they did not seek new lands in the interest of national aggrandizement, but in the service of a far nobler purpose: to safeguard and promote the cause of republicanism. As they approached the midpoint of the nineteenth century, Americans believed themselves to be locked in an ideological struggle with the forces of reaction for mastery of the continent. Bordering lands held by Britain and by a government that had only recently won its independence from Catholic Spain, Americans liked to think that their brand of imperialism was essentially defensive in nature, a crusade they had taken up not from a love of conquest but from an obligation to redeem the continent from foreign "feudal, hierarchical, and monarchical" doctrines. It was this contest between antipodal institutions, this battle between the Old World and the New, the *Review* suggested, that had made American expansionism necessary. European powers might hold sway over the far-flung reaches of the globe, but it was the sacred duty of the United States to beat back that menace whenever it appeared in the western hemisphere.[63]

No American public figure was more convinced that Great Britain aimed to subdue the United States as part of its long-term hemispheric strategy—or more alarmed by it—than Andrew Jackson. Retired and in ailing health at his plantation, the Hermitage, Jackson remained a formidable presence in the Democratic Party. Always a strident Anglophobe, in his final years the idea of Great Britain as a grave and gathering danger had taken hold in Jackson's mind and become something of a monomania. Like so many Democrats, Jackson regarded the Webster-Ashburton Treaty as little more than diplomatic sleight-of-hand, a foil to distract Americans from Whitehall's real territorial objectives in the western hemisphere. Great Britain, he was now convinced, was bent on acquiring Texas and Oregon, and further aimed to cement its control over the West Indies with the acquisition of Cuba.[64] Girding himself for one last battle against the British, the Old Hero dashed off a steady stream of frenzied missives to party leaders, warning in his cribbed scrawl that if Great Britain managed to gain a foothold in the West, it would form "an iron Hoop around the United States" that would cost "oceans of blood and millions of money to burst asunder."[65]

It should be emphasized that the expansionist impulse drew from a welter of seemingly contradictory sources. Even as jingoistic newspaper editors fulminated against British power, they often couched their appeals for more territory in racialized terms, as the inevitable march of Anglo-Saxon progress. *New York Herald* publisher James Gordon Bennett and other spread-eagle expansionists routinely derided non-white peoples as unfit for self-government, and confidently predicted that Mexi-

FIGURE 13.

"The Oregon and Texas Question." American continental expansion in the mid-1840s met with opposition from Great Britain, leading many pundits to predict a third war between the two nations. (Courtesy American Antiquarian Society)

cans and Indians would "bow and fade" as American citizens fanned out across the continent. White Americans had always subscribed to a belief in the racial inferiority of those with whom they shared the continent, views that became more virulent as they sought new rationales for conquest. Just as Americans had been torn between their pride in claiming British antecedents and their need to sever their transatlantic cultural attachments, the public discourse of expansionism was often characterized by a strange mix of racial arrogance and geopolitical anxiety.[66]

Especially alarming to the advocates of Manifest Destiny was the suspicion that non-whites could always rely on a powerful sponsor ever ready to thwart the rise of the United States. By the 1840s, Americans surveyed a veritable host of enemies arrayed against them, existing both on the periphery of the republic and within its borders, from the native tribes of the Far West, who could be armed at a moment's notice and sent to commit depredations against American settlers; to the Mexican political elite who might cede sovereignty of California to extinguish its debt to British bondholders; to the slaves toiling on American plantations and the freedmen of the West Indies, who sought to ignite a conflagration in the Southern states. All stood ready, in the febrile minds of expansionists, to do the bidding of Great Britain in its effort to undermine the republic. In short, the great danger to U.S. interests was not simply an overt threat from a world power, but a more insidious one as well, involving surrogate nations or peoples acting at its behest.

❧ ❧

In the logic that often frames a developing nation's worldview, the superpower exists as a well-oiled machine, incapable of error, its many parts all perfectly calibrated to ensure maximum performance. So it was with American perceptions of Great Britain. To citizens of the republic, imperial policies in the western hemisphere were all part of a grand design, a perfectly coordinated operation conducted with flawless precision from Whitehall. Ministries might come and go, but in the American mind, Britain's hemispheric ambitions remained unchanged.

By the early 1840s, the accretion of these anxieties would reach a point of critical mass, galvanizing broad constituencies to support a program of rapid territorial expansion. Paradoxically, such fears coexisted with, and even helped buttress, the spirit of aggressive triumphalism that infused the expansionist impulse. For the apostles of Manifest Destiny, a sense of exuberance stemmed from the belief that the republic's citizens stood shoulder to shoulder in the great task of creating a continental empire. The extension of territorial limits, they were convinced, would serve a dual purpose: uniting the nation, and freeing it from the trammels of British power. An enlarged dominion would be welcomed by those who had for so many years bristled at the anti-republican calumnies of British critics. The quest for land was also championed by members of the Young America movement, dovetailing neatly with their boisterous campaign for literary and cultural nationalism. It appealed, too, to Americans of widely divergent economic philosophies—those who strove to protect and perpetuate an agrarian way of life and who viewed industrialization as a virus of British origin, as well as those who sought an economic system to rival the British manufacturing hegemon.

There were naysayers, to be sure. Antislavery militants frantically called attention to the fact that the peculiar institution had created fissures deep within the political substrate; the steady tramp of a westward-moving people, they warned, could set off a series of tremors that would destabilize the Union. Such dire predictions went unheeded by a nation drunk on the intoxicating idiom of empire. Having often seized upon anti-British themes to mute regional, class, and ethnic antagonisms, Americans embraced the Anglophobia of expansion with special zeal.

Here, at last, was an opportunity to break, once and for all, the vestigial bonds of their colonial heritage. Here, at last, was the perfect antidote to partisan and sectional rancor. Here, at last, was an agenda for all Americans.

The fallacy of these beliefs would become all too apparent in the years ahead.

☙ 10 ☙

The Texas Question

If Johnny Bull's fat greedy boys
About our union grumble,
I'll kick up such a tarnal noise,
'T'will make 'em feel quite humble.

If Mexy, back'd by secret foes,
Still talks of taking you, gal,
Why we can lick 'em all, you know.
An' then annex 'em too, gal.

—"Uncle Sam's Song to Miss Texas"

Following Washington's rebuff of their annexation overtures in 1838, Texans now had no choice but to go it alone and carve a new country from the vast, underpopulated land that sprawled west of the Sabine River. While many Lone Star citizens were understandably chagrined at this unexpected turn of events, Mirabeau Buonaparte Lamar was one Texan who wondered if the republic might be better off. A Georgia-born slaveholder, Lamar had become alarmed by the tenor of antislavery opinion in the North and the increasingly bitter debates in Washington over the gag rule. Succeeding Sam Houston as president in 1838, he sought to chart a bold new course for Texas, and in his inaugural address urged his audience not to surrender its independence to antislavery agitators "who are known to be opposed to her peculiar and essential interests, and who are daily sending forth their denunciations against her from the fireside, the pulpit and the council chamber."[1] For Lamar, the prosperity of Texas and the peculiar institution were inextricable. With its rich cotton-growing soil, the region beckoned immigrants from the Southern states, but a Texas without slavery would return forthwith to the "pastoral ignorance" it had experienced under

Mexican rule. A visionary imbued with the spirit of the Romantic age, Lamar in 1838 did not see the Lone Star Republic as a stopgap measure until annexation could be consummated. Rather, he imagined a new, permanent republic in the American Southwest, extending from Louisiana to New Mexico, and perhaps one day as far as the Pacific Ocean. And unlike the republic that spawned it, this one would be founded by men who would not have to make concessions to hostile Northern interests. Free of abolitionist agitation, free of any qualms as to the morality of a system of bonded labor, Texas would become a slaveholders' paradise.[2]

Five years later, Lamar was advocating a very different future for Texas. By the mid-1840s, amid renewed calls for a union between the Lone Star Republic and the United States, the former president threw his support to the cause, lobbying vigorously in Washington and Texas on behalf of an annexation treaty. Abandoning his dream of a permanent Texas empire, Lamar no longer thought in grandiose terms when he contemplated the future of slavery. Fearful for the very survival of the institution, he fairly begged Texas's citizens to accept annexation to the United States, a measure he now claimed he had favored all along.

The reason for Lamar's change of mind was simple enough. After a few years of independence, Texas slave owners had come to realize that they could not inoculate themselves from antislavery extremism by severing their ties with the United States. In the early 1840s, they began to see a new and far more ominous threat—a conspiracy to destroy slavery in Texas and make the Lone Star Republic a client state of Great Britain. Lamar chose what he perceived to be the lesser of two evils. As a state in the union, Texas would add to the strength of the South; alone, it would be at the mercy of a globe-girding colossus bent on abolition. Annexation to the United States, he was now convinced, would give Texas "a shelter from the grasp of British cupidity" and a refuge "from the storms that threatened her."[3]

But the stakes were now much higher even than the institution's survival in the Lone Star Republic. What would make the fate of Texas so vitally important to Southern slaveholders was the widely held belief that British reformers had set their sights on nothing less than the complete eradication of the system throughout North America. Vigilant to potential threats against the peculiar institution in the best of times, Southern slaveholders now saw the full power of the British government arrayed against them. With feelings of trepidation that would eventually mutate into hysteria, they became convinced that the future of American slavery would be decided in Texas. A cohesive Southern bloc that included the Lone Star Republic, Lamar believed, was the only salvation for the planter class.

Slavery and the Lone Star

Had the infant Lone Star Republic prospered and become a viable nation-state in the years following its independence from Mexico, Lamar's initial dream of an empire in the Southwest might well have been realized. Instead, the new nation stumbled out of the gate and was quickly hobbled by the Panic of 1837, which left its government without credit, its currency all but worthless. From the outset, Texas looked to foreign powers for assistance. The United States, France, Holland, and Great Britain all extended diplomatic recognition, but what Texas really needed was capital investment and a steady flow of immigrants. While settlers from the Southern states trickled in, they were, on the whole, an impecunious lot, many coming to escape bad debts incurred in their own country. As the situation grew dire, Texas leaders found themselves turning more and more to European powers, even as they fretted that closer transatlantic ties might come at an unacceptable cost.

Great Britain, with its commitment to the goal of universal emancipation, seemed a particularly unlikely ally for the slaveholding republic. British visitors to the new nation were impressed with its agricultural potential, and often touted its benefits to prospective emigrants. Invariably, however, they were dismayed by the presence of slavery. To the consternation of slaveholders on both sides of the Sabine River, many British observers freely expressed the view that the peculiar institution could be undermined by a massive influx of free labor from Europe. Even more worrisome to Southern whites were reports that British abolitionists had settled upon the Lone Star Republic as a new field for their endeavors. In 1839, the renowned Irish antislavery leader Daniel O'Connell, then serving in the House of Commons, called publicly for the creation of a free black state in Texas. British abolitionist organizations discussed several plans to erect in Texas a line of defense against the spread of slavery, and although none ever materialized, rumors of these activities soon wafted across the Atlantic to play upon the troubled imagination of the planter class.[4]

Southerners committed to the westward expansion of slavery became further concerned when the conflict between Texas and Mexico that had lain dormant since San Jacinto suddenly flared anew in the early 1840s. In an attempt to rescue the ailing fortunes of the republic, President Lamar dispatched an expedition to establish a trade route with New Mexico in the summer of 1841, but Mexican troops captured the invading force with little difficulty as it neared Santa Fe. Declaring that it was now ready to make good on its repeated promises to reconquer Texas, the Mexican government launched two incursions in the spring and fall of 1842. Both forces seized San Antonio, then quickly retreated across the South Texas plains. Angry Texans clamored for retribution, and in December a small army marched to the lower Rio Grande Valley. It was defeated at Mier, a town below the river, dealing yet another blow to Texas's much-vaunted reputation for Spartan heroics. Though most Anglo citizens lived east of the Brazos River and were untouched by the conflict along the frontier, these defeats exacted a heavy toll on the fledgling republic, depleting its meager resources, discouraging foreign investment, and scaring off potential settlers.[5]

Such developments by themselves were not especially worrisome to American expansionists. With their innate contempt for Latin American political and military institutions, they never seriously entertained the possibility that Texas might be resubjugated by Mexico acting alone. Rather, their overriding concern since the Texas Revolution had been that Great Britain might seek to turn the region's instability to its own advantage. Wholly captivated by British conspiracy myths, they viewed events in the Southwest through a prism that confirmed their darkest fears. When Mexico launched its forays into Texas in 1842, Southern newspapers alleged that the expeditions had been financed by British banks.[6] They were even more indignant when Mexico purchased two warships from an English shipbuilding firm to continue the war against Texas, to be manned by English crews and commanded by officers on leaves of absence from the Royal Navy.[7]

In the final analysis, it mattered little whether Britain's intentions toward Texas were hostile or benign; either way, Southerners harbored no doubt that a stronger British presence in the American Southwest imperiled slaveholding interests. As a result, events in Texas were monitored closely in Washington, where John Tyler and others were beginning to realize that Washington's decision to reject the Lone Star Republic in 1838 had pushed it into the enfolding embrace of European powers. Even so, upon his accession to the presidency, the Virginia-born president did not regard the issue as one that demanded his immediate attention. The president first broached the subject of acquiring Texas to Secretary of State Daniel Webster in the fall of 1841, but as relations with party leaders soured over his states' rights opposition to the Whig economic agenda, his lack of political support made any attempt to revive annexation impossible. In fact, Tyler evinced a far greater interest in penetrating the lucrative markets of the Pacific Rim. In 1842, the administration made it known to Mexico that the United States would gladly sacrifice annexation in order to acquire the California harbors of Monterey and San Francisco, both seen as gateways to Asia. At the same time, the president rejected two overtures from Lone Star diplomats and

confided to the Texas minister in Washington that the outlook for annexation looked bleak.[8]

During the early months of 1843, however, news of the Texan defeat at Mier, coupled with persistent reports of British intrigues, thrust
the annexation issue once again to the foreground, and forced the Tyler
administration to rethink its expansionist priorities. Sometime in February, Tyler received a cryptic letter from Washington D. Miller, the private secretary of Sam Houston, then serving a second presidential term.
Miller wished to alert Tyler to the fact that the British had designs on
Texas, and urged him to make the cause of annexation his own before
it was too late. There can be little doubt that this letter was part of a deliberate and calculated effort by Sam Houston to put the United States
on notice that it was not Texas's only suitor. Frustrated by Washington's
foot-dragging on the issue, Houston opted for a policy designed to play
upon American fears of British encirclement. If the Tyler administration
had been slow to see the advantages of annexing Texas, Houston can-
nily believed that it must be made to see the disadvantages if it failed to
act.[9]

In his subtle campaign to raise American apprehensions of British
intrigues in Texas, Houston had a valuable, though unwitting, ally in
Charles Elliot, the British chargé d'affaires. The forty-one-year-old Elliot was already well known as an imperial troubleshooter. A captain
in the Royal Navy and scion of a prominent and well-connected family, Elliot had served as protector of slaves in Guiana in the early 1830s,
where he became a dedicated abolitionist.[10] In 1839, Elliot vaulted to
international prominence when his actions as Chief Superintendent
for Trade to China—Britain's highest-ranking representative in the Far
East—-triggered the first "Opium War." In an effort to stamp out the
British-sponsored opium trade, Chinese military forces surrounded the
opium warehouses of British traders along the Canton waterfront and
demanded that they surrender their merchandise. After a six-week siege,
Elliot persuaded the merchants to turn over their stocks—20,000 chests
of opium, totaling two and a half million pounds—with the pledge that
Her Majesty's government would indemnify them for their losses. A series of British military victories followed, leading to the Convention of
Chuanbi, by which China ceded Hong Kong to Her Majesty's government. The treaty fell well short of the concessions Parliament demanded,
however—among other things, it did not provide adequate compensation for the destroyed opium—and as a result was greeted with disbelief
and outrage when its terms were made public in England; even Queen
Victoria found Elliot's conduct "unaccountably strange." The Melbourne
government disavowed the agreement, recalled Elliot, and renewed hos-

tilities, ultimately forcing China to accept the British doctrine of free trade at gunpoint with the historic Treaty of Nanjing in 1842.[11]

If Elliot's star was no longer in the ascendant in Whitehall, the arrival of such a celebrated figure in the backwoods republic in 1842 created quite a hubbub among annexationists in Texas and the United States. Rather than view Elliot's posting as the banishing of an errant diplomat to the North American hinterlands, many took it as evidence that Texas had now become a high priority in Britain's imperial agenda.[12] Once on the ground in Texas, Elliot took stock of the situation and quickly realized that a great many residents were inclined to ascribe "perfidious purposes" to every British action, convinced that Her Majesty's government thought of little else but the best means of effecting "the strangulation of this young Hercules."[13]

Bemused though he may have been by American suspicions, Elliot soon gave anxious Anglophobes plenty to worry about. Polished and urbane, the British chargé d'affaires lost no time in making the acquaintance of Texas's leading public figures. In Galveston, he became a prominent member of the town's social scene (such as it was), holding dinner parties that he used to lobby for British interests.[14] Elliot's high profile was augmented by the absence of a reliable American diplomatic presence in the Lone Star Republic. The tropical Gulf Coast climate played havoc with the U.S. legation, with no less than three chargés succumbing to fatal malarial diseases in quick succession soon after their arrival in Galveston. Not until 1844 would Washington have an effective envoy in Texas to counter Elliot's influence.[15]

As part of his long-term strategy to arouse the jealousy of the Tyler administration, Sam Houston established a close working relationship with the British chargé that went beyond mere diplomatic protocol. The two got on so famously that Houston enlisted Elliot and the British minister in Mexico City in an effort to gain the release of Texas prisoners-of-war then languishing in Mexican jails, pointedly snubbing U.S. diplomats, who had enjoyed some success in gaining the repatriation of Texas combatants in the past. In the spring of 1843 Elliot had another opportunity to perform a valuable service for Houston, helping to arrange an armistice between Texas and Mexico, a respite that paved the way for peace negotiations later that year. Both Houston and Elliot hoped that the talks might result in Mexico's recognition of Texas sovereignty, but such optimism proved unwarranted. When negotiations between the two sides ultimately collapsed, many Texans, always suspicious of British initiatives, believed that Her Majesty's government had conspired with Mexico against them.[16]

But Elliot was not content to busy himself with routine diplomatic duties, nor satisfied with his role as the Texas president's new best friend. Presumably eager to redeem himself after his China imbroglio, Elliot sought to make the most of his new post. Within a few weeks of his arrival in Galveston, he was writing to the Foreign Office suggesting a plan that promised nothing less than the chance to remake the geopolitical framework of the North American continent. The British diplomat reasoned that if Whitehall could offer Texas a suitably attractive package of commercial loan guarantees, unrestricted trade agreements, and compensation for area slaveholders, the region could be secured as a beachhead for abolition. A free Texas would attract thousands of runaway slaves and free blacks from the Deep South, dashing forever the Southern dream of a continental slave empire. Over the long term it might even help to destabilize the peculiar institution in the United States. The scheme's economic merits were equally tantalizing. As a client state of Britain, Texas would be a customer for its capital and commerce, and could be used to help break the virtual monopoly in short staple cotton held by the South. A policy to promote antislavery in Texas, with its synchronicity of economic self-interest and humanitarian altruism, would serve the twin doctrines of open markets and emancipation that were the cornerstones of British imperial policy. Nor was this all. Perhaps most important, an independent Texas would serve as a bulwark against the further expansion of the United States, Britain's principal rival for hemispheric dominance.[17]

How could Elliot have believed that Anglo Texans, the overwhelming majority of whom hailed from the Southern states, would readily abandon the peculiar institution? The plan was not so far-fetched as it might seem. The republic's relatively small slave population had always led abolitionists to dare hope that the die was not yet cast, that Texas might yet be redeemed from the blight of slavery through a plan of compensated abolitionism. This was certainly a plausible scenario in view of Britain's success with such a program in its own colonial possessions, where slavery had been much more firmly entrenched. Wedded though white Southerners were to the peculiar institution, Elliot believed that hard times would make Texas settlers receptive to a plan in which the British government offered hard currency for the emancipation of slaves. It seemed reasonable to suppose that Texas, a nation desperately in need of capital, would follow the path of the young Latin American republics, which had opened their doors to British commerce after independence, borrowing from British banks to finance their appetite for British goods. Opposition in Texas to the Whig protectionist tariff of 1842, which imposed new restrictions on its agricultural exports to the United States, made conditions especially favorable for such a scheme.

Elliot's enthusiasm for a plan to abolish slavery in Texas must also be attributed at least in part to the hubris not uncommon to the envoys of the world's most powerful empire. Like David Turnbull in Cuba, whose antislavery activities had resulted in his expulsion from the Spanish colony, Elliot saw himself as an agent provocateur in the cause of universal emancipation, fired with a reformist's zeal that blinded him to all obstacles. Since the turn of the century, Great Britain, virtually alone among the Western nations, had waged war against those who profited from the slave trade and slavery, and could claim a number of impressive victories against the institution's vested interests. Resourceful and energetic, Elliot could hardly be blamed for regarding the emancipation of a few thousand Texas slaves as an objective well within his grasp.[18]

By the spring of 1843, Elliot's antislavery plans for Texas had become public knowledge, and the British diplomat found himself the focus of much unwanted publicity and speculation regarding Whitehall's intentions.[19] Nonetheless, Elliot remained undaunted, convinced that the advantages of abolishing slavery in the Lone Star Republic were "so immediate and so momentous," that the general public would be won over to the plan once it had the opportunity to weigh its benefits objectively.[20] Elliot convinced Stephen Pearl Andrews, a Houston lawyer, formerly of Massachusetts, to travel to London, where a second international antislavery conference was to be held that summer. Bearing letters of introduction from the British chargé, Andrews made the trip with American antislavery leaders Joshua Leavitt and Lewis Tappan, who had also been lobbying for British investment in Texas as a means to promote abolition.[21] Known as the Tappan Committee, the trio gained an audience with Foreign Secretary Lord Aberdeen and laid out their plan: Texas would receive a £1,000,000 loan from Great Britain, pledging its public lands as security, on the condition that it amend its constitution to abolish slavery. A portion of the sum would be used to emancipate the slaves already living in Texas. Ever the diplomat, Aberdeen made no promises, but led his American visitors to believe that he would do all in his power to bring about the abolition of slavery in the Lone Star Republic.[22]

No doubt Aberdeen was intrigued by the emancipation schemes floated by Elliot and the Tappan Committee, which were in keeping with the British government's long-range goal to undermine slavery in the western hemisphere.[23] At no time, however, did this solicitousness toward Texas slaves translate into concrete action. By the time the American antislavery leaders arrived in London, the Foreign Office had learned of the one-year armistice between Texas and Mexico, which offered a far less ambitious but more feasible solution to the turmoil that prevailed in the American Southwest. Mexican recognition of Texas's independence would bring an immediate halt to the border war between the two countries. Preferring a nonconfrontational course, the British foreign minister was reluctant to antagonize Washington by actively promoting abolition in Texas. With the Oregon boundary dispute still unresolved, Aberdeen sought stability and diplomatic intercourse with the republics of North America above the pursuit of Britain's long-range humanitarian goals.

Slaveholding expansionists saw the actions of the British government in an altogether different light. The proceedings of the 1843 World Antislavery Convention, whose delegates had petitioned and apparently received the sanction of the Peel government, seemed to provide compelling evidence of a vast international conspiracy to rob the South of the coveted Texas prize.[24] Following the events in London with particularly keen interest were a pair of North American envoys—Duff Green, a Tyler intimate whom the administration had sent to London as a confidential agent to discuss trade policy, and Ashbel Smith, the Texas chargé d'affaires to Great Britain. Both men lost little time in alerting their governments to the dangers of abolitionist intrigues.[25] American expansionists saw further grounds for concern when, two months after the conference, Lord Aberdeen was drawn into an exchange with the renowned abolitionist Lord Henry Brougham on the Texas question in the House of Lords. Asked to explain the government's policy toward slavery in the Lone Star Republic, the Foreign Minister replied vaguely that his office was working to negotiate an end to the conflict between Texas and Mexico, which he believed would ultimately bring about the great object Lord Brougham desired. Although Aberdeen had done little more than reiterate the British government's long-standing commitment to the eradication of slavery, to suspicious Southern politicians his remarks added to the growing body of evidence that the Peel ministry was committed to a policy that directly threatened the future of slavery in North America.[26]

Meanwhile, in Texas, Houston's campaign to arouse fears that he had succumbed to British influence appeared to be paying dividends. Letters poured into Washington from private citizens in the Lone Star Republic with new reports of British intrigues, while anti-Houston newspapers routinely excoriated the Texas president for agreeing to the British-brokered peace talks with Mexico.[27] In the fall of 1843, Houston's personal secretary penned a second disquieting missive to John Tyler. Imploring the American president to take immediate steps on behalf of annexation, Washington D. Miller noted that Britain's prospects in Texas were improving steadily as a result of the U.S. government's lassitude.[28] Such imprecations could not help but have the desired effect. "You would be amused to see their fear of England," one Texas diplomat in Washington wrote home in early 1844, "and that is the secret of our success if we do succeed."[29]

Now convinced beyond any doubt that slavery on the North American continent was imperiled by British abolitionist subterfuge, Tyler embarked upon a campaign to bring Texas into the union as the twenty-eighth state. Northern critics would later accuse the Tyler administration of acting rashly and on the basis of innuendo and misinformation in its quest to acquire Texas. Certainly there can be little doubt that the Peel ministry, with its foreign policy under the direction of the pacific and ever-cautious Aberdeen, represented a far less sinister danger than Southerners imagined. Yet by the summer of 1843, the Tyler administration saw in the Southwest an insolvent, unstable republic, its mercurial president seemingly under the sway of a gadfly British diplomat. Across the Atlantic, the Texas schemes of abolitionists were being publicly debated and, apparently, received with favor by the highest-ranking leaders of Her Majesty's government.[30]

It is probable that the Tyler administration would have reacted decisively even without such an abundance of warning signs. Allegations of Britain's nefarious intentions had saturated the political culture to such an extent that Americans had long since ceased to weigh them individually according to their intrinsic merits. A paranoid fear of Great Britain was by no means a uniquely Southern peculiarity. Northerners were equally capable of viewing the transatlantic relationship through a lens that colored every British action, in which even the vaguest slip of rumor assumed the heft of incontrovertible fact. For many in Washington, the charge of Whitehall's interference in the Texas question required little in the way of empirical verification. It was, after all, entirely consistent with their view of British policy elsewhere around the globe.

Tyler's Annexation Gambit

To promote public support for its annexation initiative, the Tyler administration orchestrated in the fall of 1843 a propaganda effort that exploited to the fullest American fears of Great Britain. The opening salvo of this campaign took the form of a series of articles in the *Daily Madisonian*, the administration news organ, believed to have been written by Tyler's new secretary of state, Abel Upshur. A childhood friend of the president's, Upshur shared Tyler's Virginia roots, proslavery sentiments, and Anglophobic proclivities.[31] While the newspaper stopped short of accusing the British government of seeking to destabilize Southern slavery, it nonetheless left no room for doubt that if emancipation—"the darling policy of England"—took root in the Lone Star Republic, the very existence of the institution in the United States would be placed in jeopardy. As a haven for runaway slaves from neighboring states, Texas threatened to unleash upon the South "the horrors of a servile war," a scenario, the *Madisonian* noted grimly, that would meet with the deep approbation of Northern "fanatics."[32]

Tyler and Upshur knew, of course, that annexation stood no hope of success if it was presented to the public as an initiative with no other purpose than to protect the interests of American slaveholders. From the outset of the campaign to acquire Texas, the administration stressed that a British client state on the southwestern border of the United States posed a serious threat to national security. With talk of a third war against Great Britain on the rise in recent years as a result of boundary disputes in Maine and Oregon, expansionist propaganda did not so much shape public opinion as capitalize upon anti-British sentiment that was already fully formed. Western Americans who could recall an earlier war against Great Britain for control of the Mississippi River Valley needed no prodding from the Tyler administration to imagine British forces using Texas as a base of military operations.[33]

As time went on, supporters of annexation bolstered their case with a host of economic arguments, which continued to keep Great Britain squarely in the foreground. Expansionists maintained that Her Majesty's government's interest in Texas stemmed from its need to find new sources of short-staple cotton. With British capital investment, the region could soon become a major source of supply, jeopardizing one of the principal mainstays of the American economy.[34] Annexation would not only eliminate these concerns, supporters of the measure contended, it would actually reverse the roles that presently existed between the two rivals, making Great Britain dependent upon the United States. With one stroke, the United States could acquire a monopoly over the cotton-producing regions of North America, giving it the leverage to neutralize Great Britain as a military and economic threat. Mindful of the calamitous effects that a cotton embargo would have on its textile industry, Great Britain would think seriously before it opposed American interests again. Southerners were hardly alone in their appreciation of the economic clout which cotton gave the United States in its commercial rivalry with the imperial parent. "Cotton bags will be much more effectual in bringing John Bull to terms," wrote a business partner of Nicholas Biddle to the Philadelphia financier, "than all the disciplined troops America could bring into the field."[35]

To a nation still feeling the sting of the Panic of 1837, expansionists presented annexation as a measure that would not only restore Ameri-

can prosperity, but one that held out the promise of an economic bonanza for generations to come. As a state in the union, Texas offered a
new and limitless market for Southern and Western agricultural products and Northern manufactures, its boosters argued.[36] Should it be
spurned again, however, the Lone Star Republic would have no choice
but to seek commercial treaties with Great Britain. British-made goods
would enter the port of Galveston duty-free, effectively eliminating U.S.
producers from the burgeoning Texas market. Great Britain might even
attempt to use Texas to circumvent high tariffs in the United States, inundating both North American republics with its surplus manufactured
products. In what was surely the most implausible claim, expansionists
tried to portray Texas as a gateway to the Pacific, asserting that the acquisition of lands in the Southwest would lead inexorably to American
control of the entire continent. In time the United States would gain access to the fabulously lucrative Asian trade and challenge Britain's global
dominance.[37]

It was, in all, an impressive list of arguments—or at the very least
a long one. But no matter how many reasons the administration mar-
shaled on behalf of its annexation initiative, there could be no hiding
the fact that the expansion of slavery would be the most conspicuous
and controversial result. Consequently, any attempt by the Tyler administration to annex Texas could expect to encounter stiff resistance,
from antislavery leaders who had blocked the measure in 1838, as well
as from centrists of both parties who had little desire to politicize the
slavery issue, especially on the eve of a presidential campaign. Treading
cautiously, the administration gave no hint that it was planning a major
policy initiative. In his 1843 annual message to Congress, the president
merely warned that Texas might fall prey to "stronger and more powerful nations," a situation the United States could not be expected to
regard with indifference. But Tyler's course was set. In the early weeks
of 1844, Secretary of State Upshur entered into secret negotiations with
Texas diplomats in Washington to hammer out a treaty of annexation.[38]

Meanwhile, support for annexation seemed to be growing steadily as
many prominent Democrats sought to develop an expansionist program
of their own. Andrew Jackson, always a political force to be reckoned
with, even in retirement, came out publicly in favor of "re-annexation"
(like many Americans, he insisted that Texas had been acquired under
the terms of the 1803 Louisiana Purchase). Bolstering the administration's claim that Texas under the aegis of Great Britain imperiled the
Western states, Jackson argued that a British army on the banks of the
Sabine River would be well poised to strike at Louisiana and Arkansas,
inciting slaves to revolt against their masters and threatening the en-

tire Mississippi River Valley.[39] Perhaps the most imaginative case for annexation was made by Mississippi senator Robert J. Walker, author of a widely influential open letter on the issue published early in 1844. Walker presented a litany of reasons for annexation, but at its core his argument skillfully played upon the Negrophobia and Anglophobia common to Americans of both sections. The growth of slavery in Texas, he argued, should be no less desirable to the North than to the South, for it would relieve the United States of the demographic pressures of an expanding black population. Texas as a state in the union, he predicted, would serve as a safety valve for thousands of slaves who might otherwise migrate to the free states as plantation agriculture receded in the Upper South. If, on the other hand, Texas should be allowed to remain independent, it would soon be overrun by English colonists who would establish a new, antislavery client state of the British empire. Like Jackson, Walker couched his argument in the language of a nation in peril. "Though saturated with blood, and gorged with power," Walker raged, Britain "yet marches on her course to universal dominion; and here, upon our own borders, Texas is next to be her prey."[40]

Critics were quick to dismiss these frenzied appeals to national unity as a cynical attempt to divert attention from the expansion of slavery. But the threat of British interference in Texas was hardly a canard cooked up by Southern extremists to frighten the country into pursuing a divisive policy of expansion for the benefit of the planter class. For Tyler and Upshur, the prospect of a British ally on the southwestern border of the United States represented a very real threat to national security. Even as he expressed his mounting irritation with the North's reluctance to stand by the South on the issue of slavery, Upshur expressed concern that the British would exploit these tensions to bring about "a separation of the Union." Conceding that annexation would be received initially with "repugnance" in the North, the secretary of state stressed that the failure to bring Texas into the union would be detrimental to the economic well-being of both sections. Troubled, like many Americans, by the growing rift over slavery, the Southern architects of annexation believed that the threat from Great Britain might well be a blessing, neutralizing these tensions and giving rise to a renewed sense of national purpose. Tyler and Upshur viewed the admission of Texas not simply as a means of protecting the institutions of the South, but as a policy initiative that would awaken both sections to their mutual advantage, strengthening the union at a time when a North/South accord was needed more than ever before.[41]

The campaign to bring Texas into the union almost came to an abrupt end in late February when President Tyler and his cabinet took a tour of the recently christened *Princeton*, a state-of-the-art warship that was the pride of the U.S. Navy. During the course of an artillery demonstration, one of the vessel's large, twelve-inch guns exploded, killing Upshur, the secretary of the navy, and six others (Tyler, who was below deck at the time of the explosion, escaped injury). To replace Upshur, the president turned to South Carolina senator John C. Calhoun, a choice he would soon have reason to regret.

In mid-March, the Whig organ in the nation's capital, the *Daily National Intelligencer*, broke the story that the Tyler administration and Texas diplomats were concluding an annexation treaty. Although word of the negotiations had been leaking out for some time, the news was greeted with anger by Whigs and many Northern Democrats. One month later, the news became official when the two governments agreed on terms by which Texas would be admitted as a territory of the United States. In his message to the Senate urging ratification, President Tyler borrowed freely from the encirclement rhetoric of Democratic expansionists, noting that the nation was "already almost surrounded" by European powers—by which he meant, of course, Great Britain—and that a commercial agreement between that country and Texas "would complete the circle."[42]

With the annexation issue now out in the open, the fragile national consensus which Tyler and Upshur had so painstakingly managed to build began to collapse. Critics brushed aside Tyler's anti-British rhetoric and seized upon the one issue the president had worked so hard to downplay, the expansion of the slave empire. What was more, they would soon receive aid from an unexpected quarter—Tyler's own secretary of state, John C. Calhoun. Only days before the Senate began to debate the treaty, Calhoun penned a letter to Richard Pakenham, the British minister to the United States, which would become one of the most controversial episodes of the South Carolinian's long and turbulent career. Written in response to a pledge from Lord Aberdeen that Whitehall would "do nothing secretly or under-handed" to abolish slavery in Texas, Calhoun, unconvinced, testily noted that his government would take strong exception to British interference. He then launched into a proslavery screed, lecturing the diplomat on the advantages of slavery to both races.[43]

Contemporaries no less anxious than Calhoun to see Texas annexed were appalled by the letter, which they regarded as a colossal blunder that would only wreck Northern support for the treaty, upon which its success depended. Andrew Jackson groaned upon reading the Secretary's letter: "How many men of talents want good common sense."[44] Writing some years later, Tyler himself laid much of the blame for the

Senate's failure to ratify the treaty on Calhoun's ill-advised and unneces-sary appeal to sectional interests. Thomas Hart Benton, one of Calhoun's fiercest critics, even charged him with purposely attempting to sabotage his own treaty in order to stir up secessionist sentiment in the South.[45]

The motives behind Calhoun's impolitic justification for Southern rights were complex. In his home state, amid rising anger over the 1842 Whig tariff and antislavery efforts to repeal the gag rule, some state lead-ers were beginning to openly question the effectiveness of Calhoun's centrist politics. Calhoun may have therefore written his letters to Pak-enham to neutralize radical insurgents in the Palmetto State by assum-ing a more stalwart defense of Southern interests, a strategy that had served him well during the nullification crisis. Yet Calhoun's rebuttal to the British minister was neither a pose nor a reluctant concession to po-litical expediency. A relentless opponent of all forms of British aggran-dizement in North America dating back to his election to the War Hawk Congress more than thirty years earlier, Calhoun did not minimize the danger of British interference. Responding to geopolitical realities as he understood them in 1844, the secretary of state was receiving new reports of British intrigues from legations and consular offices through-out the hemisphere. Like Andrew Jackson and so many Americans, Cal-houn believed that Great Britain was attempting to establish a cordon around the United States. Since taking over at the State Department two months earlier, he had become fully apprised of—and alarmed by—the determined efforts of British diplomat David Turnbull to foment a slave rebellion in Cuba. Meanwhile, in Mexico City, the U.S. chargé d'affaires warned that Mexican president Antonio López de Santa Anna was ac-tively colluding with Whitehall to enable the British government to "en-circle us on every side, & strangle our growing commerce and power in her strong embrace."[46] Certainly there is no reason to suspect that Cal-houn was being disingenuous when he stated, as he did on more than one occasion, that annexation had become nothing less than a matter of self-defense for the United States.[47]

At the same time, Calhoun's suspicions of British interference in Texas could not be extricated from the calculus of tensions between North and South. By the 1840s he had come to regard annexation as a litmus test to gauge the North's commitment to the federal compact. Since all patriotic Americans had a fundamental duty to resist British aggression in whatever form, the zeal with which some Northern politi-cal leaders championed the cause of transatlantic antislavery could only be viewed as treasonous behavior by the Southern ideologue. From Cal-houn's point of view—one that admittedly demonstrated a remarkable facility for trimming the facts to fit a Southern perspective—his section had been quick to come to the defense of the North in two wars against Great Britain, and more recently, in the region's quarrel over the Maine boundary. But now, with the South in peril, Northerners exhibited little enthusiasm when called upon to defend its institutions. In 1844 Calhoun remained faithful to the Union as he understood it, a compact based on reciprocal obligations, with each section prepared to set aside its own parochial interests and rise to the defense of the other. But the uproar over the Pakenham letter had sorely tested this system of belief, adding to the South Carolinian's growing suspicions of Northern disloyalty.[48]

During the ensuing debate over the treaty in Washington and in the national press, opponents of the measure dismissed the grim scenarios that expansionists claimed would befall the United States should it fail to annex the Lone Star Republic. Whig spokesmen made short work of the argument that a British ally on the southwestern border of the United States posed a threat to national security, pointing to the fact that the Northern states shared a 2,000-mile border with Canada, a country that, unlike Texas, was already a part of the British empire. If Great Britain intended to launch an offensive against the United States, surely it was already well poised to do so from military bases that had long been established on the Great Lakes and St. Lawrence River. Whigs also held up to ridicule the suggestion that Great Britain would strike at New Orleans from the pine forests of East Texas, observing that an attack upon the Crescent City from the sea would seem to be a far more practical military strategy. The claim that Britain intended to circumvent U.S. tariff schedules by using the Texas Republic as an entrepôt for its manufactured goods was shown to be similarly unfounded. If Her Majesty's government seriously intended to establish smuggling operations into the United States, anti-expansionists maintained, why had it not already attempted to do so from Canada?[49]

Opponents of annexation could also point to what they must have regarded as their trump card—the complete absence of hard evidence of a British conspiracy. After all, Her Majesty's government had repeatedly stated that it had no desire to interfere in the affairs of Texas. Van Buren Democrat Theodore Sedgwick wondered in frustration why Great Britain, if indeed it harbored designs on the Lone Star Republic, had not acted on them already. "She might have offered bounties upon Texas cotton; she might have colonized her with emigrants; she might have made her peace with Mexico; she might have lent her money; she might have endeavored to undermine her slavery," he declared. But Britain had done none of these things. The indisputable fact remained that Whitehall had adopted a passive posture on the question of Texas sovereignty—proof, Sedgwick argued, that the fears of Southern slaveholders were wholly unwarranted.[50]

Convincing though these counter-arguments may have been, Whig leaders were unable to entirely dispel the concerns raised by the apostles of annexation, having themselves articulated an intense distrust of British power. The Anglophobic harangues of Democratic expansionists had an uncomfortably familiar ring for many Whigs, who had accused British manufacturers of undermining American industry as recently as the debates over the tariff two years earlier. Rarely during the annexation controversy did the Whigs attempt to minimize the dangers posed by Her Majesty's government, having used equally strident invective to condemn British actions—and the timidity of the previous Democratic administration—in the *Caroline* affair.[51] And while they dismissed the idea that Texas was essential to the national defense, few Whigs questioned the encirclement theory itself, having pointed with alarm to the dangers of British military aggression in other parts of the hemisphere, such as Oregon and Maine.[52]

Even those who opposed Tyler's treaty strictly on antislavery grounds were careful to distinguish their own position from that of Great Britain. Fervent in their conviction that the expansion of slavery was immoral, they had no desire to be characterized as allies of Whitehall, and denounced British humanitarianism as a sham. Anti-expansionists acknowledged that Americans had every reason to be suspicious of England, which seemed "urged on by an insatiable lust of dominion."[53] John Quincy Adams, who had gone so far as to publicly urge the British to promote abolitionism in Texas, nonetheless viewed the altruistic rhetoric of Her Majesty's government with a hefty dose of skepticism. British efforts to maintain Texas's independence, Adams believed, had more to do with balance-of-power geopolitics—specifically, the need to protect Mexico from the territorial ambitions of the United States—than with the lofty goal of emancipating Texas slaves.[54]

In the end, neither arguments of national security nor of economic benefit could save Tyler's annexation treaty, which was soundly rejected by the Senate by a 35–16 margin in June. Calhoun's Pakenham correspondence no doubt played a role in the defeat, having undermined the administration's best efforts to promote the issue as a national measure. But the odds had always been stacked against the treaty, with most members of the Whig majority in the Senate ill-inclined to support a chief executive whom they had booted from their party two years earlier. On the Democratic side, angry Van Burenites, who blamed expansionists and Southerners for James K. Polk's upset victory over their candidate at the recent presidential convention in Baltimore, gladly cast their votes against the treaty. Others, still undecided, preferred that the issue be delayed until after the November election.

By this time, however, Texas had become an *idée fixe* for Tyler, and he refused to regard his defeated treaty as the final word on the subject. Despite his lame-duck status, the president announced that he would try again to annex Texas when the next session of Congress convened in December. A dyed-in-the-wool republican of the old school, Tyler now set aside his strict-constructionist scruples for the first time in his career (though he refused to admit to any inconsistency) and threw his support behind a proposal to admit Texas without Senate ratification. According to this plan, Texas could be incorporated by means of a joint resolution, which would require a simple majority of both houses rather than a 2/3rds majority of the Senate. Whigs denounced the scheme as unconstitutional (it was, at the very least, unprecedented), but as the summer wore on, support for annexation in some form began to gain ground. Van Burenites were obliged to accept the fact that an avowed expansionist was now the Democratic party nominee, and they clambered aboard the annexation bandwagon, though some did so with reluctance, still unhappy with the outcome of the Baltimore convention.

Although seen by historians primarily as a Southern measure, support for annexation was by no means limited to the planter class. When presented as an anti-British policy, the Democrats' expansionist agenda resonated with voters in Northern cities too, where Anglophobia, always well entrenched among the laboring classes, was gaining new strength as a result of Irish immigration. In New York City, the Texas issue briefly brought about an unusual working class alliance between George Henry Evans's land reform movement and the Spartan Association headed by political maverick Mike Walsh. The two groups even briefly merged their two newspapers and helped organize a pro-Texas mass meeting in Gotham's City Park. A crowd estimated at 10,000 heard some of the city's most prominent working-class leaders inveigh against Great Britain for allegedly seeking to block the impending union between the United States and the Lone Star Republic. The alliance proved short-lived, but working-class enthusiasm for Texas annexation helped bring New York into the Democratic column in 1844, thereby giving Polk the margin of victory in the electoral college.[55]

Expansion was not the only issue in the 1844 campaign. In New York and in many Northern states, local concerns competed with territorial ones for voters' attention. Nonetheless, pro-Texas Democrats interpreted the election result as a mandate for their agenda, and when Congress reconvened in December it set about the task of hammering out a new annexation offer. Whigs reiterated the counter-arguments they had made against the treaty in the first session, to which they added their objection to the legality of acquiring territory by means of a joint resolution. While the party line remained unchanged, several members took pains to point out that their opposition to annexation should not be construed as truckling to the British, no doubt in an effort to establish their credentials as Anglophobes more forthrightly than their party had done in the recent election. One Pennsylvania congressman assured his colleagues that he had always distrusted British foreign policy: "It is crafty, far-seeing, widely grasping, and deeply laid. It begins and ends in her own intense selfishness."[56]

After several weeks of stentorian public debate and backroom caucusing, a resolution was put before both houses admitting Texas as a state rather than as a territory. The so-called Brown Resolution allowed the Lone Star Republic to keep its public lands, providing the revenue it needed to pay off the swollen debt it had amassed during its nine-year existence. Significantly, the precise boundaries of Texas were left undefined. With Mexico and Texas both claiming the land between the Rio Grande and the Nueces River, it was widely assumed in Washington that some form of compensation would induce Mexico to surrender its claim. In February 1845 the House approved the joint resolution by a comfortable 120–98 margin, but in the Senate the vote could not have been closer: 27–25. Edward Hannegan of Illinois cast his ballot as president pro tem to avoid a tie. The most divisive issue the United States Congress had faced in its fifty-six-year history had hinged on a single vote.

⁂

The Texas annexation issue revealed the full extent to which the slavery question had come to dominate the American political scene. Debates in Washington over the Lone Star Republic's first bid for admission into the union in 1838 had pitted a small but determined cohort of antislavery leaders against an overwhelming majority on both sides of the aisle committed to preserving intersectional harmony. By the mid-1840s, this biregional and bipartisan consensus had collapsed amid Northern concerns about the expansion of slavery and the political influence of the planter class. Once a querulous minority, the antislavery lobby had gained valuable allies among Northern leaders, Whig and Democrat alike. While the two parties continued to maintain the façade of national solidarity, serious cracks in the structures of both organizations had already begun to appear, which would only grow more destabilizing in the years ahead.

Northern antislavery leaders were naturally despondent over their defeat, and did not want for explanations as to what had gone wrong. They were particularly incensed by the role that the threat of British imperialism had played in the annexation debate. In their view, Anglophobia was nothing more than a malodorous red herring employed by Democrats to deflect attention from what they regarded as the real issue—the desire of the slave power to expand into the Southwest. Nothing had had so great an impact on public opinion as "the hue-and-cry which has been so artfully raised against the alleged design of England to subjugate Texas," William Lloyd Garrison noted ruefully in the spring of 1845. The New England firebrand attached much of the blame for the defeat on Irish immigrants, whose bitter and implacable hatred of England had proved a boon to pro-annexation Democrats in the North.[57]

Evidently, Garrison had forgotten how antislavery leaders had themselves invoked the familiar theme of foreign interference in Texas. Talk of a plot to bring the Lone Star Republic within Britain's imperial orbit was not a phantom conjured up by Southern whites, but one promoted by Benjamin Lundy, John Quincy Adams, and others who, it will be recalled, had first warned of British designs in the region in 1836. Emboldened by their initial victory against annexation, American antislavery leaders had continued to make it clear in the years that followed that only the intercession of Great Britain could save Texas from the clutches of the slave power.[58] To be sure, more often than not it was Democratic expansionists who pointed with alarm to the specter of Great Britain. But in the case of Texas, it was antislavery leaders who had been the first to don John Bull fright wigs to gain political advantage. The plan backfired, enabling their adversaries to recast the annexation issue as a matter of national security. Coming at a time of heightened fears of British activities elsewhere on the continent, the possibility that Her Majesty's government might intercede in Texas was not one that Americans took lightly.

As usual, Southern planters found little satisfaction in victory, or in seeing their adversaries hoisted upon their own petard. Feeling the tightening of the antislavery noose, they had made annexation a sine qua non of the South's continued support for the union. A non-negotiable issue, amenable neither to compromise nor deferral, it had become for many Southerners a test of the North's loyalty to a federal compact of shared obligations. In their view, it was a trial that section had failed miserably, for while some in the North had rallied to the South's defense, far too many had responded with apathy or downright opposition. John C. Calhoun still regarded the Constitution as the South's ark of safety, and continued to counsel caution, but the middle ground on which he stood was fast crumbling beneath him. Ominously, Southern centrists who had once shared the South Carolina senator's commitment to the union were beginning to break rank.[59]

One of the most prominent defections was William Gilmore Simms. The bonds of union tugged at few Southerners more strongly than Simms, who had served as editor of the unionist *Charleston City Gazette* during the nullification controversy. A founding member of the Young America literary clique, Simms still liked to think of himself as a national writer, but by the 1840s he had parlayed his fame as the South's preeminent novelist into an active role in Palmetto State politics. Under the tutelage of states' rights ultra James Henry Hammond, Simms in 1844 won election to the state legislature, where he urged the acquisition of Texas as an essential safeguard against the growing Northern assault on slavery.[60]

With his deeply ingrained suspicion of the imperial parent, Simms harbored no doubt that a small cohort of Northern abolitionists was backed by "British counsels, British agents, and last, not least, British *gold.*" But Northern opposition to the expansion of slavery left Simms, like so many Southerners, severely shaken. No longer could he state with any certainty that the North would always rise in support of Southern interests. As time went on, Simms seemed less inclined to believe that the two sections would stand together against Great Britain on the Texas question (and, by extension, on the slavery issue itself). Increasingly, he came to accept the view, posited by his more radical friends, that the North and Great Britain were colleagued against the South. What Simms regarded as Northern "jealousy" of his section and its way of life, coupled with Britain's long-standing hatred of republican institutions, now seemed to be conspiring to produce the same result: "*a dissolution of the American Union.*"[61]

"Looking John Bull Straight in the Eye"

And should old England interfere,
To stop us in our bright career,
We'll teach her, as we did of yore,
This land is ours from shore to shore . . .
Let recreant statesmen fly the course,
And General Scott, the old war-horse,
Blow hot or cold his "plate of soup,"[1]
To England we will never stoop.
—Mexican War song, 1846

On March 4, 1845, Jackson protégé James K. Polk took the oath of office on the Capitol steps and, struggling to be heard over a steady rain, delivered his inaugural address to a "large assemblage of umbrellas."[2] At first blush, the foreign policy sections of the speech, with their familiar admonitions against foreign influence, seemed to vary little from the pronouncements of Polk's predecessor, John Tyler. Upon closer inspection, however, Polk's inaugural address revealed the first hints that the American expansionist agenda was about to enter a new, more militant phase. The Brown Resolution offering to annex Texas, passed by Congress a few days earlier, tacitly acknowledged the Mexican claim to the land between the Rio Grande and the Nueces River, stipulating that the Texas-Mexico boundary should be adjusted at a later date, a condition that would presumably involve some form of compensation for Mexico. But the new chief executive made no mention of Mexico's claim to the trans-Nueces. Indeed, his inaugural address seemed to brush off that country's opposition to annexation altogether, insisting that the union was a matter "belonging exclusively to the United States and Texas." Polk also departed from the moderate posture assumed by the outgoing administration on the Oregon question.

Reiterating the confrontational stand his party had taken in the Baltimore convention, Polk appeared to rule out the possibility of a compromise with Great Britain over the disputed territory, declaring American title to the Pacific Northwest to be "clear and unquestionable."[3]

This bold assertion of American territorial claims by the new president cannot be attributed to an overarching vision of a continental "manifest destiny" for the United States. Thoroughly provincial in outlook, the Tennessean had little knowledge of, or experience in, foreign affairs, nor was he known as a particularly imaginative thinker. The assets Polk brought to the White House were essentially prosaic ones—a disciplined, methodical temperament, and an unshakable faith in Jacksonian precepts. Polk had been dubbed Young Hickory by his supporters in the recent presidential campaign, and the moniker was more apt than they knew. For all intents and purposes, he was the ideological clone of the former president, a man for whom any deviation from the party line was unthinkable. While some Democrats wavered and broke rank over such issues as the Bank and the tariff, Polk remained steadfast. Jackson had recently been in a position to reward his years of loyal service, touting his protégé as a presidential contender on the eve of the Baltimore convention. In the months after the election, the two men had kept up an active correspondence, with Jackson giving advice on matters ranging from potential cabinet appointees to domestic policy. Jackson would die three months after Polk took the oath of office, but he would remain the guiding spirit of the new administration. "What would Jackson do?" would be the question Polk would ask himself with every decision he was called upon to make during the next four years.

With regard to U.S. policies toward continental neighbors, the president believed that his course was clear. One month after the election, Jackson had described the British hemispheric presence as an "iron hoop" encircling the republic. That cordon would have to be broken, and soon, if the United States was to ever have any hope of tapping the rich agricultural resources of the West or the commercial potential to be gained by access to the Pacific Ocean. And there was more than the nation's economic future at stake. As products of the republic's frontier culture, Polk and his mentor both exhibited a low tolerance for insult, which they applied in their conduct of international affairs. It was a character trait that led both men to take the defense of the nation's honor as seriously as the pursuit of any strategic objective. Above all, they were determined that the United States project an image of strength and resolve, convinced that John Bull could be relied upon to exploit any sign of weakness. In his final letters to his protégé, Jackson urged "a bold & undaunted front" as the only viable policy toward Great Britain. It was a policy that could just as well be applied to Mexico, a nation the two Ten-nesseans regarded as little more than a client state of Victoria's empire. "War is a blessing," Old Hickory wrote, "compared with national degra-dation."[4]

Polk's audience may have failed to grasp the full implications of his speech on that rainy March afternoon, but the months ahead would leave little doubt that a new, more confrontational chapter in U.S. foreign policy had begun. Henceforth, Washington would move aggressively to challenge British imperialism on the North American continent. And in the process, the nation would acquire an imperial identity of its own.

The Man in the White Hat

At the time of Polk's inaugural, Texas—the holy grail of slaveholding expansionists—appeared within reach. The last nine years had not been easy ones for Texas. Wracked by conflict with Mexico, vulnerable to In-dian depredations, and suffering from debilitating economic hardship since the Panic of 1837, the republic had never quite managed to estab-lish a firm footing for itself in the American Southwest. The overwhelm-ing majority of Anglo-Texans looked forward to annexation, believing that it would finally bring the capital investment and immigrants neces-sary for the region's prosperity.

Yet significant hurdles to a marriage of the two North American re-publics remained. Mexican leaders had repeatedly warned that any at-tempt by the United States to annex Texas, which it still claimed as its own, would constitute an act of war, though this had been dismissed as so much saber-rattling by U.S. policymakers. Now that Washington had finally acted to acquire Texas, Mexico's minister to the United States de-manded his passport, breaking off diplomatic relations. A more serious potential stumbling block, as far as the administration was concerned, was the equivocal attitude of the Lone Star Republic's leaders to the con-gressional resolution. The republic's new president, Anson Jones, hinted strongly that he favored independence. His predecessor, the enormously influential Sam Houston, whose flirtations with the British had helped goad the Tyler government into annexation talks in the first place, also remained coyly indifferent to the new proposal.[5] While the resolution offered significantly better terms than the 1844 treaty, some Texans re-mained unsatisfied. They grumbled that Washington refused to assume the republic's national debt or compensate it for its public property, and wanted a pledge that the Texas claim to the Rio Grande as the boundary with Mexico would be upheld. In his presidential valedictory address in December, Houston urged Texans not to "go begging again for admission into the United States." The Lone Star leader's friends in Washington interpreted his reluctance to endorse the Brown Resolution as a ploy, yet another of his many efforts to impress upon American policymakers that his country had other options available to it. But Houston continued to play his cards close to the vest; even Andrew Jackson did not know if his public comments on annexation were an expression of his true feelings or merely a bluff.[6]

And then there was Charles Elliot, the British chargé d'affaires to Texas. By 1844, Whitehall's real and alleged efforts to involve itself in the affairs of the Republic had created in both Texas and the United States an uneasy distrust of the Peel government, and its diplomatic agent in particular. Secretary of State James Buchanan described Elliot as a man of "transparent cunning," while the pro-annexation press vilified the chargé d'affaires, referring to him contemptuously as "the foreign meddler." The fear of British subterfuge that had driven the annexation movement from the outset now became all consuming, fueled by the widely held belief among American expansionists that Texas might be snatched from their grasp at the eleventh hour. Of course, American Anglophobes could always be relied upon to grossly exaggerate the extent of British influence. It would soon become apparent, however, that in Charles Elliot they had at last found a representative of the British government who confirmed their darkest fears.[7]

For three years, Elliot had devoted his energies to promoting an independent, stable Texas. Those efforts had all been unavailing, due in no small part to Mexico's refusal to acknowledge the Lone Star Republic's sovereignty. But now, a slender ray of hope appeared in the form of a major policy shift in Mexico City. The results of the recent U.S. presidential contest had convinced Mexican president Santa Anna that the annexation of Texas was now all but assured. In a last ditch effort to prevent the union, he was finally prepared to concede what had long been obvious—that Texas was not a Mexican province in revolt but an independent nation. This unexpected about-face gave the Foreign Office reason to believe that, even at this late stage, the westward ambitions of the United States could still be thwarted. Accordingly, in early March, Elliot received new instructions from London, asking him to prevail upon the government of Texas to delay annexation until the new Mexican position could be fully explored.[8]

Mindful that the Brown Resolution had just been passed, Elliot set off in great haste for Washington-on-the-Brazos, the Texas capital, accompanied by the French minister, Alphonse Dubois de Saligny. There the two diplomats received an attentive hearing from President Anson Jones, who agreed to delay action on the forthcoming U.S. offer for ninety days. The agreement, known as the Jones Memorandum, would allow the two European powers time to obtain the Mexican government's formal recognition of Texas's sovereignty.[9] Since Great Britain had consistently urged Mexico to recognize the independence of Texas, the proposal itself was not particularly remarkable. The same could not be said, however, for the means by which the agreement was to be conveyed to Mexico City. Evidently convinced that the situation called for bold measures, Elliot offered to carry the memorandum to its government personally. This alone constituted a serious departure from his instructions, but Elliot went further and proposed a plan that revealed, if nothing else, a flair for the dramatic. He would travel to Mexico incognito and with the British minister there obtain a formal guarantee of Texas's independence. Elliot was convinced that the Lone Star Republic would gladly spurn the U.S. annexation offer if it had nothing to fear from Mexico. Although his personal motives can only be guessed at, a secret mission to Mexico, if successful, would have represented a major coup for the career diplomat, lending new luster to a reputation tarnished by his earlier misadventures in China.

Whatever merits Elliot saw in the plan, they were not shared by his superiors in Whitehall, who were well aware that even the slightest hint of interference by Great Britain was enough to send American expansionists into fits of apoplexy. Both Aberdeen and the prime minister doubted the mission would remain secret for long, and if discovered would deal a far greater blow to British interests in the western hemisphere than if their representative in Texas had done nothing at all. If known to the public, Elliot's cloak-and-dagger diplomacy could be relied upon to excite the passions of American Anglophobes who had always accused Great Britain of meddling in their affairs.[10]

But it was too late for Peel and Aberdeen to restrain their overzealous diplomat, who had already put his plan in motion. After his meeting with Jones, Elliot returned to Galveston where, in conversations with the town's prominent citizens, he made known to all his intention to travel to Charleston, South Carolina, to visit his family. On April 5, Elliot boarded the British ship *Electra* and sailed out of Galveston Bay. Once out of sight of land, the diplomat transferred to another British vessel, the *Eurydice*, a warship helmed by his cousin, George Elliot. Six days later the *Eurydice* arrived in Vera Cruz. His face obscured by a large white hat, Charles Elliot disembarked and, in the company of his cousin, hurried toward the Mexican capital.[11]

As Whitehall feared, Elliot's plans began to go awry almost immediately. The pair's movements attracted the attention of American residents in Vera Cruz, and by the end of the month the State Department received word that "Capt. Elliot, the British agent," was on the ground in Mexico.[12] Elliot had covered his tracks so thoroughly before leaving Galveston that the State Department dismissed the report, assuming that the individual mentioned in the dispatch was George Elliot, the diplomat's relative. Events in the Mexican capital were also conspiring against the British gambit. By the time Elliot arrived, Mexican president Santa Anna had been deposed. His successor, José Joaquin Herrera, lacked the public support to undertake any major policy initiatives on his own, and referred the Jones Memorandum to Congress. There it encountered stiff resistance from legislators still bitter over the loss of Mexico's northern territory. For three weeks it deliberated before accepting the proposal, thereby formally acknowledging, nine years after San Jacinto, the independence of Texas.

Back in Texas, however, annexation, not independence, was the all-absorbing topic of the day. Since Elliot's departure, support for the Brown Resolution was clearly solidifying, especially in light of persistent—though at this point, still vague—rumors that the administration was secretly collaborating with the British to preserve Texas's independence. In early May, President Jones bowed to the public pressure and called for a convention to be held on July 4 to vote on the U.S. offer. Meanwhile, sightings of the British diplomat in Mexico continued to be received with skepticism in Texas and the United States. Though always ready to believe the worst where British diplomacy was concerned, the *New Orleans Daily Picayune*, like the State Department, gave little credence to this information at first, publishing without comment a letter from a correspondent in Vera Cruz which revealed that Elliot was indeed in Mexico on a secret mission on behalf of the Texas government. Not until it received corroboration of these reports a few days later did the paper give full attention to the episode, accompanied by an editorial tirade against British duplicity and intrigue. In the parlance of the espionage potboiler, Elliot's cover had been blown.[13]

The British diplomat returned to Galveston at the end of May to find the town in an uproar over his secret errand. Newspapers that a few weeks earlier had ignored reports of Elliot sightings in Mexico now gave voice to every rumor, contributing to the confusion and lending the affair an aura of mystery that heightened public interest in the story. It was reported by some journals that a certain "Mr. Smith," a secret agent of the Texas government, had accompanied Elliot on his trip to Mexico. The identity of this mysterious figure, who had been spotted wearing a large white hat, became the subject of enormous speculation in the Southern press. It would be several weeks before the Texas government revealed that it had not sent a diplomatic agent with Elliot to Mexico;

only then did it become clear that the now-famous "man in the white hat" was none other than Elliot himself.[14]

Elliot's dramatic eleventh-hour mission to win Mexican recognition for the Republic had come too late to be given serious consideration by most Texans, whose minds by the early summer of 1845 had long been made up. They had never placed much faith in Mexican peace overtures, especially in light of that country's warlike posturing since the annexation negotiations became public in the spring of 1844. With Mexican troop activity below the Rio Grande and rumors of an impending invasion reported daily in the press, few Anglo-Texans were inclined to view the preliminary treaty Elliot brought back from Mexico as an acceptable alternative to annexation, the guarantees of European powers notwithstanding.

Amid the furor caused by the British chargé d'affaires' errand to Mexico, what little support for Texas's independence now vanished. The *Texas National Register*, the only news organ advocating independence, conceded that Elliot's activities were bound to be misconstrued by the citizens of Texas, who looked with a jaundiced eye upon all things associated with Great Britain. "If Americans have one passion, more thorough bred than another," its editor observed, "it is jealousy of England; and Texians inherit it."[15] Sam Houston publicly declared himself in favor of the Brown Resolution in mid-May, insisting that his public avowals of friendship with Britain had all been merely a ruse and that he had "coquetted a little" with its government in an attempt to incite the jealousy of the United States.[16] A stranger to humility, Houston would harp upon this theme in several self-congratulatory speeches in the months ahead. In Tennessee, the ailing Jackson heaved a sigh of relief. "*All* safe," he wrote to his protégé in the White House. "I knew British gold could not buy Sam Houston." He could now die in peace—which he did, thirteen days later.[17]

While Houston sought to capitalize on the wave of anti-British sentiment in Texas that crested following the news of Elliot's mission in the summer of 1845, Anson Jones found himself in the eye of the storm. The "whole population," the *New Orleans Courier* declared, had been "roused to the highest pitch" by allegations that the Texas president intended "to throw the republic into the arms of England."[18] In mid-June the Texas Congress rejected the proposed treaty with Mexico, and on July 4 the special convention voted to formally accept the Brown Resolution and begin the work of drawing up a state constitution. In a public meeting held to celebrate Texas's statehood some months later, the citizens of one East Texas town noted that "a death blow" had been dealt "to the grasping ambition and arrogant pretensions of trans-Atlantic monarchs, who hoped to engraft a scion of royal despotism on the tree of American liberty."[19]

It is easy to dismiss Elliot's errand as a curiosity, a quixotic effort that could never have averted Texas's long-sought goal of annexation to the United States. But the real significance of the botched affair had less to do with results than with the methods employed. The veil of secrecy that accompanied Elliot's mission confirmed for suspicious Americans the insidious nature of British foreign policy, providing expansionists with their most potent propaganda tool. Here at last was compelling evidence that the specter of British intrigue was not simply a bugbear created by annexationists to bring Texas into the union. While the expansion of slavery remained a pressing issue for many, the threat of British meddling in North America could no longer be dismissed as Southern hysteria. Pro-annexation newspapers in the United States seized on the sensational aspects of the affair, reminding their readers that "the mountebank tricks of diplomatists . . . are completely out of date."[20]

As a result, many Northern Democrats who had heretofore expressed misgivings about the prospect of admitting Texas into the union were compelled to give new credence to allegations of a British conspiracy. Elliot's mission had caused "feelings of indignation" throughout the country, Secretary of State Buchanan exulted, transcending party and section.[21] It was a view shared by New York newspaperman John L. O'Sullivan, a Van Buren Democrat and a relative latecomer to the ultra-expansionist crusade. O'Sullivan had at one time argued that Washington should obtain Mexico's consent before annexing Texas. But now, in the flurry of excitement that surrounded Elliot's mission to Mexico, the possibility that the American thrust westward might be thwarted by European powers had convinced him that the situation required prompt, resolute action on the part of the United States. Seizing upon this new and irrefutable evidence of British subterfuge, he argued in the July issue of the *Democratic Review* that Americans must set aside their partisan and regional differences over annexation and unite to stave off this external threat. Pointing with alarm to the diplomatic intrigues of European states, O'Sullivan urged the fulfillment of the nation's "manifest destiny."[22]

Talk of an emerging national consensus on the Texas question does not appear to have been merely wishful thinking on the part of Democratic loyalists and the expansionist press. With Washington and Whitehall already at loggerheads over the Oregon boundary, Elliot's mission helped fuel a wave of anti-British feeling across the country, giving rise to speculation that Great Britain would stop at nothing short of war to block American hemispheric interests. It will be recalled that Whig standard-bearer Henry Clay had already defined his party's position with regard to annexation during the 1844 campaign, stating that any attempt by foreign powers to undermine the sovereignty of Texas should be repelled with force by the United States. Accordingly, Whig journals that had once opposed the annexation of Texas now joined in the rising cho rus of outrage against British cupidity.[23] Resentment of British interference in American affairs was even in evidence in the traditional Whig stronghold of New England, where it served to exacerbate growing tensions between anti-slavery "Conscience" Whigs and conservative party members. For the latter, British activities had clearly elbowed suspicions of slaveholding conspiracies aside, at least for the present. Massachusetts congressman Robert C. Winthrop, who had ridiculed Democrats for their Anglophobic hysteria, and who as late as January announced his opposition to annexation "now and always," threw his support behind the measure at a July 4th rally in Boston. The Boston Atlas, which had earlier urged New England Whigs to resist annexation "with the last drop of our blood," now exhorted its readers to stand and defend the country against foreign aggression.[24]

To be sure, many Northern Whigs and a sizable group of antislavery Democrats vehemently opposed annexation, as they had always done. But in the summer of 1845, anti-annexation sentiment in the North was to some degree undercut by a rising tide of Anglophobic feeling. The "man in the white hat" had failed to thwart U.S. territorial ambitions, but he had unwittingly managed to accomplish, however briefly, what ardent expansionists had always longed to do: transform annexation, an issue dangerously freighted with sectional discord, into a policy around which a large segment of the electorate could unite.

Elliot's mission may have helped mute Northern opposition toward annexation, but its greatest impact could be seen in the behavior of the expansion-minded administration in Washington. Not that Polk and his advisors needed any convincing that Great Britain exerted an inordinate degree of influence over Mexico. But there could no longer be any doubt, as far as Polk and his advisers were concerned, that "England was pulling the wires," and that Her Majesty's government had lied repeatedly in disclaiming all interest in the fate of Texas.[25]

Greatly heightening the administration's anxiety level during this crucial period was its man on the ground in Texas, chargé d'affaires Andrew Jackson Donelson. A man of impeccable Democratic credentials— a nephew of Andrew Jackson, he had served as his private secretary in the White House—Donelson was an agent whose advice Polk trusted completely. The U.S. chargé had been among those in Galveston duped by Elliot into believing that he had traveled to the United States in April.

When Donelson learned in the press of Elliot's secret trip to Mexico, he did not mince words in condemning the British diplomat's conduct to his superiors in Washington. The affair led Donelson to conclude what he had long suspected: that Mexican sovereignty was a complete fiction, its leaders little more than pawns of Her Majesty's government. Rather than view it as the last-ditch effort of a failed diplomacy, Donelson saw a deliberate attempt by Whitehall to inflame tensions between the United States and Mexico. So great was Donelson's fear of Elliot's influence that he seems to have convinced himself that the British diplomat actually had the authority to launch a Mexican invasion of Texas should annexation go forward. The U.S. chargé d'affaires concluded his dispatch with the somber assertion that he regarded a war with Mexico as "inevitable," a conflict "dictated by the British minister" for the sole purpose of defeating a union of Texas and the United States.[26]

Such apprehensions, like so many reports of British intrigues, had little basis in fact. On the other side of the Atlantic, Her Majesty's government was trying frantically to allay Washington's fears that it was seeking to manufacture a crisis in the American Southwest. Far from encouraging Mexico to embark upon a war against its northern neighbor, Lord Aberdeen had notified its leaders that they could expect no aid from Great Britain should an invasion of Texas be attempted, a warning that he would repeat to that government on numerous occasions in the months ahead. Edward Everett, the U.S. minister to London, and his successor, Louis McLane, relayed these assurances to Washington, but their reports had little if any effect on U.S. policymakers. In several meetings with the U.S. minister, the Foreign Secretary repeatedly denied, "in the most explicit terms," that Great Britain was seeking to exacerbate tensions between the United States and Mexico. But Lord Aberdeen had disavowed undue interference in the affairs of Texas in the past, and the Anglophobic president and his advisers were unwilling to take British diplomats at their word.[27]

Instead, Polk put his faith in those who shared his distrust of Great Britain, and the information he was receiving from Texas confirmed his worst apprehensions. Donelson's early June dispatches and other letters from Texas created a genuine panic within the administration. The significance of this correspondence in the chain of events that would lead up to the war with Mexico can hardly be overstated. In view of the "facts" presented by Donelson, both in regard to Mexican troop movements and "the open intermeddling" of the British chargé d'affaires, "I have lost no time in causing the most prompt and energetic measures to be adopted here," the President assured his diplomat in Galveston. Believing an invasion of Texas to be imminent, Polk ordered a naval buildup in the Gulf of Mexico and instructed General Zachary Taylor, who commanded a force of 1,500 troops in western Louisiana, to establish a new base of operations at Corpus Christi, on the Texas-Mexico frontier. Once the Texas annexation convention accepted the American proposal on July 4, the United States would be ready to protect Texas from its Mexican enemies, who had been "stimulated and excited" by British "intrigue and influence."[28]

So worried had Polk become that Texas might now be snatched from the grasp of the United States that he seems to have been wholly unaware of the extraordinary nature of these instructions. Though the annexation of Texas appeared certain, the republic was still a sovereign nation, which had not yet requested U.S. military protection. In an even more blatant disregard for the niceties of international law, the administration instructed Taylor to take up positions *below* the Nueces River, on soil claimed by Mexico as well as Texas. That Polk was more than a little rattled by Donelson's assessment of the situation in Texas is borne out by the fact that his sudden insistence on the legitimacy of the Republic's claim to the trans-Nueces was a complete departure from his earlier statements on the issue. Only one week earlier, in a letter to Sam Houston written before he learned of the war scare in Texas, Polk had alluded only vaguely to the Texas claim, no doubt confident that a negotiated settlement could be reached with Mexico that would involve some form of compensation for the land between the Nueces River and the Rio Grande.[29] But by mid-June Polk was uninterested in sorting out which nation had the more valid claim to the region. Reacting to the perceived threat of a British-sponsored Mexican invasion with a belligerence that worried even expansionist members of his own party, he was determined to send a clear and unequivocal message to wavering Texans still unhappy with the terms of the Brown Resolution that they could rely upon the United States to defend their interests. It would prove to be a fateful step in Washington's deteriorating relationship with Mexico City. Already infuriated by the annexation of Texas, many Mexicans would regard Polk's peremptory claim to the trans-Nueces as the final indignity.

On to the Pacific: Oregon and California

For all Polk's bold talk on behalf of American claims to the Pacific Northwest, the president believed that a settlement with Great Britain was still possible, and in July the administration sought to reopen negotiations with Whitehall on the Oregon question. Abandoning his "All Oregon" campaign pledge, Polk offered, as Tyler had done, to divide the territory at the 49th parallel. The president was not quite ready to go as far as his predecessor, however, and refused to grant the British navigation rights on the Columbia River. Since the Foreign Office had rejected a more advantageous settlement in its negotiations with the Tyler administration one year earlier, Britain's minister to the United States, Richard Pakenham, assumed that the new proposal would be totally unacceptable to his government and rejected the U.S. offer.

Angered by the rebuff, Polk now reverted back to his original hardline position on the boundary dispute. Convinced that further entreaties on the part of the United States would be seen as a sign of weakness, he decided to slam the door shut on the negotiations. The president's intransigence was popular with Western Democrats, though many moderates believed that with Mexico threatening to go to war over the annexation of Texas, this was no time for the administration to antagonize the British. Secretary of State Buchanan worried that Polk's action might be seen in Whitehall as an attempt to deny Great Britain an outlet on the Pacific Ocean, and prompt Her Majesty's government to work in concert with Mexico. At a cabinet meeting in August, Buchanan fairly begged the president to leave open the possibility of further negotiations. The secretary of state suggested that the administration's official reply might contain a paragraph inviting the British to make a counter-offer to the U.S. proposal, but Polk gave the idea short shrift. When Buchanan remarked that the administration's reply to Britain should at least be postponed until it could be known whether there would be a war with Mexico, Polk replied that he "saw no necessary connection between the two questions," adding that "we should do our duty towards both Mexico and Great Britain and firmly maintain our rights, & leave the rest to God and the country."[30]

Having hinted at an aggressive approach to foreign affairs in his inaugural address, the president gave a fuller, though by no means complete, view of his territorial ambitions in his first annual message in December. In a move that critics viewed as a provocative act, he called upon Congress to end the joint occupation of Oregon and assume full control of the territory, in defiance of British claims. "All attempts at compromise having failed," the President asked legislators to give Great Britain a year's notice before formally terminating the joint occupation treaty, as the agreement required. Polk also urged Congress to take appropriate measures to ensure the safety of American citizens in Oregon, and proposed that forts be built along the Oregon Trail to protect emigrants. He further suggested that Congress enact a liberal land policy to stimulate American settlement once joint occupation formally ended.

So great was the public excitement generated by the president's stand on the Oregon issue that his comments regarding affairs with Mexico passed almost unnoticed. The annexation of Texas, Polk declared, had been "a bloodless achievement," which had occurred despite the "interference of European monarchies." In a pointed reference to the Elliot mission, he noted with satisfaction that the designs of Britain and France had been thwarted, and that the impending union of the two republics had demonstrated the futility of "diplomatic arts and intrigues" on the North American continent. Sidestepping the Mexican claim to the trans-Nueces, Polk stated blandly that American dominion had now been "peacefully extended" to the Rio Grande.[31]

Unmentioned in the president's message, but very much on his mind, was the subject of California. For some months the expansionist press had been abuzz with rumors of British intrigues in the Far West. Having been foiled in its efforts to block the annexation of Texas, conspiracy theorists argued, Great Britain would now devote its full attention to gaining control of California as part of its long-term strategy to encircle the United States.[32] Convinced, now more than ever, that Mexico was little more than a British client state, the administration had been particularly disturbed by information it had recently received from Thomas O. Larkin, the U.S. consul in Monterrey, California, and a devoted propagandist for American expansion. A separatist government had recently assumed control over the territory, and Larkin claimed, among other things, that the British were financing a military expedition to bring the region back under the authority of the Mexican capital.[33] Suddenly apprehensive, just as Tyler had been when he received similar reports concerning British designs in Texas, Polk began to regard California as a matter requiring his immediate attention. Larkin was instructed to ascertain whether Great Britain or France aimed to take control of the territory, and to warn the inhabitants of California of the dangers of European interference. John D. Sloat, commander of the Pacific Squadron, was advised to remain on alert, and to seize California harbors in the event of war. Once again, Washington saw the hand of the British working actively to thwart its territorial objectives. And, once again, Americans saw Great Britain attempting to use Mexico as a surrogate to achieve its ends.[34]

Believing it vital to have a senior diplomat on the ground in Mexico as soon as possible to protect American interests, the administration in late 1845 tapped John Slidell, a Louisiana congressman, as a recess appointment to the post of U.S. minister. Although Polk was now refusing to acknowledge Mexico's claim to the trans-Nueces, he regarded the boundary dispute as the principal obstacle to normal diplomatic relations between the two countries. Accordingly, in an effort to placate the

Herrera government, he instructed Slidell to state that the United States was prepared to assume $3.25 million in American claims against Mexico in return for its recognition of the Rio Grande as the Texas boundary. Equally important, given the sense of urgency conveyed by Larkin, the president wanted his diplomat to make it clear to Mexican leaders that the United States would take aggressive measures to prevent the cession of California to any European power.[35]

It has been argued that Polk's primary objective was always California, a prize that led the president to assume an increasingly aggressive posture toward Mexico. In fact, his interest in California seems to have waxed and waned in direct proportion to his suspicions of British activities in the region. Alarmed by Larkin's assessment of the situation in the fall of 1845, the administration took a calmer view when another dispatch from the consul arrived shortly after the president's December message, seeming to indicate that California was in no immediate danger from the British after all. On the basis of this information, the president issued new instructions to Slidell: if Mexican leaders showed no interest in selling California, he should not allow the matter to upset the chances for normalizing relations between the two countries. Secure in the knowledge that Mexico would be unable to exert its sovereignty over the region, Polk was willing to shelve his territorial ambitions, at least temporarily, in the absence of a specific British threat.[36]

But suspicions of Great Britain were too deeply embedded in the national psyche to be readily dismissed, and American leaders harbored little doubt that the Foreign Office would exploit the political vacuum in the Southwest if given the opportunity. Sailing for Mexico in December 1845, Slidell found a highly volatile political environment in the nation's capital. With anger at the United States over the acquisition of Texas running high, the weakened Herrera government refused to accept his credentials. It was soon overthrown by the conservative General Mariano Paredes, who was even less disposed than his predecessor to accept compensation for the trans-Nueces on the administration's terms. The American diplomat took it for granted that the actions of the Paredes government had either been made or at the very least sanctioned by Whitehall. While he was not prepared to go so far as Donelson in Texas and accuse the British of seeking to provoke a war between the United States and Mexico, Slidell nonetheless believed that London was doing all it could to keep the two countries at odds, and was soon blaming his British counterpart for his inability to move negotiations forward.[37]

As usual, the intelligence Washington was receiving from its envoys fell well short of the mark in accurately gauging Whitehall's objectives. Even as Donelson in Texas, Larkin in California, and Slidell in Mexico inundated the State Department with dispatches describing their fears of British machinations, the Foreign Office was adhering to a strict policy of non-interference in North American affairs, urging both the United States and Mexico to resolve their differences peacefully. How could U.S. diplomats have been so utterly mistaken about British intentions? The answer can be blamed only in part on excitable American imaginations. Mexican leaders, who wished for British interference as ardently as American policymakers dreaded it, also helped fuel the wealth of misinformation contained in U.S. diplomatic dispatches. Since the Tyler administration's first signs of interest in annexing Texas, no less than three Mexican presidents—Santa Anna, Herrera, and now Paredes— had come to regard British interposition as their only salvation. Unable to reconquer Texas or to prevent its absorption by the United States, they had entertained the vain hope that the nation's honor could still be redeemed if Great Britain would move to check the American advance across the continent. Almost from the day Paredes assumed power, he had enjoined, then pleaded with Whitehall for support in the Texas crisis. But the response was always the same: the Mexican government must not expect any material assistance from London.[38]

In Washington, meanwhile, Polk was forging ahead with his plan to terminate the joint occupation agreement in Oregon. The president remained convinced that "the only way to treat John Bull was to look him straight in the eye," and that if Congress faltered, he "would immediately become arrogant and more grasping in his demands."[39] Predictably, the debates over the termination agreement saw Democratic expansionists on Capitol Hill work themselves into a rabid lather at the very thought of the British gaining a permanent foothold in the Pacific Northwest. Few were willing to concede that Britain had a legitimate claim to any part of the Oregon Territory, fewer still that British arms would prevail in a contest between the two countries. Some predicted a new sense of national purpose, in which "all local distinctions will be forgotten" should the two countries come to blows.[40]

But uncomfortable geopolitical realities invariably had a way of intruding whenever Americans proclaimed for their nation a "manifest destiny." Beneath the flood of shrill rhetoric on Capitol Hill lay an unmistakable undercurrent of anxiety, as Washington legislators fretted that the Oregon controversy might escalate beyond a war of words. In asking Congress to abrogate the agreement, was the Polk administration ruling out the possibility of further negotiations? If so, would the diplomatic impasse lead to hostilities? Southerners like John C. Calhoun, so committed to the annexation of Texas at any cost the year before, now counseled caution, alarmed by the prospect of a disruption in commercial intercourse between the two countries. Convinced that the United States would eventually establish hegemony over the Pacific Northwest as more American settlers moved into the region, the South Carolina senator argued that Washington had time on its side and had nothing to gain by forcing the issue.[41]

In the end, prudence prevailed over patriotic bluster in Washington. On Capitol Hill, an unlikely coalition of Northern and Southern legislators managed to keep the war hawks at bay. The House passed a mildly worded resolution calling for an "amicable settlement" of the dispute between the two countries, while moderates in the Senate succeeded in postponing a vote on the measure. The administration, too, adopted a much more circumspect view of the controversy, having received disturbing signals that Whitehall's patience was now at an end. Irritated by Polk's refusal to reopen negotiations or submit the matter to international arbitration, the Peel government had at last begun to consider the possibility of war. Lord Aberdeen summed up the British position succinctly: the Tory government "did not care a pin" for Oregon, but public opinion would not allow Whitehall to be bullied out of it.[42] Upon learning that the Royal Navy was outfitting thirty new warships, a chastened Polk promptly notified his minister in London that the administration would be willing to reconsider a compromise boundary at the 49th parallel after all. Now seeking to distance himself from the 54°40' extremists, the president did nothing to discourage the prevailing mood of conciliation on Capitol Hill. For all Polk's talk about looking John Bull "straight in the eye," the administration had balked when the time came to stare him down.[43]

Mr. Polk's War

While the administration moved quickly to defuse the Oregon crisis at the first sign of hostility from Whitehall, it remained utterly indifferent to the bellicose proclamations issuing from Mexico City. With no prospect of negotiating the Texas boundary issue, an angry Slidell sailed for home, still blaming the British minister for the failure of his mission. Meanwhile, in Texas, Taylor's army had broken camp at Corpus Christi and moved south to the banks of the Rio Grande. By placing U.S. troops in the disputed area, the administration hoped to pressure Mexico to adopt a more conciliatory bargaining position. It did just the opposite. Viewed in Mexico City as an egregious violation of the nation's territorial sovereignty, the presence of Taylor's army on the Rio Grande, its cannons trained on Matamoros, emboldened conservatives who cried for war. On April 25, Mexican troops crossed the river and attacked a company of U.S. dragoons. "Hostilities," General Taylor informed Washington, "may now be considered as having commenced."[44]

If Polk's bullying tactics had not been intended to provoke a war, he did not shrink from one now that hostilities had occurred. The clash along the border might still have been resolved diplomatically, but the president was in no mood to do so, Slidell's rejection having already convinced him that further negotiation would be fruitless. On May 11 he asked Congress for a declaration of war. Although both houses approved the measure by overwhelming margins, the possibility that the fighting in the trans-Nueces might escalate into a wider conflict loomed over the debate. Whig statesmen sought to forestall the nation's headlong rush into war with dire predictions of a transatlantic conflagration involving Great Britain. The most fervent Democratic war hawks, meanwhile, such as Michigan senator Lewis Cass, urged their colleagues to strike a decisive blow against Mexico before it could receive aid from London.[45]

The prospect of a British-Mexican alliance was on the minds of many Americans as the nation girded for war in the spring and early summer of 1846. In New York City, army recruitment officers were reported to have told Irish immigrants that they would be fighting a war against both countries. Tammany leader Mike Walsh (who would play such a pivotal role in the Astor Place theatre riot three years later), was already organizing a regiment of Irish volunteers in anticipation of a war over Oregon when news of the fighting in South Texas arrived. The newly formed "Oregon Guards" declared their intention to enlist anyway, asserting that Whitehall was secretly supporting Mexico.[46] A third war with Great Britain was also the subject of discussion among U.S. troops stationed along the Rio Grande. George Gordon Meade, an officer in Taylor's army (who would command Union forces at the Battle of Gettysburg), wrote home in May that he expected the war to be over in four months, unless Great Britain intervened, "in which event we shall have a war such as the world has not seen for many years."[47]

In the North, antislavery leaders saw a slaveholding conspiracy behind Washington's efforts to acquire lands in the Southwest, just as they had done in the Texas crisis, and prayed for British intervention. Northern radicals had often opined that an American defeat at the hands of the British would have one saving grace: to rid the nation of the stain of slavery.[48] Unitarian minister Samuel May wrote to a friend in England deploring a war of aggression against Mexico, as well as the painful possibility that the conflict might escalate into one involving Great Britain, a country with which he and other abolitionists felt a deep spiritual kinship. Troubled as he was by events along the Rio Grande, May discerned "one ray of hope" shining through the dark storm clouds of war: "If

England engages Mexico in a war with the United States, slavery *must fall*."⁴⁹

Blithely disregarding antiwar hand-wringing, Polk was already thinking ahead to what kinds of concessions could be won from Mexico at war's end. Although competing claims over ownership of the trans-Nueces had sparked the conflict, the president now pressed for a vastly more ambitious territorial agenda in the West in order to secure new avenues for American commerce. The threat of British intervention was a significant factor in the administration's war strategy, since Her Majesty's government had stated it would oppose any attempt by a foreign power to seize California. By acting preemptively, the president intended to present Whitehall with a fait accompli that would discourage the Peel government from further action.

American military leaders in the West shared Polk's determination to acquire California, and had been taking steps to secure Washington's territorial objectives even before the war began. At the center of these extraordinary events was the renowned explorer John Charles Frémont, who in 1846 was conducting his third expedition of the Far West for the War Department. Prior to his departure, Frémont and his father-in-law, Missouri senator Thomas Hart Benton, had discussed at length the dangers of allowing California to fall into British hands. Although Benton had no authority to speak for the administration, Frémont would later claim to have been given confidential knowledge of Polk's intentions in the event of war.⁵⁰ Frémont had indeed met with an administration messenger in early May, although there is no evidence that he received anything more than a briefing on the latest news from Washington. Nonetheless, on the basis of this information Frémont leapt to the conclusion that a British invasion was imminent. In keeping with the hotspur tradition of Andrew Jackson and Commodore Thomas ap Catesby Jones, Frémont proceeded to incite the inhabitants of California to rise up against Mexican authorities, in what would become known as the Bear Flag Revolt. Commodore Sloat sailed into Monterey harbor in early July, having caught wind of a rumor that a British fleet was preparing to seize California. Upon learning of Frémont's rebellion, and assuming that the American adventurer would never have attempted such a thing without explicit instructions from Washington, Sloat sent troops ashore and issued a proclamation declaring U.S. sovereignty over Upper California. In his memoirs written many years later, Frémont recalled his determination to secure the Pacific coast for his country: "The time has come. England must not get a foothold. We must be first."⁵¹

With a war between the United States and Mexico now underway,

American diplomats clung doggedly to the fiction that Mexican leaders were acting at the behest of their British allies. Four weeks after U.S and Mexican troops clashed in the trans-Nueces, the U.S. consul in Mexico City continued to emphasize the close relationship between Paredes and Her Majesty's government in his dispatches to Washington. Although the role of Great Britain was not a visible one, "she is the Secret Spring that has set all this Machinery in Motion," he reported. He remained convinced that Her Majesty's government aimed to mediate the dispute, in exchange for which it would receive from Mexico territory "to hem in the United States," as well as commercial privileges and loan guarantees. William S. Parrott, a confidential agent sent to Mexico, agreed, stating flatly, "Mexico may be said to be completely in the hands of England."[52]

As usual, this intelligence contrasted completely with the views of the U.S. minister to London, Louis McLane, who could find no evidence whatsoever of British machinations in the Southwest. Unwilling to do anything that might jeopardize the free trade bill then pending in Washington, the Foreign Office was anxious to remain neutral in the conflict between the two North American neighbors. Aberdeen had become so frustrated with his inability to convince Washington of Whitehall's benign intentions that he had resorted to personally reading McLane the contents of Foreign Office dispatches to Her Majesty's minister in Mexico City, in which he disclaimed any interest in siding with Mexico and urged that government to reach an accord with the United States.[53]

The Peel government's eagerness to promote British exports loomed large in the still unresolved Oregon question as well. As Congress debated the Walker tariff, Whitehall proposed a compromise similar to the one that its minister in Washington had rejected the previous year. The Foreign Office once again agreed to accept the 49th parallel compromise line, with the stipulation that Vancouver Island remain under British control. By the time Polk received the British offer in early June, he was preoccupied with the war against Mexico and in no position to insist on further modifications that might delay a negotiated settlement. Accordingly, the administration referred the British proposal to the Senate, where it encountered little opposition. Few senators were prepared to risk a war with Great Britain now that one with Mexico was well underway. Thomas Hart Benton, once one of the most vocal advocates of "all Oregon," argued that a resolution of the dispute would send a clear message to Mexico that it could expect no aid from London.[54] A passel of Western Democrats accused the administration of cowering before the British lion, which they regarded as a far greater threat to U.S. security interests than the nation it was now preparing to invade. But with new opportunities for federal patronage created by the war with Mexico, most Western Democrats were anxious to remain on good terms with the administration, and kept their displeasure largely to themselves.

Despite a series of early victories, the war against Mexico did not go entirely according to plan for Washington policymakers. Polk had assumed that Mexico would eagerly sue for peace, but its leaders lacked sufficient political capital to effect the quick negotiated settlement the president and his advisers had hoped for. In August the Paredes government collapsed, paving the way for the return of Antonio López de Santa Anna, then residing in exile in Cuba. London offered to serve as mediator for the two belligerents to resolve the conflict, a suggestion that was rejected out of hand by an administration ever wary of British intentions. When success on the battlefield failed to bring Mexican leaders to the bargaining table, some Washington Anglophobes wondered if Britain was supplying Mexico with the resources necessary to carry on the war.[55] But by the summer of 1846, any lingering fears that Great Britain would never permit the United States to establish a continental empire had been effectively laid to rest, its desire for open markets far outweighing any territorial ambitions on the North American continent it may have entertained. In striking a compromise in the Oregon boundary dispute and maintaining a position of strict neutrality while the United States seized California and New Mexico from its closest Latin American ally, Her Majesty's government had sent an unequivocal message to Washington that it preferred peace to war. The specter of British military intervention, long the bête noire of American expansionists, now faded as the nation devoted its energies to the conquest of Mexico.

✤

During the early 1840s, expansionists based their appeals for new lands on the threat of encirclement, acting on the belief that citizens of the republic—North and South, Democrat and Whig—would stand together in the face of an external enemy. This was hardly an unreasonable expectation in view of the strong anti-British feeling that manifested itself in so many aspects of American life. Slaveholding Southerners may have had particularly strong motives to favor broadening the territorial limits of the republic, but they were not alone in their apprehensions of British aggrandizement. For a mix of commercial and geopolitical reasons, as well as a simple, visceral desire to best Great Britain on the continental stage, the ideology of expansionism exerted a powerful attraction for citizens of the republic, regardless of section. Only in New England, which steadfastly opposed Southern territorial gains on antislavery grounds, did the expansionist impulse fail to truly catch fire.

But if Manifest Destiny was a phenomenon with broad national appeal, it failed miserably as an instrument of national unity. As the country grew larger, sectional antagonisms became more acute, revealing not how much Americans had in common, but how vast were the divides that lay between them. At the root of intensifying rancor between North and South was Manifest Destiny's failure to deliver on the promise of a territorial quid pro quo. Resistance to the enlargement of the slave empire, a sentiment hitherto limited to a vocal minority, was now echoed by Northern moderates, who resented the apparent eagerness of Tyler and Polk to push aggressively for Southern territorial goals in the Southwest while capitulating to Britain on the Oregon question. This growing opposition crystallized in the summer of 1846 when Pennsylvania congressman David Wilmot, heretofore unstinting in his loyalty to the Polk administration, sought to attach an amendment to an appropriations bill barring the institution in any territory that might be acquired from Mexico. The initiative drew a predictably enraged response from Southern leaders and failed to muster enough support before Congress adjourned. Nonetheless, the Wilmot Proviso made it clear that a "slave power conspiracy," a mantra of the abolitionist movement since the Texas Revolution, was beginning to acquire a convincing resonance for many Northern Democrats, who had once been indifferent to the protests of antislavery radicals.

The charge that Tyler and Polk single-mindedly pursued a proslavery agenda does not hold up under close scrutiny. Both men, as slaveholders themselves, were naturally sensitive to the needs of the South, but they could also claim to have embraced broader geopolitical aims that served the interests of the republic at large. Why, then, did Washington pursue such divergent policies toward Great Britain and Mexico? No doubt American racial attitudes undergirded the dismissive contempt in which Washington held Mexican leaders. Tyler and Polk evinced a cool disregard toward Mexico, operating always on the assumption that it lacked the resources and the will to wage war against the United States. In dealing with the world's greatest naval power, on the other hand, both men came to the conclusion—Polk perhaps more reluctantly than his predecessor—that negotiation was the better part of valor. It must also be said that Washington's decision to back down from a confrontation with one continental adversary while recklessly pursuing a collision course with another was at least in part a simple matter of military arithmetic, an acknowledgment that, as Thomas Hart Benton succinctly put it, "Great Britain is powerful and Mexico [is] weak."[56]

Yet these explanations ignore the fact that the two foreign policy initiatives were tightly meshed in the minds of U.S. leaders. In its courtship of Texas, which in turn paved the way for the conflict with Mexico, Washington was convinced that Britain could always be found lurking in the shadows, ready to thwart U.S. efforts to enlarge its domain. Polk might insist, as he did on more than one occasion, that the crises in Oregon and Mexico were unrelated, but there can be little doubt that U.S. policymakers believed that Mexican intransigence had its roots in a much broader and more serious geopolitical threat.

Any attempt to understand the different outcomes of the Oregon and Mexico crises must also take into account the fact that Washington was incapable of dealing with Great Britain and its putative surrogates in the same way. Americans invariably evinced a healthy respect for British power, yet it seemed more threatening to U.S. policymakers in veiled, indirect forms than when confronted firsthand. Whereas strictly bilateral concerns—boundary disputes over Maine and Oregon, issues of maritime rights, and the like—could all be resolved (or at least addressed) through normative diplomatic processes, Washington exhibited an altogether different set of behaviors when dealing with fledgling nation-states it believed to have succumbed to British influence. Convinced that mid-level representatives of the Foreign Office enjoyed a degree of prestige and authority that exceeded that of indigenous elites, American Anglophobes allowed their apprehensions free rein, with the result that Washington invariably limned the hand of its transatlantic rival whenever its geopolitical interests appeared threatened.

Consequently, rumors of British intrigues in Texas and California were met with anxious resolve on the part of U.S. policymakers, who placed little faith in Whitehall's repeated declarations of non-interference. That they could have been so wrong about British intentions may be attributed not so much to bad intelligence as to a cognitive dissonance resulting from the insecurities and frustrations that had long shaped the national experience. From the U.S. representatives on the ground in Texas, California, and Mexico, to their superiors in Washington, Americans drew from a deep wellspring of anti-British sentiment that tended to frame the diplomatic activities of Her Majesty's government in the western hemisphere in conspiratorial terms. When confronted with political leaders in neighboring states who resisted U.S. territorial initiatives, Americans could only believe, as they had done so many times before, that "England was pulling the wires."[57]

At no point do American expansionists seem to have paused to reflect upon the fact that their apprehensions of a wider conflict with Great Britain never materialized. With the nation in 1846 directing its energies toward war against Mexico, the British threat receded from public view without notice or comment. Mexico City, not London, now became the primary obstacle to American dominion over the continent. And with the shifting adversarial dynamics of American expansion came a new narrative in which Great Britain occupied a much less conspicuous role. American politicians and pundits no longer spoke of the urgent need to extend U.S. sovereignty to the Pacific to prevent valuable lands and harbors from falling into British hands. Rather, they gave primacy to a racialized discourse that explained American expansion as the inexorable triumph of Anglo-Saxon vigor over a dissolute, non-white people. No longer regarding the Mexican government as a puppet regime that took its marching orders from Whitehall, U.S. policymakers laid the blame for the conflict squarely on the shoulders of Mexican leaders. The transition was not a difficult one, for the champions of Manifest Destiny had long denigrated the capacity of Mexico for self-government and challenged its sovereignty of Texas and the Southwest. But in this new version of events, Great Britain, which had once been seen standing menacingly behind Mexico, orchestrating its resistance to American ambitions and ready to intercede if necessary, was nowhere to be found.

⚜ 12 ⚜

"Brother Jonathan Is Somebody"

Ye sons of freedom, hail the day
That brings Victoria's eldest son
Across the broad Atlantic Sea,
To see the land of Washington . . .

The grand-son of that King whose chains
Were broken in spite of troops and throne,
Now comes to view those fertile plains
That once Great Britain call'd her own.

He comes in peace, this Princely boy:
Then welcome him unto your shore,
That he may see free men enjoy
Those rights that God and man adore.

—A. Scott, *Prince of Wales*

With Mexico unable to enlist the support of Great Britain in its contest with the United States, the most important war ever fought between two nations in the western hemisphere quickly became a lopsided affair. Underfunded and weakened by years of political intrigue, the Mexican army proved no match for better trained and equipped U.S. troops. Zachary Taylor's army racked up a string of early victories in Texas and northern Mexico. Stephen Watts Kearny crossed the Southwest en route to California, seizing Santa Fe, New Mexico, only three months after the war began. By the spring of 1847 another force, under Winfield Scott, had landed at Vera Cruz and was marching toward the Mexican capital.

Despite these successes, Americans remained nervous about foreign interference in the region, and with the end of the war in sight some pundits and politicians began to call for the complete absorption of Mexico by the United States. As in earlier phases of American expansion, the threat of European meddling in the western hemisphere—and the intrigues of the British, in particular—proved to be among the most compelling arguments on behalf of the so-called "All Mexico" movement. A destabilized Mexico would now be vulnerable to foreign power, the apostles of Manifest Destiny argued, seemingly oblivious to the fact that its prostrate condition had been caused not by Great Britain but by the United States.[1]

Even as Washington contemplated the dismemberment of Mexico, it looked to new territorial acquisitions. In the Yucatán, which for some years had been embroiled in an on-again, off-again struggle for independence, a bloody caste war erupted between Maya Indians and *criollo* landowners. Having remained neutral during Mexico's war with the United States, the Yucatán government appealed to the Polk administration for assistance. Yucatán diplomat Justo Sierra, dispatched to Washington in 1847 to solicit American support, borrowed a page from the playbook of Sam Houston in cleverly exploiting the administration's Anglophobia. If aid from Washington was not forthcoming, he warned, his government would have no choice but to seek the protection of Great Britain. These admonitions had precisely the effect Sierra anticipated. Amid rumors that British agents were supplying the Yucatán rebels from bases in Belize, Polk resolved to take whatever steps necessary to ensure that the peninsula did not "fall into the hands of England."[2] While these negotiations were going on, expansionists turned their attention to a project that had tantalized them for many years—the acquisition of Cuba. Once again, apprehensions of Great Britain dominated expansionist thinking. Believing that Spain might surrender the island as payment of its debt to London bondholders, the Polk administration flirted with a scheme to buy Cuba for $100 million.

None of these efforts came close to fruition. The "All Mexico" movement ran into stiff resistance on Capitol Hill, not only from the Whigs, who now enjoyed a majority in the Senate, but also from many Southern expansionists, who balked at the prospect of incorporating within the boundaries of the United States Mexico's eight million *mestizos* and *indios*. The administration quickly lost interest in Yucatán affairs when an armistice between the local government and Maya insurgents brought peace to the region. Polk's Cuba initiative also proved short-lived. The Spanish foreign minister scornfully dismissed the idea, noting that before it ceded Cuba to any nation, "it would prefer seeing it sunk in the Ocean."[3]

In the end, the administration settled for its territorial demands at the outset of the war, which were by no means modest: Upper California and New Mexico, for which it agreed to pay an indemnity of $15 million. Although there were hidden costs for these spoils of war—a new round of bitter wrangling over the issue of slavery in the territories would again raise the specter of disunion—the public mood, at least for the moment, was largely one of exhilaration. Americans reveled in the sheer size of these new holdings, and the breathtaking speed with which they had been acquired. In the span of just three years the United States had annexed the cotton lands of Texas, the vast reaches west of the Rocky Mountains, and more than one thousand miles of Pacific coastline. In total, more than 1.2 million square miles had been added to the national domain. The discovery of gold in California, moreover, had fired the public imagination, and within five years more than a quarter of a million Americans would make their way to the goldfields of the Sierra Nevadas. The Far West, once hailed as an American Eden, had become the American El Dorado—proof positive, many believed, that the United States was indeed a nation smiled upon by a Divine Providence.

And there was still another benefit, one that could not be measured in square miles. Europe had formerly regarded Mexico as a counterweight to the ambitions of its neighbor to the north, and Americans took a special pride in the knowledge that the war had shattered that illusion. As the news of one battlefield triumph followed another, each seemingly more stunning than the last, the nation kept one eye trained across the Atlantic, anxious to know how its achievements were being received in the capitals of Europe. As always, Americans were especially anxious to learn of the reaction in London, desperate for the approval of the nation whose opinion mattered most. Upon learning that Vera Cruz had fallen to Scott's army, one U.S. army newspaper editor offered the hopeful prediction that John Bull "will begin to think that, after all, Brother Jonathan is somebody."[4]

And, for once, John Bull seemed suitably impressed. Americans were delighted when no less an authority on military matters than the Duke of Wellington conceded that the conquest of Mexico had established the reputation of the United States as a formidable military power. When Lord Ashburton exclaimed to U.S. minister George Bancroft in London, "You are the Lords of Mexico!" the American diplomat did not fail to pass on the remark to the White House. "They do not love us, but they are compelled to respect us," Bancroft wrote.[5] *New York Herald* editor James Gordon Bennett, who was also in Europe as the war drew to a close, happily reported that American victories had greatly elevated the United States in the eyes of Great Britain. The war, he wrote in an editorial after the fall of the Mexican capital, had given the lie to its long-

FIGURE 14.

"John Bull and Brother Jonathan." American self-confidence
grew with the onset of the war with Mexico, as evidenced by this
1846 cartoon in which Brother Jonathan, undaunted by British
power, remarks: "But a Hundred years, *and then* I will protect
you." (Negative no. 44549, Collection of The New-York Historical
Society)

standing view of American "weakness and imbecility." John Bull would
now be compelled to acknowledge his offspring "as a great and powerful
people," worthy of his respect.[6]

Even Americans who could not be counted among the war's supporters were pleased with the way in which U.S. victories in Mexico had
boosted the nation's image across the Atlantic. Despite their reluctance
to partake of the fruits of Manifest Destiny, Whigs, like all Americans,
engaged in the national pasttime of measuring the republic's development, poring over economic data and any other criteria that might serve

as evidence of the nation's progress. Reports of U.S. victories in Mexico offered a new metric by which to evaluate their place in a geopolitical hierarchy, allowing them to point with pride to the admiration of the Old World as one of "the few promising effects" of the war. "They may occasionally abuse us as an arrogant people," the New Yorker Philip Hone wrote of the British in his diary at war's end, "but the language of contempt is heard no more; the little foibles of Brother Jonathan are forgotten in the contemplation of his indomitable courage, his never-dying perseverance." A Zachary Taylor campaign tract, touting the war hero's presidential ambitions, maintained that U.S. military victories completely overshadowed recent British successes in India, even going so far as to make the extraordinary claim that, "In all modern history Buena Vista has no parallel."[7]

Of course, Americans had said much the same thing after the War of 1812. But that conflict had not seen a string of impressive victories, nor resulted in a vast increase in the national domain. For the first time, Americans had reason to suppose that their achievements had earned them a reputation as a people to be reckoned with—something they had coveted long before they had ever set their sights on Mexico's northern territories.

The End of Encirclement

The extension of U.S. territorial limits to the Pacific did not bring an end to American clashes with Great Britain in the western hemisphere. With the discovery of gold in California, the need for a transportation route linking the Atlantic and Pacific Oceans suddenly became a matter of pressing importance for U.S. policymakers. The British were already well-entrenched in Central America, a region valued for its logwood (a source of dye used in textiles) and mahogany. Belize had been a colony since the 1600s, while the Crown also claimed a protectorate over the Mosquito Indians, who occupied the eastern coast of Nicaragua. Competing British and American interests soon led to conflict, which the Clayton-Bulwer Treaty of 1850 managed to resolve, at least up to a point. Both governments promised to cooperate on a trans-isthmian canal and renounce any future territorial ambitions in the area. The agreement failed to satisfy stalwart Anglophobes, however, who complained bitterly that Britain should be compelled to withdraw from Central America entirely. Complicating Washington's policy in the region during this period were the activities of American filibusters. Throughout the decade privately financed adventurers, such as Narciso López and William Walker, mounted numerous expeditions to seize Cuba and Nicaragua. Although the United States frowned on these mercenary campaigns, their frequency and the strong public support which they enjoyed only increased the Foreign Office's wariness of American expansionist ambitions.[8]

On the surface, then, it seemed that little had changed between the two governments. Diplomatic affairs remained volatile, punctuated on occasion by bluster and the rattling of sabers, with both sides clearly reluctant to allow matters to deteriorate to the point of war. Yet the close of the Mexican War marked a new chapter in U.S.-British relations. In years past, American foreign policy had consisted chiefly of fending off British challenges (some real, others imagined) close to home. Expansionists made the case for enlarged dominion largely on national security grounds; the acquisition of Texas, Oregon, and California, they argued, had been necessary as a defensive measure to forestall British aggrandizement. For all its bombast, the rhetoric of Manifest Destiny reflected this uneasiness, a tacit admission of the inferior place which the republic occupied vis-à-vis the Old World.

By mid-century, the United States found itself in a very different position. Having reconfigured the balance of power in the western hemisphere, the war with Mexico could not fail to transform the nation's formal relations with Great Britain as well. A case in point: Washington's newfound objections to foreign spheres of influence. James K. Polk had been the first president to invoke James Monroe's "principle" during the Oregon boundary dispute, making it clear that it applied especially to North America.[9] After the Mexican War, Washington policymakers and jingoistic editors gave Monroe's 1823 statement a broader and more concrete definition. Indeed, it was not until the angry debates over the Clayton-Bulwer Treaty that the "Monroe Doctrine" entered the national vocabulary as a bold and inviolable declaration of American hemispheric power.[10] Now when expansionists thundered against British imperialism, they did so with the self-assurance that came from the knowledge that their nation, too, had forged an empire by conquest. "We are rivals but not enemies," one Boston editor declared. "We are conscious of our strength. We no longer regard England as our superior."[11]

Why, then, did this new assertiveness fail to translate into a major extension of American territorial limits? The expansionist momentum stalled in the 1850s, resulting only in the purchase of the Mesilla Valley from Mexico for a projected southern transcontinental railroad. Certainly it was not because the demand for new lands had been satiated by the acquisitions of the previous decade. Many Americans continued to preach the gospel of enlarged dominion; in the South, the dream of a Caribbean empire was still alive on the eve of the Civil War. Rising sectional tensions were the principal reason behind the expansionists' failure to build a consensus for their territorial agenda. But it is also worth noting that one of the most salient arguments for more land in the 1840s—the need to thwart British encroachment in North America—ceased to play a role in the debates over expansion after the Mexican War. The aggressive policies of the Tyler and Polk years owed much of their urgency to the belief that John Bull threatened more than just the republic's future prosperity. Hemmed in on all sides by Britain and its surrogates, the United States had regarded expansion as essential to its very survival. In the 1850s, however, the apostles of Manifest Destiny could no longer use John Bull as a convincing bogeyman. Fears of encirclement had been effectively put to rest now that the United States had an empire of its own.

In any case, Americans were now turning to the commercial possibilities which their territorial acquisitions had brought them. And for the first time they looked beyond the transatlantic axis with Great Britain that had for so long framed their worldview. Standing astride two oceans, the nation began to define its geopolitical role in increasingly expansive terms. The groundwork for an American presence in the Pacific had already been laid by the Tyler administration, which recognized the sovereignty of Hawaii and negotiated a commercial treaty with China. But the United States would not be in a position to capitalize fully on these initiatives until it acquired harbors in California, which now became the nation's gateways to the markets of Asia. By the time Commodore Perry established diplomatic relations with Japan in 1854, the belief that the republic was being restrained by an "iron hoop" of British design seemed a distant memory.[12]

Political developments in Europe also enabled Americans to shed their Anglocentric orientation. In 1848, a series of anti-monarchist uprisings from Paris to Prague threatened to bring down the established social order. A generation earlier, the reaction in the United States to an emerging republican movement in Latin America had been lukewarm at best. Not so the 1848 revolutions, which Americans followed with rapt attention; for the first time since the fall of Napoleon, events on the European continent dominated the news. Conservative, counterrevolutionary forces eventually managed to extinguish the fires of rebellion, and by 1849 the status quo had been largely restored. But the stirrings of liberal republicanism in Europe struck a chord among Americans, dovetailing neatly with their own sense of providential mission. The Hungarian revolutionary Louis Kossuth received a hero's welcome when he toured the United States in 1852, sparking a Magyar-mania that transcended party and sectional lines. Democrats and Whigs alike called for a new, aggressive foreign policy to promote American ideals, with the most jingoistic exhortations coming from the Young America wing of the Democratic Party. Like the New York literary clique of the same name, the group attracted zealous über-patriots, whose noisy bravado alienated many and produced little in the way of tangible results. Yet the rhetoric of Young America was only the most extreme manifestation of a new internationalist mood that reflected the country's eagerness to assume a geopolitical role to match its new status as an emerging power.[13]

The ascendance of the United States in the western hemisphere would give rise, naturally enough, to new opportunities for conflict with Great Britain. The irony was that it also allowed Americans to embrace the imperial parent on equal terms, making it possible for them to acknowledge, far more readily than in the past, a shared culture. While they might still insist that their efforts to "extend the area of freedom" bore little similarity to John Bull's innate love of conquest, they derived no little satisfaction from the belief that the nation's continental growth placed Brother Jonathan on the same level as his Old World rival. As a result, it was not uncommon to find American expansionists, even those who railed against British power, to credit their Anglo-Saxon heritage for the country's recent success. The desire to extend the nation's hegemonic reach, once a republican duty, now became a racial imperative. Some former Anglophobes went so far as to proclaim an end to the hostilities that had for so long governed relations between the two countries. Robert J. Walker, a spread-eagle expansionist who had played upon fears of a British conspiracy to bring about the annexation of Texas, now predicted an economic and cultural union of the two Anglophone nations (even joking, in a fit of patriotic exuberance during a trip to London, that Britain and its colonies should consider annexing themselves to the United States). Significantly, many Whigs also began to warm to the new imperialism. They had always opposed the territorial ambitions of Democrats like Walker, and had little use for the anti-British harangues that accompanied them. Yet they welcomed the opportunity for American maritime commerce to square off in a healthy competition against the world's reigning sea power. "The Englishman and American," enthused one writer in the *American Review* in 1848, "meet amid the palmy groves of Ceylon, or the coral isles of the Pacific, and hail each other brother." Americans would still find themselves divided by party and section over specific foreign policy objectives. On the rationale for empire, however, they were beginning to speak with one voice. Manifest Destiny had become "the destiny of the Anglo-Saxon . . . to conquer the whole world."[14]

Toward a New National Self-Image

The rise of an American continental empire would not only change the way Americans saw the world beyond their borders, it also changed the way they saw themselves. The nation's identity had been shaped to no small degree by its insecurities, by its eagerness to measure itself by European, and especially British, standards. Now, as the country swelled in size and stature, the once manic desire for foreign validation ebbed. "This country is so thoroughly independent of Great Britain," James Gordon Bennett asserted during the closing months of the war with Mexico, "that it matters very little whether she likes our institutions or government, our commercial or financial systems, or not." This was certainly an overstatement. Americans still did care, very much, for the high opinion of the British, as evidenced by the fact that Bennett felt obliged to make the point at all. But to a nation that had for so long grappled with its own feelings of inadequacy, the remarkable successes of recent years offered reason to hope that its self-conscious adolescence was finally behind it.[15]

In the past, nothing had betrayed these insecurities more clearly than the American reaction to the criticism of British travelers. Once notoriously thin-skinned, Americans were beginning to abandon their fixation with the opinion of foreigners. At the same time, itinerant Britons were more inclined to be impressed by what they saw, encountering a land very different from the one that greeted Frances Trollope two decades earlier. The rough-hewn nation that had once so offended tourists of delicate sensibilities and persnickety disposition now offered many of the creature comforts of home. The rapid expansion of the country's railroad network, which visitors much preferred to the hardships of traveling by stagecoach, was one reason for the change in tone. In *The Western World* (1849), the Scottish writer and lawyer Alexander Mackay endeavored to set the record straight regarding the calumnies directed against the United States by British writers, presenting what he called "a correct account of a great country, and a faithful portraiture of a great people." While Mackay was not blind to American shortcomings, his three-volume work was refreshingly free of the condescension that had characterized earlier travel memoirs, so irritating to citizens of the republic.[16] Members of the titled nobility also seemed ready to put their prejudices aside and regard the United States in a fresh light. In her *Travels in the United States* (1851), the preternaturally agreeable Lady Emmeline Stuart-Wortley even found much to praise in the slaveholding South. On the whole, she insisted, the lot of enslaved African Americans bore no relation to the brutal system portrayed by misguided moral reformers on both sides of the Atlantic. Of the oft-ridiculed American penchant for boastfulness and exaggeration, Lady Emmeline found that citizens of the republic had much to crow about. "What a future! What a country! And what a noble people," she gushed. The *North American Review*, which for so many years had despaired at the censoriousness of British travel literature, marveled at the change in tone: "We pause in wonder. This from a countrywoman of Hall, Trollope, and Hamilton!"[17]

As British fault-finding of the republic abated, Americans no longer felt the need to level their own indictments of Great Britain. During the Jacksonian period, resentment of foreign criticism could not help but color the impressions of American writers who ventured across the Atlantic. By the 1850s, the prevailing image of a corrupt parliamentary system reigning over an industrial dystopia of paupers and cotton lords faded as a spate of books acquainted the American reading public with a new representation of England, one that combined its traditional virtues as the seedbed of Western civilization with those of a stout, prosperous middle class. Not surprisingly, Ralph Waldo Emerson waxed deferential in *English Traits* (1856), a compilation of reminiscences drawn from two visits to Great Britain some years earlier. Though saddened by the "tragic spectacles" of poverty which he saw on the streets of Liverpool and Manchester, these images made but a fleeting impression; the Bostonian preferred to dwell on his personal encounters with Queen Victoria's subjects, whom he generally found to be prosperous, charming, and, above all, erudite. With each passing year, John Bull and Brother Jonathan were becoming more and more alike. "In such a people," enthused Henry T. Tuckerman in *A Month in England* (1853), "every man has a home."[18]

A robust, more diversified American economy also helped to transform the calculus of Anglo-U.S. relations. It will be recalled that the bitterly contested Walker Tariff of 1846 significantly rolled back the duties on many items, including those at the top of the protectionist list, such as textiles and iron. American manufacturers of these products, so went the conventional Whig wisdom, would be swept aside by a tidal wave of cheap British-made goods. In fact, an increase in British imports *did* occur after 1846, but not the economic ruin Whigs had predicted. On the contrary, the number of spindles during the next fifteen years would double in Massachusetts, from 800,000 to 1,600,000, while the lower duties on industrial goods such as rolled iron also failed to have an appreciable effect on domestic production.[19]

The mid-century economic boom offered compelling evidence that American industry could for the first time stand on its own, without the protection it once needed to be competitive in global markets. The period saw dramatic growth in the export of manufactured cotton goods, as the products of New England mills vied with British calicoes worldwide, especially in the new growth markets of Asia. The war with Mexico had greatly stimulated industrial growth, while the railroad-building mania of the 1850s created a surging demand for American iron, which in turn had the effect of increasing GDP by sharply reducing transportation costs. Access to Pacific commerce (an anticipated result of the war) and the discovery of gold in California (an unanticipated one) generated wealth that would provide a steady stream of capital for reinvestment in the domestic economy. The United States had not forsworn its appetite for British capital by any means—foreign loans would play a pivotal role in the nation's economic development in the second half of the nineteenth century. Yet it was becoming increasingly evident that the fortunes of the republic were no longer bound exclusively to those of the imperial parent. In years past, when the banking houses of Lombard Street sneezed, it was the American economy that invariably caught a cold. But when a panic in the late 1840s brought on by speculation and overinvestment in Britain's railroad industry dealt a severe blow to that country's financial institutions, the distress was scarcely felt across the Atlantic.

Parliament's decision to take the free trade plunge also signaled a new commercial rapprochement for the two nations. With the 1846 repeal of the Corn Laws, free trade principles had triumphed across the Atlantic, effectively undercutting the arguments of Whig protectionists. No longer could it be alleged that Her Majesty's government favored closed markets at home and open markets abroad. As a result of repeal, U.S. agricultural exports to the British Isles tripled in a single year. During the 1850s, the total value of U.S. exports to Great Britain exceeded a billion dollars, almost twice what it had been during the previous decade. Tellingly, even the *Niles' Weekly Register*, that always dependable voice of the protective principle for almost four decades, was obliged to concede in 1847 that a stronger, more diversified economy made the nation less vulnerable to foreign competition. In the years that followed, the tariff would become so depoliticized that, except for the coal-mining regions of western Pennsylvania, there would be little opposition to the further reduction of duties in 1857.[20]

Americans saw evidence of their economic progress everywhere, but one of the most gratifying signs that the gap had narrowed between the two nations came in 1851 with the opening of the Great Exhibition in London's Hyde Park. One of the defining cultural moments of the Victorian era, the exhibition was initially conceived as a showcase of British achievements in the ornamental, mechanical, and industrial arts, though organizers early in the planning stages had decided to invite the nations of the world to attend and display their wares. Housed in an architectural marvel of iron and glass dubbed the Crystal Palace, the fair offered a consumerist cornucopia of staggering proportions, the largest display of manufactured goods ever assembled under one roof. In the main pavilion, which was three times longer than St. Paul's Cathedral, 17,000 exhibitors representing thirty-two countries displayed goods in 21 acres of exhibit space.[21]

Americans greeted the opening of the trade fair with a great deal more trepidation than national pride. The U.S. commissioner had optimistically reserved 40,000 square feet of exhibit space, but the response from domestic producers had been underwhelming, to say the least. The lack of American entries was due to Washington's unwillingness to lend any financial support to the enterprise, coupled with the rumor that the exhibition was a scheme to steal foreign ideas and inventions. The American exhibit was an odd assortment of manufactures and materials: bales of cotton from Southern plantations; a McCormick reaper and other agricultural implements; daguerreotypes; revolving pistols from the Samuel Colt Company; vulcanized India rubber garments from the Goodyear Company; even a prosthetic leg—all of which was arranged around an incongruous centerpiece: Hiram Powers's "The Greek Slave," a life-size, marble female nude on a revolving turntable.[22]

Americans braced for the panning from the London press that would surely follow. But while the *Times*, ever a crusty critic of all things American, initially disdained the lack of taste and elegance of the entries, others took a kinder view, praising their inventiveness. Although the French took home the most prize medals, the smaller American exhibit, and its entries in the mechanical arts in particular, proved by all accounts to be the smashing success of the fair. In the end, even the *Times* was won over, obliged to concede that the United States had presented more useful ideas and ingenious inventions at the Exhibition than any other country.[23]

None of the awards for industrial excellence prompted as much rejoicing in the United States as the victory of an American vessel in the "One Hundred Guinea Cup," a regatta held in conjunction with the fair. In August, sixteen British vessels and a lone entry from the United States, the *America*, a schooner sponsored by the New York Yacht Club, set off from Cowes, on England's south coast, in a race around the Isle of Wight. With its unique hull design, the 101-foot craft, designed and built by George Steers, a thirty-one-year-old naval architect, got off to a slow start but soon took a commanding lead. As the *America* hove into view on its way toward the finish line without another vessel in sight, a signalman on board the royal yacht informed Queen Victoria that the American schooner was in first place. And which ship was in second, the monarch inquired? The response, as reported in the press, was cause for celebration in the United States: "Your Majesty, *there is no second.*"[24]

The American success at Crystal Palace provided tangible evidence, much as the war against Mexico had done, that the nation no longer had reason to feel inadequate when its accomplishments were placed along-side those of Great Britain. Lagging so far behind Britain and the rest of Europe in the belles artes, Americans had always been obliged to derive what comfort they could from the knowledge that they were "a practical people." To many, of course, this seemed at best a backhanded compliment, an unsatisfactory consolation prize for a nation wholly lacking in refinement and sophistication. But in a world endlessly fascinated with how things worked, distinction in the "realm of fancy" was no longer the sole standard by which cultural supremacy could be measured. The Great Exhibition represented the triumph of the practical over the ornamental, the harnessing of science and industry in the service of the public good. As such, it signaled the emergence of a bourgeois, utilitarian ethos eminently suited to American talents. Some British journals attributed American success to the country's political and social organization. Bemoaning the tendency of European business leaders to "skip over the wants of many, and rush to supply the luxuries of a few," the *London Observer* wondered if only democratic societies were capable of paying proper attention to such issues as mass-production and consumer demand. Americans agreed, lauding the mechanics—men like George Steers, a self-made shipwright—whose enterprise not only brought honor to the nation, but helped make it independent of Great Britain. The market revolution had given rise to a new cultural aesthetic, one in which "Yankee ingenuity" could feel at home.[25]

With so many legitimate achievements, Americans no longer felt the need to compete with Great Britain in those areas in which John Bull traditionally excelled. For a quarter of a century, the American play-house had served as an occasional battleground in which patrons could vent their frustrations at British cultural authority. The horror at Astor Place in 1849 brought an abrupt end to these demonstrations. Changes in entertainment culture were partly responsible for the absence of audience protest in the second half of the nineteenth century. As Lawrence Levine has noted, urban elites sought out new, "highbrow" forms of amusement—such as the opera and the symphony—which had the effect of reducing the potential for class conflict.[26] At the same time, the theater saw a dramatic drop in acts of crowd violence, because it ceased to be an appropriate venue for the expression of national antipathies.

FIGURE 15.

"The Great Exhibition of 1851." An American victory in a regatta off the Isle of Cowes—the first America's Cup—during the Crystal Palace exhibition in 1851 was the source of enormous national pride. (Courtesy Library of Congress, Prints & Photographs Division, LC-USZ62-10826)

In the past, British plays and British actors dominated the Jacksonian stage, incurring the ire of American audiences. By the 1850s, however, it was becoming increasingly common for native-born talent to share the spotlight with British imports. Indeed, an actor's nationality was not only less important, but harder to identify. Many English members of the *corps dramatique*, once viewed as interlopers by American audiences, became naturalized citizens; some, like Junius Booth, sired a new generation of native-born actors. Performers no longer existed in the public mind as combatants for their respective nations, as had been the case with Edwin Forrest and William Charles Macready. In an age of greater transatlantic exchange, the geopolitical fault lines were disappearing from the cultural landscape.

A similar détente was taking shape in the belles lettres, where Britain's preeminence had also been a major source of republican resentment. It will be recalled that the intellectual community had once regarded a respectable literature as nothing less than a sine qua non of cultural legitimacy. But while nationalists remained hopeful that a "Master Writer," to borrow Hawthorne's phrase, would one day usher in a new, golden age of American letters, they no longer waited in a state of anxious anticipation. They had come to accept the need for patience, realizing that it was not necessary to completely repudiate the British literary canon. Evert A. Duyckinck, a founder of the Young America movement, would retreat so far from the literary chauvinism of his youth that in 1856 he would edit a volume of the collected writings of Sydney Smith, who had once raised republican hackles by posing the question "Who reads an American book?" Duyckinck could now shrug off Smith's jibe as nothing more than "an historical landmark, from which to date extensive national achievements."[27]

The 1850s would see the emergence of a new constellation of writers who did not wear their patriotism self-consciously on their sleeve. Theirs was a new brand of national feeling, one that was not defined in oppositional terms. Unlike an earlier generation of writers that included Cooper and Paulding, the preeminent figures of the so-called American Renaissance defined their nationalism as something more than anti-British. Not only did they share with other Americans at mid-century a broader view of the world and their nation's place in it, they could also appreciate, perhaps more than most, the increasing diversity of their own society. With the influx of more than four million immigrants from Ireland and Central Europe, the country's literati were quick to embrace—at least in theory—the idea of a hybrid culture. Here, at last, was the answer to that most humiliating of indictments leveled against American writers: that they could never be anything more than mimics of British literary forms. At mid-century, Walt Whitman could proudly announce that America was no longer the offspring of the British Isles, but of "all continents," while Herman Melville declared in the semi-autobiographical *Redburn* (1849): "You can not spill a drop of American blood without spilling the blood of the whole world."[28] To be sure, a great many Americans were troubled by this unprecedented surge of new arrivals. Yet the belief that the republic's literary future lay in the ethno-cultural diversity of its people could even be embraced, if somewhat more tentatively, by the most stalwart Anglophile. Henry Wadsworth Longfellow, a longtime critic of literary nationalism who believed that the best of American belles lettres was not so much an imitation of English literature but a natural extension of it, was nonetheless willing to concede that the country's ethnic pluralism was not without its belletristic advantages. "As the blood of all nations is mingling with our own," says a character in Longfellow's *Kavanagh*, speaking for the author, "so will their thoughts and feelings finally mingle in our literature. We shall draw from the Germans tenderness; from the Spaniards, passion; from the French, vivacity; to mingle more and more with our English solid sense. And this will give us universality, so much to be desired."[29]

In the political sphere, anti-British expression was also on the wane.

For more than half a century, bearding the British lion had been as much a staple of American political culture as the stump speech and the whiskey barrel. Charges that candidates had fallen under the sway of foreign enemies had been an ever-present fixture of every national campaign (and for that matter, a good many local ones). But by the early 1850s the great figures of the Jacksonian era had passed from the scene, succeeded by a new generation of leaders who could not recall a time when British troops occupied American soil. In addition, the recent war with Mexico had given the nation a new crop of military heroes, who had not fought against the Crown and its "savage myrmidons." As a result, this traditional demonology disappeared abruptly from American political discourse. Democrats, whose rhetoric had been especially informed by an historical narrative, ceased to be haunted by the ghostly apparitions of the past. Unlike Andrew Jackson, they no longer spoke of "Hartford Convention men," or "blue light Federalists" or "British Whigs." Instead, party leaders began to employ a new political lexicon, one better suited to the challenges the nation faced at mid-century.[30]

Even so, old habits died hard, and a reflexive hostility toward Great Britain remained a signature issue for many Democrats. The Young America faction railed against anyone, even party members, who expressed an unhealthy regard for British opinions and policies, charging them with "Old Fogyism" (a term it applied generally to any behaviors of which it disapproved).[31] Increasingly, however, the Democratic Party's anti-British tirades struck many observers as a transparent attempt to shift the focus away from worrisome domestic affairs. When the growing slavery controversy exploded with new intensity with the passage of the Kansas-Nebraska Act, some Democrats made no secret of their desire to use geopolitics as a diversion. The *Richmond Examiner*, for example, called explicitly for a "bold and decided foreign policy," to prevent the public mind from becoming "hopelessly engrossed in sectional strife . . . and domestic discord." The Pierce administration seems to have heeded this advice, opting for a showdown with the Aberdeen ministry when it learned that the Royal Army was seeking to recruit troops in the United States during the Crimean War.[32] In May, 1856, only one week before the Democrats met to choose their party's nominee, the administration took the unprecedented step of expelling the British minister and three consuls for violating U.S. neutrality laws. The campaign to gin up a crisis against Great Britain failed to have any appreciable effect on Pierce's popularity with party leaders, who unceremoniously dumped the incumbent from their ticket at the convention.[33]

Predictably, the resurgence of sectional rancor prompted new allegations of a British-backed antislavery conspiracy. Such claims were fueled by the publication of Harriet Beecher Stowe's *Uncle Tom's Cabin* in 1852, which was received with unmixed praise in Britain, selling an astonishing two million copies in that country. The most famous American author of her day, Stowe made three visits to the British Isles before the outbreak of the Civil War at the request of antislavery organizations there. Yet even the worshipful adulation that Britons bestowed upon the novelist could not fully revive the once widely held belief that the antislavery crusade was a plot hatched in Whitehall to drive a wedge between North and South. As in so many aspects of American life, allegations of outside interference had become impossible to sustain in the absence of concrete evidence. Rendering these shopworn charges even more obsolete was the fact that the transatlantic antislavery movement in recent years had ceased to play a major role in the debate over the peculiar institution in the United States. The campaign against American slavery had initially been waged under the broad banner of Christian benevolence, inviting accusations of foreign involvement. Proslavery Northerners had little reason to doubt that the Liberty Party was a tool of transatlantic philanthropists; its first and only presidential candidate, after all, had spent the 1840 campaign season raising money in the British Isles. But as the debate over slavery became more heated, its basic structural properties changed. Humanitarian concerns alone were never enough to galvanize the Northern electorate; rather, it was the advent of a free soil ideology determined to block the spread of slavery in the territories that would bring the simmering controversy to a rapid boil. For decades antislavery had been a transatlantic moral question; by the 1850s it had become a national, economic one. As such, it ceased to be an issue that lent itself to allegations of British influence. Whichever side Northern voters took on the free soil question, the role of Great Britain was far from their minds.[34]

In the South, too, allegations of British antislavery activism had grown stale. Anglophobia had once provided a welcome refuge from the Sturm und Drang of sectional strife, as moderates struggled to undercut the appeal of radicals who argued that it was more important to defend slavery than the union itself. And there were still a few centrists who gamely swallowed the old British conspiracy theories long after their shelf life had obviously expired. As late as 1849, William Gilmore Simms was still blaming Northern antislavery agitation on foreign propaganda, accusing Great Britain of having subsidized "the Lundys and Garrisons" to promote disunion and wreak havoc on the Southern states. "Are we to allow, then, this foreign public opinion to mingle with our principles, and to control and alter our American institutions?" he asked. But Simms had grown suspicious of Northern motives, and his nationalism was already on the wane. As editor of the *Southern Quarterly Review* from 1849 to 1856, he championed Southern letters with the same dogged enthusiasm he had once reserved for an American literature. Having devoted much of his career, both as a novelist and an historian, to chronicling Britain's domination of the thirteen colonies, Simms spied after the Compromise of 1850 a new form of tyranny, in which the Northern states lorded their own economic and political power over the South. And as the specter of disunion loomed, Simms's lifelong Anglophobia all but vanished. A political alliance with Great Britain, he believed, represented his beloved South's only salvation in the coming contest with the North.[35]

In short, the American practice of transatlantic scapegoating did not disappear altogether in the 1850s. Yet the lack of conviction with which such arguments were uttered was inescapable. When public figures referenced Great Britain, more often than not they did so out of habit, or a desperate need to change the political conversation. In any case, Americans were already blotting from their collective consciousness all memory of their former subordinate status. Unencumbered by the narratives that had shaped the post-Revolutionary generation, they sought out new avenues by which to arrive at an understanding of who they were, as a people and as a nation. As the storm clouds over slavery darkened, they would seek refuge in their regional affiliations; as Northerners and Southerners, they developed wholly divergent visions of what the republic should be. But one thing was certain: the transatlantic binary that had once played such a vital role in the process of national self-definition suddenly seemed a quaint relic of a bygone era. No longer held captive by the structures of the past, the nation had come of age.

And as the country changed, so too, quite literally, did its self-image. During the American Revolution British soldiers had used the term "Brother Jonathan" to refer to the colonial insurgents, and in the years that followed the name had slowly worked its way into the national lexicon. Appearing in stage plays as a Yankee rustic in the early nineteenth century, Brother Jonathan emerged by the 1830s as a fixture of political cartoons on both sides of the Atlantic. British and American illustrators gradually endowed Brother Jonathan with a set of standardized physical features and attributes that made him as easily recognizable as his British counterpart, John Bull. Unlike the portly, ruddy-cheeked symbol of British prosperity, Brother Jonathan frequently appeared as a down-at-the-heels provincial, a long-legged, gangly youth who has outgrown his swallowtail coat and striped pants. In time, the American icon would undergo certain modifications. As the slavery controversy festered, Brother Jonathan took on a distinctively Southern appearance for some British cartoonists, who gave him a slave driver's whip and replaced his low-crowned top hat with a broad-brimmed one. During the 1850s, however, it was American cartoonists who gave Brother Jonathan a makeover, as they searched for a national symbol that would better reflect the United States' growing stature. Some abandoned the rustic Brother Jonathan altogether, but when he did appear, it was as a figure that had little in common with his original incarnation as a Yankee bumpkin. The transition can be seen in an illustration commemorating the laying of the first transatlantic telegraph cable in 1858. Brother Jonathan stands erect, dignified, elegantly dressed (though still wearing his familiar striped pants) as he clasps John Bull's hand in friendship. He has become the prototype of the figure Americans would recognize after the Civil War as "Uncle Sam."[36]

The high point of this new spirit of transatlantic amity came in the fall of 1860, when Albert Edward, the nineteen-year-old Prince of Wales, toured the United States after an official state visit to the Canadian provinces. With their fascination for foreign celebrities, Americans turned out en masse for a glimpse of the heir to the British throne and his entourage. The fact that the eldest son of Queen Victoria was considered to be one of the most eligible bachelors in the Western world only added to the mania surrounding the event. The royal procession prompted the usual breathlessness among the privileged classes, anxious to project an image of cosmopolitan sophistication. Not everyone was overawed. In New York City, the state militia's Sixty-ninth Regiment, composed mainly of Irishmen, boycotted the parade in the prince's honor, a decision applauded by the city's sizable Irish community. On balance, however, the first visit of a member of the royal family to North America was deemed a great success, with newspapers across the country hailing both the prince and the reception which Americans accorded him. Caught up in the euphoria of the moment, pundits waxed sentimental as they spoke of two great branches of the Anglo-Saxon family and the kindred ties that united them. "America at that time had no reason to feel envy or ill will to England," declared one observer some years later. "Bygones were bygones." The conciliatory attitude said much about Americans' growing self-confidence. "We could afford to forgive all the injuries and insults of the past, and to be generous to a power that could not hope long to keep up with us in the great race of empire."[37]

Of course, Americans had always drawn a distinction between the British people and their government, and declarations of kinship could be quickly forgotten when disputes arose between Washington and Whitehall. Within a month of the prince's departure, Lincoln's victory in the presidential election would provide the flashpoint for disunion.

FIGURE 16.

"The Laying of the Cable." In this illustration commemorating the laying of the first transatlantic telegraph cable in 1858, Brother Jonathan clasps John Bull's hand in friendship. No longer the Yankee bumpkin seen in earlier illustrations, Brother Jonathan has become the prototype of the figure Americans would recognize after the Civil War as "Uncle Sam." (Courtesy Library of Congress, Prints & Photographs Division, LC-DIG-pga-00117)

In the spring of 1861, as the new Republican administration struggled to cope with the crisis, Lincoln's secretary of state seized upon an extraordinary scheme to save the union. William H. Seward urged the new president to precipitate an international crisis serious enough to cause a surge of patriotism and deflect attention from conflict at home. The president's chief diplomat advised that any effort by the Palmerston government to recognize the Confederacy should be met immediately by a declaration of war. Great Britain was not the only European nation Seward believed could induce Americans to set aside their grievances; he counseled a similar course against France and Spain for their own interference in hemispheric affairs. Lincoln wisely refused to entertain such proposals, convinced that a day of reckoning between North and South could no longer be averted. Still, the secession crisis inevitably gave rise to long-held concerns that Great Britain would seek to turn American domestic strife to its advantage. Despite the Palmerston government's avowed neutrality, the prospect of British intervention on the side of the Confederacy remained a source of no small anxiety in Washington. The tenuous nature of official British-U.S. relations would be highlighted by the *Trent* affair, when a U.S. naval commander caused a diplomatic uproar by seizing two Confederate diplomats from a British steamship.[38]

Americans' conflicted, love/hate relationship with the imperial parent lingered for many years, still shaped by a strange mix of cultural affinity and competing geopolitical interest. But while British policies could occasionally arouse the anger of Washington and the public at large, such episodes would be confined largely to contretemps within the diplomatic sphere. After the Civil War, few Americans could recall that John Bull had once intruded upon virtually every facet of civic life; fewer still would remember the feelings of national inadequacy and insecurity that had made relations between the two countries so contentious. Be that as it may, John Bull could claim a major, if indirect role in the architectural design of the American nation-state. In the first half of the nineteenth century American resentment of Great Britain had provided an ideological scaffolding from which a national sense of self could be constructed. This scaffolding consisted of many separate planks—the censure of American life and institutions by British travelers; the dominance of British culture, from literature to the performing arts; the influence which a seemingly all-powerful empire allegedly exerted over American politics, commerce, and banking; the leadership role which Britain played in the assault on slavery in the western hemisphere; and, finally, Whitehall's opposition to U.S. territorial expansion. Together they formed a platform from which Americans crafted for themselves a separate and unique identity. The framework had been necessary while the American edifice was being built. But once the bricks set and the mortar cured, it no longer served any useful purpose. As soon as the nation could stand alone, the scaffolding could be easily disassembled and removed, leaving no evidence that it had been there at all.[39]

❧ ❧

John Bull had helped Americans define their republic, but whether he united them was an entirely different matter. The mere presence of an external threat had never been a guarantee of internal solidarity. As the preceding chapters have shown, the country's favorite bête noire did precious little to instill in its citizens a gauzy, feel-good togetherness. It mattered little that anti-British sentiment managed to insinuate itself into virtually every aspect of American life, or that charges of "foreign influence" served as a mantra which Americans invoked at every possible opportunity. The nation remained divided despite its apprehensions of Great Britain, and, at least in part, because of them. And herein lay the paradox of Anglophobia. For while it seemed to be a highly versatile and useful device in the process of nation-building, it actually served to reveal the preexisting fissures in American society. Even as it was employed to draw Americans together, anti-British sentiment succeeded only in driving them further apart.

This was due largely to the fact that, for many citizens, internal enemies lurked alongside external ones. Americans had never been united in past conflicts with Great Britain, and there existed the widely held belief that Tories could still be found, eager to undermine the republic from within. As a result, partisan disagreements led inevitably to charges and countercharges of foreign collusion, with each party labeling their opponents as willing allies of the Crown. Helping to lend credence to such allegations was the fact that Americans could never agree as to what the nation's precise relationship to the imperial parent should be. When citizens of the republic in the first half of the nineteenth century discussed their cultural, political, and economic future, they invariably did so within a postcolonial framework which they interpreted in different ways. Some were determined to repudiate British norms and models; others tended to believe that national greatness could only be achieved by emulating them. This fundamental tension was hardly unique to the United States, but was repeated time and again throughout the nineteenth and twentieth centuries in fledgling nation-states that had won their independence from European powers. Whether the former colony was composed of Old World migrants or indigenous peoples, the battle lines were usually sharply drawn, pitting citizens of privilege who still harbored a fondness for the ancien regime on one side, against a rising class that laid claim to an anti-imperialist ideology on the other. The political dominance of the party of Andrew Jackson may be understood in this context. Far more than their opponents, the Jacksonians reflected the postcolonial anxieties that continued to shape the American experience long after the Revolution. Their rhetoric resonated with an electorate still fearful of foreign agents, still convinced that John Bull was being assisted by homegrown accomplices.

In other ways, too, fears of Great Britain offered at best a cosmetic sense of solidarity, and served ultimately to focus attention upon, not away from, the tensions imbedded in American life. As the nation pushed westward, it was widely assumed that Americans would unite behind a program of territorial growth to thwart British hemispheric designs. To their dismay, expansionists discovered that the agenda was impossible to implement; Americans could all agree that Britain sought to check the rise of the United States, but each section viewed the precise nature of the threat differently. Alarmed by alleged British ambitions insofar as their own region or interests were concerned, they reacted with feelings that ranged from ambivalence, skepticism, and even hostility when the cry of British aggression was raised in other quarters. It was no small irony that Manifest Destiny—the clarion call of American nationalism—laid bare the fact that the United States was still a nation of disparate parts; a threat to one was not automatically perceived as a threat to all.

And as the British threat abruptly receded in the 1850s, Americans were left with the manifold disagreements that had divided them all along. Domestic adversaries could no longer be maligned as dupes of the British; they would now have to be viewed strictly as legitimate dangers in their own right. This is not to suggest that the slavery issue, the most serious source of domestic rancor, only became intractable when the nation's anxieties toward Britain faded. Extremists on both sides—Southern ultras and Northern abolitionists—were always more focused on dangers at home than abroad. But the same could not be said for those who occupied the political center, who had routinely raised the call of foreign influence with every domestic crisis. Anglophobia's dwindling appeal meant there was one less diversion to occupy the country's attention, one less opportunity to cast internal problems in broader terms.

It is perhaps fitting that James Fenimore Cooper should be given the last word, for he had done as much as anyone to draw attention to the deep sense of inferiority that informed the American relationship with Great Britain. The "American Scott" had once accepted the conventional wisdom that the War of 1812 provided the coda in the nation's struggle for independence. But the years that followed had only led to disappointment, as the republic seemed utterly incapable of shaking off the bonds that tied it to the imperial parent. By mid-century, however, Cooper looked to the future with renewed optimism. Like many Americans, he saw in the war with Mexico something more than the defeat of a weaker neighbor. With U.S. armies occupying the Mexican capital, he dared hope that his country's long process of separation from Great Britain might finally be complete. Penning an introduction to a new edition of his novel *The Spy* more than a quarter of a century after its initial publication, the author took the opportunity to reflect on the republic's newfound stature. The United States was emerging as the western hemisphere's dominant power, and in so doing it could not help but make great strides "toward real independence and high political influence." But Cooper offered an intriguing caveat. With telling prophecy that could only guess at the conflagration that lay ahead, he added: "There is now no enemy to fear, but the one that resides within."[40]

Notes

INTRODUCTION

1. The so-called special relationship looms large over our understanding of the web of associations that have historically connected the United States and Great Britain. Yet it is important to remember that the unusually close friendship that Americans and Britons today take for granted did not fully take shape until the twentieth century. The term is generally attributed to Winston Churchill, who used the phrase in a speech in Fulton, Missouri, in 1946. Profoundly influenced by the alliances of two world wars and the emerging struggle against the Soviet bloc, Churchill and scholars on both sides of the Atlantic tended to stress the affinities that linked the two nations. This is evidenced by the work of H. C. Allen (see *Great Britain and the United States: A History of Anglo-American Relations, 1783 to 1952*); and Frank Thistlethwaite (see *The Anglo-American Connection in the Early Nineteenth Century*). In recent years, academic interest in the linkages that define the Atlantic world has prompted scholars to pay more attention to the cultural relations between Great Britain and its former colonies. Elisa Tamarkin describes a republican citizenry hopelessly infatuated with all things British in *Anglophilia: Deference, Devotion, and Antebellum America*, while Frank Prochaska takes a similar view in *The Eagle and the Crown: Americans and the British Monarchy*. In "Post-Colonial America: Transatlantic Networks of Exchange in the Early National Period," Kariann Yokota finds evidence of deep-seated cultural insecurities in American consumer habits during the early national period. Recently, two sweeping syntheses have examined the relationship between the two Anglophone nations from the colonial period to the present day: see Kevin Phillips, *The Cousins' Wars: Religion, Politics, and the Triumph of Anglo-America*; and Kathleen Burk, *Old World, New World: Great Britain and America from the Beginning*. For a study of U.S.-British power relations from a British perspective, see Duncan Andrew Campbell, *Unlikely Allies: Britain, America, and the Victorian Origins of the Special Relationship*. There are, of course, many studies that examine specific aspects of U.S.-British relations during the early national period, which will be cited in relevant chapters.

2. The role of invented narratives in constructing a sense of national belonging is explored in Benedict Anderson's seminal work, *Imagined Communities*. The relational nature of national identity has long been recognized by historians. Linda Colley, for example, in *Britons: Forging the Nation, 1707–1837*, has made especially effective use of "otherness" as an argument for social cohesion in demonstrating that the British developed a national consciousness in the eighteenth century largely as a result of their protracted military struggle with France.

1 THE AXIALS OF INDEPENDENCE

1. *Army and Navy Chronicle*, March 26, 1842, 147.

2. Mackay, *The Western World, or, Travels in the United States in 1846–47*, 1:65–66. Mac-

kay was not alone in his impressions of the artillery display; the always jingoistic *New York Herald* was obliged to concede that the guns of the *Warspite* "created marked expressions of their force and superiority" over the U.S. ships in the harbor ("The Fourth and Its Events," *New York Herald,* July 6, 1842).

3. "History of the United States," *United States Magazine and Democratic Review,* January 1850, 44 [hereafter cited as the *Democratic Review*].

4. Historians have long held the view that, as Henry Adams put it in 1891, "a new episode in American history began in 1815" (Adams, *History of the United States of America during the Second Administration of James Madison,* 241). Moreover, they have generally accepted the popular nationalism of the period as evidence of the republic's growing self-confidence (see, e.g., Dangerfield, *The Awakening of American Nationalism;* and Van Alstyne, *The Rising American Empire).* More recent scholarship has buttressed the view of a muscular nation on the rise. In her social history of Americans born in the late eighteenth century, Joyce Appleby also finds a citizenry conscious of the republic's "emergent greatness" (see Appleby, *Inheriting the Revolution,* 24). Similarly, in recounting the political events that followed the war, Carl Edward Skeen sees a nation on the cusp of maturity (see Skeen, *1816).* On the other hand, some historians have detected in the postwar years a decidedly less sanguine national mood (see Somkin, *Unquiet Eagle;* and Nagel, *This Sacred Trust).*

5. Bell, *Men and Things in America,* 31.

6. Combe, *Notes on the United States of America,* 1:284. Some of the larger urban centers held their own annual celebrations to honor their role in the Revolution. Bostonians celebrated the Battle of Bunker Hill every June 17; the residents of Charleston, South Carolina, observed Palmetto Day, June 28, to commemorate the defense of Fort Moultrie; while New York City residents observed Evacuation Day on November 25, to celebrate the final departure of British troops from the city in 1783. Revolutionary War monuments built during the early nineteenth century included Savannah's Pulaski Monument (completed in 1825); Boston's Bunker Hill Monument (1827); the Fort Griswold Obelisk in Groton, Connecticut (1830); and in Baltimore, Battle Monument (1825) and the Washington Monument (1829). The public rituals through which Americans commemorated and reified their national past have been the subject of a great deal of fruitful historical inquiry in recent years: see Newman, *Parades and the Politics of the Street;* Travers, *Celebrating the Fourth;* and Waldstreicher, *In Pursuit of Perpetual Fetes.* For more on the 1826 celebrations, see Burstein, *America's Jubilee;* Purcell, *Sealed With Blood;* and Somkin, *Unquiet Eagle,* 131–74.

7. Addington, *Youthful America,* 68.

8. Strange, *Oration of Robert Strange, Esq.,* 10. See also James, *An Address, Delivered at the Columbian College, in the District of Columbia, in the Celebration of the National Anniversary, July 4, 1826,* 8; and Pinckney, *An Oration, Delivered in St. Michael's Church,* 8. There were, of course, exceptions. The English visitor C. H. Wilson reported being treated to "an unnecessary and malign invective" against his country by a minister in New York City in 1820 (see Wilson, *The Wanderer in America,* 27).

9. Cooper, *Gleanings in Europe: England,* 11; Marryat, *Second Series of A Diary in America,* 130; Addington, *Youthful America,* 27; Hall, *Travels in North America,* 2:150–51.

10. Marryat, *Second Series of A Diary in America,* 135.

11. Taylor, *The Transportation Revolution,* 450, table 10.

12. Warburton, *Hochelaga,* 2:107. Other British travelers remarked on the American appetite for the latest London news; see, e.g., Hall, *Travels in North America,* 1:230; and Maury, *An Englishwoman in America,* 135.

13. Thomas Jefferson to Elbridge Gerry, May 13, 1797, in *The Writings of Thomas Jef-*

ferson, 9:385; Thomas Jefferson to Horatio G. Spafford, March 17, 1814, ibid., 14:120. For an examination of these frustrations in the 1780s and 1790s, see Friedman, *Inventors of the Promised Land*, 3–43.

14. For a traditional interpretation of American nationalism that emphasized the intellectual origins of national identity, see Kohn, *American Nationalism*, 3–24. Yehoshua Arieli, in *Individualism and Nationalism in American Ideology*, also stressed the importance of ideas, specifically the concept of individual freedom, as the primary adhesive of American national identity. More recently, historians have borrowed from other disciplines to arrive at a more textured understanding of the ways in which people with seemingly little in common develop a unitary view of national belonging; see, e.g., Anderson, *Imagined Communities*. For a cultural approach to the complex process of identity formation in postcolonial states (although with an emphasis on indigenous societies rather than the settler cultures of North America), see Bhabha, *The Location of Culture*; and Bhabha, "DissemiNation."

15. "Public Documents on Foreign Relations: The United States and Great Britain," *New York Review* 10 (April 1842): 375–420. For more on the familial imagery Americans employed to describe the transatlantic relationship, see Clark, "John Bull's American Connection."

16. Poinsett to [Frances Tyrell], May 12, 1842, in Pennsylvania Historical Survey, *Calendar of Joel R. Poinsett Papers in the Henry D. Gilpin Collection*, 162. Despite fond childhood memories of England, Poinsett exhibited a lively Anglophobia as the first U.S. minister to Mexico in the early 1820s (see chap. 9, this volume). When the nullification controversy flared in his home state a few years later, Poinsett, a staunch Unionist, blamed the crisis on British free trade agents. With tensions mounting and state leaders hinting at secession, Poinsett journeyed once again to England, where he reconnected with the friends of his youth. Returning to the Palmetto State some months later, he threw himself once more into the political fray, again reminding South Carolina voters of the dangers that awaited the state should it seek the protective embrace of the British empire (see Rippy, *Joel Poinsett, Versatile American*; and Poinsett, *Joel R. Poinsett, Substance of a Speech, Delivered by the Hon. Joel R. Poinsett, at a Public Meeting Held at Seyle's, October 5th, 1832*).

17. "House of Representatives," *Niles' Weekly Register*, February 5, 1842.

18. Fisher, *A Philadelphia Perspective*, 16.

19. Grund, *Aristocracy in America*, 176; Paulding, *Letters from the South*, 2:60. See also Kasson, *Rudeness and Civility*; and Bushman, *The Refinement of America*.

20. Hill, *Scenes from the Life of an Actor*, 130; Buckingham, *America, Historical, Statistic, and Descriptive*, 1:173. James Fenimore Cooper, who had traveled widely in Europe, was irritated by the unseemly love of rank and privilege that well-to-do Americans exhibited on their tours abroad. Speaking through the character Paul Powis in *Home As Found*, a novel written upon his return stateside, Cooper noted: "Whenever I felt in the mood to hear high monarchical and aristocratical doctrines blindly promulgated, I used to go to the nearest American Legation" (370).

21. "He will not take me for a noodle next time," Legaré declared (see O'Brien, *A Character of Hugh Legaré*, 30–31); Faust, *James Henry Hammond and the Old South*, 191). For more on Southern travelers in Europe, see Kilbride, "Travel, Ritual, and National Identity." See also Sedgwick, *Letters from Abroad to Kindred at Home*, 1:6.

22. Marryat, *Second Series of a Diary in America*, 133. Although Maxwell refers here to the New England population as a whole, he concedes that he moved primarily in upper-class circles and had only limited contact with working-class Americans (Maxwell, *A Run through the United States, during the Autumn of 1840*, 2:94).

23. "Public Documents on Foreign Relations: The United States and Great Britain,"

New York Review 10 (April 1842): 406. The English visitor, Matilda Houstoun, observed widespread hatred of the English among the Irish. "It is sad, indeed," she wrote, "when one's foes are those of one's own household" (Houston, *Hesperos,* 1:178–79). For more on the anti-British attitudes of the urban poor, see Fidler, *Observations on Professions, Literature, Manners, and Emigration in the United States and Canada,* 88–89; and Marryat, *Second Series of A Diary in America,* 133, 135. British immigration is the focus of Van Vogt, *Britain to America.* See also Shepperson, *British Emigration to North America;* and Erickson, *Invisible Immigrants.*

24. Marryat, *A Diary in America, with Remarks on Its Institutions,* 1:46. Thomas Hamilton found "far more English feeling in Boston than I was prepared to expect. The people yet feel pride in the country of their forefathers, and even retain somewhat of a reverence for her ancient institutions" (see Hamilton, *Men and Manners in America,* 242; see also Warburton, *Hochelaga,* 2:270). Not all British visitors viewed New England's Anglophilia with approbation, however. Harriet Martineau, no admirer of the political and social institutions of her own country, observed that "the veneration for England is greater than I think any one people ought to feel for any other" (see Martineau, *Society in America,* 23).

25. Putnam, *American Facts,* 152–53.

26. "Southern Wealth and Northern Profits," *De Bow's Review* 4 (August 1860), 200–203; Taylor, *Cavalier and Yankee.* The Tidewater elite's desire to model itself after Britain's landed aristocracy had deep roots in the colonial era (see Rozbicki, *The Complete Colonial Gentleman;* and Prentiss, *A Memoir,* 2:536, 353).

27. "Editorial Comments," *Kentucky Yeoman,* April 12, 1844. Traveling through Kentucky, Matilda Houston, curious as to the state of feeling that existed among the Scots-Irish and English emigrants toward the "old country," was dismayed to find that many, regardless of class, looked back upon the land of their birth with little fondness, and were inclined to renounce their nationality "once and for ever" (see Houston, *Hesperos,* 1:292).

28. Ascending to the throne in 1837, Victoria was crowned the following year. For more on Americans' views of the coronation, see Prochaska, *The Eagle and the Crown,* 43–61.

29. Ludlow, *A Thanksgiving Sermon,* 9–13.

30. U.S. Congress, *Register of Debates,* 21st Cong., 1st sess., 244. Not surprisingly, the work on British influences in early American political thought is voluminous. See, e.g., Bailyn, *The Ideological Origins of the American Revolution;* Wood, *The Making of the American Republic;* Shalhope, "Toward a Republican Synthesis"; and Rodgers, "Republicanism."

31. Simms, "Travels in the United States," no. 1, *Magnolia* 4 (April 1842): 203. James Fenimore Cooper agreed, maintaining that an American "has just as good a right to claim Milton, and Shakespeare, and all the old masters of the language," as any English subject (see Cooper, *Notions of the Americans,* 2:100; Elson, *Guardians of Tradition,* 121).

32. The Boston mayor's declaration of fealty prompted a stern reproof from *New York Evening Post* editor William Cullen Bryant, who objected to the metaphor on the grounds that it suggested a subordinate role for the American republic. While a parent was due the respect of a child, the United States owed no such deference to Great Britain (see Bryant, *Power for Sanity,* 175–76; Beman, *The Intellectual Position of Our Country,* 8–9). Pundits of the period commonly used the term "leading strings" to describe the American relationship to Great Britain. Sewn, usually on the shoulders, of children's clothing, leading strings served as a walking aid for toddlers, as well as a restraining device for older, more rambunctious children. The practice came under sharp criticism as too restrictive during the eighteenth century, and gradually declined.

33. Lindsley, *An Address Delivered at Nashville, Tenn. Feb. 22, 1832*, 6–7; "Anniversary Address," *Southern Literary Messenger* 5 (November 1839): 730; "English Traits," in Emerson, *Works*, 5:39; Beman, *The Intellectual Position of Our Country*, 10. See also Welter, *The Mind of America*, 31–44.

34. Simpson, *The Working Man's Manual*, 12 (the reference to "hewers of wood, drawers of water" is from Joshua 9:21). Also, Sampson, *An Anniversary Discourse delivered Before the New York Historical Society on the Common Law*, 57. Nationalistic intellectuals complained incessantly of their fellow citizens' inability to distance themselves from British norms. "We imitate foreign fashions, and follow foreign opinions, with a degree of docility which approaches abjectness," James Kirke Paulding observed (see Paulding, "American Literature, Number Two," *Knickerbocker* 5 [May 1835]: 380). Boston editor Orestes Brownson expressed similar sentiments: Americans may have thought they had thrown off the yoke of colonial subjugation, but "the mother country exerts an almost absolute spiritual dominion over the colonies, which may be continued long after events shall have severed the political ties which bind them together" (see "American Literature," in Brownson, *Works*, 19:24). Only those Americans whose patriotism inclined toward the emotional maintained that there was no connection whatsoever between parent and progeny. It was this kind of reflexive chauvinism that British author Basil Hall encountered while visiting a Boston high school for boys in 1827. When the schoolmaster called upon two youths to exhibit their oratorical skills for their foreign guest, Hall was surprised to find himself subjected to a furious diatribe against his native land. Warming to the task, one of the students declared, "Gratitude! Gratitude to England! What does America owe to her?" (see Hall, *Travels in North America*, 1:302).

35. For more on American exceptionalism during the late eighteenth century, see Greene, *The Intellectual Construction of America*; and Guyatt, *Providence and the Invention of America*. The influence of European Romanticism on American thought is examined in Miller, *The Life of the Mind in America*; and Sanford, *The Quest for Paradise*.

36. "Sam Slick in England," *North American Review*, 58 (January 1844): 214; "The Works of James Fenimore Cooper," *North American Review* 74 (January 1852): 159; "National Feelings and Prejudices," *Niles' Weekly Register*, April 3, 1819, 106; James Fenimore Cooper to William Bradford Shubrick, November 8, 1837, in Cooper, *Letters and Journals*, 3:300.

37. "History for the Purposes of Art," in Simms, *Views and Reviews in American Literature, History, and Fiction*, 58; Lindsley, *An Address Delivered at Nashville, Tenn., Feb. 22, 1832*, 6, 19, 28.

38. Marsh, *The Goths in New-England*, 14; see also Miles, "The Young American Nation and the Classical World."

39. Sampson and Thompson, *Sampson's Discourse*, 69, 201–2; Fisk, *Labor the Only True Source of Wealth*, 16. See also Fisk's philippic against English jurisprudence, in "Lawyers and the Common Law," *Working Man's Advocate*, August 1840. For more recent studies of the codification movement, see Cook, *The American Codification Movement*; Widmer, *Young America*, 155–84; and Miller, *Life of the Mind in America*, 239–65.

40. "Americanisms," *Southern Literary Messenger*, 2 (March 1836): 257; Joseph C. Hart, *Geographical Exercises*, quoted in Abdy, *Journal of a Residence and Tour in the United States*, 2:332; "Americanism in Literature," in Simms, *Views and Reviews in American Literature, History, and Fiction*, 10; "American Women," *Democratic Review* 6 (August 1839): 129. For more on the early debate over American English, see Unger, *Noah Webster*; and Ellis, *After the Revolution*, 212.

41. "The Epochs and Events of American History," in Simms, *Views and Reviews in American Literature, History, and Fiction*, 59.

2 "WHAT DO YOU THINK OF OUR COUNTRY?"

1. For bibliographies on British travelers to the United States during the period under review, see Mesick, *The English Traveler in America*; Berger, *The British Traveller in America*; and Nisbet, *British Comment on the United States*.

2. Meigs, *The Life of Charles Jared Ingersoll*, 42. For more on Ingersoll, see "Political Portraits with Pen and Pencil, No. XVI, Charles Jared Ingersoll," *Democratic Review* 6 (October 1839): 339–54; Maury, *The Statesmen in America*, 155–61; and Watts, *The Republic Reborn*, 93–100.

3. Janson, *The Stranger in America*, 297, 87.

4. Ingersoll, *Inchiquin*, 137; Eldridge, "The Paper War between England and America."

5. For evidence of Federalist anger at Ingersoll's apostasy, see Fischer, *The Revolution in American Conservatism*, 350.

6. Ingersoll, *Historical Sketch of the Second War between the United States of America and Great Britain*, 1:17.

7. "Inchiquen's [*sic*] Favourable View of the United States," *Quarterly Review* 10 (January 1814): 502–39.

8. Dwight, *Remarks on the Review of Inchiquin's Letters*, 171. For more on the Federalists' twilight years, see Kerber, *Federalists in Dissent*. For more on the Connecticut Wits, see Giles, *Transatlantic Insurrections*, 40–69.

9. Faux, *Memorable Days in America*; Fearon, *Sketches of America*; Howitt, *Selections from Letters Written during a Tour of the United States*. For a more complimentary view of American institutions during this period, see Bristed, *America and Her Resources*.

10. "English Writers on America," in Irving, *The Sketch Book of Geoffrey Crayon, Gentleman*, 75.

11. Walsh, *An Appeal from the Judgments of Great Britain*, vi; *Dictionary of American Biography*, 19:391.

12. Review of "An Appeal from the Judgments of Great Britain," by Robert Walsh Jr., *Port Folio* 8 (December 1819): 495; Review of "An Appeal from the Judgments of Great Britain Respecting the United States of America," by Robert Walsh Jr., *North American Review* 1 (April 1820): 335, 339. For more on the "Paper War," see McCloskey, "The Campaign of Periodicals after the War of 1812 for a National Literature." For more on the cultural nationalism of the early republic's conservative elite, see Foletta, *Coming to Terms with Democracy*.

13. Review of *Statistical Annals of the United States of America*, by Adam Seybert, *Edinburgh Review* 33 (January 1820): 79–80.

14. "Mr. Adams' July 4 Oration," *Niles' Weekly Register*, July 21, 1821, 332.

15. See, e.g., Walsh, *Appeal from the Judgments of Great Britain*, viii; Paulding, *A Sketch of Old England*, 2:176–77.

16. William I. Paulding, *Literary Life of James K. Paulding*, 24. See also Reynolds, *James Kirke Paulding*.

17. Paulding, *The Lay of the Scottish Fiddle*, xii.

18. Paulding, *The United States and England*.

19. Paulding also poked fun at British travelers in *The Bucktails, or, Americans in England*, although the play was never performed.

20. Paulding, *A Sketch of Old England*, 2:54–59, 291; Paulding, *John Bull in America*, 40.

21. Hall, *Travels in North America*.

22. *Philadelphia Monthly Magazine* 1 (October 1829): 858. For an account of the Amer-

ican reception of Hall's book, see Trollope, *Domestic Manners of the Americans*, 354–65. See also Boardman, *America, and the Americans*, 255.

23. Trollope, *Domestic Manners of the Americans*, 404.

24. For a sampling of reviews of *Domestic Manners*, see "Domestic Manners of the Americans," *Illinois Monthly Magazine* 2 (August 1832): 505–26; and "Prince Puckler Muscau and Mrs. Trollope," *North American Review* 36 (January 1833): 1–49.

25. Isaac Fidler reported that the belief that Hall and Trollope were one and the same "was entertained by almost every American I spoke to on the subject" (see Fidler, *Observations on Professions, Literature, Manners, and Emigration in the United States and Canada*, 237).

26. Martineau, *Society in America*, 25; Combe, *Notes on the United States of America during a Phrenological Visit in 1838–9–40*, 1:240.

27. Hall, *Travels in North America*, 1:240.

28. Abdy, *Journal of a Residence and Tour in the United States of North America*, 2:337; Hall, *Travels in North America*, 1:239; Trollope, *Domestic Manners of the Americans*, 355; Tudor, *Narrative of a Tour in North America*, 2:423.

29. See, e.g., "Travels in North America," *North American Review* 29 (October 1829): 545–46.

30. Trollope, *Domestic Manners of the Americans*, 354.

31. Coke, *A Subaltern's Furlough*, 1:148; Warburton, *Hochelaga*, 2:86–87; Fidler, *Observations on Professions, Literature, Manners, and Emigration in the United States and Canada*, 283.

32. In 1833 the following travel memoirs were released by British publishing houses: Boardman, *America, and the Americans*; Coke, *A Subaltern's Furlough*; Hamilton, *Men and Manners in America*; Fidler, *Observations on Professions, Literature, Manners, and Emigration in the United States and Canada*; Finch, *Travels in the United States of America and Canada*; Mackenzie, *Sketches of Canada and the United States*; and Stuart, *Three Years in North America*.

33. Marryat, *A Diary in America*, 17. See also Hone, *Diary*, 1:260.

34. Hone, *Diary*, 1:323–34.

35. According to initial newspaper accounts, the author had been caught *in flagrante delicto* by the phrenologist, although the doctor subsequently issued a statement dismissing the entire episode as a misunderstanding—an explanation viewed by some as an attempt to avoid a duel with the British captain (see Marryat, *A Diary in America*, 23–25).

36. Often published anonymously, parodies of the works of British travel writers included Green, *Travels in America, by George Fibbleton*; Cutler, *My Conscience!*; and Shelton, *The Trollopiad*. For more serious replies to the British critique, the works of Charles Jared Ingersoll and Robert Walsh have already been cited. See also Cooper, *Notions of the Americans, Picked up by a Travelling Bachelor*; Biddle, *Captain Hall in America*; Colton, *The Americans*; and Wood, *Change for the American Notes*.

37. "The Tone of British Criticism," *North American Review* 31 (July 1830): 28; "American Society," *Knickerbocker* 8 (July 1836): 30.

38. "Review," *Niles' Weekly Register*, August 31, 1816, 6; "Slavery in the Southern States," *Southern Quarterly Review* 8 (October 1845): 333.

39. "British Opinions of America," *American Quarterly Review* 20 (December 1836): 411.

40. "National Views," in Simms, *The Charleston Book*, 278.

41. [James Kirke Paulding,] "American Literature, Number Three," *Knickerbocker* 5 (June 1835): 477.

42. "Capt. Marryatt, and His Diary," *Southern Literary Messenger* 7 (April 1841): 262–63.

43. Hall, *Travels in North America*, 2:48; review of *Travels in North America* by Basil Hall, *North American Review* 20 (October 1829): 538; "The Tone of British Criticism," *North American Review* 31 (July 1830): 30.

44. Barnard, *An Oration, Delivered before the Honorable the Corporation and the Military and Civic Societies of the City of Albany, on the Fourth of July, 1835*, 15; "American Literature," *Western Monthly Magazine and Literary Journal* 1 (April 1833): 188; Lindsley, *An Address Delivered at Nashville, Tenn. Feb. 22, 1832, at the Request of the Citizens of Nashville and Its Vicinity, on the Occasion of the Centennial Birth Day of George Washington*, 17.

45. Marryat, *Second Series of A Diary in America*, 136; "American Literature," *Western Monthly Magazine* 1 (April 1833): 185; Hall, *Travels in North America*, 1:242.

46. Pinckney, *An Oration, Delivered in the College Chapel, before the Clariosophic Society Incorporate*, 14, 25; Grayson, *An Oration, Delivered in the College Chapel, before the Clariosophic Society Incorporate*, 17–18.

47. "Dr. Channing and the Edinburgh Review," *Southern Literary Messenger* 6 (January 1840): 3–12; "Captain Marryat and his Diary," *Southern Literary Messenger* 7 (April 1841): 255, 276.

48. "The Tone of British Criticism," *North American Review* 31 (July 1830): 26–67; "On American Literature," *Ladies' Literary Cabinet* 1 (December 18, 1819): 42; "The Tone of British Criticism," *North American Review* 31 (July 1830): 29.

49. For an examination of American attitudes toward England during this period, see Strout, *The American Image of the Old World*, 62–106.

50. Mrs. Felton, *American Life*, 11. See also Buckingham, *America, Historical, Statistic, and Descriptive*, 1:283–85.

51. Featherstonaugh, *Excursion through the Slave States*, vi; Warburton, *Hochelaga*, 2:313.

52. "The Laboring Classes of Europe," *North American Review* 41 (October 1835): 364.

53. Lester, *The Glory and the Shame of England*. Not all American visitors painted so bleak a picture as Lester; see, e.g., Colton, *Four Years in Great Britain*.

54. Mackay, *The Western World, or, Travels in the United States in 1846–47*, 2:208–9.

55. "National Views," in Simms, *The Charleston Book*, 280–81. For examples of the American conviction that Great Britain had been resting on its cultural laurels, see "Seybert's Statistical Annals of America," *The Literary and Scientific Repository, and Critical Review* 1 (June 1820): 185–86; and "Young England. Coningsby," *Southern Literary Messenger* 10 (December 1844). George Putnam's essay was published anonymously as "The Poets and Poetry of America" (*North American Review* 59 [July 1844]: 32, 33). For more on Putnam, see Greenspan, *George Palmer Putnam, Representative American Publisher*.

56. Godley, *Letters from America*, 2:180.

57. "British Opinions of America," *American Quarterly Review* 20 (December 1836): 413.

58. For more on Charles Dickens' first American tour, see Meckier, *Innocent Abroad*, chaps. 2–3.

59. Charles Dickens to Thomas Mitton, January 31, 1842, in Dickens, *Letters*, 3:43; Nichols, *Forty Years of American Life*, 182. An effusive Philip Hone described the affair as "the greatest event in modern times" (see Hone, *Diary*, 2:586).

60. *Spirit of the Times*, February 1, 1842, quoted in Reynolds, *George Lippard, Prophet of Protest*, 230.

61. *Brother Jonathan*, quoted in Barnes, *The Quest for an Anglo-American Copyright Agreement*, 29.

62. Dickens to John Forster, February 24, 1842, in Dickens, *Letters*, 3:82–83.

63. McGill, *American Literature and the Culture of Reprinting*, 22–23; Nevins, *America through British Eyes*, 90; Peach, *British Influence on the Birth of American Literature*, 11.

64. Dickens, *American Notes for General Circulation*, 69.

65. "Dickens' American Notes," *Southern Quarterly Review* 3 (January 1843): 168.

66. Dickens, *Martin Chuzzlewit*, chap. 16.

67. For Dickens' second, more enjoyable tour of the United States, see Meckier, *Innocent Abroad*, 133–82.

68. Wright, *Views of Society and Manners in America*; Martineau, *Society in America*; Murray, *Travels in North America during the Years 1834, 1835 & 1836*, 2:327; Tudor, *Narrative of a Tour in North America*, 2:40; Hall, *Travels in North America*, 2:191–94; Dickens, *American Notes*, 45–47. For similarly favorable accounts, see Boardman, *America, and the Americans*; and Ouseley, *Remarks on the Statistics and Political Institutions of the United States*.

69. "Travels in North America," *Western Monthly Review* 3 (December 1829): 295.

70. Fearon, *Sketches of America*, 369–70.

3 "Who Reads an American Book?"

1. Edmund Quincy to R. D. Webb, May 23, 1846, in *British and American Abolitionists*, 268. For more on Emerson's Phi Beta Kappa address, see Sacks, *Understanding Emerson*; Sealts, *Emerson on the Scholar*, 97–110; Wilson, *Waldo Emerson*, 298–303; and Ziff, *The Declaration of Cultural Independence in America*, 18–21.

2. "The American Scholar," in Emerson, *Works*, 1:113; "Letters to Various Persons," *North American Review* 101 (October 1865): 600; Holmes, *Ralph Waldo Emerson*, 115

3. "Remarks on National Literature," in Channing, *Works*, 1:243–80; "The Naturalist," in *The Early Lectures of Ralph Waldo Emerson*, 1:75.

4. "On the Uses of Natural History," in Emerson, *Works*, 13:226.

5. Emerson, *Journals and Miscellaneous Notebooks*, 4:297. Although Emerson is generally considered to be a staunch Anglophile, Lawrence Buell takes a contrary view in *Emerson*.

6. Washington Allston, "America to Great Britain," in Morris, *American Melodies*, 161.

7. Paulding, *Letters from the South*, 2:60.

8. Preston, *Reminiscences*, 34.

9. Irving, *Bracebridge Hall*, 8, 5. For more on Irving, see Burstein, *The Original Knickerbocker*; and Rubin-Dorsky, *Adrift in the Old World*.

10. Lindsley, *Baccalaureate Address, Pronounced on the Seventh Anniversary Commencement of the University of Nashville, October 3, 1832*, 18.

11. In the *Port Folio*, see, e.g., the review of *An Appeal from the Judgments of Great Britain* by Robert Walsh, Jr. (vol. 8 [December 1819]: 493–515); and "Intelligence in Literature, Science, and the Arts" (vol. 9 [February 1820]: 502–10). For similar sentiments in the *North American Review*, see "Reflection on the Literary Delinquency of America" (vol. 2 [November 1815]: 33–43); and "England and America" (vol. 13 [July 1821]: 20–47). In the *American Quarterly Review*, see "London Quarterly Review" (vol. 3 [June 1828]: 491–56); and "The Life and Adventures of Jonathan Jefferson Whitlaw" (vol. 20 [December 1836]: 405–32). See also "Editorial Miscellany," *Broadway Journal*, October 4, 1845, 199. The case for Poe's authorship is made in O'Neill, "The Poe-Griswold-Harrison Texts of the 'Marginalia,'" 246–48.

12. "The Red Rover," *North American Review* 27 (July 1828): 143.

13. Prescott to Charles Sumner, October 16, 1840, in Prescott, *Papers*, 165.

14. Whitman, *The Gathering of the Forces*, 2:243; Paulding, "American Literature," *Knickerbocker* 5 (April 1835): 320.

15. Grayson, *An Oration Delivered in the College Chapel before the Clariosophic Society,* 9.

16. Whitman, *Gathering of the Forces,* 2:243; "Our Struggle for Independence," *Knickerbocker* 5 (February 1835): 122; "American Women," *Democratic Review* 6 (August 1839): 129.

17. William Gilmore Simms to P. C. Pendleton, December 1, 1843, in Simms, *Letters,* 1:203–6.

18. "American Women," *Democratic Review* 6 (August 1839): 128, 130.

19. "Introduction," *Democratic Review* 1 (October 1837): 15; "Moral Poisons, The Antidote," *The Mother's Magazine* (May 1845): 150.

20. "American Literature," *Knickerbocker* 5 (May 1835): 383. See also Frost, *The Duty of the American Scholar to the Literature of His Country,* 17. For more on American fears of the corrupting influences of British literature, see Spencer, *The Quest for Nationality,* 81–90.

21. "American Literature," in Brownson, *Works,* 19:26. Edgar Allan Poe shared Brownson's sentiments, believing that "gentlemen of elegant leisure" were predisposed to imitate British literary models (see Poe, *The Complete Works,* 9:345–46). See also "Our Struggle for Independence," *Knickerbocker* 5 (February 1835): 123.

22. For expressions of these cultural anxieties, see Cooper, *Notions of the Americans,* 2:108; Ingersoll, *A Discourse concerning the Influence of America on the Mind,* 13; and "Travels in North America," *American Quarterly Review* 18 (December 1836): 424–25. For more on this predicament for American writers, see Orians, "The Romance Ferment after Waverly," *American Literature* 3 (January 1932): 408–31.

23. "The Spy," *North American Review* 15 (July 1822): 252–53.

24. Neal, *American Writers,* 25. Neal struggled with much the same dilemma that has confronted authors in other postcolonial societies (see Gayatri Chakravorty Spivak's seminal essay, "Can the Subaltern Speak?"). The question of whether American literature should be considered postcolonial is posed by Lawrence Buell in "American Literary Emergence as a Postcolonial Phenomenon." For a critique of Buell's thesis, see McClintock, "Angel of Progress."

25. Fuller, "American Literature, Its Position in the Present Time, and Prospects for the Future." See also Thomas, *James Freeman Clarke, Apostle of German Culture to America;* and "Remarks on National Literature," in Channing, *Works,* 1:276.

26. Du Ponceau, *A Discourse on the Necessity and the Means of Making Our National Literature Independent of That of Great Britain,* 24.

27. "International Copyright," *Southern Literary Messenger* 10 (June 1844): 341.

28. For an examination of British influences on American literature, see Lease, *Anglo-American Encounters;* Peach, *British Influence on the Birth of American Literature;* Weisbuch, *Atlantic Double-Cross;* Gravil, *Romantic Dialogues;* Ziff, *Literary Democracy;* and Giles, *Transatlantic Insurrections.*

29. Cooper, *Gleanings in Europe: England,* 11.

30. Cooper's patrician background has led some historians to emphasize his innate Anglophilia: see Schacterle, "Cooper's Attitudes toward England"; and Hartung, "James Fenimore Cooper's Attitude toward England." For more on Cooper before his years in Europe, see Franklin, *James Fenimore Cooper.*

31. Cooper, *The Spy,* 1:iii.

32. For more on Cooper's treatment at the hands of British reviewers, see Cairns, *British Criticism of American Writings,* 111–57 passim; and Cooper, *Lionel Lincoln,* xxxi–xxxii.

33. James Fenimore Cooper to Mrs. Peter Augustus Jay, March 26, 1827, in Cooper, *Letters and Journals,* 1:200–206; and Cooper to Benjamin Silliman, May 12, 1827, ibid., 1:216–17.

34. Cooper, *The Red Rover,* 3:341.

35. Cooper to Mrs. Peter Augustus Jay, March 26, 1827, in Cooper, *Letters and Journals*, 1:209.

36. [Mrs. Cooper to sister,] ibid., 1:254.

37. Cooper, *Gleanings in Europe: England*, 185. For more examples of Cooper's unfavorable impressions of his London visit, see ibid., 164, 128, 119.

38. Cooper to Charles Wilkes, April 27, 1831, in Cooper, *Letters and Journals*, 2:75; Cooper to William Dunlap, November 14, 1832, ibid., 2:358.

39. Cooper, *Notions of the Americans*, 2:127.

40. Cooper to William Gilmore Simms, January 5, 1844, in Cooper, *Letters and Journals*, 4:438; Cooper to Cornelius Mathews and Evert Augustus Duyckinck, December 6, 1841, ibid., 4:203.

41. For Cooper's difficulties readjusting to life in the United States, see Waples, *The Whig Myth of James Fenimore Cooper*.

42. Cooper, *A Letter to His Countrymen*, 98. Cooper's intemperate response to his critics is examined in Cooper, *Letters and Journals*, 3:6–7.

43. Cooper, *Gleanings in Europe: England*, 247.

44. Ibid., 180, 205.

45. The *Southern Literary Messenger* pronounced the work "vapid, pointless, inane" (see "Editorial Remarks," *Southern Literary Messenger* 5 [July 1834]: 652). See also brief mentions of the book in "Literary Notices," *Knickerbocker* 6 (August 1835): 152; and "The Monikins," *American Monthly Magazine* 5 (August 1835): 487.

46. His colleagues in the American literary fraternity, Cooper wrote, "are afraid of their popularity, and half of them have a most profound and provincial awe of the old island" (Cooper to William Bradford Shubrick, November 8, 1837, in Cooper, *Letters and Journals*, 3:300).

47. Cooper, *Homeward Bound*, 55; Waples, *The Whig Myth of James Fenimore Cooper*, 205.

48. Cooper, *Home As Found*, 98.

49. Ibid., 413.

50. Ibid., 271.

51. *New York Courier and Enquirer*, November 22, 1838.

52. At the height of the controversy over Cooper's patriotism, the Southern novelist William Gilmore Simms came to the New Yorker's defense (see "Cooper: His Genius and Writings," *Magnolia* [1 September 1842]: 129–40).

53. Bryant, *Prose Writings*, 1:312–13. See also "The Works of James Fenimore Cooper," *North American Review* 74 (January 1852): 147–61. The essay was widely attributed to Francis Parkman.

54. See, e.g., James Kirke Paulding, "American Literature," *Knickerbocker* 5 (April 1835): 317–26. For similar expressions of cultural nationalism in the *Knickerbocker*, see Timothy Flint, "Obstacles to American Literature" (vol. 2 [September 1833]: 161–70); and S[amuel] L[orenzo] K[napp], "Our Struggle for Independence" (vol. 5 [February 1835]: 117–23).

55. "Introduction," *Democratic Review* 1 (October 1837): 14.

56. For an in-depth study of O'Sullivan's career, see Sampson, *John L. O'Sullivan and His Times*. For more on O'Sullivan's Anglophobic rhetoric, see Lee, "Hawthorne's Politics of Storytelling."

57. For an excellent study of Young America, both as a literary and cultural movement, see Widmer, *Young America*, chaps. 1–3.

58. "Sectional Literature," *Magnolia* 4 (April 1842): 251.

59. Higham, "The Loyalties of William Gilmore Simms."

60. William Gilmore Simms to George F. Holmes, August 15, 1842, in Simms, *Letters*, 1:319.

61. Wakelyn, *The Politics of a Literary Man*; McCardell, *The Idea of a Southern Nation*, 143–74.

62. Not all members of the Young America clique favored a copyright law. John L. O'Sullivan, for example, regarded the measure as a form of literary protectionism. For a defense of the protectionist argument, see "American Literature," *Southern Literary Messenger* 11 (July 1845): 393–400.

63. "Reply to E. D. and William Gilmore Simms," *Southern Literary Messenger* 10 (April 1844): 194–95.

64. "Public Documents on Foreign Relations: The United States and Great Britain," *New York Review* 10 (April 1842): 409–10.

65. Ibid., 410.

66. "Literary Prospects of 1845," *American Review* 1 (February 1845): 149.

67. "Simms' Stories and Reviews," *North American Review* 63 (October 1846); "Literary Notices," *Knickerbocker* 22 (November 1843): 473–79. The feud between Lewis Gaylord Clark and Cornelius Mathews is examined fully in Miller, *The Raven and the Whale*, 88–279 passim.

68. "Simms' Stories and Reviews," *North American Review* 63 (October 1846): 378.

69. "American Letters—Their Character and Advancement," *American Whig Review* 1 (June 1845). For more on the copyright debate, see "Community of Copy-right," *Knickerbocker* 6 (October 1835): 285–90; "International Copy-right," *Knickerbocker* 22 (October 1843): 360–65; and "Reply to E. D. and William Gilmore Simms," *Southern Literary Messenger* 10 (April 1844): 193–99.

70. "Political independence hath given us wings," declared the grammarian James Brown. "Literary freedom will enable us to soar to fame" (Brown, *An Appeal from the British System of English Grammar, to Common Sense*, xi).

71. Even Edgar Allan Poe unsuccessfully sought to obtain a federal clerkship, in a desperate bid to be relieved from his "miserable life of literary drudgery" (see Edgar Allan Poe to James Kirke Paulding, July 19, 1838, Letters of Edgar Allan Poe website, http://www.eapoe.org/WORKS/letters/p3807190.htm).

4 "AMERICA RULES ENGLAND TONIGHT, BY JESUS"

1. Wilmeth, *George Frederick Cooke, Machiavel of the Stage*, 256–74.

2. William Dunlap drew the unenviable assignment of keeping Cooke in line. For a detailed glimpse into the strange final months of the actor's life, see Dunlap, *The Life of George Fred. Cooke*, vol. 2, chaps. 26–35 passim; and Playfair, *Kean*, 200.

3. For more on the Incledon riot, see Odell, *Annals of the New York Stage*, 2:498–99.

4. Hillebrand, *Edmund Kean*; Proctor, *The Life of Edmund Kean*, 2:190–91.

5. Hillebrand, *Edmund Kean*, 217.

6. "Drury-Lane Theatre," *New York Mirror*, March 19, 1825, 267.

7. Hillebrand, *Edmund Kean*, 258–59; Stone, *Personal Recollections of the Drama*, 15–16; "Riot at the Theatre," *New York Mirror*, November 19, 1825, 135.

8. Kean's apology to the people of Boston appeared in the *New York Mirror*, November 19, 1825. For accounts of the demonstrations organized against him in Boston, see "Federal Street Theatre," *Bowen's Boston News*, December 31, 1825, 15–17. See also Clapp, *A Record of the Boston Stage*, 231–35; Wood, *Personal Recollections of the Stage*, 309; and Cowell, *Thirty Years Passed among the Players in England and America*, 70–71.

9. The major New York theater riots are: the Incledon riot, Park Theatre, 1817; the Kean riot, Park Theatre, 1825; the Anderson riot, Park Theatre, 1831; the Anderson riot,

Richmond Theatre, 1832; the Farren riot, Bowery Theatre, 1834; the Wood riot, Park Theatre, 1836; the Turnbull riot, Bowery Theatre, 1848; and the Macready riot, Astor Place Opera House, 1849.

10. Of the sixty professional theaters in the United States, only ten were owned and operated by Americans (see "Dramatic and Histrionic Talent," *Spirit of the Times,* July 2, 1836).

11. Wood, *Personal Recollections of the Stage,* 187–88.

12. "The Drama," *The Mirror of Taste and Dramatic Censor* 2 (November 1810): 372.

13. "The Drama," *Broadway Journal,* January 11, 1845, 30; Rees, *The Dramatic Authors of America,* viii. These sentiments were echoed by the playwright Anne Royall (see Royall, *Sketches of History, Life, and Manners in the United States,* 199–200; see also Nichols, "The Prejudice against Native American Drama from 1778 to 1830").

14. *Account of the Terrific and Fatal Riot at the New-York Astor Place Opera House on the Night of May 10th, 1849,* 7.

15. *Working Man's Advocate,* February 16, 1833; Kemble, *Fanny Kemble, Journal of a Young Actress,* 145–47.

16. See, e.g., "Foreign Insolence Again," *Philadelphia Public Ledger,* June 10, 1836; and "Mr. Wood and the Courier," *Philadelphia Public Ledger,* June 1, 1836.

17. Marryat, *Second Series of A Diary in America,* 138–39. One of the Providence actors was allowed to return the following season; the other never worked in the theater again, dying in poverty a decade later (see Willard, *History of the Providence Stage,* 123–25).

18. Maud and Otis Skinner, *One Man in His Time,* 220, 90.

19. "Row at the Bowery Theatre," *New York Herald,* August 16, 1848.

20. Joseph Jefferson, *Autobiography,* 48–49.

21. "New York," *New York Sun,* July 14, 1834.

22. Odell, *Annals of the New York Stage,* 4:272–73, 279; "Mathews and his Chere Amie Again," *Spirit of the Times,* September 8, 1838. For Mathews's version of events, see "Park Theatre," *Albion,* November 17, 1838.

23. Odell, *Annals of the New York Stage,* 3:179. See also "The Morality of the Stage," *Dramatic Mirror,* October 30, 1841.

24. Stone, *Personal Recollections of the Drama,* 51–52.

25. *Memoir of Mr. and Mrs. Wood,* 22–29; "Park Theatre," *New York Courier and Enquirer,* May 27, 1836. The couple returned to the United States in 1840–41, but once again the penny-wise Wood ran afoul of his American hosts. Wood's refusal to perform to a small house evoked the anger of theater patrons in Philadelphia, causing the couple to cut short their tour.

26. Wemyss, *Twenty-six Years of the Life of an Actor and Manager,* 103.

27. Vandenhoff, *Leaves from an Actor's Note-Book,* 214–15.

28. Lawrence Levine offers a different analysis than the one presented here, arguing that a fair degree of cultural consensus within the urban audience existed during the early national and Jacksonian periods. The emergence of cultural hierarchies in the world of commercial entertainment, he suggests, did not begin until mid-century (see Levine, *Highbrow/Lowbrow,* chap. 1 passim).

29. "Theatrical Hubbub—Anderson Withdrawn," *New York Courier and Enquirer,* October 18, 1831; *New York Evening Post,* October 14, 1831.

30. Hone, *Diary,* 1:49; *New York Evening Post,* October 17, 1831; Odell, *Annals of the New York Stage,* 3:548–49; "Theatrical Hubbub—Anderson Withdrawn," *New York Courier and Enquirer,* October 18, 1831; *New York Evening Post,* October 17, 1831. Subsequent engagements in Boston and New York City resulted in further disturbances (see Clapp, *A Record of the Boston Stage,* 293–94; "Richmond Hill Theatre," *Spirit of the Times,* March 24, 1832).

31. Buckley, "To the Opera House," 178; Shank, "The Bowery Theatre," 304–5.

32. Odell, *Annals of the New York Stage*, 3:628–29; "The Drama," *New York Mirror*, November 30, 1833, 174; Hone, *Diary*, 1:103–4.

33. Buckley, "To the Opera House," 139–61. For more on the American theater during this period, see Wilmeth and Bigsby, *The Cambridge History of American Theatre: Beginnings to 1870*. See also McConachie, *Melodramatic Formations*, 1–28; Grimsted, *Melodrama Unveiled*; and Bank, *Theatre Culture in America*.

34. Harlow, *Old Bowery Days*, 291.

35. *New York Evening Post*, July 10, 1834.

36. Hone, *Diary*, 1:134–35; Haswell, *Reminiscences of an Octogenarian*, 289–90; *New York Sun*, July 11, 1834; *New York Evening Post*, July 10, 1834; "Disturbance in the City," *New York Courier and Enquirer*, July 10, 1834. See also Headley, *The Great Riots of New York*, 85.

37. *New York American*, August 6, 1834, quoted in Shank, "The Bowery Theatre," 386–87.

38. "Bowery Theatre," *New York Mirror*, August 20, 1836, 63.

39. For more on the transatlantic interchange that occurred in theater culture during this period, see Meserve, *Heralds of Promise*. See also Gallagher, *The Foreigner in Early American Drama*.

40. Hamilton, *Men and Manners in America*, 51. See also Boardman, *America, and the Americans*, 80–81; and Coke, *A Subaltern's Furlough*, 1:35.

41. Moody, *Dramas from the American Theatre*, 155–74.

42. Hodge, *Yankee Theatre*, 106–7; Haswell, *Reminiscences of an Octogenarian*, 295.

43. For a synopsis of "A Trip to Niagara," see the *New York American*, November 28, 1828, quoted in Shank, "The Bowery Theatre," 220–21.

44. Paulding, *Lion of the West*.

45. Shank, "The Bowery Theatre," 460.

46. Northall, *Before and Behind the Curtain*, 124.

47. Coke, *A Subaltern's Furlough*, 1:129.

48. Trollope, *Domestic Manners of the Americans*, 134.

49. "American Theatre," *New York Mirror*, June 8, 1833, 387.

50. "Selections from New Works: A German Mrs. Trollope," *New York Mirror*, November 15, 1834, 157.

51. Wilson, *A History of the Philadelphia Theatre*, 6–7; Odell, *Annals of the New York Stage*, 4:635; "Park Theatre," *New York Mirror*, September 13, 1834, 86.

52. Hamilton, *Men and Manners in America*, 52–53.

53. "Mr. Forrest," *New York Mirror*, September 6, 1828, 71.

54. *New York Evening Post*, July 17, 1834.

55. "Theatrical Talent and Diplomacy," *New York Herald*, September 15, 1836.

56. See, e.g., "Forrest in London," *New York Mirror*, December 10, 1836, 190.

57. Litto, "Edmund Simpson of the Park Theatre, New York," 45–46.

58. Joseph Jefferson, *Autobiography*, 41; An American Citizen, *A Rejoinder to "The Replies from England, etc." to Certain Statements Circulated in This Country respecting Mr. Macready,"* 68.

59. Moody, *Edwin Forrest, First Star of the American Stage*, 227–29; Macready, *Diaries*, 2:327.

60. "American Actors in England," *Democratic Review* 19 (September 1846), 188; Wemyss, *Twenty-six Years of the Life of an Actor and Manager*, 389; "Forrest and Macready—The Great Theatrical Excitement," *New York Herald*, May 9, 1849.

61. Moody, *Edwin Forrest, First Star of the American Stage*, 237.

62. Macready, *Diaries*, 2:420.

63. "The Theatrical Prize-Fight," *New York Herald*, April 5, 1849. For more on the escalating tensions leading up to the riot, see "Forrest and Macready—Another Letter from Mr. Forrest," *New York Herald*, April 10, 1849; and "Another Letter from Edwin Forrest," *New York Herald*, April 24, 1849.

64. For more on the career of Isaiah Rynders, see Kaplan, "The World of the B'hoys, 113–32; and E. J. Edwards, "Tammany: Early Spoilsmen and the Reign of the Plug-Uglies," *McClure's Magazine* (May 1895): 576–79.

65. Wilentz, *Chants Democratic*, 327–35; Walsh, *Sketches*, 31–32.

66. "Secret History of the Astor Place Riot, with Glimpses of the Forrest Divorce Case, by Andrew Stevens," Astor Place Riot Scrap-Book, p. 61, Charles P. Daly Papers, New York Public Library.

67. Northall, *Before and Behind the Curtain*, 140; Macready, *Diaries*, 2:424.

68. Wallack, *Memories of Fifty Years*, 131. Forrest was fond of this particular line, and never failed to give it special emphasis.

69. Buckley, "To the Opera House," 214; Harlow, *Old Bowery Days*, 327.

70. "Secret History of the Astor Place Riot," Astor Place Riot Scrap-Book, p. 62, Charles P. Daly Papers, New York Public Library; "The Great Theatrical War—Macready Yet in the Field," *New York Herald*, May 10, 1849.

71. Walling, *Recollections of a New York City Police Chief*, 47.

72. Monaghan, *The Great Rascal*, 177; *Account of the Terrific and Fatal Riot at the New York Astor Place Opera House*, 20.

73. "The Tragedy at Astor Place," *New York Herald*, May 12, 1849. Rynders would later be acquitted of inciting a riot. Judson was also charged, and would be sentenced to a year in prison on Blackwell's Island. While awaiting trial he again managed to make headlines. In a well-publicized stunt, the journalist sailed his yacht down the East River, where a British merchant vessel lay at anchor. As a crowd on the Battery watched and cheered, Judson stuffed a Union Jack into the mouth of a cannon on deck, then fired it at the British steamer as he passed under its stern (see Monaghan, *The Great Rascal*, 187).

74. For a summary of contemporary analyses of the riot, see Buckley, "To the Astor Place Opera House," 18–23.

75. Rees, *The Life of Edwin Forrest*, 371.

76. "Additional Particulars of the Terrible Riot at the Astor Place Opera House," *New York Herald*, May 12, 1849.

5 THE POLITICS OF ANGLOPHOBIA

1. Hildreth, *History of the United States of America*, 6:467.

2. Andrew Jackson to James Monroe, January 6, 1817, in Jackson, *Correspondence*, 2:272–73. For more on the demise of the Federalist Party, see Banner, *To the Hartford Convention*; and Fischer, *The Revolution in American Conservatism*.

3. *Washington Extra Globe*, October 12, 1840, 343. See, e.g., Andrew Jackson to James K. Polk, February 5, 1845, in Jackson, *Correspondence*, 6:404.

4. Not uncommon was the statement issued by a group of Democratic congressmen after their party's defeat at the hands of William Henry Harrison's followers in the 1840 presidential contest, who sullenly posed the question in a joint letter to their constituents: "Where are all the living members of the Hartford Convention?" They had a ready answer: "In the Harrison ranks!" (see *An Address of the Democratic Members of Congress from the State of Tennessee to their Constituents*, 26).

5. Hone, *Diary*, 1:486–87.

6. For more on the attacks on Hamilton in the post-Federalist era, see Knott, *Alexander Hamilton and the Persistence of Myth*, 23–46.

7. For more on the public memory of the nation's first president, see Bryan, *George Washington in American Literature;* Longmore, *The Invention of George Washington;* Cunliffe, *George Washington, Man and Monument;* and Schwartz, *George Washington: The Making of an American Symbol.*

8. de Beaumont, *Marie, or, Slavery in the United States,* 106.

9. Given the fact that Jackson's name has often been used to denote the age in which he lived, it is not surprising that Old Hickory's biographers have been inclined to view their subject as a representation of larger themes in American life. Exactly what Jackson's career tells us about his times, however, has been a matter of frustratingly broad disagreement. The debate over the nation's seventh president rages on, as evidenced by very different perspectives taken by Jackson's most recent biographers. In *The Passions of Andrew Jackson,* Andrew Burstein emphasizes his volatile temperament, vindictive character, and anti-intellectualism. Sean Wilentz (in *Andrew Jackson*), on the other hand, admires the populist and democratic ideology (for white males, at least) that informed Old Hickory's politics.

10. British minister Henry Unwin Addington, who witnessed Lafayette's reception in the nation's capital, experienced no hostility during the nation's jubilee (see Addington, *Youthful America,* 68). For more on Lafayette's tour, see Somkin, *Unquiet Eagle.* The outpouring of national pride during the year-long celebration is examined in Burstein, *America's Jubilee.*

11. "Pennsylvania. Address of the Committee of the Harrisburg Convention," *Niles' Weekly Register,* March 20, 1824, 41.

12. Nagel, "The Election of 1824."

13. Eaton, *The Letters of Wyoming to the People of the United States,* 6.

14. Ibid., 47.

15. Jackson to L. H. Coleman, April, 26, 1824, in Jackson, *Correspondence,* 3:250.

16. "Presidential," *Niles' Weekly Register,* March 20, 1824, 41; Hay, "'The Presidential Question,'" 180.

17. *Proceedings and Address of the New Jersey State Convention,* 15; *Address of the Republican General Committee of the Young Men of the City and County of New York,* 35.

18. "Adams and Monarchy," *United States' Telegraph,* May 4, 1827.

19. *A Fair and Just Comparison of the Lives of the Two Candidates, Andrew Jackson and John Quincy Adams,* pts. 1, 2; Josiah Quincy, *Memoir of the Life of John Quincy Adams.*

20. "An Address to the Freemen of Kentucky," *Kentucky Reporter,* January 9, 1828.

21. Remini, *The Election of Andrew Jackson,* 153.

22. *An Impartial and True History of the Life and Services of Major General Andrew Jackson,* quoted in Ward, *Andrew Jackson, Symbol for an Age,* 64.

23. Crawford, *Address to the People of Connecticut, Adopted at the State Convention, Held at Middletown, August 7, 1828,* 7.

24. Benns, *The American Struggle for the British West Indian Carrying Trade.* For criticism of Jackson's West Indian trade policy, see U.S. Congress, *Register of Debates,* 22nd Cong., 1st sess., 750–51.

25. Belohlavek, *Let the Eagle Soar!* 53–73 (quote on p. 73).

26. Prucha, "Andrew Jackson's Indian Policy."

27. *Washington Globe,* quoted in the *Pennsylvanian,* October 18, 1832.

28. Chevalier, *Society, Manners, and Politics in the United States,* 146.

29. For more insight on the complex personality of the seventh president, in addition to the previously cited works by Burstein and Wilentz, see Rogin, *Fathers and Children;* and Curtis, *Andrew Jackson and the Search for Vindication.*

30. Rantoul, *An Oration Delivered before the Democrats and Antimasons, of the County of*

Plymouth, at Scituate, on the Fourth of July, 1836, 19. See also Rantoul, *An Oration Delivered before the Democratic Citizens of the County of Worcester, Worcester, July 4, 1837,* 17.

31. Dusenbery, *Monument to the Memory of General Andrew Jackson,* 47.

32. "British Influence and British Money," *Washington Globe,* October 3, 1840.

33. Dix, *Address of John A. Dix, before the Democracy of Herkimer County, on the 4th of July,* 10.

34. "The British Journals," *Daily Madisonian,* January 30, 1843.

35. *Pennsylvanian,* October 10, 1832.

36. *New York Evening Star,* quoted in *New York Evening Post,* September 17, 1838.

37. *Congressional Globe,* 29th Cong., 1st sess., Appendix, 83.

38. M. J. Heale makes a similar argument, which he labels the "presidential anti-image" (see Heale, *The Presidential Quest*).

39. *Congressional Globe,* 29th Cong., 1st sess., Appendix, 346.

40. Mackay, *The Western World, or, Travels in the United States in 1846–47,* 1:305.

41. *Address of the Democratic Whig Association of the City and County of Philadelphia,* 14–16.

42. For opposition to Webster's Baring connections during his term as secretary of state, see Brownson, *Oration of Orestes A. Brownson, Delivered at Washington Hall, July 5th, 1841,* 10.

43. "Who Is To Be Our Next President?" *New York Herald,* November 23, 1846.

44. Thompson, *An Examination of the Claims of Mr. Van Buren and Gen. Harrison to the Support of the South,* 2. Van Buren was also accused of consistently upholding the dictum, widely attributed to Walpole, that "Every man has his price" (see "The Walpole Maxim," *Charleston Mercury,* August 23, 1837).

45. *Daily National Intelligencer,* September 21, 1836.

46. Hildreth, *William Henry Harrison versus Martin Van Buren,* 44–46; "Mr. Van Buren's Coach," *Washington Globe,* July 27, 1840; "Aristocracy and Democracy," *Louisville (Ky.) Daily Journal,* July 27, 1836. See also Crockett, *The Life of Martin Van Buren,* 80.

47. *New York Evening Post,* August 31, 1838.

48. Ogle, *Speech of Mr. Ogle, of Pennsylvania, on the Regal Splendor of the President's Palace. Delivered in the House of Representatives, April 14, 1840,* 7, 12; Wilson, *The Presidency of Martin Van Buren,* 196–97.

49. "Old Tip and the Log-Cabin Boys," quoted in Norton, *The Great Revolution of 1840,* 82. Another Whig song included the following bit of doggerel: "My light English coach, though often it flew,/Couldn't match the hard gray of old Tippecanoe" (quoted in Lynch, *An Epoch and a Man,* 455).

50. "The Election of 1800 and of 1840," *Washington Globe,* August 7, 1840.

51. Tract no. V, in Colton, *The Junius Tracts,* p. 16. Throughout the summer and fall of 1840 the *Washington Globe* offered its readers a surfeit of breathless editorials linking the Whig nominee to transatlantic abolitionism (see, e.g., "Harrison and Abolition," May 12, 1840; "General Harrison an Abolitionist," July 29, 1840; "British Influence," September 23, 1840; and "The Abolition Ticket," November 5, 1840).

52. Daniel Webster had made a well-publicized trip to England the year before, giving rise to the suspicion in Democratic circles that Harrison would require the federal government to assume or otherwise secure the states' foreign loans (see "The Great Money Conspiracy between the British Whigs in England and America," *Washington Extra Globe,* October 12, 1840).

53. "British Influence," *Pennsylvanian,* September 15, 1840; "More Humbug," *Pennsylvanian,* August 27, 1840; "England Is Now within Forty-Eight Hours of a State of Barter," *Washington Globe,* October 10, 1840.

54. *Congressional Globe,* 26th Cong., 2nd sess., Appendix, 114–20 (quote on p. 120). Benton was not the only Democrat to blame the British for the outcome; see Woodbury, *Speech of the Hon. Levi Woodbury, Delivered at the Democratic Meeting in Jefferson Hall, Portsmouth (N.H.) November, 18, 1841,* 11. For the Whigs' response, see the *Congressional Globe,* 28th Cong., 1st sess., Appendix, 321.

55. W. A. Richmond to Lucius Lyon, April 15, 1844, Lucius Lyon Papers, William L. Clements Library, University of Michigan.

56. *Pennsylvanian,* April 23, 1842.

57. Paul, *Rift in the Democracy,* 37–38.

58. Henry Clay to the Editors of the *Washington Daily National Intelligencer,* April 27, 1844, in Clay, *Papers,* 10:41–46; *Washington Globe,* April 27, 1844.

59. Barton, *The Randolph Epistles.* Michael A. Morrison argues that Van Buren's role as party standard-bearer, though seriously compromised by his anti-Texas stand, was already in serious jeopardy before he issued his famous letter opposing annexation (see Morrison, "Martin Van Buren, the Democracy, and the Partisan Politics of Texas Annexation").

60. "Great Britain," *Niles' Weekly Register,* May 6, 1843, 145.

61. Lyon to Cass, May 2, 1844, Michigan Pioneer and Historical Society, *Historical Collections,* 27:578.

62. "General Cass' Letter in Favor of Immediate Annexation," *Detroit Free Press,* May 22, 1844.

63. Edwin A. Miles correctly notes that the Oregon issue did not play as prominent a role in the 1844 campaign as was once commonly supposed (see Miles, "'Fifty-Four Forty or Fight,'—An American Political Legend"). Nonetheless, for a sampling of Democratic charges that the Whigs were weak on the issue of national defense, see "General Jackson's Letter," *Niles' Weekly Register,* October 5, 1844; and "Political-Presidential, The South in Danger!!" *Niles' Weekly Register,* 140.

64. Yeadon, *Speech of Richard Yeadon, Esq., of Charleston, South Carolina, . . . at the Court-House in Madison Georgia;* "James K. Polk's Ancestors," *Niles' Weekly Register,* August 3, 1844, 372–73.

65. Green, *The Voice of Warning,* 1–2.

66. See, e.g., "British Gold and the Tariff," *Niles' Weekly Register,* September 21, 1844, 39; "British Gold," October 5, 1844, *Niles' Weekly Register,* 77; *British Gold to Buy!!,* undated broadside from Zanesville, Ohio, in Coffinberry Family Papers, Western Reserve Historical Society.

67. Clayton, *Speech of the Hon. John M. Clayton, at the Delaware Mass Whig Convention, held at Wilmington, June 15, 1844,* 2–3.

68. George T. M. Davis et al., to Henry Clay, November 19, 1844, in Clay, *Papers,* 10:151.

69. Warburton, *Hochelaga,* 366–67.

6 "Politically Free, Commercial Slaves"

1. Cohen, "The Auction System in the Port of New York."

2. See, e.g., Carey, *Essays on Political Economy;* List, *The National System of Political Economy;* and List, *Outlines of American Political Economy.*

3. Niles's journalistic career is examined in Luxon, *Niles' Weekly Register: News Magazine of the Nineteenth Century.* See also Schmidt, *Hezekiah Niles and American Economic Nationalism;* and Stone, *Hezekiah Niles as an Economist.*

4. Largely for this reason, Niles was slow to accept the need for a central bank, another key feature of Clay's economic agenda and an institution Niles suspected of contrib-

uting to the maldistribution of wealth and the creation of paper fortunes at the expense of the labor (see "A Nation's Wealth," *Niles' Weekly Register*, May 17, 1817, 177–78).

5. "Southern Excitement," *Niles' Weekly Register*, September 20, 1828, 60.

6. "Brandywine," *Niles Weekly Register*, July 23, 1825, 321–22.

7. "Great Britain, &c.," *Niles' Weekly Register*, January 27, 1827, 339.

8. "The British Parliament," *Niles' Weekly Register*, June 16, 1825, 241–42.

9. Colton, *The Life, Correspondence, and Speeches of Henry Clay*, 5:221. The statement would become a rallying cry for protectionist Whigs (see Clayton, *Speech of the Hon. John M. Clayton, at the Delaware Mass Whig Convention, held at Wilmington, June 15, 1844*, 13).

10. Andrew Jackson, for example, favored modest protection for defense-related industries during his brief career as a Tennessee senator (see Andrew Jackson to L. H. Coleman, April 26, 1824, in Jackson, *Correspondence*, 3:249–51). The tariff as a means of safeguarding the national domain was still being used as late as the 1840s; see, e.g., *Report of the Discussion at Pottsville—August 10, 1844, Between J. G. Clarkson & F. W. Hughes, on the Course of Henry Clay and James K. Polk, Relative to the Protective System*, 11.

11. *Annals of Congress*, 14th Cong., 1st sess., 1335.

12. White, *Memoir of Samuel Slater, the Father of American Manufactures*, 14; "Return of Thanks!" *Niles' Weekly Register*, September 26, 1829, 65.

13. "British Distresses," *Niles' Weekly Register*, December 28, 1816, 284.

14. *Annals of Congress*, 16th Cong., 1st sess., 1926; Rothbard, *Panic of 1819*.

15. *Annals of Congress*, 16th Cong., 1st sess., 1916–46 (quote on p. 1926).

16. Hezekiah Niles, not surprisingly, took an especially cynical view of Britain's new-found advocacy of free trade (see "The British Parliament," *Niles' Weekly Register*, June 16, 1825, 241–42).

17. *Annals of Congress*, 18th Cong., 1st sess., 1635.

18. Ibid., 1977.

19. For a typical rebuttal to Clay's American System, see *Annals of Congress*, 18th Cong., 1st sess., 2101, 2115. Andrew Jackson declared that Clay's so-called American system was but a "British system of corrupt influence in Embryo" (see "Paper Read to the Cabinet," September 18, 1833, in Jackson, *Correspondence*, 5:194).

20. Following passage of the Tariff of Abominations in 1828, Cooper predicted that South Carolina and Georgia would secede from the Union within a year (see Thomas Cooper to Joseph Parker, February 21, 1829, Thomas Cooper Papers, Caroliniana Library, University of South Carolina).

21. For a comprehensive summary of Cooper's economic views, see his *Lectures on the Elements of Political Economy*. For more on Thomas Cooper, see Malone, *The Public Life of Thomas Cooper*; and Kilbride, "Slavery and Utilitarianism."

22. "Querist," *Charleston City Gazette*, August 14, 1827. Similar allegations were leveled at Robert Turnbull, author of *The Crisis*, who had been born in West Florida when it was under Spanish control and who was educated in England.

23. Eckes, *Opening America's Market*, 23.

24. *Niles' Weekly Register*, September 20, 1828, 49. More than two and a half years later, Niles was still attributing Southern agitation over the tariff to a transatlantic conspiracy (See "Southern Excitement," *Niles' Weekly Register*, May 14, 1831, 177). More circumspect observers agreed with Niles. The Philadelphia economist Matthew Carey, for example, not normally one to succumb to anti-British conspiratorial apparitions, was disturbed by the extent to which Cooper's writings were influenced by the theorists of the Manchester school (see Carey, *Collectanea*, 12).

25. See, e.g., *Charleston Courier*, March 5, 1830. See also "Disunion!" *Charleston Courier*, November 14, 1832.

26. *New York Courier and Enquirer*, August 20, 1830; "The State of the Country," *Niles' Weekly Register*, July 3, 1830, 342.

27. Jackson's July 4, 1831 address is reprinted in Capers, *The Life and Times of C. G. Memminger*, 46–47.

28. "The State of the Country," *Niles' Weekly Register*, July 3, 1830, 342.

29. "From the Beaufort, S.C. Gazette," *Niles' Weekly Register*, September 20, 1828, 61.

30. The quote is taken from a list of resolves issued by a Unionist meeting in the back-country Chester district (see "Anti-Nullification," *Niles' Weekly Register*, April 7, 1832, 92). For similar accounts of Washington Society meetings, see *Proceedings of a General Meeting, Held at Columbia Courthouse*, 14–15; and *Address of the Washington Society to the People of South Carolina*, 4. See also Grimké, *Speech of Thomas S. Grimké, One of the Senators from St. Philip's and St. Michael's, Delivered in the Senate of South Carolina, in December, 1828, during the Debate on Sundry Resolutions, of the Senate and House of Representatives, respecting the Tariff*, 80–81.

31. South Carolina, *The Debate in the South Carolina Legislature, in December, 1830, on the Reports of the Committees of Both Houses in Favor of Convention*, 106.

32. *Charleston Courier*, July 30, 1832, quoting the *Augusta Courier*.

33. "Southern Movements," *Niles' Weekly Register*, July 5, 1828, 301. For similar expressions of nullifiers' confidence that Britain would support the state in its trial with Washington, see *Charleston Courier*, July 30, 1832; and "The Secret History of Nullification," *Washington Globe*, December 22, 1832. Some leaders of the movement, however, perhaps mindful that they had overplayed their hand, sought to stifle Anglophobic alarmism. George McDuffie, for example, dismissed the war scare in 1831 as an attempt to "alarm the timid" (see McDuffie, *Speech of the Hon. George McDuffie, May 19, 1831*, 28).

34. In an effort to demonstrate their anti-protection bona fides, Unionists often vied with their opponents in condemning federal tariff policy. In doing so, however, they may well have contributed to the prevailing mood of economic anxiety that gripped the state, thus undercutting their own appeals for caution (see "Speech before the Union Party, July 4th, 1831," in Legaré, *Writings*, 1:271; and Ford, *The Origins of Southern Radicalism*).

35. *Address of the Washington Society to the People of South Carolina*, 3. See also *Charleston Courier*, September 25, 1830; and Grimké, *Speech of Thomas S. Grimké, One of the Senators from St. Philip's and St. Michael's, Delivered in the Senate of South Carolina, in December, 1828, during the Debate on Sundry Resolutions, of the Senate and House of Representatives, respecting the Tariff*, 80–81.

36. U.S. Congress, *Register of Debates*, 21st Cong., 1st sess., 923.

37. "The State of the Country," *Niles' Weekly Register*, July 3, 1830, 343.

38. *Proceedings of a General Meeting, Held at Columbia Courthouse*, November 18, 1831.

39. "Old '76," *Charleston City Gazette*, August 14, 1827. See also "A Native Carolinian," *Charleston Courier*, August 25, 1832, in which the followers of Thomas Cooper were castigated as "submissionists to the Tories of Great Britain!"

40. Turnbull, *The Crisis, or, Essays on the Usurpations of the Federal Government*.

41. *Address of the Washington Society to the People of South Carolina*, 4. See also U.S. Congress, *Register of Debates*, 21st Cong., 1st sess., 940–41; and "To the Union Party of the Congressional District of Charleston," *Charleston Courier*, August 20, 1833. Turnbull himself sought to allay these fears, arguing that South Carolina, unlike the British West Indies, was strong enough "to grapple with any set of usurpers, foreign and domestic" (see Turnbull, *The Crisis*, 129).

42. U.S. Congress, *Register of Debates*, 22nd Cong., 1st sess., 3643; U.S. Congress, *Register of Debates*, 22nd Cong., 1st sess., 597.

43. See, e.g., John Quincy Adams's 1832 report on the tariff (House Committee on Manufactures, *Tariff—Manufactures: May 23, 1832.*)

44. Clay, *Speech of Henry Clay, in Defence of the American System*, 11.

45. "Proclamation," in U.S. President, *A Compilation of the Messages and Papers of the Presidents*, 3:1217. Jackson's private correspondence offers no evidence that he believed the threat of British interference to be a credible one, although widespread rumors of British intrigue may have served to harden the Anglophobic president's determination to summarily quash the states' rights movement. The administration news organ, on the other hand, was considerably less circumspect in predicting that "colonial bondage" would be the result should South Carolina separate from the Union (see "What Next?" *Washington Globe*, December 4, 1832).

46. *Congressional Globe*, 27th Cong., and sess., Appendix, 918.

47. Robert J. Walker, "Report from the Secretary of the Treasury," in *State Papers and Speeches on the Tariff*. Walker's role in spearheading the measure in Congress is briefly examined in Shenton, *Robert John Walker: A Politician from Jackson to Lincoln*, 70–86.

48. Although Britain's repeal of the Corn Laws is generally attributed to domestic political pressure (i.e., the demand for a steady supply and lower price of foodstuffs), some economists draw attention to British free trade advocates' interest in gaining access to lucrative American markets (see James and Lake, "The Second Face of Hegemony").

49. For a sampling of Whig charges, see the following pages from the *Congressional Globe*, 29th Cong., 1st sess.: Appendix, 964; 1006; 1067; Appendix, 964. See also Eiselen, *The Rise of Pennsylvania Protection*, 188.

50. Taussig, *The Tariff History of the United States*, 77.

51. "Fourth Annual Message," in U.S. President, *Messages and Papers of the Presidents*, 5:2504.

7 THE MONEY POWER OF ENGLAND

1. For more on Taylor, see Mudge, *The Social Philosophy of John Taylor of Caroline*; Shalhope, *John Taylor of Caroline: Pastoral Republican*; Tate, *Conservatism and Southern Intellectuals*, 12–20, 77–87; and O'Brien, *Conjectures of Order*, 785–99.

2. Taylor, *Tyranny Unmasked*, 131.

3. Ibid., 310.

4. Taylor, *An Enquiry into Principles and Tendency of Certain Public Measures*, 22.

5. Taylor, *Construction Construed, and Constitutions Vindicated*, 251.

6. Taylor, *Tyranny Unmasked*, 19, 166, 219.

7. Ibid., 163. In a similar vein, Taylor likened the protectionist lobby's many promises of prosperity to those of an unscrupulous polygamist intent on wooing several women at once (see *Annals of Congress*, 18th Cong., 1st sess., 686–87).

8. Hone, *Diary*, 2:722.

9. Simms, *The Social Principle*, 35. For similar remarks from Hezekiah Niles, see "Review," *Niles' Weekly Register*, August 31, 1816, 6.

10. *An Address to the Workingmen of the City and County of Philadelphia*, 6. See also Churchill Cambreleng, "House of Representatives," *Niles' Weekly Register*, May 8, 1830, 208; and Rantoul, *Memoirs, Speeches and Writings of Robert Rantoul, Jr.*, 277.

11. Simpson, *The Working Man's Manual*, 39.

12. *Republican Meeting of the Citizens of Washington City Friendly to the Re-election of Andrew Jackson to the Presidency* [1832], 11.

13. "The Question, " *Washington Globe*, November 1, 1834.

14. *The Man*, June 29, 1835, quoted in *A Documentary History of American Industrial So-*

ciety, 6:41. For an overview of the emerging divisions within American labor, see Laurie, *Artisans into Workers*, 47–73. The most in-depth analysis of this issue as it pertains to the laboring classes of New York City is Wilentz, *Chants Democratic*.

15. Prominent English-born labor leaders included George Henry Evans, a founder of the New York's Working Men's movement, and Philadelphia's William Heighton, who helped organize the Mechanics' Union of Trade Association. For more on the transatlantic connections among artisan labor groups, see Wilentz, *Chants Democratic*, 176–90; and Jentz, "Artisans, Evangelicals, and the City," 119–21. The symbiotic relationship between American and British working-class political activism is examined in Boston, *British Chartists in America*; and Yearley, *Britons in American Labor*.

16. *Pennsylvanian*, April 2, 1834.

17. *Evening Star*, January 18, 1834, quoted in Shank, "The Bowery Theatre," 379–80.

18. *New York Journal of Commerce*, June 10, 1835, quoted in *A Documentary History of American Industrial Society*, 5:308–9. Other examples in which master mechanics characterized union organizing among their journeymen as an "evil of foreign growth" include the Philadelphia House Carpenters' Strike of 1836 and the Boston House Carpenters' Strike of 1825 (see ibid., 6:52, 76–77).

19. *New York Evening Post*, quoted in *A Documentary History of American Industrial Society*, 4:325–33. Also quoted in "Tailors' Combination Trial," *Niles' Weekly Register*, June 25, 1836; "The Recent Strike," *New York Herald*, August 2, 1836; and *New York Herald*, October 19, 1835.

20. *Register of Debates*, 22nd Cong., 1st sess., 3384.

21. "Lowell," *Niles' Weekly Register*, July 11, 1835, 324. For more on Appleton and the Lowell Mills experiment, see Gregory, *Nathan Appleton*; and Sanford, "The Intellectual Origins and New-Worldliness of American Industry."

22. *Voice of Industry*, October 9, 1839, in *A Documentary History of American Industrial Society*, 7:88–89. See also Massachusetts House Document, no. 50, March, 1845, ibid., 8:133–87 passim; and *Workingmen's Advocate*, June 29, 1844, ibid., 8:88.

23. "The Working People of Manayunk to the Public," *Pennsylvanian*, August 28, 1833; "The Factory System," *Working Man's Advocate*, March 24, 1832; Sullivan, *The Industrial Worker in Pennsylvania*, 48; Laurie, *Working People of Philadelphia*. Cynthia J. Shelton argues that these instances of labor militancy reached across occupational lines, enlisting support from local artisans and mechanics, and thereby creating, if only briefly, a transatlantic working-class ideology (see Shelton, *The Mills of Manayunk*).

24. "Remarks of Mr. Commerford," *Workingmen's Advocate*, March 30, 1844. See also *The Man*, September 17, 1834.

25. For more on British-American financial relations, see Smith and Cole, *Fluctuations in American Business*; and Hidy, "The Organization and Function of Anglo-American Merchant Bankers." For more on the Baring financial empire, see Ziegler, *The Sixth Great Power*; and Hidy, *The House of Baring in American Trade and Finance*.

26. Wallis, "The Depression of 1839 to 1843," 16.

27. Clark and Hall, *Legislative and Documentary History of the Bank of the United States*, 273.

28. *Congressional Globe*, 26th Cong., 1st sess., Appendix, 136. For more on the impact of easy credit on American manufacturing, see Cohen, "The Auction System in the Port of New York."

29. Godwin, *Democracy, Constructive and Pacific, 1844*, 20. See also Hale, *Useful Knowledge for the Producers of Wealth*, 14–15; and Stubblebine, *The Man Child Ruling the Nations with a Rod of Iron, and Breaking to Pieces the Great Red Dragon of the European Laws in America*.

30. "Debate on the Prospective Pre-Emption Bill," *Niles' Weekly Register*, February 6, 1841, 365.

31. *Legislative and Documentary History of the Bank of the United States*, 183, 203.

32. Gouge, *A Short History of Paper Money and Banking*, 44. Echoing American anxieties was a cohort of Britons, including William Cobbett, who denounced their government's policies of economic imperialism (see "The Infernal Paper Money," *The Man*, August 26, 1834). For more on Cobbett's influence in the United States, see Wilson, *Paine and Cobbett*.

33. Catterall, *The Second Bank of the United States*, 201.

34. *Register of Debates*, Senate, 22nd Cong., 1st sess., 538.

35. Benton, *Thirty Years' View*, 1:261.

36. "The Veto and the Bank," *Washington Globe*, August 6, 1832.

37. *Proceedings and Address, of the Committee of the Anti Jackson Men of Franklin County, Pennsylvania*, 34.

38. At the time of the "bank war," banking historian Bray Hammond estimates, foreign shareholders owned only $8 million of the bank's $35 million total capital (see Hammond, *Banks and Politics in America*, 407–8).

39. "Speech of Mr. King, of Georgia," *Niles' Weekly Register*, October 21, 1837, 122.

40. Marshall, "The Authorship of Jackson's Bank Veto Message," 469; "Veto Message," in U.S. President, *A Compilation of the Messages and Papers of the Presidents*, 3:1144.

41. *Register of Debates*, 23rd Cong., 1st sess., 2282.

42. Sexton, *Debtor Diplomacy*, 23.

43. While economic historians disagree over the impact of the Jackson administration's banking policies, most notably the famous Specie Circular in 1836, they are in general agreement that the Bank of England's decision to sharply raise its bank rate in 1837 precipitated the crisis (see Hammond, *Banks and Politics in America*, 457–58; and Temin, *The Jacksonian Economy*, 137–38).

44. Jenks, *The Migration of British Capital to 1875*, 87.

45. "Speech of Mr. Clay, of Ky. on the Sub-Treasury Bill," *Niles' Weekly Register*, February 22, 1840, 405.

46. Colton, *The Crisis of the Country*, 11. See also Sullivan, *Considerations Which Tend to Prove That a States' National Bank, is Necessary to Countervail the Injurious Effects of the New Banking System of England on the Revenue, Domestic Commerce, Manufactures, and Internal Improvements of the United States, Respectfully Addressed to the President*, 4.

47. Govan, *Nicholas Biddle*, 333.

48. Among the many anti-bank *Globe* editorials, see "Policy of the Bank of England and its Branch in the United States," *Washington Globe*, May 1, 1837.

49. *Washington Globe*, quoted in the *Pennsylvanian*, August 12, 1837.

50. "Great Meeting in Baltimore," *Niles' Weekly Register*, June 3, 1837, 215. Ironically, Biddle, though no Anglophobe, was an economic nationalist and a firm believer in American fiscal independence (see Govan, *Nicholas Biddle*, 349, 356, 358).

51. D'Arusmont, *What is the Matter? A Political Address as Delivered in Masonic Hall, October 28th, 1838*, 20.

52. Govan, *Nicholas Biddle*, 352–407; Dickens, *American Notes for General Circulation*, 67.

53. Sullivan, *Popular Explanation of the System of Circulating Medium Recently Published in the Form of an Act of Congress*, 18; "Thoughts on the Times," *Democratic Review* 6 (December 1839): 452–59.

54. The eight states were Mississippi, Michigan, Pennsylvania, Maryland, Indiana, Illinois, Arkansas, and Louisiana. In addition, the Florida Territory also defaulted on its interest payments (see Jenks, *Migration of British Capital*, 88).

55. *The Cause of the Hard Times*, 2.

56. For more on the independent treasury debate, see Wilson, *The Presidency of Martin Van Buren*, 61–146 passim.

57. "Third Annual Message," in U.S. President, *A Compilation of the Messages and Papers of the Presidents*, 4:1762–63.

58. *Congressional Globe*, 26th Cong., 1st sess., Appendix, 136; *Congressional Globe*, 26th Cong., 1st sess., Appendix, 122; Wilson, *Martin Van Buren*, 87.

59. Evidence for the latter allegation stemmed from an October 1839 circular issued by Barings, expressing the opinion that Washington might be required to guarantee future loans to the states (see "The Great Money Conspiracy between the British Whigs in England and America," *Washington Extra Globe*, October 12, 1840; and "Letter No. 2, June 15, 1840," in Sutherland, *Three Political Letters, Addressed to D. Wolfred Nelson*, 30–31).

60. Timberlake, "The Specie Standard and Central Banking in the United States before 1860," 338.

61. Sullivan, *Considerations Which Tend to Prove that a States' National Bank is Necessary to Countervail the Injurious Effects of the New Banking System of England on the Revenue, Domestic Commerce, Manufactures, and Internal Improvements of the United States, Respectfully Addressed to the President*, 5.

62. Benton, *Thirty Years' View*, 2:313–14.

63. Aldrich, *Address of the Phi Gamma Society of Cokebury Seminary, Abbeville District*, 6.

64. Pickens, *Remarks of Hon. F. W. Pickens, on the Separation of the Government from All Banks. Delivered in the House of Representatives, Oct. 10, 1837*, 12.

65. Aldrich, *Address of the Phi Gamma Society of Cokebury Seminary, Abbeville District*, 6. See also "Is Southern Civilization Worth Preserving?" *Southern Quarterly Review* 3 (January 1851): 32–33.

66. Pickens, *Remarks of Hon. F. W. Pickens, on the Separation of the Government from All Banks. Delivered in the House of Representatives, Oct. 10, 1837*, 12.

67. Pickens, *Speech of Hon. F. W. Pickens, of South Carolina, on the Loan Bill*, 3.

8 "An Army of Fanatics"

1. The only full-length study of the American Colonization Society is Staudenraus, *The African Colonization Movement*. For a yearly table of colonists sent to Liberia, see p. 251. More recently, Douglas R. Egerton has argued that proslavery leaders within the organization operated behind the scenes to shape the group's agenda (see Egerton, "'Its Origin Is Not a Little Curious'").

2. In charting the rise of radical antislavery doctrine, David Brion Davis describes the similarities of the two movements as "a striking coincidence," but adds that American abolitionists modeled their campaigns after those established in Great Britain (see Davis, "The Emergence of Immediatism in British and Antislavery Thought," 226, 227). For more on the connections between the American and British antislavery movements, see Fladeland, *Men and Brothers*.

3. *The Liberator*, January 1, 1831.

4. Before sailing for England, Garrison published *Thoughts on Colonization*, a pamphlet attacking the ACS, which gained wide distribution in British antislavery circles before his arrival.

5. For more on the Garrison-Cresson feud, see Stuart, *British Opinions of the American Colonization Society*; and Blackett, "Anglo-American Opposition to Liberian Colonization."

6. *New York Commercial Advertiser*, October 3, 1833.

7. "Mr. Editor . . . ," *New York Courier and Enquirer*, September 30, 1833. For more on the public unrest following Garrison's return, see Richards, "*Gentlemen of Property and Standing*," 23–30; and Wyatt-Brown, *Lewis Tappan and the Evangelical War against Slavery*, 104–5.

8. "Letter from London—Wilberforce—O'Connell," *The Liberator*, August 23, 1834.

9. "Mr. Walsh's Appeal," *North American Review* 10 (April 1820): 368. See also "Cant-Cant-Cant," *Niles' Weekly Register*, May 14, 1825, 162.

10. According to Adam Rothman, 3,600 slaves were taken from the Chesapeake area, while 200 more were evacuated after the Battle of New Orleans (see Rothman, "The Expansion of Slavery in the Deep South," 278). For more on African American collaboration with Great Britain during the Revolution and the War of 1812, see Schama, *Rough Crossings*; Frey, *Water from the Rock*; Buckley, *Slaves in Red Coats*, 150–51; and Richardson, *Moral Imperium*, 170–71.

11. "Savage Barbarity!" *The Liberator*, October 1, 1831.

12. Fearon, *Sketches of America*, 239–40, 57–61.

13. Faux, *Memorable Days in America*, 1:85, 88.

14. For more on Northern anti-abolition sentiment, see Richards, *Gentlemen of Property and Standing*; Ratner, *Powder Keg*; and Tise, *Pro-Slavery*.

15. "Faux's Memorable Days in America," *North American Review* 19 (July 1824): 105. For additional examples of New England resentment of British antislavery criticism, see "The Little Master and His Little Slave," in Child, *Evenings in New England*, 138; and Child, *An Appeal in Favor of That Class of Americans Called Africans*, 79.

16. "Annexation of Texas," *Southern Quarterly Review* 6 (October 1844): 504; Cunliffe, *Chattel Slavery and Wage Slavery*.

17. Leggett, *Democratick Editorials*, 194.

18. "Hammond's Letters on Slavery," in *The Pro-Slavery Argument as Maintained by the Most Distinguished Writers of the Southern States containing the Several Essays, on the Subject, of Chancellor Harper, Governor Hammond, Dr. Simms, and Professor Dew*, 139.

19. Whitman, *The Gathering of the Forces*, 1:43.

20. See, e.g., *Annals of Congress*, 16th Cong., 1st sess., 404–5; "The Slave Trade," *Niles' Weekly Register*, October 6, 1821, 83; and "Cant-Cant-Cant," *Niles' Weekly Register*, May 14, 1825, 162.

21. William Lloyd Garrison to the Liberator, May 24, 1833, in Garrison, *Letters*, 1:233.

22. Gross, "The Abolition of Negro Slavery and British Parliamentary Reform."

23. Adams, *Memoirs*, 11:406–7.

24. *Annals of Congress*, 15th Cong., 2nd sess., 307; *Annals of Congress*, 15th Cong., 2nd sess., 1211; *Annals of Congress*, 16th Cong., 1st sess., 388.

25. Foster, *An Errand of Mercy*, 53.

26. For a discussion of the Unitarian contribution to the slavery crusade, see Stange, *British Unitarians against Slavery*.

27. *Fourth Annual Report of the Board of Managers of the New England Anti-Slavery Society, 1836*, 41.

28. Anderson, *Joyous Greetings*; Sklar, "'Women Who Speak for an Entire Nation.'"

29. Maria Weston Chapman to Elizabeth Pease, August 30, 1838, in *British and American Abolitionists*, 66.

30. Walker, *Walker's Appeal, in Four Articles*, 47. Less incendiary African American spokesmen expressed similar sentiments; see, e.g., "God Bless Great Britain," *The Liberator*, April 4, 1835.

31. Fearon, *Sketches of America*, 57. For an indication of the gratitude African Ameri-

cans who had fled to Canada felt for Great Britain, see Steward, *Twenty-two Years a Slave, and Forty Years a Freeman,* 323–26. See also Charles Dickens to John Forster, April 15, 1842, in Dickens, *Letters,* 3:198.

32. *First Annual Report of the Board of Managers of the New England Anti-Slavery Society, 1833,* 13; Garrison and Garrison, *William Lloyd Garrison,* 1:283.

33. "Address," *Anti-Slavery Reporter,* October 1833.

34. Barnes, *The Anti-Slavery Impulse,* 33.

35. "Sentiments and Sympathies of British Christians," *New York Evangelist,* October 4, 1834.

36. Edmund Quincy to R. D. Webb, May 23, 1846, in *British and American Abolitionists,* 268.

37. "London Missionary Society," *New York Observer and Chronicle,* June 28, 1834.

38. Wendell Phillips to George Thompson, July 29, 1839, in *British and American Abolitionists,* 74.

39. William Lloyd Garrison to Samuel May, September 6, 1840, in Garrison, *Letters,* 2:696; Garrison to Harriet Minot, March 19, 1833, ibid., 1:215.

40. William Lloyd Garrison to Helen E. Garrison, July 3, 1840, ibid., 2:661.

41. "Riot in New York," *The Liberator,* October 12, 1833.

42. *Declaration of Sentiments Adopted by the Peace Convention, held in Boston, September 18, 19, and 20, 1838.*

43. Garrison to Elisha Pease, September 30, 1840, in Garrison, *Letters,* 2:708.

44. Louis Cowan to William Lloyd Garrison, June 21, 1834, in *British and American Abolitionists,* 32.

45. See, e.g., Trollope, *Domestic Manners of the Americans,* , 247; Martineau, *Society in America,* 2:119; and Martineau, *The Martyr Age of the United States,* 1.

46. "For the Courier," *Charleston Courier,* July 19, 1833; "To the Union Party of the Congressional District of Charleston," *Charleston Courier,* August 20, 1833. For more on the impact of Britain's antislavery crusade in the South, see Wilkins, "Window on Freedom." Kenneth S. Greenberg examines the ways in which British and New England antislavery movements merged in the minds of Southern slaveholders in *Masters and Statesmen,* 107–23.

47. William Harper, "Anniversary Oration," *Charleston Mercury,* April 23, 1836.

48. "English Views," *Charleston Mercury,* November 4, 1835.

49. Barker, *Captain Charles Stuart, Anglo-American Abolitionist,* 89, 119.

50. Thompson gave his account of the incident in Thompson and Breckenridge, *Discussion of American Slavery,* 99–100.

51. "Cowardice and Ruffianism," *The Liberator,* December 6, 1834. For more on Thompson's American tour, see Rice, "The Anti-Slavery Mission of George Thompson to the United States."

52. "The Voice of New York," *Niles' Weekly Register,* September 5, 1835, 9. The residents of Barnstead, New Hampshire, drafted a similar list of resolves (see *Congressional Globe,* 24th Cong., 1st sess., Appendix, 91).

53. "George Thompson," *The Religious Intelligencer,* September 19, 1835, 249. The Garrisonians had clearly failed to anticipate the anti-British hostility that accompanied Thompson's visit, and sought to minimize the damage, comparing the Agency Committee speaker to another famous foreigner, the Marquis de Lafayette (see "George Thompson," *The Liberator,* September 12, 1835; see also "British and Foreign Society for the Abolition of Slavery," *The Liberator,* June 6, 1835).

54. "Mr. Garrison's Policy," *Boston Recorder,* October 23, 1835; "George Thompson in the Right," *Boston Recorder,* November 13, 1845; "British Abolitionists and American Politics," *Boston Recorder,* October 7, 1836.

55. Wise, *Speech of Mr. Wise, of Virginia, on the Subject of Abolition of Slavery within the District of Columbia.*

56. "Seventh Annual Message," in U.S. President, *A Compilation of the Messages and Papers of the Presidents,* 3:1394.

57. "Slavery and the Abolitionists," *Niles' Weekly Register,* October 3, 1835, 80; Grimsted, *American Mobbing,* 116–17.

58. *New York Star,* October 23, 1835, quoted in "Abolition Troubles," *Niles' Weekly Register,* October 31, 1835, 145–46.

59. *Papers Relating to the Garrison Mob,* 14.

60. C. Duncan Rice argues that Thompson's greatest contribution to the transatlantic antislavery movement may have been to whip up support for American abolitionist groups upon his return to Great Britain (see Rice, "The Anti-Slavery Mission of George Thompson to the United States," 29).

61. Lerner, *The Grimké Sisters from South Carolina,* 119–20.

62. See, e.g., Ludlow, *A Thanksgiving Sermon, Preached in the Church Street Church, New Haven, Nov. 19, 1840,* 17–18.

63. Channing, *Remarks on the Slavery Question in a Letter to Jonathan Phillips,* 72.

64. "The Bondmen of the South," *North American Magazine* 4 (August 1834): 252.

65. Paulding, *Letters from the South,* 2:211–12; Paulding, *Slavery in the United States,* 123.

66. "Abolition," *Charleston Mercury,* May 15, 1839.

67. Preston, *Speech of Mr. Preston, of South Carolina, in the Senate of the United States, March 1, 1836, on the Abolition Question.*

68. Harwood, "British Evangelical Abolitionism and American Churches in the 1830s," 294; Mathews, *Slavery and Methodism.*

69. "Efforts to Raise a Mob," *The Philanthropist,* July 22, 1836.

70. *Guernsey Times and Farmers' and Mechanics' Advocate,* August 15, 1836.

71. Folk, "'The Queen City of Mobs,'" 335–38.

72. Richards, *Gentlemen of Property and Standing,* 107.

73. "Perfectly Right," *Philadelphia Public Ledger,* December 1, 1838.

74. Sturge, *A Visit to the United States in 1841,* 143.

75. *Congressional Globe,* 24th Cong., 1st sess., Appendix, 99; *Congressional Globe,* 25th Cong., 3rd sess., Appendix, 238.

76. *Congressional Globe,* 24th Cong., 2nd sess., Appendix, 308. See also *Congressional Globe,* 27th Cong., 1st sess., Appendix, 72.

77. Temperley, *British Antislavery,* 206–7.

78. Of the 409 delegates in attendance, all hailed from Great Britain or its colonial possessions save for 40 Americans and half a dozen delegates from France (see Maynard, "The World's Anti-Slavery Convention of 1840").

79. Stewart, *Wendell Phillips, Liberty's Hero.*

80. For more on the impact of the conference on the women's rights movement, see Sklar, "'Women Who Speak for an Entire Nation.'"

81. Playfair, *Brother Jonathan,* 3:203.

82. *New York Herald,* quoted in Playfair, *Brother Jonathan,* 2:59. For more on the American delegates post-conference activities, see Elizabeth Cady Stanton, *Reminiscences,* chap. 5 passim; and Henry B. Stanton, *Random Recollections,* chaps. 9–12 passim.

83. *Congressional Globe,* 27th Cong., 2nd sess., 171. For more on the mercurial Virginian, see Simpson, *A Good Southerner.* For more on the Wise-Adams exchange, see Miller, *Arguing about Slavery,* 429–42. For evidence of the conference's impact on the election of 1840, see *Congressional Globe,* 26th Cong., 1st sess., Appendix, 253; Playfair, *Brother*

Jonathan, 3:203; and Tyson, *The Doctrines of the "Abolitionists" Refuted, in a Letter from J. Washington Tyson, the Democratic Harrison Candidate for Congress, in the First District, of Pennsylvania* , 7.

84. "Our Relations with England," *Southern Literary Messenger* 8 (June 1842): 387.

85. "The Fanatics and Mr. O'Connell," *New York Courier and Enquirer*, January 1, 1834.

86. Rhett, *Speech of Hon. R. Barnwell Rhett, of South Carolina on the Annexation of Texas to the United States, January 31, 1845,* 7.

87. *Greenville Mountaineer*, October 10, 1835, quoted in Wilkins, "Window on Freedom," 81. See also *Washington Globe*, October 28, 1835.

88. *Congressional Globe*, 27th Cong., 1st sess., Appendix, 72.

89. Drayton, *The South Vindicated from the Treason and Fanaticism of the Northern Abolitionists*, 289. For another example of the proslavery conspiracy thesis during this period, see Reese, *Letters to the Hon. William Jay*.

9 BREAKING THE "IRON HOOP"

1. Stacey, "The Myth of the Unguarded Frontier."

2. For more on the destruction of Negro Fort, see Landers, *Black Slavery in Spanish Florida*, 231–35; Owsley and Smith, *Filibusters and Expansionists;* and Lewis, *The American Union and the Problem of Neighborhood*.

3. Monroe to Jackson, June 2, 1817, in Jackson, *Correspondence*, 2:296.

4. "Military Affairs," no. 164, *Annals of Congress*, 15th Cong., 2nd sess., 688.

5. Jackson to Calhoun, May 5, 1818, in Jackson, *Correspondence*, 2:367; Jackson to Monroe, June 2, 1818, ibid., 2:378.

6. Remini, *Andrew Jackson and His Indian Wars*. See also Prucha, "Andrew Jackson's Indian Policy."

7. "Our Relations with Great Britain," *North American Review* 27 (October 1828): 481.

8. For diplomatic overviews of U.S.-British relations during this period, see Pletcher, *The Diplomacy of Annexation;* Jones, *To the Webster-Ashburton Treaty;* and Jones, *The American Problem in British Diplomacy*.

9. Indian Bureau superintendent Thomas McKenney attributed the trading posts' lack of success to "the influence (principally British) which is spread so generally over that region" (see Thomas McKenney to Calhoun, July 7, 1820, in Calhoun, *Papers*, 5:242–43).

10. Calhoun to A. Smyth, December 29, 1819, in Calhoun, *Papers*, 4:522; Viola, *Thomas L. McKenney, Architect of America's Early Indian Policy*. For more on the efforts of the U.S. government to monitor British activities in Canada and establish control over the northwestern frontier, see Goetzmann, *Army Exploration in the American West*, 3–21.

11. Lewis Cass to Calhoun, August 3, 1819, in Calhoun, *Papers*, 4:201–2. See also Lewis Cass to Calhoun, October 8, 1819, ibid., 4:367; and Lewis Cass to Calhoun, October 9, 1819, ibid., 4:368. Other correspondents with the War Department reported similar findings of British influence (see Jacob Brown to Calhoun, August 23, 1819, ibid., 4:265).

12. Calhoun was particularly anxious that the boundary line between the United States and Canada be well established, to prevent future conflict with the British empire (see Calhoun to Stephen Long, March 8, 1819, in Calhoun, *Papers*, 3:639; Calhoun to A. Smyth, December 29, 1819, ibid., 4:523; and S. Bernard, J. D. Elliot, and Joseph G. Totten to Calhoun, February 7, 1821, ibid., 5:607). Road-building along the New York-Canada border was a special concern for General Jacob Brown, commander of the U.S. Army's Northern Division (see Jacob Brown to Calhoun, September 15, 1819, ibid., 4:327; and Jacob Brown to Calhoun, September 27, 1819, ibid., 4:345–46).

13. Thomas Jefferson to Alexander von Humboldt, December 6, 1813, quoted in

Keller, "Philanthropy Betrayed," 56. Not surprisingly, Jefferson's views on assimilation were complex and often suffered from inconsistency. For more on this issue, see Wallace, *Jefferson and the Indians*; and Sheehan, *Seeds of Extinction*.

14. "Indian Removal," *North American Review* 30 (January 1830): 62–121; Klunder, *Lewis Cass and the Politics of Moderation*; Warrick, "The American Indian Policy in the Upper Old Northwest Following the War of 1812."

15. Deposition of John Barrell, [November 2, 1831], in Whitney, *The Black Hawk War*, 2:175.

16. Rumors of British collusion with the Sauk and Fox tribes were rife in the early 1830s. See, e.g., Edmund P. Gaines to Roger Jones, June 14, 1831, in Whitney, *The Black Hawk War*, 2:49; Joseph M. Street to Lewis Cass, August 26, 1831, ibid., 2:149–50; John Bliss to Henry Atkinson, April 6, 1832, ibid., 2:227; and John Bliss to Henry Atkinson, April 9, 1832, ibid., 2:237. For an overview of these events, see Trask, *Black Hawk*, 121–40.

17. James Fenimore Cooper to Martin Van Buren, March 15, 1840, in Cooper, *Letters and Journals*, 4:25; Satz, *American Indian Policy in the Jacksonian Era*, 224–27.

18. For more on the Canadian rebellions, see Ryerson, *Unequal Union*; Greer, "1837–38: Rebellion Reconsidered"; and Stephen, "The Canadian Rebellion and the Limits of Historical Perspective."

19. Stevens, *Border Diplomacy*; Wilson, *The Presidency of Martin Van Buren*, 147–69.

20. Guillet, *The Lives and Times of the Patriots*.

21. Jones, "Anglophobia and the Aroostook War."

22. The thesis that American expansion stemmed from the drive for new Asiatic markets was first posited by Norman A. Graebner in *Empire on the Pacific: A Study in American Continental Expansion*. Though still useful, Graebner's thesis gave short shrift to one of the most salient aspects of antebellum expansion: the push for lands into the Southwest. For a thorough examination of the Oregon boundary issue, see Merk, *The Oregon Question*; and Rakestraw, *For Honor or Destiny*.

23. U.S. Congress, House Committee on Foreign Affairs, *Territory of Oregon: To Accompany Bill H.R. No. 976 . . . Report*. In the Senate, Missouri Democrat Lewis F. Linn echoed Cushing's alarmism, demanding the abrogation of the 1827 joint agreement on the grounds of national defense (see U.S. Congress, Senate Select Committee on Bill to Authorize the President to Occupy the Oregon Territory, *Report [to Accompany Senate Bill No. 206]*).

24. Adams, *Memoir*, 11:37. For more on Cushing's expansionist views, see Belohlavek, "Race, Progress, and Empire."

25. Perkins, *The Monroe Doctrine*, 74.

26. Quoted in Pratt, "Anglo-American Commercial and Political Rivalry in the Plata," 316, 317.

27. For a meticulous study of British nineteenth-century investment in Mexico, see Costeloe, *Bonds and Bondholders*.

28. Ward, *Mexico in 1827*; Gilmore, "Henry George Ward, British Publicist for Mexican Mines." The Poinsett-Ward rivalry is discussed in some detail in the work of J. Fred Rippy; see his *Rivalry of the United States and Great Britain over Latin America*, and *Joel Poinsett, Versatile American*, 107–11. For an examination of Western diplomacy during this period, see Langhorne and Hamilton, *The Practice of Diplomacy*, 89–182.

29. Forbes, *California*; Engelson, "Proposals for Colonization of California by England in Connection with the Mexican Debt to British Bondholders."

30. Smith, *Thomas ap Catesby Jones*, 93–122.

31. Rumors of British designs on Cuba first appeared as Spain's colonial empire col-

lapsed after the Napoleonic Wars, and continued intermittently throughout much of the century. For early evidence of American fears of British designs on Cuba, see J. R. Mullany to Calhoun, October 7, 1819, in Calhoun, *Papers*, 4:365; and Calhoun to Andrew Jackson, January 22, 1820, ibid., 4:591. See also "Cuba and the Floridas," *Niles' Weekly Register*, January 8, 1820, 305–6.

32. da Costa, *Crowns of Glory, Tears of Blood*; Turner, *Slaves and Missionaries*.

33. Wilkins, "Window on Freedom," 217; Thomas, *Jamaica and Voluntary Laborers from Africa*, 8–9; Green, *British Slave Emancipation*, 191–228; Heuman, "The British West Indies."

34. Thome and Kimball, *Emancipation in the West Indies*, 347. A thorough examination of Harrison's Anglophobic rants in his capacity as U.S. consul in Havana can be found in Wilkins, "Window on Freedom," 107–65; and Rugemer, *The Problem of Emancipation*, 180–221. See also Mitton, "The Upshur Inquiry."

35. The thesis that West Indian slavery was undermined by sugar interests in India is developed in *Southern Quarterly Review* 1 (April 1842): 446–94.

36. Paquette, *Sugar is Made with Blood*, 183–205 passim; Robert M. Harrison to Calhoun, August 23, 1844, in Calhoun, *Papers*, 19:634–35.

37. "War with America a Blessing to Mankind," *Fraser's Magazine for Town and Country* 23 (1841): 494–502. For an example of Southern reaction to the article, see "Speculations on the Consequences of a War with Great Britain," *Southern Literary Messenger* 8 (July 1842): 445–47.

38. Calhoun to William R. King, August 12, 1844, in Calhoun, *Papers*, 19:576–77.

39. "The Life of Commodore Oliver Hazard Perry," *North American Review* 53 (July 1841): 90.

40. "Abolition and Slavery," *Louisville (Ky.) Democrat*, September 15, 1845.

41. Rippy, *Rivalry of the United States and Great Britain over Latin America*, 91–99.

42. Houston to Jackson, February 13, 1833, in Sam Houston, *Writings*, 1:275.

43. [Unsigned] to David Lee Child, October 8, 1835, in *British and American Abolitionists*, 41–42. Southern slaveholders also considered British intervention in Texas a real possibility if the war proved to be a long one (see John Catron to Andrew Jackson, June 8, 1836, in Jackson, *Correspondence*, 5:401–2).

44. Smith, *The Annexation of Texas*, 60.

45. "Lo Here! Lo There!" *The Genius of Universal Emancipation*, January 1823.

46. Lundy, *The Origin and True Causes of the Texas Insurrection*.

47. *Congressional Globe*, 24th Cong., 1st sess., 1836, Appendix, 450.

48. "Slavery in Texas," *Niles' Weekly Register*, September 17, 1836, 38–40.

49. See, e.g., Channing, *A Letter to the Hon. Henry Clay on the Annexation of Texas to the United States*, 28–34; and Thornton, *An Inquiry into the History of Slavery*, 295. For more on the public discourse of annexation, see Rathbun, "The Debate over Annexing Texas and the Emergence of Manifest Destiny."

50. Current, "Webster's Propaganda and the Ashburton Treaty"; Soulsby, *The Right of Search and the Slave Trade in Anglo-American Relations*, 78–116.

51. Young, *Sketch of the Life and Public Services of General Lewis Cass*; *Congressional Globe*, 28th Cong., 1st sess., Appendix, 299.

52. For a full treatment of the Webster-Ashburton Treaty, see Jones, *To the Webster-Ashburton Treaty*. On the Canadian boundary issue, see Carroll, *A Good and Wise Measure*.

53. "The Great Nation of Futurity," *Democratic Review* 4 (November 1839): 427.

54. *Congressional Globe*, 29th Cong., 1st sess., Appendix, 272.

55. Mackay, *The Western World, or, Travels in the United States in 1846–47*, 1:297.

56. "Annexation," *Democratic Review* 17 (July 1845): 5. The provenance of the term

"Manifest Destiny" has recently been challenged by Linda S. Hudson, who believes the unsigned article was written not by *Democratic Review* editor O'Sullivan, but by Jane McManus Storms (see Hudson, *Mistress of Manifest Destiny*, 59–62).

57. The triumphalist nature of Manifest Destiny has dominated the historical literature of the period. See, e.g., Frederick Merk, with Lois Bannister Merk, *The Monroe Doctrine and American Expansionism*; and Merk, *Manifest Destiny and Mission in American History: A Reinterpretation*. This perspective has been echoed by cultural historians such as Albert Boime, who has argued that American landscape painters' fixation on panorama reflected the national "desire for dominance" (see Boime, *The Magisterial Gaze*, 21). A notable exception to this body of literature is Hietala, *Manifest Design*; Hietala argues that a host of anxieties, including Anglophobia, fueled the American desire for more land during the 1840s.

58. Maury, *The Statesmen of America in 1846*, 159–60.

59. *Congressional Globe*, 28th Cong., 1st sess., Appendix, 301.

60. *Congressional Globe*, 29th Cong., 1st sess., Appendix, 80.

61. *Congressional Globe*, 29th Cong., 1st sess., Appendix, 88.

62. Cushing, *Lecture on Oregon*, 2.

63. "European Interference on the American Continent," *American Review* 3 (January 1846): 19.

64. Andrew Jackson to Andrew Jackson Donelson, December 2, 1844, *Correspondence of Andrew Jackson*, 6:335.

65. Andrew Jackson to Sam Houston, March 15, 1844, in Sam Houston, *Writings*, 4:266.

66. Horsman, *Race and Manifest Destiny*, 208–28 passim

10 The Texas Question

1. Inaugural Address, November 10, 1838, in Lamar, *Papers*, 2:319–21. Lamar's ideas on the subject of Texas nationalism were undoubtedly influenced by the former South Carolina governor, James Hamilton (see Hamilton to Lamar, November 3, 1838, ibid., 2:277).

2. In this view Lamar was by no means alone. More than a few Southern slaveholders were so concerned for their section's future in a Union dominated by Northern interests that they too urged Texans to pursue an independent course (see West, "Southern Opposition to the Annexation of Texas").

3. Lamar to T. P. Anderson and Others, November 18, 1845, in Lamar, *Papers*, 4:113.

4. Ashbel Smith, the Texas minister to the Court of St. James's, kept his government routinely informed of the Texas colonization schemes of British antislavery organizations, none of which ever materialized (see Ashbel Smith to Isaac Van Zandt, January 25, 1843, in Texas (Republic) Department of State, *Diplomatic Correspondence of the Republic of Texas*, vol. 2, pt. 2, 1106–7). For more on British colonization efforts, see Narrett, "A Choice of Destiny."

5. For more on the simmering border war between the Texas Republic and Mexico during the years 1842–44, see Haynes, *Soldiers of Misfortune*.

6. Nance, *Attack and Counter-Attack*, 138; Smith, *The Annexation of Texas*, 72. In December 1842, British bondholders had once again been obliged to restructure Mexico's debt, but the arrangement had done little to alleviate the indigent government's cash flow problems.

7. Adams, *British Interests and Activities in Texas*, chap. 4 passim. William Kennedy, the British consul in Texas, complained to the Foreign Office that the American press had been especially active in creating the impression that Great Britain was goading Mexico

to undertake its border harassment of Texas (see Kennedy to Aberdeen, June 15, 1842, in *British Diplomatic Correspondence concerning the Republic of Texas*, 69; see also Anderson, *The Letter of Alexander Anderson of Tennessee in Reply to the Committee of Invitation to Attend a Dinner Given by the Democracy of Maury, Tennessee on the 13th July to the Delegation from That State to the National Convention*). For an historian's view of the extent and limits of British influence over Mexico, see Roeckell, "Bonds over Bondage."

8. Van Zandt to Jones, April 19, 1843, in *Diplomatic Correspondence of the Republic of Texas*, vol. 2, pt. 2, 165. Historians have traditionally characterized Tyler as a narrow-minded sectionalist dedicated to the pursuit of slaveholding interests. See, e.g., Merk, *Slavery and the Annexation of Texas*; Merk regards Tyler's Anglophobia as a red herring that masked his single-minded pursuit of annexation. For an important and, in my view, persuasive corrective to this argument, see Crapol, "John Tyler and the Pursuit of National Destiny"; as well as Crapol's recent biography of the tenth president, *John Tyler: Accidental President*.

9. Washington D. Miller to President Tyler, January 30, 1843, Washington Daniel Miller Papers, Texas State Library and Archives.

10. Elliot to Addington, November 15, 1842, in *British Diplomatic Correspondence concerning the Republic of Texas*, 129.

11. Fay, *The Opium War* (the Queen Victoria quote is on p. 311). The *Times* of London was blunter, concluding that Elliot was "unfit to manage a respectable apple stall" (see Fay, *Opium War*, 342). See also Hoe and Roebuck, *The Taking of Hong Kong*; and Blake, *Charles Elliot, R.N., 1801–1875*, 22–61.

12. Elliot's activities in China were naturally the subject of much commentary in the United States; see, e.g., "The Opium Trade—England and China," *Merchant's Magazine and Commercial Review* 2 (May 1840): 406–18.

13. Elliot to Addington, November 15, 1842, in *British Diplomatic Correspondence concerning the Republic of Texas*, 127.

14. "Our Relations with Mexico—Peace or War?" *New York Herald*, June 19, 1845.

15. Joseph Eve (1841–43), William Murphy (1843–44), and Tilgham Howard (1844) all died of yellow fever.

16. Elliot to Aberdeen, January 28, 1843, in *British Diplomatic Correspondence concerning the Republic of Texas*, 156; see also Elliot to Aberdeen, February 5, 1843, ibid., 162. For more on the Peel Ministry's diplomatic policy toward Texas, see Adams, *British Interests and Activities in Texas*, chaps. 5–6. See also Spence, "British Interests and Attitudes regarding the Republic of Texas and its Annexation to the United States." The 1843 armistice talks are examined in Haynes, *Soldiers of Misfortune*, 155, 166–67.

17. Elliot to Addington, November 15, 1842, in *British Diplomatic Correspondence concerning the Republic of Texas*, 127–30.

18. Elliot was not the first British diplomat to alert the Foreign Office to Texas's potential as a beachhead against the rising tide of slavery (see Francis Sheridan to Joseph Garroway, July 12, 1840, in *British Diplomatic Correspondence concerning the Republic of Texas*, 18–26; and James Hook to Palmerston, April 30, 1841, ibid., 29–39).

19. Yates to Elliot, July 12, 1843, ibid., 229–33; Smith, *Annexation of Texas*, 113.

20. Elliot to Addington, March 26, 1843, in *British Diplomatic Correspondence concerning the Republic of Texas*, 168.

21. Lewis Tappan to Joseph Sturge, undated, in Tappan, *A Side-Light on Anglo-American Relations*, 148, 59–60; Lewis Tappan to John Scoble, May 13, 1843, ibid., 138.

22. Smither, "English Abolitionism and the Annexation of Texas."

23. For an example of Lord Aberdeen's interest in the status of slavery in the Lone

Star Republic, see Aberdeen to Kennedy, May 30, 1843, in *British Diplomatic Correspondence concerning the Republic of Texas*, 199–200.

24. *Proceedings of the General Anti-Slavery Convention Called by the Committee of the British and Foreign Anti-slavery Society, and Held in London from Tuesday, June 13th, to Tuesday, June 20th, 1843.*

25. Smith, *Reminiscences of the Texas Republic*, 54–58; Merk, *Slavery and the Annexation of Texas*, 12–19. For more on the role of Duff Green in Texas affairs, see Belko, *The Invincible Duff Green, Whig of the West*, 332–403.

26. "Later from England," *Daily Madisonian*, September 23, 1843.

27. Anonymous Texan to Calhoun, April 20, 1844, in John C. Calhoun, *Papers*, 18:296; W. W. T. Smith to Calhoun, May 20, 1844, ibid., 18:547. By the summer of 1844, American suspicions of foreign intrigues ran so high that even the mere presence of British citizens on the streets of Galveston was enough to convince U.S. chargé d'affaires William S. Murphy when he arrived in the port city that a plot was afoot to infiltrate Texas with British agents (see William S. Murphy to John Tyler, March 16, 1844, ibid., 18:85; see also William S. Murphy to Hugh S. Legaré, June 5, 1843, reel no. 1, Despatches from U.S. Ministers in Mexico, 1823–1906, RG 59, U.S. National Archives, Washington, D.C.).

28. Washington D. Miller to John Tyler, September 16, 1843, Washington Daniel Miller Papers, Texas State Library and Archives.

29. Friend, *Sam Houston, The Great Designer*, 131.

30. British diplomatic historian Ephraim D. Adams finds little evidence to support allegations of undue British influence in Texas affairs (see Adams, *British Interests and Activities in Texas*, 142–43).

31. *Daily Madisonian*, September 23, 25, 27, and 28, 1843.

32. "Lord Brougham and the President," *Daily Madisonian*, September 28, 1843.

33. See, e.g., Guy Bryan to Rutherford B. Hayes, December 21, 1843, in Bryan and Hayes, "The Bryan-Hayes Correspondence," 111. For more on the role of anti-British sentiment in the annexation debates, see Haynes, "The Quest for National Security: Anglophobia and the Annexation of Texas."

34. *Annals of Congress*, 16th Cong., 1st sess., 1924.

35. Hammond, *Banks and Politics in America from the Revolution to the Civil War*, 548.

36. Ximenes, *Mr. Calhoun—Mr. Van Buren—Texas*.

37. Andrew Jackson to Aaron V. Brown, February 9, 1843, in Jackson, *Correspondence*, 6:202.

38. "Third Annual Message," in U.S. President, *A Compilation of the Messages and Papers of the Presidents*, 5:2114.

39. Andrew Jackson to Aaron V. Brown, February 9, 1843, in Jackson, *Correspondence*, 6:202. Though written in 1843, the letter was not released to the public until the following year.

40. Walker, *Letter of Mr. Walker, of Mississippi, Relative to the Annexation of Texas*, 31. Historians have generally focused on the Democratic leader's novel argument that Texas, if annexed, would serve as a safety valve for slavery, drawing off the growing black population from the Upper South, where the need for slave labor was declining. Ultimately, Walker predicted, the African American population would migrate into Mexico, thereby solving the "Negro problem," for white Americans. For analyses of Walker's safety valve thesis, see Merk, *Slavery and the Annexation of Texas*, 9–11; and Hietala, *Manifest Design*, 10–54 passim.

41. Upshur to Calhoun, August 14, 1843, in Calhoun, *Papers*, 17:536. The view that annexation was a policy engineered by Southern slaveholders to advance a proslavery

agenda enjoyed wide credence in the mid-1840s, and has informed the analysis of many historians. Few have accepted the proslavery conspiracy thesis more uncritically than Frederick Merk, who argues that Tyler and his two Southern secretaries of state viewed slavery with a monomania that led them to press forward on annexation with a reckless disregard for either the facts or national unity (see Merk, *Slavery and the Annexation of Texas*). William W. Freehling has argued that the Tyler administration's determination to acquire Texas was not a deliberate campaign of disinformation, but rather was consistent with a coherent commitment to the ideology of slavery (see Freehling, *The Road to Disunion*, 356). See also Haynes, "Anglophobia and the Quest for National Security"; and Silbey, *Storm Over Texas*.

42. *Daily National Intelligencer*, March 16, 1844; "To the Senate of the United States," in U.S. President, *Messages and Papers of the Presidents*, 5:2163.

43. Aberdeen to Pakenham, December 26, 1843, no. 341, in Senate Documents, 28th Cong., 1st sess., *U.S. Congressional Serial Set*; Calhoun to Pakenham, April 18, 1844, in Calhoun, *Papers*, 18:276–78.

44. Andrew Jackson to Francis Blair, May 11, 1844, in Jackson, *Correspondence*, 6:287.

45. Benton, *Thirty Years' View*, 2:581–90. Several historians, equally perplexed by the Pakenham letter, have offered various theories to explain Calhoun's conduct. For a summary of various viewpoints, see Cooper, *The South and the Politics of Slavery*, 375–76.

46. Ben E. Green to John C. Calhoun, June 17, 1844, in Calhoun, *Papers*, 19:102.

47. John C. Calhoun to Benjamin Green, April 19, 1844, ibid., 18:283. Chauncey S. Boucher also notes Calhoun's fears of a British plot to acquire Texas as an explanation for his conduct as secretary of state (see Boucher, "The Annexation of Texas and the Bluffton Movement in South Carolina," 15–16). It is worth noting that many of Calhoun's friends and associates did not initially view the Pakenham letter as a Southern call to arms. From Northern states, Calhoun received letters from supporters who, like so many of their fellow citizens, had long resented British criticism of American customs and institutions, and praised the secretary of state on that basis alone. Boston essayist and editor Orestes Brownson read the letter "with a glow of patriotic pride," thankful that at least one public figure had dared to rebuke an "insolent foreign government" for its presumptuousness in lecturing Americans on the morality of their institutions (see "The Presidential Nominations," in Brownson, *Works*, 15:490).

48. Calhoun to Francis Wharton, May 28, 1844, in Calhoun, *Papers*, 18:649.

49. For a sampling of the Whig rebuttal of Democratic annexation arguments, see "Annexation of Texas," tract no. IX, in Colton, *The Junius Tracts*; *Congressional Globe*, 28th Cong., 2nd sess., Appendix, 335.

50. Sedgwick, *Thoughts on the Proposed Annexation of Texas to the United States*, 26–27.

51. Benton, *Thirty Years' View*, 2:300.

52. For an example of the Whigs' use of the encirclement argument, see Clay, *Speech of Cassius M. Clay, against the Annexation of Texas to the United States of America* . . . . In 1846, the Whig journal *American Review* would employ the argument in defense of an aggressive policy to seize California. Firmly entrenched in the West Indies, Canada, and Halifax, and with a loyal ally in Mexico, Her Majesty's government aimed to acquire California in order to ensnare the American republic "as completely in her net, as the bloodiest intentions of extermination could possibly desire!" (see "California," *American Review* 3 [January 1846]: 94).

53. Sedgwick, *Thoughts on the Proposed Annexation of Texas to the United States*, 25.

54. John Quincy Adams, *Memoirs*, 11:406–7.

55. "Great Texas Meeting in the Park," *Working Man's Advocate*, May 11, 1844. The

land reform movement has been the subject of considerable recent scholarly attention. See Bronstein, *Land Reform and the Working-Class Experience in Britain and the United States*; Earle, *Jacksonian Antislavery and the Politics of Free Soil*; and Lause, *Young America*.

56. *Congressional Globe*, 28th Cong., 2nd sess., Appendix, 356. See also *Congressional Globe*, 28th Cong., 2nd sess., Appendix, 369.

57. William Lloyd Garrison to R. D. Webb, March 1, 1846, in *British and American Abolitionists*, 234.

58. Lewis Tappan to John Scoble, October 19, 1843, in Tappan, *A Side-Light on Anglo-American Relations*, 148.

59. Calhoun to Henry Conner, July 3, 1844, in Calhoun, *Papers*, 19:254.

60. Higham, "The Loyalties of William Gilmore Simms," 215.

61. "British Opinions of Texas," *Magnolia* 1 (October 1842), 237. See also Simms, *Sources of American Independence, An Oration, on the Sixty-ninth Anniversary of American Independence, delivered at Aiken, South Carolina*; Faust, *A Sacred Circle*. For more on Simms's changing political views, see Wakelyn, *The Politics of a Literary Man*; and McCardell, *The Idea of a Southern Nation*, 143–74.

11 "Looking John Bull Straight in the Eye"

1. The reference to a "plate of soup" alludes to a comment made by Winfield Scott in an 1846 letter to Secretary of War William Marcy. Scott, a prominent Whig, had complained that he had been sitting down to dinner when he received new instructions from the War Department that seemed to undercut his authority as commander of the war effort. The Polk administration, wishing to discredit Scott and replace him with a more loyal subordinate, published the letter, and the phrase became associated with the general for the rest of his life.

2. John Quincy Adams, *Memoirs*, 12:179.

3. "Inaugural Address," in U.S. President, *A Compilation of the Messages and Papers of the Presidents*, 5:2230–31.

4. Andrew Jackson to James K. Polk, May 2, 1845, in Polk, *Correspondence*, 9:333.

5. Valedictory to the Texas Congress, December 9, 1844, in Houston, *Writings*, 4:403; Elliot to Aberdeen, December 28, 1844, in *British Diplomatic Correspondence concerning the Republic of Texas*, 398.

6. See, e.g., Houston to Andrew Jackson Donelson, April 8, 1845, in Houston, *Writings*, 4:410–17.

7. James Buchanan to Andrew Jackson Donelson, June 15, 1845, in Buchanan, *Works*, 6:174; *Washington Union*, quoted in *Texas National Register*, July 10, 1846, 246; *New Orleans Daily Picayune*, April 17, 1845.

8. Bankhead to Aberdeen, November 29, 1844, in *British Diplomatic Correspondence concerning the Republic of Texas*, 433–36; Aberdeen to Elliot, January 23, 1845, ibid., 430–31.

9. Elliot to Aberdeen, April 2, 1845, ibid., 466; *Treaty of Peace and Independence with Mexico*, June 4, 1845, ibid., 473–75.

10. Aberdeen to Peel, May 11, 1845, and Peel to Aberdeen, May 12, 1845, quoted in Merk, *Slavery and the Annexation of Texas*, 170–71.

11. *New York Herald*, May 29, 1845.

12. William S. Parrott to James Buchanan, April 19, 1845, Despatches from U.S. Ministers in Mexico, 1823–1906, Department of State, RG 59, U.S. National Archives, Washington, D.C.

13. *New Orleans Daily Picayune*, May 21, 1845; *New Orleans Daily Picayune*, May 24, 1845.

14. *New Orleans Daily Picayune,* May 24, 1845, *New Orleans Daily Picayune,* June 23, 1845; *Texas National Register,* July 17, 1845, 251; Jones, *Memoranda and Official Correspondence,* 443.

15. *Texas National Register,* June 26, 1845, 226. For reports of the rise of annexation sentiment in Texas following Elliot's mission, see Donelson to Jackson, May 24, 1845, in Jackson, *Correspondence,* 6:409–10; and Saligny to Guizot, June 10, 1845, in Barker, *The French Legation in Texas,* 2:666.

16. "A Review of the Summer Campaign: A Speech at Houston in the Summer of 1845," in Houston, *Writings,* 6:12–13; *Telegraph and Texas Register,* June 4, 1845. Houston later claimed that he had been misquoted, insisting that he had said only that such "coquetry" would have been excusable in view of Washington's reluctance to annex Texas (see *Congressional Globe,* 30th Cong., 1st sess., Appendix, 607).

17. Andrew Jackson to James K. Polk, May 26, 1845, in Polk, *Correspondence,* 9:410.

18. *New Orleans Courier,* June 24, 1845, quoted in Smith, *The Annexation of Texas,* 453–54.

19. Sheppard, *An Editor's View of Early Texas as Depicted in the Northern Standard (1842–1846),* 348.

20. *New York Morning News,* May 30, 1845.

21. Edward Everett to Buchanan, July 4, 1845, in Manning, *Diplomatic Correspondence of the United States,* 7:270; Buchanan to Donelson, June 15, 1845, in Buchanan, *Works,* 6:174.

22. "Annexation," *Democratic Review* 17 (July 1845): 5.

23. See "Foreign Interference in American Affairs," *New York Herald,* June 8, 1845; "Coming Round," *New Orleans Daily Picayune,* June 14, 1845; Smith, *Annexation of Texas,* 464–66.

24. *Congressional Globe,* 28th Cong., 1st sess., Appendix, 321; Brauer, *Cotton versus Conscience,* 106, 128; *Boston Atlas,* March 21, 1844, quoted in Smith, *Annexation of Texas,* 183; *New Orleans Daily Picayune,* July 6, 1845.

25. *Texas National Register,* July 24, 1845, 257.

26. Donelson to Buchanan, June 2, 1845, and June 4, 1845, no. 1, pp. 64–67, in Senate Documents, 29th Cong., 1st sess., *U.S. Congressional Serial Set.* See also Middleton, "Donelson's Mission to Texas in Behalf of Annexation." The *Washington Union* is quoted in *Texas National Register,* July 10, 1845, 246. For more on the influential American diplomat, see Cheathem, *Old Hickory's Nephew,* 187–207.

27. Louis McLane to James Buchanan, September 26, 1845, in Manning, *Diplomatic Correspondence of the United States,* 7:271; Louis McLane to James Buchanan, May 18, 1846, ibid., 7:274. For the views of Everett and McLane, who both had come to the conclusion that Great Britain had no desire to intervene in the affairs of the two American neighbors, see Edward Everett to James Buchanan, July 4, 1845, in Manning, *Diplomatic Correspondence of the United States,* 7:270; and Louis McLane to James Buchanan, September 26, 1845, ibid., 7:270–71.

28. James K. Polk to Donelson, June 15, 1845, in Polk, "Letters of James K. Polk to Andrew J. Donelson, 1843–1848." See also Buchanan to Donelson, June 15, 1845, in Buchanan, *Works,* 6:172.

29. James K. Polk to Sam Houston, June 6, 1848, in Polk, *Correspondence,* 9:431.

30. Polk, *Diary,* 1:4–5.

31. "First Annual Message," in U.S. President, *Messages and Papers of the Presidents,* 5:2245; ibid., 5:2237–38.

32. "Texas—Oregon—and California," *New York Herald,* July 30, 1845. The administration read sinister import into every rumor, expressing concern when reports reached

Washington that the Mormons, then preparing to embark on their great trek from Illinois to Utah, were cooperating with the British and the Mexican government (see John McN to James K. Polk, December 24, 1845, in Polk, *Correspondence*, 10:521).

33. Thomas O. Larkin to James Buchanan, July 10, 1845, in Manning, *Diplomatic Correspondence of the United States*, 8:736. For more on Larkin, see Hague and Langum, *Thomas O. Larkin*; and Hawgood, *First and Last Consul*. Information from other U.S. agents in the days that followed seemed to lend credence to such reports (see Pletcher, *The Diplomacy of Annexation*, 281–82.

34. Cleland, "The Early Sentiment for the Annexation of California." See also two articles by Sheldon G. Jackson, which discuss British activities in California: "The British and the California Dream: Rumors, Myths and Legends"; and "Two Pro-British Plots in Alta California."

35. Although Secretary of State Buchanan urged Slidell to be vigilant against the efforts of France, he left no doubt that the cession of California to Great Britain, "our principal commercial rival," was the administration's paramount concern (see James Buchanan to John Slidell, November 10, 1845, in Buchanan, *Works*, 6:294, 304). Buchanan echoed these concerns in his correspondence with Thomas Larkin (see Buchanan to Larkin, October 17, 1845, ibid., 6:275–76). Fear of British activities in California was not limited to ultra-expansionists. Even prominent Whigs, mindful of the enormous commercial potential of California harbors, could wax Anglophobic when discussing Mexico's northernmost province (see, e.g., Thompson, *Recollections of Mexico*, 235; and "California," *American Review* 3 [January 1846]): 98).

36. Thomas O. Larkin to James Buchanan, September 29, 1845, in Manning, *Diplomatic Correspondence of the United States*, 8:755; James Buchanan to John Slidell, December 17, 1845, ibid., 8:184.

37. Slidell maintained that Charles Bankhead, the British minister, had advised the Mexican government to reject his credentials as U.S. minister, a charge the British diplomat denied (see John Slidell to James Buchanan, December 29, 1845, in Manning, *Diplomatic Correspondence of the United States*, 8:805). Washington's anxiety regarding European interference in the affairs of its Latin American neighbor increased still further with the news that Paredes was considering a plan to return Mexico to Spanish monarchical rule, which Slidell believed had the covert sanction of Great Britain (see Soto, "The Monarchist Conspiracy and the Mexican War").

38. Pletcher, *The Diplomacy of Annexation*, 370; Tymitz, "British Influence in Mexico, 1840–1848," 147.

39. Polk, *Diary*, 1:155.

40. *Congressional Globe*, 29th Cong., 1st sess., Appendix, 299.

41. *Congressional Globe*, 29th Cong., 1st sess., Appendix, 474. Other members of the South Carolina delegation expressed similar sentiments; see, e.g., *Congressional Globe*, 29th Cong., 1st sess., Appendix, 165–67. For a rebuttal to Southern opinions, see *Congressional Globe*, 29th Cong., 1st sess., Appendix, 388.

42. Smith, *Reminiscences of the Texas Republic*, 41. See also Cramer, "British Magazines and the Oregon Question"; Jones and Vinson, "British Preparedness and the Oregon Settlement"; Merk, "British Government Propaganda and the Oregon Treaty."

43. Polk, *Diary*, 1:244–45.

44. For more on the outbreak of the war from a Mexican perspective, see Henderson, *A Glorious Defeat*.

45. *Congressional Globe*, 29th Cong., 2nd sess., Appendix, 25; *Congressional Globe*, 29th Cong., 1st sess., Appendix, 647.

46. Foos, *A Short, Offhand, Killing Affair*, 75.

47. Meade, *The Life and Letters of George Gordon Meade*, 1:96.

48. In a speech calling for the termination of the Oregon boundary agreement with Great Britain earlier in the year, Ohio congressman Joshua Giddings suggested that a transatlantic conflict would eventually devolve into a war uniting the North and Britain against slavery (see *Congressional Globe*, 29th Cong., 1st sess., Appendix, 74).

49. Samuel May to J. B. Estlin, May 30, 1846, in *British and American Abolitionists*, 266.

50. John Charles Frémont, *Memoirs of My Life*, 1:423. Whether Frémont had secret instructions from the Polk administration is a question of some debate (see Wiltsee, *The Truth about Frémont*; Stenberg, "Polk and Frémont, 1845–1846"; Marti, *Messenger of Destiny*; and Tays, "Frémont Had No Secret Instructions."

51. Frémont, *Memoirs of My Life*, 1:489; Nevins, *Frémont, Pathmarker of the West*, 244; Pletcher, *The Diplomacy of Annexation*, 426–38.

52. John Black to James Buchanan, May 23, 1846, in Manning, *Diplomatic Correspondence of the United States*, 8:854; Smith, *The War with Mexico*, 1:443n.

53. McLane to Buchanan, June 18, 1846, in Manning, *Diplomatic Correspondence of the United States*, 7:283.

54. *Congressional Globe*, 29th Cong., 1st sess., Appendix, 869.

55. *Congressional Globe*, 29th Cong., 1st sess., Appendix, 920; *New York Herald*, May 21, 1846.

56. Benton, *Thirty Years' View*, 2:610.

57. *Texas National Register*, July 24, 1845, 257.

12 "BROTHER JONATHAN IS SOMEBODY"

1. James Gordon Bennett, predictably, could be found in the vanguard of the clamor for "All Mexico," arguing that annexation would deal a fatal blow to the power of British capitalists in the western hemisphere (see "Rumors of Peace with Mexico," *New York Herald*, January 22, 1848). For a similar argument, see the Senate speech of Henry S. Foote, in *Congressional Globe*, 30th Cong., 1st sess., Appendix, 128. For scholarly treatments of the "All Mexico" movement, see Fuller, *The Movement for the Acquisition of All Mexico*; and Lambert, "The Movement for the Acquisition of All Mexico."

2. De Armond, "Justo Sierra O'Reilly and Yucatecan United States Relations," 426; Polk, *Diary*, 3:445.

3. Pletcher, *The Diplomacy of Annexation*, 574.

4. "News for John Bull," *American Flag*, May 1, 1847.

5. Bauer, *The Mexican War*, 332; George Bancroft to James K. Polk, May 14, 1847, in Howe, *The Life and Letters of George Bancroft*, 2:17; George Bancroft to James K. Polk, January 19, 1847, ibid., 2:7.

6. "The Mexican War . . . Its Influences Abroad . . . Its Benefits to the United States," *New York Herald*, October 26, 1847.

7. Hone, *Diary*, 2:862; *The Rough and Ready Songster*, 9. For more on the cultural impact of the U.S.-Mexican War, see Streeby, *American Sensations*.

8. Gray, "American Attitudes toward British Imperialism, 1815–1860"; May, *Manifest Destiny's Underworld*, 119–23.

9. Although Monroe had referred in 1823 to "the American continents," Polk left no doubt that the North American continent was his primary concern, referring to it specifically in his 1845 annual message no less than four times (see "First Annual Message," in U.S. President, *A Compilation of the Messages and Papers of the Presidents*, 5:2248–49).

10. Perkins, *A History of the Monroe Doctrine*, 99.

11. "Great Britain and the United States," in Brownson, *Works*, 16:484. For a simi-

lar argument, see "A Letter to John Bull," *Putnam's Monthly Magazine* (February 1853): 221–30.

12. Crapol, *John Tyler: The Accidental President,* 129–73 passim.

13. Curti, "Young America"; Edward L. Widmer makes the case for a clear connection between the literary and political movements that adopted the name Young America during the 1840s and 1850s (see Widmer, *Young America*).

14. Shenton, *Robert John Walker,* 134–36; "The Anglo-Saxon Race," *American Review* 1 (January 1848): 29; "The Anglo-Saxon Race," *North American Review* 73 (July 1851): 35–36; "The Anglo-Saxons and the Americans: European Races in the United States," *American Whig Review* 8 (September 1851): 187–94.

15. "The Position of Political, Commercial, and Financial Affairs in the United States," *New York Herald,* August 14, 1847.

16. Mackay, *The Western World, or, Travels in the United States in 1846–47* (quote on p. xix).

17. Stuart-Wortley, *Travels in the United States,* 127; "English Travellers of Rank in America," *North American Review* 74 (January, 1852): 207. Other writers were more inclined to express feelings of trepidation at the republic's budding power; see, e.g., Mrs. Houston, *Hesperos,* 1:244; and Warburton, *Hochelaga,* 2:363–64. For more on the changing mood of British travelers at this time, see Crawford, "British Travellers and the Anglo-American Relationship in the 1850s."

18. Emerson, *English Traits;* Tuckerman, *A Month in England.* See also Coxe, *Impressions of England.* For a review of these travel memoirs, see "Recent Books on England," *North American Review* 83 (October 1856). See also Sealts, *Emerson on the Scholar,* 221–33.

19. Taussig, *The Tariff History of the United States,* 87–88; Irwin and Temin, "The Antebellum Tariff on Cotton Textiles Revisited."

20. U.S. Bureau of the Census, *Historical Statistics of the United States, Colonial Times to 1957,* 551; "The American Institute," *Niles' Weekly Register,* October 30, 1847, 131–33; Taussig, *Tariff History of the United States,* 71.

21. The structure was disassembled after the exhibition and rebuilt in Sydenham Park, south of London, in 1852. It was destroyed by fire in 1936.

22. "Official Catalogue of the Great Exhibition," *North American Review* 76 (October 1852): 357–87; "London Matters," *Scientific American,* August 9, 1851; [Article 3], *Scientific American,* August 23, 1851. For descriptions of the exhibition through American eyes, see Greeley, *The Crystal Palace and Its Lessons;* and Bartlett, *London by Day and Night,* 322. For an overview of the exhibition, see Auerbach, *The Great Exhibition of 1851.*

23. "Travels in America," *North American Review* 74 (January 1852): 200. For a detailed description of the American entries, see Rodgers, *American Superiority at the World's Fair.*

24. "The Great Yacht Race," *The Independent,* September 26, 1901, p. 2291. Steers and the crew of the *America* returned to New York with the trophy (later renamed the *America's* Cup) to a heroes' welcome. The obligatory dinner in Steers's honor provided the opportunity for an orgy of chest thumping at Great Britain's expense (see Rodgers, *American Superiority at the World's Fair,* 77).

25. "Official Catalogue of the Great Exhibition," *North American Review* 76 (October 1852): 357–86; "American Progress," *Scientific American,* November 1, 1851.

26. Levine, *Highbrow/Lowbrow,* chap. 2 passim.

27. "Kavanagh," *North American Review* 69 (January 1849): 210; Smith, *Wit and Wisdom of the Rev. Sydney Smith,* 188n.

28. Peach, *British Influence on the Birth of American Literature,* 26–27; Melville, *Red-*

burn, 169. For a trenchant analysis of Melville's internalized Anglophilia, see Buell, "Melville and the Question of Decolonization," passim. Similarly, Sohui Lee finds Hawthorne deeply conflicted in his efforts to combat American "Anglomania" (see Lee, "Hawthorne's Politics of Storytelling."

29. "Hawthorne and His Mosses," *Literary World*, August 17, 1850; Longfellow, *Kavanagh, A Tale*, 118. Even American colloquial speech, once a profound source of shame for those who held fast to English linguistic and orthographic conventions, now bore the mark of respectability, as evidenced by the success of Bartlett's *Dictionary of Americanisms*, first published in 1848.

30. Andrew Jackson to James K. Polk, in Polk, *Correspondence*, 9:332.

31. "Progress of Democracy, vs. Old Fogy Retrogrades," *Democrat's Review* (April 1852): 289; "John Bull, Esquire," *United States Review* (March 1853): 236; "The United States and the United Kingdom," *United States Review* (May 1853): 385.

32. *Richmond Examiner*, quoted in "Foreign War—A Remedy for Domestic Agitation," *National Era*, June 22, 1854. For more on the recruitment controversy, see Hill, "The Anglo-American Recruitment Crisis, 1854–56; and Dowty, *The Limits of American Isolationism*.

33. Poore, *Perley's Reminiscences of Sixty Years in the National Metropolis*, 474; Hamlin, *The Life and Times of Hannibal Hamlin*, 282. For more on the ways in which U.S. foreign policy intruded upon the growing sectional crisis, see Belohlavek, *Broken Glass*, 242–82 passim.

34. For more on the contemporary response to Stowe's book in the British Isles, see "British Philanthropy and American Slavery, By a Southern Lady," *DeBow's Review* 14 (March 1853): 258–80; "Blackwood's Magazine," *United States Review* 1 (April 1853): 289; "The Conspiracy of Fanaticism," *Democratic Review* 26 (May 1850): 385; and "North and South; or, the Policy of Ignorance," *United States Review* (October 1854): 354.

35. "Slavery and the Abolitionists," *Southern Quarterly Review* 15 (April 1849): 221; "The Southern Convention," *Southern Quarterly Review* 16 (September 1850): 207; Higham, "The Loyalties of William Gilmore Simms," 221–23.

36. For more on the origins of the early American character, see Morgan, *An American Icon*.

37. Nichols, *Forty Years of American Life, 1821–1861*, 186. Prince Albert Edward's tour of North America is examined thoroughly in Radforth, *Royal Spectacle*; see chapters 9–10 for the prince's tour of the United States. For a contemporary perspective of Albert Edward's travels, see Engleheart, *Journal of the Progress of H. R. H. the Prince of Wales through British North America; and His Visit to the United States, 10th July to 15th November, 1860*.

38. Brauer, "Seward's 'Foreign War Panacea'"; Ferris, *Desperate Diplomacy*. Martin Crawford examines the deterioration in U.S.-British relations during this period from a British perspective in *The Anglo-American Crisis of the Mid-Nineteenth Century*.

39. Relations between the two countries were sometimes stormy after the Civil War; see Crapol, *America for the Americans*.

40. Cooper, *The Spy; A Tale of the Neutral Ground*, ix–x.

Bibliography

ARCHIVAL SOURCES

Dolph Briscoe Center for American History. University of Texas at Austin.
    Anson Jones Papers
    Isaac Van Zandt Papers
    Charles A. Wickliffe Letters
William L. Clements Library. University of Michigan, Ann Arbor.
    Lucius Lyon Papers
Harvard Theatre Collection. Houghton Library, Harvard University, Cambridge,
    Mass.
    Edmund Kean Papers
    Noah Miller Ludlow Papers
    Playbill Collection
Historical Society of Pennsylvania. Philadelphia, Pa.
    Joel Roberts Poinsett Papers
Library Company of Philadelphia
    American Theatre Playbill Collection
    Charles Durang, History of the Philadelphia Stage Scrap-book
    Political Pamphlet Collection
New York Public Library
    Charles P. Daly Papers
South Caroliniana Library. University of South Carolina, Columbia.
    Thomas Cooper Papers
    William Drayton Papers
    Francis W. Pickens Papers
Southern Historical Collection. University of North Carolina, Chapel Hill.
    Duff Green and Benjamin Green Papers
Texas State Library and Archives Commission. Austin.
    Andrew Jackson Houston Papers
    Mirabeau Lamar Papers
    Washington Daniel Miller Papers
United Kingdom. Public Record Office, London.
    FOREIGN OFFICE PAPERS
    Series 50 (Mexico)
    Series 75 (Texas)

United States. National Archives, Washington, D.C.
    RECORD GROUP 59 (DEPARTMENT OF STATE)
    Despatches from U.S. Ministers in Mexico, 1823–1906
    Diplomatic Instructions of the Department of State, 1801–1906
Western Reserve Historical Society. Cleveland, Ohio.
    Coffinberry Family Papers

                              NEWSPAPERS

American & Commercial Daily Advertiser   New York Commercial Advertiser
American Flag (Matamoros, Mexico)   New York Courier and Enquirer
Boston Atlas   New York Evangelist
Bowen's Boston News   New York Evening Post
Charleston City Gazette   New York Herald
Charleston Courier   New York Mirror
Charleston Mercury   New York Morning News
Cincinnati Advertiser   New York Observer and Chronicle
Cincinnati Enquirer   New York Sun
Daily Madisonian (Washington, D.C.)   Niles' Weekly Register
Daily National Intelligencer   Pennsylvanian (Philadelphia)
    (Washington, D.C.)   Philadelphia Public Ledger
Detroit Free Press   The Philanthropist (Cincinnati, Ohio)
Guernsey Times and Farmers' and   Telegraph and Texas Register (Houston)
    Mechanics' Advocate (Cambridge,   Texas National Register (Washington-
    Ohio)   on the-Brazos)
Kentucky Reporter (Lexington)   Times (London)
Kentucky Yeoman (Frankfort)   United States' Telegraph (Washington,
Louisville (Ky.) Daily Journal   D.C.)
Louisville (Ky.) Democrat   Washington Globe [Saturday edition is
The Man (New York City)   called Washington Extra Globe]
New Orleans Bee   Working Man's Advocate (New York
New Orleans Daily Picayune   City)
New York Albion

                              PERIODICALS

American Monthly Magazine   Edinburgh Review
American Quarterly Review   Fraser's Magazine for Town and Country
American Review   The Genius of Universal Emancipation
American Whig Review   Illinois Monthly Magazine
Anti-Slavery Reporter   The Independent
Army and Navy Chronicle   John Donkey
Broadway Journal   Knickerbocker
Brother Jonathan   Ladies' Literary Cabinet
De Bow's Review   The Liberator
Democrat's Review   Literary World
Dramatic Mirror   The Literary and Scientific Repository,

and Critical Review
McClure's Magazine
Magnolia
Merchant's Magazine and Commercial
    Review
The Mirror of Taste and Dramatic Censor
The Mother's Magazine
National Era
New York Review
North American Magazine
North American Review
Philadelphia Monthly Magazine

Port Folio
Putnam's Monthly Magazine
Quarterly Review
The Religious Intelligencer
Scientific American
Southern Literary Messenger
Southern Quarterly Review
United States Magazine and Democratic
    Review
United States Review
Western Monthly Magazine and Literary
    Journal

Government Documents

Great Britain. Foreign Office. *British Diplomatic Correspondence concerning the Republic of Texas, 1838–1846.* Edited by Ephraim Douglass Adams. Austin: Texas State Historical Association, [1918].

Manning, William R. *Diplomatic Correspondence of the United States: Inter-American Affairs, 1831–1860.* Washington, D.C.: Carnegie Endowment for International Peace, 1932–39.

South Carolina. *The Debate in the South Carolina Legislature, In December, 1830, on the Reports of the Committees of Both Houses in Favor of Convention.* Columbia: Printed by S. J. M'Morris, 1831.

Texas. (Republic) Department of State. *Diplomatic Correspondence of the Republic of Texas.* Edited by George P. Garrison. 3 vols. Washington, D.C.: Government Printing Office, 1908.

United States. Bureau of the Census. *Historical Statistics of the United States, Colonial Times to 1957: A Statistical Abstract Supplement.* Washington, D.C.: U.S. Dept. of Commerce, Bureau of the Census: For sale by the Supt. of Docs., U.S. Govt. Print. Off., 1961, 1960.

United States. Congress. *Annals of the Congress of the United States, 1789–1824.* 42 vols. Washington, D.C., 1834–56.

———. *Congressional Globe.* 46 vols. Washington, D.C., 1834–73.

———. *Register of Debates.* 14 vols. Washington, D.C., 1824–37.

———. House. Committee on Foreign Affairs. *Territory of Oregon: To Accompany Bill H.R. No. 976 . . . Report.* Washington, D.C.: T. Allen, printer, 1839.

———. House. Committee on Manufactures, and John Quincy Adams. *Tariff—Manufactures: May 23, 1832.* Washington, D.C.: n.p., 1832.

———. Senate. Select Committee on Bill to Authorize the President to Occupy the Oregon Territory. *Report (to Accompany Senate Bill No. 206).* [Washington, D.C.]: Blair and Rives, 1838.

United States. President. *A Compilation of the Messages and Papers of the Presidents.* Compiled by James D. Richardson. 20 vols. New York: Bureau of National Literature, ©1897–©1929.

U.S. Congressional Serial Set. Washington, D.C.: Government Printing Office, 1817– .

Published Primary Sources

Abdy, Edward S. *Journal of a Residence and Tour in the United States of North America, from April, 1833, to October, 1834.* 3 vols. London: J. Murray, 1835.

Account of the Terrific and Fatal Riot at the New-York Astor Place Opera House on the Night of May 10th, 1849. New York: H. M. Ranney, 1849.

Adams, John Quincy. *Memoirs of John Quincy Adams: Comprising Portions of His Diary from 1795 to 1848.* 12 vols. Edited by Charles Francis Adams. Philadelphia: J. B. Lippincott and Co., 1874–77.

Addington, Henry Unwin. *Youthful America: Selections from Henry Unwin Addington's Residence in the United States of America, 1822, 23, 24, 25.* Edited by Bradford Perkins. Berkeley: University of California Press, 1960.

Address of the Democratic Whig Association of the City and County of Philadelphia. N.d.

Address of the Republican General Committee of the Young Men of the City and County of New York. New York: Alexander Ming, 1828.

Address of the Washington Society to the People of South Carolina. Charleston: P. S. Burges, 1832.

Aldrich, A. P. *Address of the Phi Gamma Society of Cokebury Seminary, Abbeville District.* Columbia: A. S. Johnston, 1847.

An Address of the Democratic Members of Congress from the State of Tennessee to their Constituents. Washington, D.C.: Blair and Rives, 1841.

An Address to the Workingmen of the City and County of Philadelphia. Philadelphia: 1839.

An American Citizen. *A Rejoinder to "The Replies from England, etc." to Certain Statements Circulated in This Country respecting Mr. Macready."* New York: Stringer and Townsend, 1849.

Anderson, Alexander. *The Letter of Alexander Anderson of Tennessee in Reply to the Committee of Invitation to Attend a Dinner Given by the Democracy of Maury, Tennessee on the 13th July to the Delegation from That State to the National Convention.* N.p., 1844.

Barker, Nancy Nichols, trans. and ed. *The French Legation in Texas.* 2 vols. Austin: Texas State Historical Association, 1971–73.

Barnard, Daniel D. *An Oration, Delivered before the Honorable the Corporation and the Military and Civic Societies of the City of Albany, on the Fourth of July, 1835.* Albany: E. W. and C. Skinner, 1835.

Bartlett, David W. *London by Day and Night; or, Men and Things in the Great Metropolis.* New York: Hurst, 1852.

Bartlett, John Russell. *Dictionary of Americanisms: A Glossary of Words and Phrases, Usually Regarded as Peculiar to the United States.* New York: Bartlett and Wellford, 1848.

[Barton, Seth.] *The Randolph Epistles: To the Delegates of the National Democratic Convention: Texas and the nomination . . . .* N.p., [1844].

Bell, Andrew. *Men and Things in America, or the Experiences of a Year's Residence in the United States.* Southampton, U.K.: E. Paul and Son, 1862.

Beman, Nathan S. S. *The Intellectual Position of Our Country . . . .* Troy, N.Y.: N. Tuttle, 1839.

Benton, Thomas Hart. *Thirty Years' View, or, A History of the Working of the American*

Government for Thirty Years from 1820 to 1850. 2 vols. New York: D. Appleton and Co., 1854–56.

Biddle, Richard. *Captain Hall in America*, by An American. Philadelphia: Carey and Lea, 1830.

Boardman, James. *America, and the Americans*, by a Citizen of the World. London: Longman, Rees, Orme, Brown, Green, and Longman,, 1833.

Bristed, John. *America and Her Resources, or, A View of the Agricultural, Commercial, Manufacturing, Financial, Political, Literary, Moral and Religious Capacity and Character of the American People.* London: Henry Colburn, 1818.

British and American Abolitionists: An Episode in Transatlantic Understanding. Compiled by Clare Taylor. Edinburgh: Edinburgh University Press, 1974.

Brown, James. *An Appeal from the British System of English Grammar, to Common Sense*. Philadelphia: John Fennimore, 1836.

Brownson, Orestes A. *Oration of Orestes A. Brownson, Delivered at Washington Hall, July 5th, 1841*. New York: 1841.

———. *The Works of Orestes A. Brownson*. Edited by Henry F. Brownson. 20 vols. Detroit: Thorndike Nourse, 1882–87.

Bruce, James C. *An Address Delivered Before the Alumni and Graduating Class of the University of North Carolina, at Chapel Hill, on the Afternoon of June Third, 1841.* Raleigh: North Carolina Standard, 1841.

Bryan, Guy, and Rutherford B. Hayes. "The Bryan-Hayes Correspondence." *Southwestern Historical Quarterly* 25 (October 1921). 98–120.

Bryant, William Cullen. *Power for Sanity: Selected Editorials of William Cullen Bryant, 1832–1860*. New York: Fordham University Press, 1994.

———. *Prose Writings*. Edited by Parke Godwin. 2 vols. in 1. Reprint of the 1884 edition. New York: Russell and Russell, 1964.

Buchanan, James. *Works, Comprising his Speeches, State Papers, and Private Correspondence*. Collected and edited by John Bassett Moore. 12 vols. 1908–11; reprint, New York: Antiquarian Press, 1960.

Buckingham, J. S. *America, Historical, Statistic, and Descriptive*. 3 vols. London: Fisher, Son and Co., [1841].

Calhoun, John C. *The Papers of John C. Calhoun*. Edited by Robert Lee Meriwether et al. 28 vols. Columbia: Published by the University of South Carolina Press for the South Caroliniana Society, 1959–2003.

Capers, Henry. *The Life and Times of C. G. Memminger*. Richmond, Va.: Everett Waddey, 1893.

Carey, M[athew]. *Collectanea: Displaying the Rise and Progress of the Tariff System*. Philadelphia: Thomas B. Town, 1833.

———. *Essays on Political Economy; or, The Most Certain Means of Promoting the Wealth, Power, Resources, and Happiness of States, Applied Particularly to the United States by Matthew [sic] Carey*. Reprint of the 1882 edition. New York: A. M. Kelley, 1968.

The Cause of the Hard Times. N.p., [1840].

Channing, William E. *A Letter to the Hon. Henry Clay on the Annexation of Texas to the United States*. Boston: James Munroe and Company, 1837.

———. *Remarks on the Slavery Question in a Letter to Jonathan Phillips*. Boston: James Munroe and Company, 1839.

——. *The Works of William E. Channing, D.D.* Boston: James Munroe and Co., 1845.

Chevalier, Michel. *Society, Manners, and Politics in the United States.* 1839. Reprint, New York: Augustus M. Kelley, 1966.

Child, Lydia Maria. *An Appeal in Favor of that Class of Americans Called Africans.* Boston: Allen and Ticknor, 1833.

——. *Evenings in New England: Intended for Juvenile Amusement and Instruction.* Boston: Cummings, Hilliard and Co., 1824.

Clapp, William W. *A Record of the Boston Stage.* Boston: James Munroe and Co., 1853.

Clark, M. St. Clair, and D. A. Hall, comps. *Legislative and Documentary History of the Bank of the United States.* Washington, D.C.: Printed by Gales and Seaton, 1832.

Clarke, Mary. *A Concise History of the Life and Amours of Thomas S. Hamblin, Late Manager of the Bowery Theatre.* N.p., n.d.

Clay, Cassius. *Speech of Cassius M. Clay, against the Annexation of Texas to the United States of America . . . : In Reply to Col. R. M. Johnson and Others, in a Mass Meeting of Citizens of the Eighth Congressional District . . . on . . . Dec. 30, 1843.* Lexington: Printed at the Observer and Reporter Office, 1844.

Clay, Henry. *The Papers of Henry Clay.* Edited by James F. Hopkins et al. Lexington: University of Kentucky Press, 1959–92.

——. *Speech of Henry Clay, in Defence of the American System.* Washington, D.C.: Gales and Seaton, 1832.

Clayton, John M. *Speech of the Hon. John M. Clayton, at the Delaware Mass Whig Convention, held at Wilmington, June 15, 1844.* [Albany, New York: n.p.,] 1844.

Coke, E. T. *A Subaltern's Furlough: Descriptive of Scenes in Various Parts of the United States, Upper and Lower Canada, New-Brunswick, and Nova Scotia, during the Summer and Autumn of 1832.* 2 vols. New York: J. and J. Harper, 1833.

Colton, Calvin. *The Americans.* London: F. Westly and A. H. Davis, 1833.

——. *The Crisis of the Country,* by Junius. New York: Egbert Benson, 1840.

——. *Four Years in Great Britain, 1831–1835.* New York: Harper Brothers, 1835.

——. *The Junius Tracts.* Nos. I–X. New York: Greeley and McElrath, 1844.

——. *The Life, Correspondence, and Speeches of Henry Clay.* 6 vols. New York: A. S. Barnes and Co., 1857.

Combe, George. *Notes on the United States of America during a Phrenological Visit in 1838–9–40.* 2 vols. Philadelphia: Carey and Hart, 1841.

Cooper, James Fenimore. *Gleanings in Europe: England* (1837). Historical introduction and explanatory notes by Donald A. Ringe and Kenneth W. Staggs; text established by James P. Elliott, Kenneth W. Staggs, and R. D. Madison. Albany: State University of New York Press, 1982.

——. *Home As Found.* 1838. Reprint, New York: Hurd and Houghton, 1872.

——. *Homeward Bound; or, The Chase. A Tale of the Sea.* 1838. Reprint, New York: Hurd and Houghton, 1871.

——. *A Letter to His Countrymen.* New York: John Wiley, 1834.

——. *Letters and Journals of James Fenimore Cooper.* Edited by James Franklin Beard. 6 vols. Cambridge, Mass.: Harvard University Press, 1960–64.

——. *Lionel Lincoln.* Edited by Donald A. Ringe and Lucy B. Ringe. Albany: State University of New York Press, 1984.

———. *Notions of the Americans, Picked Up by a Travelling Bachelor.* 1828. Reprint, New York: Frederick Ungar, 1963.

———. *The Red Rover: A Tale.* London: H. Colburn, 1828.

———. *The Spy; A Tale of the Neutral Ground.* 1821. Reprint, New York: George P. Putnam, 1851.

Cooper, Thomas. *Lectures on the Elements of Political Economy.* 1830. Reprint, New York: Augustus Kelley, 1971.

Cowell, Joe. *Thirty Years Passed among the Players in England and America: Interspersed with Anecdotes and Reminiscences of a Variety of Persons, Directly or Indirectly Connected with the Drama during the Theatrical Life of Joe Cowell, Comedian.* New York: Harper and Brothers, 1843.

Coxe, A. Cleveland. *Impressions of England.* New York: Dana, 1856.

[Crawford, Ingoldsby W.] *Address to the People of Connecticut, Adopted at the State Convention, Held at Middletown, August 7, 1828.* Hartford: J. Russell, 1828.

Crockett, Davy, and Augustin S. Clayton. *The Life of Martin Van Buren, Heir-Apparent to the "Government," and the Appointed Successor of General Andrew Jackson.* . . . Philadelphia: R. Wright, 1837.

Cushing, Caleb. *Lecture on Oregon.* Boston, 1845.

Cutler, Fanny Thimble. *My Conscience! Fanny Thimble Cutler's Journal of a Residence in America whilst Performing a Profitable Theatrical Engagement: Beating the Non-sensical Fanny Kemble Journal All Hollow !!!* Philadelphia, 1835.

D'Arusmont, Frances [Wright]. *What is the Matter? A Political Address as Delivered in Masonic Hall, October 28th, 1838.* New York: Published for the author, 1838.

de Beaumont, Gustave. *Marie, or, Slavery in the United States.* Translated by Barbara Chapman. Baltimore: John Hopkins University Press, 1999.

Declaration of Sentiments Adopted by the Peace Convention, held in Boston, September 18, 19, and 20, 1838. Boston: T. Moore's Lithography, 1838.

Dickens, Charles. *American Notes for General Circulation.* London: Chapman and Hall, 1850.

———. *The Letters of Charles Dickens.* Edited by Madeline House et al. 8 vols. Oxford: Clarendon Press, 1974.

———. *Martin Chuzzlewit.* London: Wordsworth Classics, 1994.

Dix, John A. *Address of John A. Dix, before the Democracy of Herkimer County, on the 4th of July.* [New York, 1840].

A Documentary History of American Industrial Society. Edited by John R. Commons et al. 10 vols. Cleveland: Arthur H. Clark Co., 1910.

[Drayton, William.] *The South Vindicated from the Treason and Fanaticism of the Northern Abolitionists.* Philadelphia: H. Manly, 1836.

Dunlap, William. *The Life of George Fred. Cooke.* 2 vols. London: Henry Colburn, 1815.

Du Ponceau, Peter S. *A Discourse on the Necessity and the Means of Making Our National Literature Independent of That of Great Britain; Delivered before the Members of the Pennsylvania Library of Foreign Literature and Science, on Saturday, Feb. 15, 1834.* Philadelphia: E. G. Dorsey, Printer, 1834.

Dusenbery, B. M., comp. *Monument to the Memory of General Andrew Jackson: Containing Twenty-five Eulogies and Sermons Delivered on the Occasion of His Death.* Philadelphia: James A. Bill, 1848.

Dwight, Timothy. *Remarks on the Review of Inchiquin's Letters*. Boston: Samuel T. Armstrong, 1815.

[Eaton, John.] *The Letters of Wyoming to the People of the United States*. Philadelphia: S. Simpson and J. Conrad, 1824.

Emerson, Ralph Waldo. *The Early Lectures of Ralph Waldo Emerson*. Edited by Stephen E. Whicher and Robert E. Spiller. 3 vols. Cambridge, Mass.: 1959.

———. *English Traits*. Boston: Phillips, Sampson, and Co., 1856.

———. *The Journals and Miscellaneous Notebooks of Ralph Waldo Emerson*. Edited by William H. Gillman. Cambridge, Mass.: Belknap Press of Harvard University Press, 1960–82.

———. *The Works of Ralph Waldo Emerson*. Edited by James Elliot Cabot. 14 vols. Boston: Houghton Mifflin, 1883–93.

Engelson, Lester D. "Proposals for Colonization of California by England in Connection with the Mexican Debt to British Bondholders, 1837–1846." *California Historical Society Quarterly* 18 (June 1939): 136–48.

Engleheart, Gardner D. *Journal of the Progress of H. R. H. the Prince of Wales through British North America; and His Visit to the United States, 10th July to 15th November, 1860*. Privately printed, [1861].

A Fair and Just Comparison of the Lives of the Two Candidates, Andrew Jackson and John Quincy Adams. N.p., 1828.

Faux, W[illiam]. *Memorable Days in America*. London: W. Simpkin and R. Marshall, 1823.

Fearon, Henry Bradshaw. *Sketches of America: A Narrative of a Journey of Five Thousand Miles through the Eastern and Western States of America . . .* London: Longman, Hurst, Rees, Orme, and Brown, 1818.

Featherstonaugh, G[eorge] W. *Excursion Through the Slave States*. New York: Harper and Brothers, 1844.

Felton, Mrs. *American Life: A Narrative of Two Years' City and Country Residence*. London: Simpkin, Marshall and Co., 1842.

Fidler, Isaac. *Observations on Professions, Literature, Manners, and Emigration in the United States and Canada: Made during a Residence There in 1832*. New York: J. and J. Harper, 1833.

Finch, John. *Travels in the United States of America and Canada*. London: Longman, Rees, Orme, Brown, Greem, and Longman, 1833.

First Annual Report of the Board of Managers of the New England Anti-Slavery Society, 1833. Westport, CT: Negro University Press, 1970.

Fisher, Sidney George. *A Philadelphia Perspective: The Diary of Sidney George Fisher Covering the Years 1834–1871*. Edited by Nicholas B. Wainwright. Philadelphia: Historical Society of Pennsylvania, 1967.

Fisk, Theophilus. *Labor the Only True Source of Wealth, or, The Rottenness of the Paper Money Banking System Exposed . . . .* N.p., 1837.

Forbes, Alexander. *California: A History of Upper and Lower California*. London: Smith, Elder and Co., 1839.

Fourth Annual Report of the Board of Managers of the New England Anti-Slavery Society, 1836. Westport, Conn.: Negro University Press, 1970.

Frémont, John Charles. *Memoirs of my Life by John Charles Fremont. Including in* the Narrative Five Journeys of Western Exploration, during the Years 1842, 1843–4, 1845–6–7, 1848–9, 1853–4. Chicago: Belford, Clark and Co., 1887.

Frost, John. The Duty of the American Scholar to the Literature of His Country: An Address, Delivered before the Goethean & Diagnothian Societies, of Marshall College, at Their Annual Celebration, September 28, 1841. Philadelphia: J. Crissy, 1841.

Fuller, Margaret, S. "American Literature, Its Position in the Present Time, and Prospects for the Future." In Papers on Literature and Art. New York: Wiley and Putnam, 1846.

Garrison, William Lloyd. The Letters of William Lloyd Garrison. Edited by Walter Macintosh Merrill and Louis Ruchames. 6 vols. Cambridge, Mass.: Belknap Press of Harvard University Press, 1971–81.

———. Thoughts on African Colonization. 1832. Reprint, New York: Arno Press, 1968.

Godley, John Robert. Letters From America. 2 vols. London: John Murray, 1844.

Godwin, Parke. Democracy, Constructive and Pacific, 1844. 1844. Reprint, Philadelphia: Porcupine Press, 1972.

Gouge, William M. A Short History of Paper Money and Banking in the United States, including an Account of Provincial and Continental Paper-Money. Philadelphia: Printed by T. W. Ustick, 1833.

Grayson, William J. An Oration Delivered in the College Chapel before the Clariosophic Society. Charleston: Printed by A. E. Miller, 1813.

———. An Oration, Delivered in the College Chapel, before the Clariosophic Society Incorporate and the Inhabitants of Columbia, on the 3d December, 1827. Charleston, S.C.: Printed by A. E. Miller, 1828.

Greeley, Horace. The Crystal Palace and Its Lessons. A Lecture. New York: Dewitt and Davenport, 1852.

Green, Asa [George Fibbleton, pseud.] Travels in America. New York: William Pearson, 1833.

Green, Willis. The Voice of Warning: To the Independent Voters of the United States. Washington, D.C.: Whig Standard Office, 1844.

Grimké, Thomas S. Speech of Thomas S. Grimké, One of the Senators from St. Philip's and St. Michael's, Delivered in the Senate of South Carolina, in December, 1828, during the Debate on Sundry Resolutions, of the Senate and House of Representatives, respecting the Tariff. Charleston, S.C.: W. Riley, 1829.

Grund, Francis J. Aristocracy in America, from the Sketch-Book of a German Nobleman. 1839. Reprint, New York: Harper, 1959.

Guillet, Edwin C. The Lives and Times of the Patriots: An Account of the Rebellion in Upper Canada, 1837–1838, and the Patriot Agitation in the United States, 1837–1842. 1938. Reprint, Toronto: University of Toronto Press, 1968.

Hale, William H. Useful Knowledge for the Producers of Wealth: Being an Enquiry into the Nature of Trade, the Currency, the Protective and Internal Improvement Systems, and into the Origin and Effects of Banking and Paper Money. New York: G. H. Evans, 1833.

Hall, Basil. Travels in North America, in the Years 1827 and 1828. 2 vols. Philadelphia: Carey, Lea and Carey, 1829.

[Hamilton, Thomas.] Men and Manners in America. 1833. Reprint, New York: Augustus M. Kelly, 1968.

Haswell, Chas. H. *Reminiscences of an Octogenarian*. New York: Harper and Brothers, 1896.

[Hildreth, Richard.] *William Henry Harrison versus Martin Van Buren*. Boston: Weeks, Jordan & Co., 1840.

Hill, George. *Scenes from the Life of an Actor*. New York: Garrett and Co., 1853.

Historical Collections of Piscataquis County, Maine: Consisting of Papers Read at Meetings of Piscataquis County Historical Society: Also, The North Eastern Boundary Controversy and the Aroostook War, with Documentary Matter Pertaining Thereto. Dover: Observer Press, 1910.

Hone, Philip. *The Diary of Philip Hone, 1828–1851*. Edited by Allan Nevins. 2 vols. New York: Dodd, Mead and Co., 1927.

Houston, Mrs. (Matilda Charlotte). *Hesperos: or, Travels in the West*. London: J. W. Parker, 1850.

Houston, Sam. *The Writings of Sam Houston, 1813–1863*. Edited by Amelia W. Williams and Eugene C. Barker. 8 vols. Austin: University of Texas Press, 1938–43.

Howitt, E[manuel]. *Selections from Letters Written during a Tour of the United States, in the Summer and Autumn of 1819; . . . .* Nottingham: Printed and sold by J. Dunn, 1820.

Ingersoll, C. J. *A Discourse Concerning the Influence of America on the Mind*. Philadelphia: Abraham Small, 1823.

———. *Historical Sketch of the Second War between the United States of America and Great Britain*. 3 vols. Philadelphia: Lea and Blanchard, 1845.

———. *Inchiquin, the Jesuit's Letters, during a Late Residence in the United States of America*. New York: L. Riley, 1810.

Irving, Washington. *Bracebridge Hall*. Pocantico Ed. New York: G. P. Putnam's, n.d.

———. *The Sketch Book of Geoffrey Crayon, Gentleman*. 1822. Reprint, Boston: George P. Putnam's, 1848.

Jackson, Andrew. *Correspondence of Andrew Jackson*. Edited by John Spencer Bassett. Washington D.C.: Carnegie Institute of Washington, 1926–35.

James, John W. *An Address, Delivered at the Columbian College, in the District of Columbia, in the Celebration of the National Anniversary, July 4, 1826*. Washington D.C.: Columbian Star Office, 1826.

Janson, Charles William. *The Stranger in America: Containing Observations Made during a Long Residence in that Country*. 1807. Reprint, New York: The Press of the Pioneers, 1935.

Jefferson, Joseph. *The Autobiography of Joseph Jefferson*. New York: The Century Co., 1889.

Jefferson, Thomas. *The Writings of Thomas Jefferson*. Edited by Andrew A. Lipscomb and Albert Ellery Bergh. 20 vols. Washington, D.C., 1903–4.

Jones, Anson. *Memoranda and Official Correspondence relating to the Republic of Texas, Its History and Annexation*. 1859. Reprint, Chicago: Rio Grande Press, 1966.

Kemble, Fanny. *Fanny Kemble, Journal of a Young Actress*. Edited by Monica Gough. New York: Columbia University Press, 1990.

Lamar, Mirabeau Buonaparte. *The Papers of Mirabeau Buonaparte Lamar*. Edited from the original papers in the Texas State Library by Charles Gulick; with the assistance of Katherine Elliott. 6 vols. in 7. Austin, Tex.: A. C. Baldwin and Sons, Printers, 1921–27.

Legaré, Hugh S. *Writings of Hugh Swinton Legaré*. 1846. Reprint, New York: Da Capo Press, 1970.

Lester, C. Edwards. *The Glory and the Shame of England*. 2 vols. New York: Harper and Brothers, 1841.

Lindsley, Philip. *An Address Delivered at Nashville, Tenn. Feb. 22, 1832, at the Request of the Citizens of Nashville and Its Vicinity, on the Occasion of the Centennial Birth Day of George Washington*. Nashville: Hunt, Tariff and Co., 1832.

———. *Baccalaureate Address, Pronounced on the Seventh Anniversary Commencement of the University of Nashville, October 3, 1832*. Nashville: Hunt, Tardiff, 1832.

List, Friedrich. *The National System of Political Economy*. 1885. Reprint, A. M. Kelley, 1966.

———. *Outlines of American Political Economy: In a Series of Letters Addressed by Frederick List to Charles J. Ingersoll; to Which is Added the Celebrated Letters of Mr. Jefferson to Benjamin Austin, and of Mr. Madison to the Editors of the Lynchburg Virginian*. Philadelphia: S. Parker, 1827.

Littell, John S. *The Clay Minstrel*. New York: Greeley and McElrath, 1844.

Longfellow, Henry Wadsworth. *Kavanagh, A Tale*. Boston: Ticknor and Fields, 1849.

Lowell, James Russell. *A Fable for Critics, or, Better—A Glance at a Few of Our Literary Progenies, from the Tub of Diogenes; that is, a Series of Jokes by a Wonderful Quiz*. New York: G. P. Putnam, 1848.

Ludlow, H. G. *A Thanksgiving Sermon, Preached in the Church Street Church, New Haven, Nov. 19, 1840*. New Haven: B. L. Hamlen, 1840.

Lundy, Benjamin. *The Origin and True Causes of the Texas Insurrection*. Philadelphia, 1836.

Luxon, Norval Neil. *Niles' Weekly Register, News Magazine of the Nineteenth Century*. Baton Rouge: Louisiana State University Press, 1947.

Mackay, Alexander. *The Western World, or, Travels in the United States in 1846–47: Exhibiting Them in Their Latest Development, Social, Political and Industrial: Including a Chapter on California*. 2nd ed. 3 vols. London: Richard Bentley, 1849.

Mackenzie, William Lyon. *Sketches of Canada and the United States*. London: E. Wilson, 1833.

Macready, William Charles. *The Diaries of William Charles Macready, 1833–1851*. 2 vols. 1912. Reprint, New York: B. Blom, 1969.

Marryat, Frederick. *A Diary in America, With Remarks on Its Institutions*. 2 vols. Philadelphia: Carey and Hart, 1839.

———. *Diary in America*. Edited by Jules Zanger. Bloomington: Indiana University Press, 1960.

———. *Second Series of A Diary in America, with Remarks on Its Institutions*. Philadelphia: T. K. and P. G. Collins, 1840.

Marsh, George Perkins. *The Goths in New-England: A Discourse Delivered at the Anniversary of the Philomathesian Society of Middlebury College, August 15, 1843*. Middlebury: J. Cobb, 1843.

Martineau, Harriet. *The Martyr Age of the United States*. Newcastle-upon-Tyne: Finley and Charlton, 1840.

———. *Society in America*. London: Saunders and Otley, 1837.

Mathews, [Anne]. *A Continuation of the Memoirs of Charles Mathews, Comedian*. 2 vols. Philadelphia: Lea and Blanchard, 1839.

Mathews, Charles James. *The Life of Charles James Mathews.* Edited by Charles Dickens. 2 vols. London: Macmillan and Co., 1879.

Maury, Sarah Mytton. *An Englishwoman in America.* London: Thomas Richardson and Son, 1848.

———. *The Statesmen in America.* Philadelphia: Carey and Hart, 1847.

Maxwell, A. M. *A Run through the United States, during the Autumn of 1840.* 2 vols. London: Henry Colburn, Publisher, 1841.

McDuffie, George. *Speech of the Hon. George McDuffie, May 19, 1831.* Charleston, S.C.: A. E. Miller, 1831.

Meade, George Gordon. *The Life and Letters of George Gordon Meade.* New York: Charles Scribner's Sons, 1913.

Melville, Herman. *Redburn, His First Voyage; Being the Sailor-Boy Confessions and Reminiscences of the Son-of-a-Gentleman, in the Merchant Service.* Evanston, Ill.: Northwestern University Press, 1969.

Memoir of Mr. and Mrs. Wood, Containing an Authentic Account of the Principal Events in the Lives of These Celebrated Vocalists. Philadelphia: Turner and Fisher, 1840.

Morris, George P., ed. *American Melodies.* New York: Linen and Fennell, 1841.

Mowatt, Anna Cora. *Autobiography of an Actress; or, Eight Years on the Stage.* Boston: Ticknor, Reed, and Fields, 1853.

Murray, Charles Augustus. *Travels in North America during the Years 1834, 1835 & 1836.* 2 vols. London: R. Bentley, 1839.

Neal, John. *American Writers: A Series of Papers Contributed to Blackwood's Magazine (1824–1825).* Edited by Fred Lewis Pattee. Durham, N.C.: Duke University Press, 1937.

Nichols, Thomas Low. *Forty Years of American Life, 1821–1861.* New York: Stackpole Sons, 1937.

Northall, William Knight. *Before and Behind the Curtain.* New York: W. F. Burgess, 1851.

Ogle, Charles. *Speech of Mr. Ogle, of Pennsylvania, on the Regal Splendor of the President's Palace. Delivered in the House of Representatives, April 14, 1840.* [Washington, D.C., 1840.]

Ouseley, William G. *Remarks on the Statistics and Political Institutions of the United States.* Philadelphia: Carey and Lea, 1832.

Papers Relating to the Garrison Mob. Edited by Theodore Lyman 3d. Cambridge, Mass.: Welch, Bigelow, and Co., Printers to the University, 1870.

Paulding, James Kirke. *John Bull in America, or, The New Munchausen.* New York: Charles Wiley, 1825.

———. *The Lay of the Scottish Fiddle: A Poem in Five Cantos.* London: Whittingham and Rowland, Printers, 1814.

———. *Letters from the South, by A Northern Man.* New ed. 2 vols. New York: Harper and Brothers, 1835.

———. *Lion of the West; Retitled The Kentuckian, or A Trip to New York.* Edited by James N. Tidwell. Stanford, Calif.: Stanford University Press, 1954.

———. *A Sketch of Old England, by a New-England Man.* 2 vols. New York: Charles Wiley, 1822.

———. *The United States and England: Being a Reply to the Criticism of Inchiquin's Letters contained in the Quarterly review for January, 1814.* Philadelphia, 1815.

Pennsylvania Historical Survey. *Calendar of Joel R. Poinsett Papers in the Henry D. Gilpin Collection*. Edited by Grace E. Heilman and Bernard S. Levin. Philadelphia: The Gilpin Library of the Historical Society of Pennsylvania, 1941.

Pickens, F. W. *Remarks of Hon. F. W. Pickens, on the Separation of the Government from All Banks. Delivered in the House of Representatives, Oct. 10, 1837*. Washington, D.C.: Printed at the Globe Office, 1837.

———. *Speech of Hon. F. W. Pickens, of South Carolina, on the Loan Bill*. [1841.]

Pinckney, Henry Laurens. *An Oration, Delivered in St. Michael's Church*. Charleston: W. P. Young, 1818.

———. *An Oration, Delivered in the College Chapel, before the Clariosophic Society Incorporate*. Charleston, A. E. Miller, 1828.

Playfair, Hugo. *Brother Jonathan, the Smartest Nation in All Creation*. 3 vols. London: Saunders and Otley, 1844.

Poe, Edgar Allan. *The Complete Works of Edgar Allan Poe*. Edited by James Albert Harrison, New York: AMS Press, 1965.

Poinsett, Joel R. *Joel R. Poinsett, Substance of a Speech, Delivered by the Hon. Joel R. Poinsett, at a Public Meeting Held at Seyle's, October 5th, 1832*. Charleston: J. S. Burges, 1832.

Polk, James K. *Correspondence of James K. Polk*. Edited by Herbert Weaver, Wayne Cutler et al. 11 vols. Nashville: Vanderbilt University Press, 1969- .

———. *The Diary of James K. Polk during His Presidency*. Edited by Milo M. Quaife. 4 vols. Chicago: A. C. McClurg and Co., 1910.

———. "Letters of James K. Polk to Andrew J. Donelson, 1843–1848." *Tennessee Historical Magazine* 3 (March–December 1917): 67-68.

Poore, Ben[jamin] Perley. *Perley's Reminiscences of Sixty Years in the National Metropolis*. Philadelphia: Hubbard Bros., 1886.

Prescott, William Hickling. *The Papers of William Hickling Prescott*. Edited by C. Harvey Gardiner. Urbana: University of Illinois Press, 1969.

Preston, William C. *The Reminiscences of William C. Preston*. Edited by Minnie Clare Yarborough. Chapel Hill: University of North Carolina Press, 1933.

———. *Speech of Mr. Preston, of South Carolina, in the Senate of the United States, March 1, 1836, on the Abolition Question*. Washington, D.C.: Gales and Seaton, 1836.

Proceedings and Address, of the Committee of the Anti-Jackson Men of Franklin County, Pennsylvania. George K. Harper, Printer [1832].

Proceedings and Address of the New Jersey State Convention. Trenton: Joseph Justice, 1828.

Proceedings of a General Meeting, Held at Columbia Courthouse, November 18, 1831. Columbia: A. Landrum, 1832.

Proceedings of the General Anti-Slavery Convention Called by the Committee of the British and Foreign Anti-slavery Society, and Held in London from Tuesday, June 13th, to Tuesday, June 20th, 1843. By J. F. Johnson, Short-Hand Writer. 1843. Reprint, Miami: Mnemosyne Publishing Co., 1969.

The Pro-Slavery Argument as Maintained by the Most Distinguished Writers of the Southern States containing the Several Essays, on the Subject, of Chancellor Harper, Governor Hammond, Dr. Simms, and Professor Dew. Charleston: Walker, Richards, and Co., 1852.

Putnam, George Palmer. *American Facts.* London: Wiley and Putnam, 1845.

Quincy, Josiah. *Memoir of the Life of John Quincy Adams.* Boston: N. Phillips, Sampson and Company, 1859.

Rantoul, Robert, Jr. *Memoirs, Speeches and Writings of Robert Rantoul, Jr.* Edited by Luther Hamilton. Boston: John P. Jewett and Co., 1854.

———. *An Oration Delivered before the Democratic Citizens of the County of Worcester, Worcester, July 4, 1837.* Worcester, Mass.: Mirick and Bartlett, 1837.

———. *An Oration Delivered before the Democrats and Antimasons, of the County of Plymouth, at Scituate, on the Fourth of July, 1836.* Boston: Beals and Greene, 1836.

Rees, James. *The Dramatic Authors of America.* Philadelphia: G. B. Zeiber and Co., 1845.

Reese, David M. *Letters to the Hon. William Jay.* New York: Leavitt, Lord and Co., 1835.

Report of the Discussion at Pottsville—August 10, 1844, Between J. G. Clarkson & F. W. Hughes, on the Course of Henry Clay and James K. Polk, Relative to the Protective System. Philadelphia, 1844.

Republican Meeting of the Citizens of Washington City Friendly to the Re-election of Andrew Jackson to the Presidency. [1832.]

Rhett, Barnwell. *Speech of Hon. R. Barnwell Rhett of South Carolina on the Annexation of Texas to the United States, January 31, 1845.* [Washington, D.C.: n.p., 1845].

Rodgers, Charles T. *American Superiority at the World's Fair.* Philadelphia: John J. Hawkins, 1852.

The Rough and Ready Songster: Embellished with Twenty-five Splendid Engravings, Illustrative of the American Victories in Mexico. By an American Officer. New York: Nafis and Cornish, 1848.

[Royall, Anne Newport.] *Sketches of History, Life, and Manners in the United States.* New Haven, Conn., 1826.

Sampson, William. *An Anniversary Discourse Delivered before the New York Historical Society on the Common Law.* New York: E. Bliss and E. White, 1824.

Sampson, William, and Pishey Thompson. *Sampson's Discourse, and Correspondence with Various Learned Jurists upon the history of the law.* Washington City: Printed by Gales and Seaton, 1826.

Schmidt, Philip R. *Hezekiah Niles and American Economic Nationalism.* New York: Arno Press, 1982.

Scott, A. *Prince of Wales.* New York: H. De Marsan, [1859].

Sedgwick, [Catherine Maria]. *Letters from Abroad to Kindred at Home.* 2 vols. New York: Harper and Brothers, 1841.

[Sedgwick, Theodore.] *Thoughts on the Proposed Annexation of Texas to the United States.* 1844.

Shelton, Frederick William. *The Trollopiad, or, Travelling Gentlemen in America: A Satire, by Nil Admirari, Esq.* New York: C. Shepard, 1837.

Sheppard, Lorna Geer, ed. *An Editor's View of Early Texas as Depicted in the Northern Standard (1842–1846).* Austin: Eakin Press, 1998.

Simms, William Gilmore. *The Charleston Book: A Miscellany in Prose and Verse.* Charleston, S.C., 1845.

———. *Letters of William Gilmore Simms.* Edited by Mary C. Simms Oliphant, Alfred

Taylor Odell, and T. C. Duncan Eaves. 6 vols. Columbia: University of South Carolina Press, 1952–82.

——. *The Social Principle, the True Source of National Permanence: An Oration Delivered before the Erosophic Society of the University of Alabama, December 13, 1842.* Tuscaloosa: Erosophic Society, 1843.

——. *Sources of American Independence, An Oration, on the Sixty-ninth Anniversary of American Independence, Delivered at Aiken, South Carolina.* Aiken, S.C., 1844.

——. *Views and Reviews in American Literature, History, and Fiction: First Series.* Cambridge, Mass.: Belknap Press of Harvard University Press, 1962.

Simpson, Stephen. *The Working Man's Manual: A New Theory of Political Economy, on the Principle of Production the Source of Wealth.* Philadelphia: Thomas L. Bonsal, 1831.

Smith, Ashbel. *Reminiscences of the Texas Republic.* 1876. Reprint, Austin, Tex.: Pemberton Press, 1967.

Smith, Sydney. *Wit and Wisdom of the Rev. Sydney Smith.* Edited by Evert A. Duyckinck. New York: J. S. Redfield, 1856.

Stanton, Elizabeth Cady. *Eighty Years and More (1815–1897): Reminiscences of Elizabeth Cady Stanton.* New York: European Publishing Co., 1898.

Stanton, Henry B. *Random Recollections.* New York: Harper and Brothers, 1887.

State Papers and Speeches on the Tariff. Edited by F. W. Taussig. Cambridge, Mass.: Harvard University Press, 1893.

Steward, Austin. *Twenty-two Years a Slave, and Forty Years a Freeman: Embracing a Correspondence of Several Years while President of Wilberforce Colony, London, Canada West.* Rochester: William Alling, 1857.

Stone, Henry Dickinson. *Personal Recollections of the Drama: or Theatrical Reminiscences, Embracing Sketches of Prominent Actors and Actresses, Their Chief Characteristics, Original Anecdotes of Them, and Incidents Connected Therewith.* Albany, N.Y.: Charles Van Benthuysen and Sons, 1873.

Stone, Richard Gabriel. *Hezekiah Niles as an Economist.* Baltimore: Johns Hopkins University Press, 1933.

Strange, Robert. *Oration of Robert Strange, Esq., Delivered at Fayetteville, N.C., on the Jubilee of American Independence, July 4, 1826.* Fayetteville: E. J. Hale, 1826.

Stuart, Charles. *British Opinions of the American Colonization Society.* Boston: Garrison and Knapp, 1833.

Stuart, James. *Three Years in North America.* New York: J. and J. Harper, 1833.

Stuart-Wortley, Emmeline. *Travels in the United States, Etc., during 1849 and 1850.* New York: Harper and Brothers, 1851.

Stubblebine, Daniel. *The Man Child Ruling the Nations with a Rod of Iron, and Breaking to Pieces the Great Red Dragon of the European Laws in America.* Reading, Pa., 1845.

Sturge, Joseph. *A Visit to the United States in 1841.* Boston: Dexter S. King, 1842.

Sullivan, George. *Popular Explanation of the System of Circulating Medium Recently Published in the Form of an Act of Congress.* New York: Samuel Colman, 1839.

Sullivan, John L. *Considerations Which Tend to Prove That a States' National Bank, is Necessary to Countervail the Injurious Effects of the New Banking System of England on the Revenue, Domestic Commerce, Manufactures, and Internal Improvements of the United States, Respectfully Addressed to the President.* New Haven, Conn.: Printed by B. L. Hamlen, 1838.

Sutherland, Th[omas] Jefferson. *Three Political Letters, Addressed to D. Wolfred Nelson.* New York: 1840.

Tappan, Lewis. *A Side-Light on Anglo-American Relations, 1839–1858: Furnished by the Correspondence of Lewis Tappan and Others with the British and Foreign Anti-Slavery Committee.* Edited with an introduction and notes by Heloise Abel and Frank J. Klingberg. New York: Augustus M. Kelley, 1970.

Taylor, John. *Construction Construed, and Constitutions Vindicated.* Richmond, Va.: Shepherd and Pollard, 1820.

———. *An Enquiry into Principles and Tendency of Certain Public Measures.* Philadelphia: Dobson, 1794.

———. *Tyranny Unmasked.* Washington, D.C.: Davis and Force, 1822.

Thome, Ja[me]s A. and J. Horace Kimball. *Emancipation in the West Indies: A Six Months' Tour in Antigua, Barbadoes, and Jamaica, in the Year 1837.* New York: The American Anti-Slavery Society, 1838.

Thompson, George, and Robert J. Breckinridge. *Discussion of American Slavery: Between George Thompson, Esq., . . . and Rev. Robert J. Breckinridge . . . .* Boston: Isaac Knapp, 1836.

Thompson, Waddy. *An Examination of the Claims of Mr. Van Buren and Gen. Harrison to the Support of the South.* 1840.

———. *Recollections of Mexico.* New York: Wiley and Putnam, 1846.

Thornton, T. C. *An Inquiry into the History of Slavery.* Washington, D.C.: William M. Morrison, 1841.

Tippecanoe Song Book: A Collection of Log Cabin and Patriotic Melodies. Philadelphia: Marshall, Williams, and Butler, 1840.

Towles, James. *Desperation of Whigery: Lying Outright, and Forgery to Sustain It.* Washington, D.C.: 1844.

Trollope, Frances. *Domestic Manners of the Americans* (1832). Edited, with a history of Mrs. Trollope's adventures in America, by Donald Smalley. New York: Alfred A. Knopf, 1949.

Tuckerman, Henry T. *A Month in England.* New York: Redfield, 1853.

Tudor, Henry. *Narrative of a Tour in North America.* 2 vols. London: James Duncan, 1834.

Turnbull, Robert J. *The Crisis, or, Essays on the Usurpations of the Federal Government.* Charleston, S.C.: A. E. Miller, 1827.

Tyson, J. Washington. *The Doctrines of the "Abolitionists" Refuted, in a Letter from J. Washington Tyson, the Democratic Harrison Candidate for Congress, in the First District, of Pennsylvania.* Philadelphia, 1840.

Vandenhoff, George. *Leaves from an Actor's Note-Book; with Reminiscences and Chit-Chat from the Green-Room and the Stage, in England and America.* New York: D. Appleton and Co., 1860.

Walker, David. *Walker's Appeal, in Four Articles: Together with a Preamble, to the Coloured Citizens of the World . . . .* Boston, 1829.

Walker, Robert J. *Letter of Mr. Walker, of Mississippi, Relative to the Annexation of Texas: In Reply to the Call of the People of Carroll County, Kentucky, to Communicate His Views on That Subject.* St. Louis: Missourian Office, 1844.

Wallack, Lester. *Memories of Fifty Years*. London: Sampson, Low, Marston, Searle, and Rivington, 1889.

Walling, George. *Recollections of a New York City Police Chief*. New York: Caxton Book Concern, 1887.

Walsh, Michael. *Sketches of the Speeches and Writings of Michael Walsh: Including his Poems and Correspondence, Compiled by a Committee of the Spartan Association*. New York, 1843.

Walsh, Robert, Jr. *An Appeal from the Judgments of Great Britain*. Philadelphia: Mitchell, Ames and White, 1819.

Ward, Henry George. *Mexico in 1827*. 2 vols. London: Henry Colburn, 1829.

Warburton, George. *Hochelaga; or, England in the New World*. 2 vols. London: Henry Colburn, Publisher, 1846.

Wemyss, Francis Courtney. *Twenty-six Years of the Life of an Actor and Manager*. New York: Burgess, Stringer, and Co., 1847.

Whig Songs: Selected, Sung, and Published, by the Choir of the National Clay Club. Philadelphia, 1844.

White, George. *Memoir of Samuel Slater, the Father of American Manufactures*. Philadelphia, 1836.

Whitman, Walt. *The Gathering of the Forces: Editorials, Essays, Literary and Dramatic Reviews and other Material Written as Editor of the Brooklyn Daily Eagle in 1846 and 1847*. Edited by Cleveland Rodgers and John Black. 2 vols. New York: G. P. Putnam's Sons, 1920.

Wilson, C. H. *The Wanderer in America: Or, Truth at Home*. Northallerton, U.K.: Printed for the author, by J. Langdale, 1820.

Winthrop, Robert. *Addresses and Speeches on Various Occasions*. Boston: Little, Brown and Co., 1852.

Wise, Henry A. *Speech of Mr. Wise, of Virginia, on the Subject of Abolition of Slavery within the District of Columbia*. Washington, D.C.: National Intelligencer, 1835.

Wood, Henry, Yorkshire Journalist. *Change for the American Notes: In Letters from London to New York, by an American Lady*. New York: Harper and Brothers, 1843.

Wood, William B. *Personal Recollections of the Stage*. Philadelphia: Henry Carey Baird, 1855.

Woodbury, Levi. *Speech of the Hon. Levi Woodbury, Delivered at the Democratic Meeting in Jefferson Hall, Portsmouth (N.H.) November, 18, 1841*. Alexandria, Va.: "Index," 1841.

Wright, Frances. *Address to the People of Philadelphia, Delivered in the Walnut Street Theatre, on the Morning of the Fourth of July, Common Era 1829, and the Fifty-Fourth Year of Independence*. New York: George Evans, Printer, 1829.

———. *Views of Society and Manners in America: In a Series of Letters from That Country to a Friend in England, during the Years 1818, 1819, and 1820, by an English-woman*. London: Printed for Longmont, Hurst, Rees, Orme, and Brown, 1821.

Ximenes [pseud.]. *Mr. Calhoun—Mr. Van Buren—Texas* [broadside]. [July 1, 1843.]

Yeadon, Richard. *Speech of Richard Yeadon, Esq., of Charleston, South Carolina, . . . at the Court-House in Madison Georgia*. 1844.

Young, William T. *Sketch of the Life and Public Services of General Lewis Cass*. Detroit: Markham and Elwood, 1852.

The Young Hickory and Annexation Minstrel, or, Polk and Dallas Melodist. Philadelphia: J. M. Davis, 1844.

Secondary Sources

Adams, Ephraim D. *British Interests and Activities in Texas.* 1909. Reprint, Gloucester, Mass.: Peter Smith, 1963.

Adams, Henry. *History of the United States of America during the Second Administration of James Madison.* 1921. Reprint, New York: Antiquarian Press, 1962.

Allen, H. C. *Great Britain and the United States: A History of Anglo-American Relations, 1783 to 1952.* New York: St. Martin's Press, 1955.

Anderson, Benedict. *Imagined Communities: Reflections on the Origin and Spread of Nationalism.* London: Verso, 1983.

Anderson, Bonnie. *Joyous Greetings: The First International Women's Movement, 1830–1860.* New York: Oxford University Press, 2000.

Appleby, Joyce. *Inheriting the Revolution: The First Generation of Americans.* Cambridge, Mass.: Harvard University Press, 2000.

Arieli, Yehoshua. *Individualism and Nationalism in American Ideology.* Baltimore: Peregrine Books, 1966.

Auerbach, Jeffrey A. *The Great Exhibition of 1851: A Nation on Display.* New Haven, Conn.: Yale University Press, 1999.

Bailyn, Bernard. *The Ideological Origins of the American Revolution.* Cambridge, Mass.: Belknap Press of Harvard University Press, 1967.

Bank, Rosemarie K. *Theatre Culture in America, 1825–1860.* New York: Cambridge University Press, 1997.

Banner, James M., Jr. *To the Hartford Convention: The Federalists and the Origins of Party Politics in Massachusetts, 1789–1815.* New York: Alfred A. Knopf, 1970.

Barker, Anthony J. *Captain Charles Stuart, Anglo-American Abolitionist.* Baton Rouge: Louisiana State University Press, 1986.

Barnes, Gilbert Hobbs. *The Anti-Slavery Impulse, 1830–1844.* New York: Harcourt, Brace, and World, 1964.

Barnes, James J. *The Quest for an Anglo-American Copyright Agreement, 1815–1854.* Columbus: Ohio State University Press, 1974.

Bauer, K. Jack. *The Mexican War, 1846–1848.* New York: Macmillan, 1974.

Belko, W. Stephen. *The Invincible Duff Green, Whig of the West.* Columbia: University of Missouri Press, 2006.

Belohlavek, John M. *Broken Glass: Caleb Cushing and the Shattering of the Union.* Kent, Ohio: Kent State University Press, 2005.

———. *Let the Eagle Soar! The Foreign Policy of Andrew Jackson.* Lincoln: University of Nebraska Press, 1984.

———. "Race, Progress, and Empire: Caleb Cushing and the Quest for American Empire." In *Manifest Destiny and Empire: American Antebellum Expansionism,* edited by Sam W. Haynes and Christopher Morris, 21–47. College Station: Texas A&M University Press, 1997.

Benns, F. Lee. *The American Struggle for the British West Indian Carrying Trade, 1815–1830.* Indianapolis, 1923.

Berge, Dennis E. "Mexican Response to United States' Expansionism, 1841–1848." Ph.D. diss., University of California at Berkeley, 1965.

Berger, Max. *The British Traveller in America, 1836–1860.* New York: AMS Press, 1943.

Bhabha, Homi K. "DissemiNation: Time, Narrative, and the Margins of the Modern Nation." In *Nation and Narration,* edited by Homi Bhabha, 291–320. London: Routledge, 1990.

———. *The Location of Culture.* London: Routledge, 1994.

Blackett, Richard J. "Anglo-American Opposition to Liberian Colonization, 1831–1833." *Historian* 41 (February 1979): 276–94.

Blake, Clagette. *Charles Elliot, R.N., 1801–1875: A Servant of Britain Overseas.* London: Cleaver-Hume Press, 1960.

Boime, Albert. *The Magisterial Gaze: Manifest Destiny and American Landscape Painting, 1830–1865.* Washington, D.C.: Smithsonian Institution, 1991.

Boston, Ray. *British Chartists in America, 1839–1900.* Manchester, U.K.: Manchester University Press, 1971.

Boucher, Chauncey S. "The Annexation of Texas and the Bluffton Movement in South Carolina." *Mississippi Valley Historical Review* 6 (June 1919): 3–33.

Brauer, Kinley J. *Cotton versus Conscience: Massachusetts Whig Politics and Southwestern Expansion, 1843–1848.* Lexington: University of Kentucky Press, 1967.

———. "Seward's 'Foreign War Panacea': An Interpretation." *New York History* 55 (April 1974): 132–57

Brock, William. "The Image of England and American Nationalism." *Journal of American Studies* 5 (December 1971): 225–45.

Bronstein, Jamie I. *Land Reform and the Working-Class Experience in Britain and the United States, 1800–1862.* Stanford, Calif.: Stanford University Press, 1999.

Brown, T. Allston. *A History of the New York Stage, from the First Performance in 1732 to 1901.* New York: Dodd, Mead, and Co., 1903.

Bryan, William Alfred. *George Washington in American Literature, 1775–1865.* New York: Columbia University Press, 1952.

Buckley, Norman. *Slaves in Red Coats: The British West India Regiments, 1795–1815.* New Haven, Conn.: Yale University Press, 1979.

Buckley, Peter George. "To the Opera House: Culture and Society in New York City, 1820–1860." Ph.D. diss., State University of New York at Stony Brook, 1984.

Buell, Lawrence. "American Literary Emergence as a Postcolonial Phenomenon." *American Literary History* 4 (Autumn 1992): 411–42.

———. *Emerson.* Cambridge, Mass.: Belknap Press of Harvard University Press, 2003.

———. "Melville and the Question of Decolonization." *American Literature* 64 (June 1992): 215–37.

Burk, Kathleen. *Old World, New World: Great Britain and America from the Beginning.* New York: Atlantic Monthly Press, 2008.

Burstein, Andrew. *America's Jubilee: How in 1826 a Generation Remembered Fifty Years of Independence.* New York: Alfred A. Knopf, 2001.

———. *The Original Knickerbocker: The Life of Washington Irving.* New York: Basic Books, 2007.

———. *The Passions of Andrew Jackson*. New York: Alfred A. Knopf, 2003.

Bushman, Richard L. *The Refinement of America: Persons, Houses, Cities*. New York: Random House, 1992.

Cairns, William B. *British Criticism of American Writings, 1815–1833*. Madison: University of Wisconsin Press, 1922.

Campbell, Duncan Andrew. *Unlikely Allies: Britain, America, and the Victorian Origins of the Special Relationship*. London: Hambledon Continuum, 2007.

Carroll, Francis M. *A Good and Wise Measure: The Search for the Canadian-American Boundary, 1783–1842*. Toronto: University of Toronto Press, 2001.

Catterall, Ralph C. H. *The Second Bank of the United States*. Chicago: University of Chicago Press, 1902.

Charvat, William. *Literary Publishing in America, 1790–1850*. Philadelphia: University of Pennsylvania Press, 1959.

———. *The Origins of American Critical Thought, 1810–1835*. Philadelphia: University of Pennsylvania Press, 1936.

Cheathem, Mark R. *Old Hickory's Nephew: The Political and Private Struggles of Andrew Jackson Donelson*. Baton Rouge: Louisiana State University Press, 2007.

Clark, Jennifer. "John Bull's American Connection." *Huntington Library Quarterly* 53 (Winter 1990): 15–39.

Cleland, Robert Glass. "The Early Sentiment for the Annexation of California: An Account of the Growth of American Interest in California, 1835–1846." *Southwestern Historical Quarterly* 18 (January 1915): 231–60.

Cohen, Ira. "The Auction System in the Port of New York, 1817–1837." *Business History Review* 45 (Winter 1971): 488–510.

Cook, Charles M. *The American Codification Movement: A Study of Antebellum Legal Reform*. Westport, Conn.: Greenwood Press, 1981.

Cooper, William J., Jr. *The South and the Politics of Slavery, 1828–1856*. Baton Rouge: Louisiana State University Press, 1978.

Costeloe, Michael P. *Bonds and Bondholders: British Investors and Mexico's Foreign Debt, 1824–1888*. Westport, Conn.: Praeger, 2003.

Cramer, Richard S. "British Magazines and the Oregon Question." *Pacific Historical Review* 32 (1963): 369–82.

Crapol, Edward P. *America for the Americans: Economic Nationalism and Anglophobia*. Westport, Conn.: Greenwood Press, 1973.

———. *John Tyler: The Accidental President*. Chapel Hill: University of North Carolina Press, 2006.

———. "John Tyler and the Pursuit of National Destiny." *Journal of the Early American Republic* 17 (October 1997): 467–91.

Crawford, Martin. *The Anglo-American Crisis of the Mid-Nineteenth Century: The Times and America, 1850–1862*. Athens: University of Georgia Press, 1987.

———. "British Travellers and the Anglo-American Relationship in the 1850s." *Journal of American Studies* 12 (August 1978): 203–19.

Crouthamel, James L. "James Watson Webb and the New York Courier and Enquirer, 1827–1861." Ph.D. diss., University of Rochester, 1958.

Cunliffe, Marcus. *Chattel Slavery and Wage Slavery: The Anglo-American Context, 1830–1860*. Athens: University of Georgia Press, 1979.

——. *George Washington, Man and Monument.* Boston: Little, Brown and Co., 1958.

Current, Richard N. "Webster's Propaganda and the Ashburton Treaty." *Mississippi Valley Historical Review* 34 (September 1947): 187–200.

Curti, Merle E. "Young America." *American Historical Review* 32 (October 1926): 34–55.

Curtis, James. *Andrew Jackson and the Search for Vindication.* New York: Longman, 1988.

Da Costa, Emilia Viotti. *Crowns of Glory, Tears of Blood: The Demerara Slave Rebellion of 1823.* New York: Oxford University Press, 1994.

Dangerfield, George. *The Awakening of American Nationalism, 1815–1828.* New York: Harper Torchbooks, 1965.

Davis, David Brion. "The Emergence of Immediatism in British and Antislavery Thought." *Mississippi Valley Historical Review* 49 (September 1962): 209–30.

De Armond, Louis. "Justo Sierra O'Reilly and Yucatecan United States Relations, 1847–1848." *Hispanic American Historical Review* 31 (August 1951): 426.

Dictionary of American Biography. Edited by A. Johnson et al. 22 vols. New York: Scribner's, 1936.

Dowty, Alan. *The Limits of American Isolationism: The United States and the Crimean War.* New York: New York University Press, 1971.

Earle, Jonathan H. *Jacksonian Antislavery and the Politics of Free Soil, 1824–1854.* Chapel Hill: University of North Carolina Press, 2004

Eckes, Alfred E. *Opening America's Market: U.S. Foreign Trade Policy since 1776.* Chapel Hill: University of North Carolina Press, 1995.

Egerton, Douglas R. "'Its Origin Is Not a Little Curious': A New Look at the American Colonization Society." *Journal of the Early Republic* 5 (Spring 1985): 463–80.

Eiselen, Malcolm R. *The Rise of Pennsylvania Protection.* Philadelphia: Porcupine Press, 1974.

Eldridge, Herbert G. "The Paper War between England and America: The Inchiquin Episode, 1810–1815." *Journal of American Studies* 16 (April 1982): 49–68.

Ellis, Joseph J. *After the Revolution: Profiles of Early American Culture.* New York: W. W. Norton, 1979.

Elson, Ruth Miller. *Guardians of Tradition: American Schoolbooks of the Nineteenth Century.* Lincoln: University of Nebraska Press, 1964.

Erickson, Charlotte. *Invisible Immigrants: The Adaptation of English and Scottish Immigrants in Nineteenth-Century America.* Leicester, U.K.: Leicester University Press, 1972.

Faust, Drew Gilpin. *James Henry Hammond and the Old South.* Baton Rouge: Louisiana State University Press, 1982.

——. *A Sacred Circle: The Dilemma of the Intellectual in the Old South, 1840–1860.* Baltimore: Johns Hopkins University Press, 1977.

Fay, Peter. *The Opium War, 1840–1842: Barbarians in the Celestial Empire in the Early Part of the Nineteenth Century and the War by Which They Forced Her Gates Ajar.* Chapel Hill: University of North Carolina Press, 1975.

Ferris, Norman B. *Desperate Diplomacy: William H. Seward's Foreign Policy, 1861.* Knoxville: University of Tennessee Press, 1976.

Fischer, David Hackett. *The Revolution in American Conservatism: The Federalist Party in the Era of Jeffersonian Democracy.* New York: Harper and Row, 1965.

Fladeland, Betty. *Men and Brothers: Anglo-American Antislavery Cooperation.* Urbana: University of Illinois Press, 1972.

Foletta, Marshall. *Coming to Terms with Democracy: Federalist Intellectuals and the Shaping of American Culture.* Charlottesville: University Press of Virginia, 2001.

Folk, Patrick Allen. "'The Queen City of Mobs': Riots and Community Reactions in Cincinnati, 1788–1848." Ph.D. diss., University of Toledo, 1978.

Foos, Paul. *A Short, Offhand, Killing Affair: Soldiers and Social Conflict during the Mexican-American War.* Chapel Hill: University of North Carolina Press, 2002.

Ford, Lacy. *The Origins of Southern Radicalism: The South Carolina Upcountry, 1800–1860.* New York: Oxford University Press, 1991.

Foster, Charles I. *An Errand of Mercy: The Evangelical United Front, 1790–1837.* Chapel Hill: University of North Carolina Press, 1960.

Franklin, Wayne. *James Fenimore Cooper: The Early Years.* New Haven, Conn.: Yale University Press, 2007.

Freehling, William W. *Prelude to Civil War: The Nullification Controversy in South Carolina, 1816–1836.* New York: Harper and Row, 1966.

———. *Road to Disunion: Secessionists at Bay, 1776–1854.* New York: Oxford University Press, 1991.

Frey, Sylvia R. *Water from the Rock: Black Resistance in a Revolutionary Age.* Princeton, N.J.: Princeton University Press, 1991.

Friedman, Lawrence J. *Inventors of the Promised Land.* New York: Alfred A. Knopf, 1975.

Friend, Llerena. *Sam Houston, The Great Designer.* 1954. Reprint, Austin: University of Texas Press, 1969.

Fuller, John Douglas Pitts. *The Movement for the Acquisition of All Mexico, 1846–1848.* Baltimore: Johns Hopkins University Press, 1936.

Gallagher, Kent. *The Foreigner in Early American Drama: A Study in Attitudes.* The Hague: Mouton and Co., 1966.

Garrison, Wendell Phillips, and Francis Jackson Garrison. *William Lloyd Garrison, 1805–1879: The Story of His Life, Told by His Children.* 4 vols. New York: Century, 1885.

Giles, Paul. *Transatlantic Insurrections: British Culture and the Formation of American Literature, 1730–1860.* Philadelphia: University of Pennsylvania Press, 2001.

Gilje, Paul A. *The Road to Mobocracy: Popular Discontent in New York City, 1763–1834.* Chapel Hill: University of North Carolina Press, 1987.

Gilmore, N. Ray. "Henry George Ward, British Publicist for Mexican Mines." *Pacific Historical Review* 32 (February 1963): 35–47.

Goetzmann, William H. *Army Exploration in the American West, 1803–1863.* Lincoln: University of Nebraska Press, 1980.

Govan, Thomas Payne. *Nicholas Biddle: Nationalist and Public Banker. 1786–1844.* Chicago: University of Chicago Press, 1959.

Graebner, Norman A. *Empire on the Pacific: A Study in American Continental Expansion.* New York: Ronald Press, 1955.

Gravil, Richard. *Romantic Dialogues: Anglo-American Continuities, 1776–1862.* New York: St. Martin's Press, 2000.

Gray, Elizabeth Kelly. "American Attitudes toward British Imperialism, 1815–1860." Ph.D. diss., College of William and Mary, 2002.

Green, William A. *British Slave Emancipation: The Sugar Colonies and the Great Experiment, 1830–1865.* Oxford: Clarendon Press, 1976.

Greenberg, Kenneth S. *Masters and Statesmen: The Political Culture of American Slavery.* Baltimore: Johns Hopkins University Press, 1985.

Greene, Jack P. *The Intellectual Construction of America: Exceptionalism and Identity from 1492 to 1800.* Chapel Hill: University of North Carolina Press, 1993.

Greenspan, Ezra. *George Palmer Putnam, Representative American Publisher.* University Park: Pennsylvania State University Press, 2000.

Greer, Allan. "1837–38: Rebellion Reconsidered." *Canadian Historical Review* 76 (March 1995): 1–18.

Gregory, Frances W. *Nathan Appleton: Merchant and Entrepreneur, 1779–1861.* Charlottesville: University Press of Virginia, 1975.

Grimsted, David. *American Mobbing, 1828–1861: Toward Civil War.* New York: Oxford University Press, 1998.

———. *Melodrama Unveiled: American Theatre and Culture, 1800–1850.* Chicago: University of Chicago Press, 1968.

Gross, Izhak. "The Abolition of Negro Slavery and British Parliamentary Reform, 1832–33." *Historical Journal* 23 (March 1980): 63–85.

Guyatt, Nicholas. *Providence and the Invention of America, 1607–1876.* New York: Cambridge University Press, 2007.

Hague, Harlan, and David J. Langum. *Thomas O. Larkin: A Life of Patriotism and Profit in Old California.* Norman: University of Oklahoma Press, 1990.

Hamlin, Charles Eugene. *The Life and Times of Hannibal Hamlin.* Cambridge, Mass.: Riverside Press, 1899.

Hammond, Bray. *Banks and Politics in America: From the Revolution to the Civil War.* Princeton, N.J.: Princeton University Press, 1957.

Harlow, Alvin. *Old Bowery Days.* New York: D. Appleton and Co., [1931].

Hartung, George Westebee. "James Fenimore Cooper's Attitude Toward England." Ph.D. diss., University of Wisconsin, 1957.

Harwood, Thomas F. "British Evangelical Abolitionism and American Churches in the 1830s." *Journal of Southern History* 28 (August 1962): 287–306.

Hawgood, John, ed. *First and Last Consul, Thomas Oliver Larkin and the Americanization of California: A Selection of Letters.* San Marino, Calif.: Huntington Library, 1962.

Hay, Robert P. "'The Presidential Question': Letters to Southern Editors." *Tennessee Historical Quarterly* 31 (Summer 1972): 170–86.

Haynes, Sam W. "Anglophobia and the Annexation of Texas: The Quest for National Security." In *Manifest Destiny and Empire: American Antebellum Expansionism,* edited by Sam W. Haynes and Christopher Morris, 115–45. College Station: Texas A&M University Press, 1997.

Haynes, Sam W. *James K. Polk and the Expansionist Impulse.* New York: Longman, 1997.

———. *Soldiers of Misfortune: The Somervell and Mier Expeditions.* Austin: University of Texas Press, 1990.

Headley, Joel Tyler. *The Great Riots of New York, 1712–1873.* New York: E. B. Treat, 1873.

Heale, M. J. *The Presidential Quest: Candidates and Images in American Political Culture, 1787–1852*. London: Longman, 1982.

Henderson, Timothy J. *A Glorious Defeat: Mexico and Its War with the United States*. New York: Hill and Wang, 2007.

Heuman, Gad. "The British West Indies." In *The Oxford History of the British Empire: The Nineteenth Century*, edited by Andrew Porter, 3:470–94. New York: Oxford University Press, 1999.

Hidy, Ralph W. *The House of Baring in American Trade and Finance: English Merchant Bankers at Work, 1763–1861*. Cambridge, Mass.: Harvard University Press, 1949.

———. "The Organization and Function of Anglo-American Merchant Bankers, 1815–1860." *Journal of Economic History* 1 (December 1941): 53–66.

Hietala, Thomas R. *Manifest Design: Anxious Aggrandizement in Late Jacksonian America*. Ithaca, N.Y.: Cornell University Press, 1985.

Higham, John W. "The Loyalties of William Gilmore Simms." *Journal of Southern History* 9 (May 1943): 210–23.

Hildreth, Richard. *History of the United States of America*. 6 vols. New York: Harper and Brothers, 1852.

Hill, Franklin William. "The Anglo-American Recruitment Crisis, 1854–56: Origins, Events and Outcomes." Ph.D. diss., Washington State University, 1996.

Hillebrand, Harold Newcomb. *Edmund Kean*. New York: AMS Press, 1966.

Hodge, Frank. *Yankee Theatre: The Image of American on the Stage, 1825–1850*. Austin: University of Texas Press, 1964.

Hoe, Susanna, and Derek Roebuck. *The Taking of Hong Kong: Charles and Clara Elliot in China Waters*. Richmond, Surrey, U.K.: Curzon, 1999.

Holmes, Oliver Wendell, Sr. *Ralph Waldo Emerson*. Boston: Houghton Mifflin, 1885.

Holt, Michael F. *The Rise and Fall of the American Whig Party: Jacksonian Politics and the Onset of the Civil War*. New York: Oxford University Press, 1999.

Horsman, Reginald. *Race and Manifest Destiny: The Origins of American Racial Anglo-Saxonism*. Cambridge, Mass.: Harvard University Press, 1981.

Howe, Daniel Walker. *The Political Culture of the American Whigs*. Chicago: University of Chicago Press, 1979.

———. *What Hath God Wrought: The Transformation of America, 1815–1848*. New York: Oxford University Press, 2009.

Howe, M. A. DeWolfe. *The Life and Letters of George Bancroft*. 2 vols. 1908. Reprint, New York: Kennikat Press, 1971.

Hudson, Linda S. *Mistress of Manifest Destiny: A Biography of Jane McManus Storms Cazneau, 1807–1878*. Austin: Texas State Historical Association, 2001.

Ireland, Joseph N. *Records of the New York Stage, from 1750 to 1860*. 2 vols. New York: T. H. Morrell, 1866.

Irwin, Douglas A., and Peter Temin. "The Antebellum Tariff on Cotton Textiles Revisited." *Journal of Economic History* 61 (September 2001), 777–98.

Jackson, George Stuyvesant. *Early Songs of Uncle Sam*. Boston: B. Humphries, 1933.

Jackson, Sheldon G. "The British and the California Dream: Rumors, Myths, and Legends." *Southern California Quarterly* 57 (Summer 1975): 251–68.

———. "Two Pro-British Plots in Alta California." *Southern California Quarterly* 55 (Summer 1973): 105–40.

James, Scott C., and David A. Lake. "The Second Face of Hegemony: Britain's Repeal of the Corn Laws and the American Walker Tariff of 1846." *International Organization* 43 (Winter 1989): 1–29.

Jenks, Leland Hamilton. *The Migration of British Capital to 1875*. New York: Alfred A. Knopf, 1927.

Jentz, John Barkley. "Artisans, Evangelicals, and the City: A Social History of Abolition and Labor Reform in Jacksonian New York." Ph.D. diss., City University of New York, 1977.

Jones, Howard. "Anglophobia and the Aroostook War." *New England Historical Quarterly* 48 (December 1975): 519–39.

———. *To the Webster-Ashburton Treaty: A Study in Anglo-American Relations, 1783–1843*. Chapel Hill: University of North Carolina Press, 1977.

Jones, Wilbur Devereux. *The American Problem in British Diplomacy, 1841–1861*. London: Macmillan Press, 1974.

Jones, Wilbur Devereux, and Chad J. Vinson. "British Preparedness and the Oregon Settlement." *Pacific Historical Review* 22 (November 1953): 353–64.

Kaplan, Michael. "The World of the B'hoys: Urban Violence and Political Culture of Antebellum New York City, 1825–1860," Ph.D. diss., New York University, 1996.

Kasson, John F. *Rudeness and Civility: Manners in Nineteenth-Century Urban America*. New York: Farrar, Straus and Giroux, 1990.

Kasson, Joy. *Artistic Voyager: Europe and the American Imagination in the Works of Irving, Allston, Cole, Cooper, and Hawthorne*. Westport, Conn.: Greenwood Press, 1982.

Keller, Christian B. "Philanthropy Betrayed: Thomas Jefferson, the Louisiana Purchase, and the Origins of Federal Indian Removal Policy." *Proceedings of the American Philosophical Society* 144 (March 2000): 39–66.

Kerber, Linda K. *Federalists in Dissent: Imagery and Ideology in Jeffersonian America*. Ithaca, N.Y.: Cornell University Press, 1980.

Kilbride, Daniel. "Slavery and Utilitarianism: Thomas Cooper and the Mind of the Old South." *Journal of Southern History* 59 (August 1993): 469–86.

———. "Travel, Ritual, and National Identity: Planters on the European Tour, 1820–1860." *Journal of Southern History* 69 (August 2003): 549–84.

Klunder, William Carl. *Lewis Cass and the Politics of Moderation*. Kent, Ohio: Kent State University Press, 1996.

Knott, Stephen F. *Alexander Hamilton and the Persistence of Myth*. Lawrence: University Press of Kansas, 2002.

Kohn, Hans. *American Nationalism: An Interpretative Essay*. New York: Macmillan, 1957.

Lambert, Paul F. "The Movement for the Acquisition of All Mexico." *Journal of the West* 11 (April 1972): 317–27.

Landers, Jane G. *Black Slavery in Spanish Florida*. Urbana: University of Illinois Press, 1999.

Langhorne, Richard, and Keith A. Hamilton. *The Practice of Diplomacy: Its Evolution, Theory, and Administration*. London: Routledge, 1995.

Laurie, Bruce. *Artisans Into Workers: Labor in Nineteenth-Century America*. New York: Hill and Wang, 1989.

————. *Working People of Philadelphia, 1800–1850.* Philadelphia: Temple University Press, 1980.

Lause, Mark A. *Young America: Land, Labor, and the Republican Community.* Urbana: University of Illinois Press, 2005.

Lease, Benjamin. *Anglo-American Encounters: England and the Rise of American Literature.* Cambridge: Cambridge University Press, 1981.

Lee, Sohui. "Hawthorne's Politics of Storytelling: Two 'Tales of the Province House' and the Specter of Anglomania in the Democratic Review." *American Periodicals* 14, no. 1 (2004): 35–62.

Leggett, William. *Democratick Editorials: Essays in Jacksonian Political Economy.* Indianapolis: Liberty Press, 1984.

Lerner, Gerda. *The Grimké Sisters from South Carolina: Rebels against Slavery.* Boston: Houghton Mifflin, 1967.

Levine, Lawrence W. *Highbrow/Lowbrow: The Emergence of Cultural Hierarchy in America.* Cambridge, Mass.: Harvard University Press, 1988.

Lewis, James E. *The American Union and the Problem of Neighborhood: The United States and the Collapse of the Spanish Empire, 1783–1829.* Chapel Hill: University of North Carolina Press, 1998.

Lincove, David A., and Gary R. Treadway. *The Anglo-American Relationship: An Annotated Bibliography of Scholarship, 1945–1985.* Westport, Conn.: Greenwood Press, 1988.

Litto, Fredric M. "Edmund Simpson of the Park Theatre, New York, 1809–1848." Ph.D. diss., Indiana University, 1969.

Longmore, Paul K. *The Invention of George Washington.* Berkeley: University of California Press, 1988.

Lynch, Denis Tilden. *An Epoch and a Man: Van Buren and His Times.* Port Washington, N.Y.: Kennikat Press, 1929.

Malone, Dumas. *The Public Life of Thomas Cooper, 1783–1839.* Columbia: University of South Carolina Press, 1961.

Marshall, Lynn L. "The Authorship of Jackson's Bank Veto Message." *Mississippi Valley Historical Review* 50 (December 1963): 466–77.

Marti, Herman. *Messenger of Destiny: The California Adventures, 1846–1847, of Archibald Gillespie, U.S. Marine Corps.* San Francisco: J. Howell Books, 1960.

Mathews, Donald C. *Slavery and Methodism: A Chapter in American Morality, 1780–1845.* Princeton, N.J.: Princeton University Press, 1965.

Matthews, Jean V. *Toward a New Society: American Thought and Culture, 1800–1830.* Boston: Twayne Publishers, 1991.

May, Robert E. *Manifest Destiny's Underworld: Filibustering in Antebellum America.* Chapel Hill: University of North Carolina Press, 2002.

Maynard, Douglas H. "The World's Anti-Slavery Convention of 1840." *Mississippi Valley Historical Review* 47 (December 1960): 452–71.

McCardell, John. *The Idea of a Southern Nation: Southern Nationalists and Southern Nationalism, 1830–1860.* New York: W. W. Norton, 1979.

McCarty, William, comp. *National Songs, Ballads, and Other Patriotic Poetry, Chiefly Relating to the War of 1846.* Philadelphia: W. M'Carty, 1846.

McClintock, Anne. "Angel of Progress: Pitfalls of the Term Post-colonialism." In Williams and Chrisman, *Colonial Discourse and Post-colonial Theory,* 291–304.

McCloskey, John C. "The Campaign of Periodicals after the War of 1812 for a National Literature." *Publications of the Modern Language Association of America* 50 (March 1935): 262–73.

McConachie, Bruce. *Melodramatic Formations: American Theatre and Society, 1820–1870.* Iowa City: University of Iowa Press, 1992.

McGill, Meredith L. *American Literature and the Culture of Reprinting, 1835–1853.* Philadelphia: University of Pennsylvania Press, 2003.

Meckier, Jerome. *Innocent Abroad: Charles Dickens's American Engagements.* Lexington: University Press of Kentucky, 1990.

Meigs, William Montgomery. *The Life of Charles Jared Ingersoll.* 1897. Reprint, New York: Da Capo Press, 1970.

Merk, Frederick. "British Government Propaganda and the Oregon Treaty." *American Historical Review* 40 (October 1934): 38–62.

———. *Manifest Destiny and Mission in American History: A Reinterpretation.* New York: Alfred A. Knopf, 1963.

———. *The Oregon Question: Essays in Anglo-American Diplomacy and Politics.* Cambridge, Mass.: Harvard University Press, 1967.

Merk, Frederick, with Lois Bannister Merk. *The Monroe Doctrine and American Expansionism, 1843–1849.* New York: Alfred A. Knopf, 1966.

Meserve, Walter J. *Heralds of Promise: The Drama of the American People during the Age of Jackson, 1829–1849.* Westport, Conn.: Greenwood Press, 1986.

Mesick, Jane Louise. *The English Traveler in America, 1785–1835.* 1922. Reprint, Westport, Conn.: Greenwood Press, 1970.

Michigan Pioneer and Historical Society. *Historical Collections, Collections and Researches Made by the Michigan Pioneer and Historical Society.* 29 vols. Lansing: Robert Smith Printing Co., 1897.

Middleton, Annie. "Donelson's Mission to Texas in Behalf of Annexation." *Southwestern Historical Quarterly* 24 (April 1921): 247–91.

Miles, Edwin A. "'Fifty-Four Forty or Fight,'—An American Political Legend." *Mississippi Valley Historical Review* 44 (September 1957): 291–309.

———."The Young American Nation and the Classical World." *Journal of the History of Ideas* 35 (April–June 1974): 259–74.

Miller, Perry. *The Life of the Mind in America, from the Revolution to the Civil War.* New York: Harcourt, Brace and World, 1965.

———. *The Raven and the Whale: Poe, Melville, and the American Literary Scene.* Baltimore: Johns Hopkins University Press, 1956.

Miller, William Lee. *Arguing About Slavery: The Great Battle in the United States Congress.* New York: Oxford University Press, 1996.

Mitton, Steven Heath. "The Upshur Inquiry: Lost Lessons of the Great Experiment." *Slavery and Abolition* 27 (April 2006): 89–124.

Monaghan, Jay. *The Great Rascal: The Life and Adventures of Ned Buntline.* New York: Bonanza Books, 1951.

Monroe, Dan. *The Republican Vision of John Tyler.* College Station: Texas A&M University Press, 2003.

Moody, Richard. *Dramas from the American Theatre, 1762–1909.* Cleveland: World Publishing Co., 1969.

———. *Edwin Forrest, First Star of the American Stage.* New York: Alfred Knopf, 1960.

Morgan, Winifred. *An American Icon: Brother Jonathan and American Identity.* Newark: University of Delaware Press, 1988.

Morrison, Michael A. "Martin Van Buren, the Democracy, and the Partisan Politics of Texas Annexation." *Journal of Southern History* 61 (November 1995): 695–724.

Mudge, Eugene Tenbroeck. *The Social Philosophy of John Taylor of Caroline: A Study in Jeffersonian Democracy.* 1939. Reprint, New York: AMS Press, 1968.

Nagel, Paul C. "The Election of 1824: A Reconsideration Based on Newspaper Opinion." *Journal of Southern History* 26 (August 1960): 315–29.

———. *This Sacred Trust: American Nationality, 1798–1898.* New York: Oxford University Press, 1971.

Nance, Joseph Milton. *Attack and Counter-Attack: The Texas-Mexican Frontier, 1842.* Austin: University of Texas Press, 1964.

Narrett, David E. "A Choice of Destiny: Immigration Policy, Slavery, and the Annexation of Texas." *Southwestern Historical Quarterly* 100 (January 1997): 270–302.

Nevins, Allan. *America through British Eyes.* New York: Oxford University Press, 1948.

———. *Frémont, Pathmarker of the West.* New York: Ungar, 1961.

Newman, Simon P. *Parades and the Politics of the Street: Festive Culture in the Early American Republic.* Philadelphia: University of Pennsylvania Press, 1997.

Nichols, Harold J. "The Prejudice against Native American Drama from 1778 to 1830." *Quarterly Journal of Speech* 60 (February 1974): 279–88.

Nichols, Thomas Low. *Forty Years of American Life, 1821–1861.* New York: Stackpole Sons, 1937.

Nisbet, Ada B. *British Comment on the United States: A Chronological Bibliography, 1832–1919.* Berkeley: University of California Press, 2001.

Norton, A. B. *The Great Revolution of 1840: Reminiscences of the Log Cabin and Hard Cider Campaign.* Dallas: A. B. Norton and Co., 1880.

O'Brien, Michael. *A Character of Hugh Legaré.* Knoxville: University of Tennessee Press, 1985.

———. *Conjectures of Order: Intellectual Life and the American South, 1810–1860.* 2 vols. Chapel Hill: University of North Carolina Press, 2004.

Odell, George C. D. *Annals of the New York Stage.* 15 vols. New York: Columbia University Press, 1927–49.

O'Neill, E. H. "The Poe-Griswold-Harrison Texts of the 'Marginalia.'" *American Literature* 15 (November 1943): 238–50.

Orians, G. Harrison. "The Romance Ferment after Waverly." *American Literature* 3 (January 1932): 408–31.

Owsley, Frank, Jr., and Gene A. Smith. *Filibusters and Expansionists: Jeffersonian Manifest Destiny, 1800–1821.* Tuscaloosa: University of Alabama Press, 1997.

Paquette, Robert L. *Sugar is Made with Blood: The Conspiracy of La Escalera and the Conflict between Empires over Slavery in Cuba.* Middletown, Conn.: Wesleyan University Press, 1988.

Paul, James C. N. *Rift in the Democracy.* Philadelphia: University of Pennsylvania Press, 1951.

Paulding, William I. *Literary Life of James K. Paulding,* compiled by his son. New York: C. Scribner, 1867.

Peach, Linden. *British Influence on the Birth of American Literature*. New York: St. Martin's Press, 1982.

Perkins, Dexter. *A History of the Monroe Doctrine*. Boston: Little, Brown and Co., 1941.

———. *The Monroe Doctrine, 1823–1826*. Cambridge, Mass.: Harvard University Press, 1927.

Phillips, Kevin. *The Cousins' Wars: Religion, Politics, and the Triumph of Anglo-America*. New York: Basic Books, 1999.

Playfair, Giles. *Kean: The Life and Paradox of a Great Actor*. London: Reinhardt and Evans, 1950.

Pletcher, David M. *The Diplomacy of Annexation: Texas, Oregon, and the Mexican War*. Columbia: University of Missouri Press, 1973.

Pratt, Edwin J. "Anglo-American Commercial and Political Rivalry in the Plata, 1820–1830." *Hispanic American Historical Review* 11 (August 1931): 302–35.

Prentiss, S. S. *A Memoir of S. S. Prentiss, Edited by His Brother*. 2 vols. New York: Charles Scribner, 1856.

Prochaska, Frank. *The Eagle and the Crown: Americans and the British Monarchy*. New Haven, Conn.: Yale University Press, 2008.

Proctor, B. W. *The Life of Edmund Kean*. 1835. Reprint, New York: Benjamin Blom, 1969.

Prucha, Francis Paul. "Andrew Jackson's Indian Policy: A Reassessment." *Journal of American History* 56 (December 1969): 527–39.

Purcell, Sarah J. *Sealed With Blood: War, Sacrifice, and Meaning in Revolutionary America*. Philadelphia: University of Pennsylvania Press, 2002.

Radforth, Ian. *Royal Spectacle: The 1860 Visit of the Prince of Wales to Canada and the United States*. Toronto: University of Toronto Press, 2004.

Rakestraw, Donald A. *For Honor or Destiny: The Anglo-American Crisis over the Oregon Territory*. New York: Peter Lang, 1995.

Rathbun, Lyon. "The Debate over Annexing Texas and the Emergence of Manifest Destiny." *Rhetoric and Public Affairs* 4 (2001): 459–93.

Ratner, Lorman. *Powder Keg: Northern Opposition to the Anti-Slavery Movement, 1831–1840*. New York: Basic Books, 1968.

Rees, James. *The Life of Edwin Forrest*. Philadelphia: T. B. Peterson and Brothers, 1874.

Remini, Robert V. *Andrew Jackson and His Indian Wars*. New York: Viking, 2001.

———. *The Election of Andrew Jackson*. Philadelphia: Lippincott, 1963.

Reynolds, David S. *George Lippard, Prophet of Protest*. New York: Peter Lang, 1986.

Reynolds, Larry J. *James Kirke Paulding*. Boston: Twayne Publishers, 1984.

Rice, C. Duncan. "The Anti-Slavery Mission of George Thompson to the United States, 1834–1835." *Journal of American Studies* 2 (April 1968): 13–31.

Richards, Leonard L. *"Gentlemen of Property and Standing": Anti-Abolition Mobs in Jacksonian America*. New York: Oxford University Press, 1970.

Richardson, Ronald Kent. *Moral Imperium: Afro-Caribbeans and the Transformation of British Rule, 1776–1838*. New York: Greenwood Press, 1987.

Richmond, Douglas, W., ed. *Essays on the Mexican War*. College Station: Texas A&M University Press, 1986.

Rippy, J. Fred. *Joel Poinsett, Versatile American.* Durham, N.C.: Duke University Press, 1957.

———. *Rivalry of the United States and Great Britain over Latin America.* New York: Octagon Books, 1964.

Rodgers, Daniel T. "Republicanism: The Career of a Concept." *Journal of American History* 79 (June 1992): 11–39.

Roeckell, Lelia. "Bonds over Bondage: British Opposition to the Annexation of Texas." *Journal of the Early Republic* 19 (Summer 1999): 257–78.

Rogin, Michael Paul. *Fathers and Children: Andrew Jackson and the Subjugation of the American Indian.* New York: Random House, 1988.

Rothbard, Murray N. *Panic of 1819: Reactions and Policies.* New York: Columbia University Press, 1962.

Rothman, Adam. "The Expansion of Slavery in the Deep South, 1790–1820." Ph.D. diss., Columbia University, 2000.

Rozbicki, Michal J. *The Complete Colonial Gentleman: Colonial Legitimacy in Plantation America.* Charlottesville: University Press of Virginia, 1998.

Rubin-Dorsky, Jeffrey. *Adrift in the Old World: The Psychological Pilgrimage of Washington Irving.* Chicago: University of Chicago Press, 1988.

Rugemer, Edward Bartlett. *The Problem of Emancipation: The Caribbean Roots of the American Civil War.* Baton Rouge: Louisiana State University Press, 2009.

Ryerson, Stanley B. *Unequal Union: Confederation and the Roots of Conflict in the Canadas, 1815–1873.* New York: International Publishers, 1968.

Sacks, Kenneth S. *Understanding Emerson: "The American Scholar" and His Struggle for Self-Reliance.* Princeton, N.J.: Princeton University Press, 2003.

Sampson, Robert. *John L. O'Sullivan and his Times.* Kent, Ohio: Kent State University Press, 2005.

Sanford, Charles L. "The Intellectual Origins and New-Worldliness of American Industry." *Journal of Economic History* 18 (March 1958): 1–16.

———. *The Quest for Paradise: Europe and the American Moral Imagination.* Urbana: University of Illinois Press, 1961.

Satz, Ronald N. *American Indian Policy in the Jacksonian Era.* Lincoln: University of Nebraska Press, 1976.

Schacterle, Lance. "Cooper's Attitudes toward England." In *James Fenimore Cooper: His Country and His Art,* edited by George A. Test, 33–54. Oneonta and Cooperstown, N.Y., 1982.

Schama, Simon. *Rough Crossings: Britain, the Slaves, and the American Revolution.* New York: HarperCollins, 2005.

Schwartz, Barry. *George Washington: The Making of an American Symbol.* New York: Free Press, 1997.

Sealts, Merton M., Jr. *Emerson on the Scholar.* Columbia: University of Missouri Press, 1992.

Sexton, Jay. *Debtor Diplomacy: Finance and American Foreign Relations in the Civil War Era, 1837–1873.* Oxford: Clarendon Press, 2005.

Shalhope, Robert E. *John Taylor of Caroline: Pastoral Republican.* Columbia: University of South Carolina Press, 1980.

———. "Toward a Republican Synthesis: The Emergence of an Understanding of

Republicanism in American Historiography." *William and Mary Quarterly* 29 (January 1972): 49–80.

Shank, Theodore. "The Bowery Theatre, 1826–1836." Ph.D. diss., Stanford University, 1956.

———, ed. *A Digest of 500 Plays; Plot Outlines and Production Notes.* New York: Crowell-Collier Press, 1963.

Sheehan, Bernard W. *Seeds of Extinction: Jeffersonian Philanthropy and the American Indian.* New York: W. W. Norton, 1974.

Sheidley, Harlow W. *Sectional Nationalism: Massachusetts Conservative Leaders and the Transformation of America, 1815–1836.* Boston: Northeastern University Press, 1998.

Shelton, Cynthia J. *The Mills of Manayunk: Industrialization and Social Conflict in the Philadelphia Region, 1787–1837.* Baltimore: Johns Hopkins University Press, 1986.

Shenton, James P. *Robert John Walker: A Politician from Jackson to Lincoln.* New York: Columbia University Press, 1961.

Shepperson, Wilbur. *British Emigration to North America: Projects and Opinions in the Early Victorian Period.* New York: Blackwell, 1957.

Sidbury, James. *Becoming African in America: Race and Nation in the Early Black Atlantic* New York: Oxford University Press, 2009.

Silbey, Joel H. *Storm Over Texas: The Annexation Controversy and the Road to Civil War.* New York: Oxford University Press, 2005.

Simpson, Craig M. *A Good Southerner: The Life of Henry A. Wise of Virginia.* Chapel Hill: University of North Carolina Press, 1985.

Sinha, Minisha. *The Counterrevolution of Slavery: Politics and Ideology in Antebellum South Carolina.* Chapel Hill: University of North Carolina Press, 1999.

Skeen, Carl Edward. *1816: America Rising.* Lexington: University of Kentucky Press, 2003.

Skinner, Maud and Otis, eds. *One Man in His Time: The Adventures of H. Watkins, Strolling Player, 1845–1863, from His Journal.* Philadelphia: University of Pennsylvania Press, 1938.

Sklar, Kathryn Kish. "'Women Who Speak for an Entire Nation'": American and British Women at the World Anti-Slavery Convention, London, 1840." In *The Abolitionist Sisterhood: Women's Political Culture in Antebellum America,* edited by John C. Van Horne and Jean Fagan Yellin, 301–33. Ithaca, N.Y.: Cornell University Press, 1994.

Smith, Gene A. *Thomas ap Catesby Jones: Commodore of Manifest Destiny.* Annapolis: Naval Institute Press, 2000.

Smith, Justin H. *The Annexation of Texas.* 1911. Reprint, New York: AMS Press, 1971.

———. *The War with Mexico.* 2 vols. New York: Macmillan, 1919.

Smith, Walter Buckingham, and Arthur Harrison Cole. *Fluctuations in American Business, 1790–1860.* Cambridge, Mass.: Harvard University Press, 1935.

Smither, Harriet. "English Abolitionism and the Annexation of Texas." *Southwestern Historical Quarterly* 32 (January 1929): 193–205.

Somkin, Fred. *Unquiet Eagle: Memory and Desire in the Idea of American Freedom, 1815–1850.* Ithaca, N.Y.: Cornell University Press, 1967.

Soto, Miguel E. "The Monarchist Conspiracy and the Mexican War." In *Essays on the Mexican War*, edited by Douglas W. Richmond, 66–84. College Station: Texas A&M University Press, 1986.

Soulsby, Hugh G. *The Right of Search and the Slave Trade in Anglo-American Relations, 1814–1862*. Baltimore: Johns Hopkins University Press, 1933.

Spencer, Benjamin T. *The Quest for Nationality: An American Literary Campaign*. Syracuse, N.Y.: Syracuse University Press, 1957.

Spivak, Gayatri Chakravorty. "Can the Subaltern Speak?" In Williams and Chrisman, *Colonial Discourse and Post-colonial Theory*, 66–111.

Stacey, C. P. "The Myth of the Unguarded Frontier, 1815–1871." *American Historical Review* 56 (October 1950): 1–18.

Stange, Douglas Charles. *British Unitarians against Slavery, 1833–65*. Rutherford, N.J.: Fairleigh Dickinson University Press, 1984.

Staudenraus, P. J. *The African Colonization Movement, 1816–1865*. New York: Columbia University Press, 1961.

Stenberg, Richard R. "Polk and Frémont, 1845–1846." *Pacific Historical Review* 7 (September 1938): 211–27.

Stephen, Kenny. "The Canadian Rebellion and the Limits of Historical Perspective." *Vermont History* 58 (Summer 1990): 179–98.

Stevens, Kenneth R. *Border Diplomacy: The Caroline and McLeod Affairs in Anglo-American-Canadian Relations, 1837–1842*. Tuscaloosa: University of Alabama Press, 1989.

Stewart, James Brewer. *Wendell Phillips, Liberty's Hero*. Baton Rouge: Louisiana State University Press, 1986.

Streeby, Shelly. *American Sensations: Class, Empire, and the Production of Popular Culture*. Berkeley: University of California Press, 2002.

Strout, Cushing. *The American Image of the Old World*. New York: Harper and Row, 1963.

Sullivan, William A. *The Industrial Worker in Pennsylvania, 1800–1840*. Harrisburg: Pennsylvania Historical and Museum Commission, 1955.

Tamarkin, Elisa. *Anglophilia: Deference, Devotion, and Antebellum America*. Chicago: University of Chicago Press, 2008.

Tate, Adam L. *Conservatism and Southern Intellectuals, 1789–1861: Liberty, Tradition, and the Good Society*. Columbia: University of Missouri Press, 2005.

Taussig, F. W. *The Tariff History of the United States*. New York: A. M. Kelley, 1931.

Taylor, George Rogers. *The Transportation Revolution, 1815–1860*. New York: Rinehart and Co., 1951.

Taylor, William R. *Cavalier and Yankee: The Old South and American National Character*. New York: Oxford University Press, 1957.

Tays, George. "Frémont had no Secret Instructions." *Pacific Historical Review* 9 (June 1940): 157–72.

Temin, Peter. *The Jacksonian Economy*. New York: W. W. Norton, 1969.

Temperley, Howard. *British Antislavery, 1833–1870*. London: Longman, 1972.

Thistlethwaite, Frank. *The Anglo-American Connection in the Early Nineteenth Century*. New York: Russell and Russell, 1959.

Thomas, J. W. *James Freeman Clarke, Apostle of German Culture to America*. Boston: J. W. Luce, 1949.

Thomas, Mary Elizabeth. *Jamaica and Voluntary Laborers from Africa, 1840–1865.* Gainesville: University of Florida Press, 1974.

Timberlake, Richard H., Jr. "The Specie Standard and Central Banking in the United States Before 1860." *Journal of Economic History* 21 (September 1961): 318–41.

Tise, Larry E. *Pro-Slavery: A History of the Defense of Slavery in America, 1701–1840.* Athens: University of Georgia Press, 1988.

Trask, Kerry A. *Black Hawk: The Battle for the Heart of America.* New York: Henry Holt, 2006.

Travers, Len. *Celebrating the Fourth: Independence Day and the Rites of Nationalism in the Early Republic.* Amherst: University of Massachusetts Press, 1997.

Turner, Mary. *Slaves and Missionaries: The Disintegration of Jamaican Slave Society, 1787–1834.* Urbana: University of Illinois Press, 1982.

Unger, Harlow Giles. *Noah Webster: The Life and Times of an American Patriot.* New York: John Wiley and Sons, 1998.

Van Alstyne, Richard W. *The Rising American Empire.* New York: W. W. Norton, 1974.

Van Vogt, William E. *Britain to America: Mid-Nineteenth-Century Immigrants to the United States.* Urbana: University of Illinois, 1999.

Viola, Herman J. *Thomas L. McKenney, Architect of America's Early Indian Policy. 1816–1830.* Chicago: Sage Books, 1974.

Wakelyn, Jon. *The Politics of a Literary Man: William Gilmore Simms.* Westport, Conn.: Greenwood Press, 1973.

Waldstreicher, David. *In Pursuit of Perpetual Fetes: The Making of American Nationalism, 1776–1820.* Chapel Hill: University of North Carolina Press, 1997.

Wallace, Anthony F. C. *Jefferson and the Indians: The Tragic Fate of the First Americans.* Cambridge, Mass.: Harvard University Press, 1999.

Wallis, John Joseph. "The Depression of 1839 to 1843: States, Debts, and Banks." National Bureau of Economic Research Working Paper, 1–58.

Waples, Dorothy. *The Whig Myth of James Fenimore Cooper.* New Haven, Conn.: Yale University Press, 1938.

Ward, John William. *Andrew Jackson, Symbol for an Age.* New York: Oxford University Press, 1953.

Warrick, W. Sheridan. "The American Indian Policy in the Upper Old Northwest Following the War of 1812." *Ethnohistory* 3 (Spring 1956): 109–25.

Watts, Steven. *The Republic Reborn: War and the Making of Liberal America, 1790–1820.* Baltimore: Johns Hopkins University Press, 1987.

Weisbuch, Robert. *Atlantic Double-Cross: American Literature and British Influence in the Age of Emerson.* Chicago: University of Chicago Press, 1986.

Welter, Rush. *The Mind of America, 1820–1860.* New York: Columbia University Press, 1975.

West, Elizabeth Howard. "Southern Opposition to the Annexation of Texas." *Southwestern Historical Quarterly* 18 (July 1914): 74–82.

White, Laura A. "The United States in the 1850s as Seen by British Consuls." *Mississippi Valley Historical Review* 19 (March 1933): 530–32.

Whitney, Ellen M., comp. and ed. *The Black Hawk War, 1831–1832.* Springfield: Illinois Historical Society, 1973.

Widmer, Edward L. *Young America: The Flowering of Democracy in New York City.* New York: Oxford University Press, 1999.

Wilentz, Sean. *Andrew Jackson.* New York: Times Books, 2005.

———. *Chants Democratic: New York City and the Rise of the American Working Class, 1788–1850.* New York: Oxford University Press, 1986.

———. *The Rise of American Democracy: Jefferson to Lincoln.* New York: W. W. Norton, 2005.

Wilkins, Joe Bassette, Jr.. "Window on Freedom: The South's Response to the Emancipation of Slaves in the British West Indies, 1833–1861." Ph.D. diss., University of South Carolina, 1977.

Willard, George O. *History of the Providence Stage.* Providence: The Rhode Island News Company, 1891.

Williams, Patrick, and Laura Chrisman, eds. *Colonial Discourse and Post-colonial Theory: A Reader.* New York: Columbia University Press, 1994.

Wilmeth, Don B. *George Frederick Cooke, Machiavel of the Stage.* Westport, Conn.: Greenwood Press, 1980.

Wilmeth, Don B., and C. W. E. Bigsby, eds. *The Cambridge History of American Theatre: Beginnings to 1870.* New York: Cambridge University Press, 1998.

Wilson, Arthur Herman. *A History of the Philadelphia Theatre, 1835 to 1855.* Philadelphia: University of Pennsylvania Press, 1935.

Wilson, David A. *Paine and Cobbett: The Trans-Atlantic Connection.* Ottawa: National Library of Canada, 1985.

Wilson, Gay Allen. *Waldo Emerson: A Biography.* New York: Viking Press, 1981.

Wilson, Major L. *The Presidency of Martin Van Buren.* Lawrence: University of Kansas Press, 1984.

Wiltsee, Ernest A. *The Truth about Frémont: An Inquiry.* San Francisco: J. H. Nash, 1936.

Wood, Gordon S. *The Making of the American Republic, 1776–1787.* Chapel Hill: University of North Carolina Press, 1998.

Wyatt-Brown, Bertram. *Lewis Tappan and the Evangelical War against Slavery.* Cleveland: The Press of Case Western Reserve University, 1969.

Yearley, Clifton K. *Britons in American Labor: A History of the Influence of United Kingdom Immigrants on American Labor, 1820–1914.* Baltimore: Johns Hopkins University Press, 1957.

Yokota, Kariann. "Post-Colonial America: Transatlantic Networks of Exchange in the Early National Period." Ph.D. diss., University of California at Los Angeles, 2002.

Ziegler, Philip. *The Sixth Great Power: A History of One of the Greatest Banking Families, The House of Barings, 1762–1929.* New York: Alfred A. Knopf, 1988.

Ziff, Larzer. *The Declaration of Cultural Independence in America.* New York: Viking Press, 1981.

Index

Italicized pages refer to illustrations.